# World Civilizations

# World Civilizations

## Sources, Images, and Interpretations

*Fourth Edition · Volume II*

*Edited by*

**Dennis Sherman**
John Jay College of Criminal Justice, City University of New York

**A. Tom Grunfeld**
Empire State College, State University of New York

**Gerald Markowitz**
John Jay College of Criminal Justice, City University of New York

**David Rosner**
Columbia University

**Linda Heywood**
Boston University

Boston   Burr Ridge, IL   Dubuque, IA   Madison, WI   New York   San Francisco   St. Louis
Bangkok   Bogotá   Caracas   Kuala Lumpur   Lisbon   London   Madrid   Mexico City
Milan   Montreal   New Delhi   Santiago   Seoul   Singapore   Sydney   Taipei   Toronto

*A Division of The McGraw-Hill Companies*

WORLD CIVILIZATIONS: SOURCES, IMAGES, AND INTERPRETATIONS, VOLUME II

Published by McGraw-Hill, a business unit of The McGraw-Hill Companies, Inc., 1221 Avenue of the Americas, New York, NY, 10020.

5 6 7 8 9 0 VNH/VNH 0 9

ISBN-13: 978-0-07-313338-6

ISBN-10: 0-07-313338-8

Publisher: *Lyn Uhl*
Senior sponsoring editor: *Jon-David Hague*
Editorial assistant: *Sean Connelly*
Marketing manager: *Katherine Bates*
Lead producer: *Sean Crowley*
Senior project manager: *Jill Moline-Eccher*
Senior production supervisor: *Carol A. Bielski*
Design manager: *Laurie J. Entringer*
Photo research coordinator: *Alexandra Ambrose*
Art manager: *Robin Mouat*
Freelance photo researcher: *Christine Pullo*
Art director: *Jeanne Schreiber*
Cover design: *Laurie J. Entringer*
Interior design: *JoAnne Schopler*
Typeface: *10.5/12.5 Goudy*
Compositor: *Cenveo*
Printer: *Von Hoffmann Corporation*

Cover credits: Prince Mahadaji Sindhia entertaining a British army officer and a naval officer to a nautch, Delhi artist, c. 1820 (gouache on paper), Indian School, (19th century) / British Library, London, UK / Bridgeman Art Library

Back cover credits: Musee Conde, Chantilly, France/Giraudon-Bridgeman Art Library (top); The National Gallery, London (center); Victoria & Albert Museum, London/Art Resource, NY (bottom)

**Library of Congress Cataloging-in-Publication Data**

World civilizations: sources, images, and interpretations / edited by Dennis Sherman ...
    [et al.].—4th ed.
     p. cm.
    ISBN 0-07-312759-0 (V. 1: softcover: alk. paper)—ISBN 0-07-313338-8 (V. 2: softcover: alk. paper)
     1. Civilization—History—Sources—Textbooks. 2. Civilization—History—Textbooks. I.
Sherman, Dennis.
CB69.W66 2006
909—dc22
                                                     2004058798

www.mhhe.com

# About the Editors

**Dennis Sherman** is professor of history at John Jay College of Criminal Justice, the City University of New York. He received his B.A. (1962) and J.D. (1965) degrees from the University of California at Berkeley, and his Ph.D. (1970) from the University of Michigan. He was visiting professor at the University of Paris (1978–79, 1985). He received the Ford Foundation Prize Fellowship (1968–69, 1969–70), a fellowship from the Council for Research on Economic History (1971–72), and fellowships from the National Endowment for the Humanities (1973–76). His publications include *The West in the World: A Mid-Length Narrative History*, Second Edition (co-author), *A Short History of Western Civilization*, Eighth Edition (coauthor), *Western Civilization: Images and Interpretations*, Sixth Edition, a series of introductions in the Garland Library of War and Peace, several articles and reviews on 19th-century French economic and social history in American and European journals, and several short stories in literary reviews.

**A. Tom Grunfeld** is a professor of history at the State University of New York/Empire State College, where he has just been appointed a State University of New York (SUNY) Distinguished Teaching Professor. He received his B.A. (1972) from the State University of New York/College at Old Westbury, his M.A. (1973) from the University of London/School of Oriental and African Studies, and his Ph.D. (1985) from New York University. He has received numerous travel and research grants from, among others, the National Endowment for the Humanities (1984), the Research Foundation of the City University of New York (1985), the State University of New York, and the Ford Foundation (1993). His publications include over 100 articles in periodicals published in over a dozen countries, *The Making of Modern Tibet* (1996), *On Her Own: Journalistic Adventures from the San Francisco Earthquake to the Chinese Revolution, 1917–1927* (1933), and *The Vietnam War: A History in Documents* (with Marilyn Young and John Fitzgerald) (2001). He has lived and traveled extensively throughout Asia since 1966 and is a frequent commentator on Chinese and Tibetan matters for BBC Radio and CNN International.

**Gerald Markowitz** is Distinguished Professor of History at John Jay College of Criminal Justice and the CUNY Graduate Center. He is also Adjunct Professor in the Department of Sociomedical Sciences at Columbia's Mailman School of Public Health. He and David Rosner have recently published *Deceit and Denial: The Deadly Politics of Industrial Pollution* (2002). He has been awarded numerous grants, including those from the National Endowment for the Humanities, the National Science Foundation, the Milbank Memorial Fund, and the Robert Wood Johnson Foundation. He was a recipient of the Viseltear Prize from the Medical Care Section of the American Public Health Association for "Outstanding Contributions" to the history of public health. He has co-authored and edited numerous books and articles, including *Deadly Dust: Silicosis and the Politics of Occupational Disease in Twentieth Century America* (1991; 1994), *Children, Race, and Power: Kenneth and Mamie Clark's Northside Center* (1996), *Dying for Work* (1987), *"Slaves of the Depression," Workers' Letters about Life on the Job* (1987), *Democratic Vistas: Post Offices and Public Art in the New Deal* (1984), and *The Anti-Imperialists: 1898–1902* (1976).

**David Rosner** is Professor of History and Public Health at Columbia University and Director of the Center for the History of Public Health at Columbia's Mailman School of Public Health. He and Gerald Markowitz have recently authored *Deceit and Denial: The Deadly Politics of Industrial Pollution* (2002). He was University Distinguished Professor of History at the City University of New York. He has been a Guggenheim Fellow, a National Endowment for the Humanities Fellow, and a Josiah Macy Fellow. Presently, he is the recipient of a Robert Wood Johnson Investigator Award. He has been awarded the Distinguished Scholar's Prize from the City University, the Viseltear Prize for Outstanding Work in the History of Public Health from the APHA, and the Distinguished Alumnus Award from the University of Massachusetts. He is author of *A Once Charitable Enterprise* (1982; Princeton University Press, 1987), and editor of *"Hives of Sickness," Epidemics and Public Health in New York City* (1986). In addition, he has co-authored and edited numerous books and articles, including *Deadly Dust: Silicosis and the Politics of Occupational Disease in Twentieth Century America* (1991; 1994), *Children, Race, and Power: Kenneth and Mamie Clark's*

*Northside Center* (1996; 2000), *Dying for Work* (1987), "*Slaves of the Depression,*" *Workers' Letters about Life on the Job* (1987), and *Health Care in America: Essays in Social History* (1979).

**Linda Heywood** is an associate professor of African history and the history of the African Diaspora at Boston University. She received her Ph.D. (1984) from Columbia University. Her publications include *Contested Power in Angola, 1840's to the Present* (2000), *Black Diaspora: Africans and the Descendants in the Wider World,* Parts One and Two (1988 revised ed., co-editor), and numerous articles on Angolan and African Diasporic history. She is the editor of *Central Africans and Cultural Transformations in the American Diaspora* (Cambridge, forthcoming), and is co-authoring a study on the first generation of Africans in the Dutch- and English-speaking Americas.

We Look Backward,
All of Us,
To Know,
All of Us,
If We Can.

# Contents

# Topical Contents

# Preface

We compiled *World Civilizations: Sources, Images, and Interpretations* with three main goals in mind. First, we wanted to show readers the variety of sources that historians use to write about history. Therefore, we have included not only primary documents, but also visual and secondary sources. Second, this collection is intended to be relatively concise, so we wanted the sources to "get to the point." To do that, we have carefully edited each selection to highlight its historical meanings as efficiently as possible. Third, we sought to structure the book in a way that makes sense to the reader and does not dominate the organization of a course that may be following a textbook or using other books. To this end, we arranged the sources along clear chronological and regional lines.

This book thus provides a broad introduction to the sources that historians use, the ways in which they interpret historical evidence, and the challenges they face in studying the evolution of civilizations around the world over the past 6,000 years. Each selection—whether a document, photograph, or map—is presented with an introduction, commentary, and questions designed to provide meaningful context and to facilitate readers' understanding of the selection's historical significance.

Moreover, the book overall addresses the course of human history as a whole, as it has ebbed and flowed over various parts of the globe. Individual chapters then examine particular civilizations as they have risen, developed, and interacted with other civilizations. We have also selected sources that provide a general balance among political, economic, social, intellectual, religious, and cultural history. However, different chapters highlight particular themes that are important for understanding certain eras of a civilization's history. For example, some chapters offer more sources on social and women's history, while others might emphasize political and religious history.

A book of this size can contain only a small portion of the historical material that is available. Thus *World Civilizations* is truly an introduction. Indeed, it is our hope that the materials presented here will serve primarily as a jumping-off point for further exploration into history and the historian's discipline.

## New in This Edition

This new edition includes some important changes.

- The larger format and the use of full color add to the book in several ways. Since the images in each chapter's Visual Sources section are presented in ways to encourage students to "read" and analyze what they are seeing as historical documents, the color and increased size of the paintings and photographs make this popular section more useful. Maps within the Visual Sources section are presented similarly and now are easier to read and understand. Finally, the use of color in the graphics should make the book more appealing to the reader.

- To take greater advantage of the new color format, we added many new Visual Sources.

- In response to reviewers' requests, we added several new primary and secondary sources.

- To reflect changing developments, we reorganized and revised the material in the final chapter. In particular, we have added several sources on international terrorism.

Otherwise, the structure, approach, and approximate length of this edition remain as in previous editions.

## Structure of the Book

As the **table of contents** indicates, each of the book's two volumes contains chapters of manageable length. The chapter divisions are based on how the different civilizations of the world have developed over time and within certain geographic contexts. A **topical table of contents** further facilitates cross-chapter comparisons among different civilizations and over time.

All the chapters are structured similarly. Specifically, each opens with a **chapter introduction** that previews the period of history and the topics covered. A **time line** follows, outlining the relevant dates, individuals, events, and developments focused on in the chapter.

Then come the three categories of historical sources. First are **primary sources,** usually written documents which give voice to the individuals who lived through the events described. These are followed by the **visual sources**—paintings, drawings, sculpture, ceramics, photographs, buildings, monuments, coins, and so forth—that provide valuable historical insights that are difficult to gain solely through written documents. Included within this category are **maps.** Finally, **secondary sources**—most written by scholars looking back on the time in question—offer interpretations of primary sources.

Each source is preceded by a **headnote,** which identifies the nature of the source, places it in historical context, and indicates its particular focus. Headnotes for visual sources—including maps—are extensive, to help readers see their unique value as historical evidence.

The headnotes end with **points to consider.** These are not simply facts that readers must search for in the selection. Rather, they are designed to stimulate thought about the selections and to indicate the uses of each source.

Each chapter then ends with **chapter questions** that challenge readers to draw major themes together.

Finally, what immediately follows the **acknowledgments** is a section on **Using This Book,** aimed at helping readers to use all the features in this book to their best advantage. Within this section are three models: **Using Primary Sources, Using Visual Sources,** and **Using Secondary Sources.** These models offer suggestions for interpreting and using these different kinds of sources.

## For the Instructor

The *Instructor's Guide to Classroom Discussion* is designed to show some of the ways in which the materials in *World Civilizations: Sources, Images, and Interpretations* can be used for classroom discussion. The *Guide* suggests a number of ways to organize discussion based on the selected sources.

## Videos

A wide range of videos on classic and contemporary topics in history is available through the Films for the Humanities and Sciences Collection. Instructors can illustrate classroom discussion and enhance lectures by selecting from a series of videos. Contact your McGraw-Hill sales representative for further information.

## Slide Set

Available through your McGraw-Hill sales representative, instructors can choose from a list of hundreds of fine art slides to create a customized slide set to complement the text and enhance classroom lectures.

## For the Student

*Magellan Geographix World History Atlas* is a printed collection of maps from early civilizations to the states of the world in 2000.

## Acknowledgments

McGraw-Hill and the authors would like to thank reviewers of this and the previous edition of this book for their many helpful comments and suggestions. They are Jacob Abadi, U.S. Air Force Academy; Edward Anson, University of Arkansas at Little Rock; Karl F. Bahm, University of Southern Mississippi; Myrna Chase, Baruch College; Denise Davidson, Georgia State University; Gayle V. Fischer, Salem State College; Anita Fisher, Clark College; David J. Gerleman, Southern Illinois University at Carbondale; Paul B. Goodwin, University of Connecticut; Steven W. Guerrier, James Madison University; Hines Hall, Auburn University; Udo Heyn, California State University, Los Angeles; Thomas Kay, Wheaton College; Gretchen Knapp, State University of New York, Buffalo; Patricia Kollander, Florida Atlantic University; Steven Leibo, Sage College, SUNY Albany; Daniel Lewis, San Bernadino Valley College; Marilyn Morris, University of North Texas; Oliver Pollack, University of Nebraska, Omaha; Patrice C. Ross, Columbus State Community College; Wendy St. Jean, Springfield College; Linda Walton, Portland State University; Lawrence Watkins, University of Kansas; John Weakland, Ball State University; Joseph Whitehorne, Lord Fairfax Community College; and Richard Williams, Washington State University.

*Dennis Sherman*
*A. Tom Grunfeld*
*Gerald Markowitz*
*David Rosner*
*Linda Heywood*

# Using This Book

In using this book, you face a task similar to that confronting all historians: discover *what* people in the past thought and did, and *why*, and to organize this information into a chronological record. To do this, historians must search for evidence from the past, and this evidence comes in many different forms. Most sources consist of written materials, ranging from government records to gravestone inscriptions, memoirs, and poetry. Other sources include paintings, photographs, sculpture, buildings, maps, pottery, and oral traditions. Historians also use secondary sources—accounts of a particular topic or period written by other scholars. But in searching for sources, historians usually have something in mind—some particular interest or tentative conclusions that shape their search. Thus, in working with sources, historians make numerous decisions about which ones to include and emphasize, and how to interpret them. What historians write is ultimately a synthesis of the questions they posed, the sources they used, and their own ideas.

This book provides examples of all these materials and lets you try your hand at thinking as a historian does. However, working with sources takes practice. Each piece of historical evidence is usually mute. It's up to the historian (or "you") to unlock the message in the evidence—to give voice, in a sense, to the people who created that document or those paintings so long ago. The historian (or "you") therefore must be a skilled detective. Here are some guidelines to help you hone your detecting skills:

1. **What Is the Context?** Get a sense of the **context** of the source you are about to read or analyze. This book gives you three ways to do this. First, read the brief introduction to the chapter in which the source appears. This preview sketches some of the most important developments in the period covered by the chapter. It introduces the topics, issues, and questions that the sources in the chapter focus on, and places these sources in the larger historical context of the civilizations being examined.

Second, look at the time line, which shows the period covered by the chapter and indicates the approximate dates and lifespans of the developments and people depicted in the sources. Third, read the headnote—the one or two paragraphs in italics that precede each source. These provide the immediate context to the source, introduce the source's author or creator, and indicate what the source is about.

2. **What Kind of Source Is It?** Each chapter is divided into three kinds of sources: primary, visual, and secondary. Primary sources are "firsthand" or "eyewitness" accounts of historical events or issues. Historians consider these documents their main building blocks for learning about and interpreting the past. These pieces of evidence are the most direct links possible to what people thought, how and why they acted as they did, and what they accomplished.

The visual sources in the book—such as paintings, sculpture, photographs, and buildings—are far more than just ornamentation or examples of renowned pieces of art and architecture. These sources reveal just as much of the past as written materials do—if you know how to interpret them. The extensive headnotes accompanying the visual sources will help you with this challenge.

Finally, secondary sources are accounts or analyses of events by someone (usually a scholar looking back on the past) who did not witness the event or live through the particular era described in the source. Secondary-source writers usually base their interpretations of what occurred on their examination of numerous primary documents and other sources. The analyses in these sources reflect the authors' choices and their own understanding of what happened. Often scholars differ on how to interpret significant historical developments.

At times the distinction between primary and secondary sources blurs, as when the author of a source lived during the events he or she is interpreting but did not witness it directly. If a historian views such a document as an *interpretation* of what occurred, the document is considered a secondary source. However, if the historian treats the document as evidence of the *assumptions and attitudes* of the author's times, the document is considered a primary source.

3. **What Does the Source Seem to Be Saying?** All sources reveal some information (whether directly or indirectly) about people and societies of the past. As you consider each source, ask yourself: What does this document or image tell me about this topic, society, individual, or era? The **"Consider"** questions that follow the headnote to each source will help you identify the important information contained in the sources.

**4. Who Created the Source, and Why?** To critically examine a source, ask yourself four questions. First, *who* created the source? Knowing the author or creator—a religious figure? scholar? worker?—may give you clues to the point reflected in the view expressed in the source. Second, what might be the author's *biases and assumptions*, such as political sympathies, group allegiances, or religious beliefs? Discerning these can give you valuable information that the author did not intend to convey. Third, *why* was the document written or created? Perhaps the author was trying to advocate a particular point of view or satisfy the wishes of a powerful group. Identifying the motivation behind the source sheds further light on its meaning. Fourth, who were the source's *intended readers or viewers*? Were they scholars? nobles? women? Knowing this can help you interpret a document's message or decipher the meaning of a painting.

Each kind of source—primary, visual, and secondary—poses its own challenge to historians who are trying to analyze them critically. Some primary documents, for example, may be forgeries or contain errors. There may also be inconsistencies within the document. These problems call into question the credibility of a document. The kind of primary source may limit its usefulness as well. For example, a law may not tell you anything about whether people followed it or whether it was enforced. And just because a book was published doesn't necessarily mean that it was widely read at the time. A formal written statement may reveal less about an individual's feelings and actual behavior than a diary entry can. Moreover, language constantly evolves, so the meanings of words and phrases may have changed over time. To fully understand a primary source, try to imagine yourself living during the time and in the society in which the source was first created.

Visual sources require especially careful interpretation. For example, a painter's intentions can be difficult to discern. Furthermore, a particular painting might mean something completely different to a sixteenth-century viewer than it does to a twenty-first-century viewer. Similarly, it makes a great difference whether a photograph was posed or spontaneous. Scholars differ greatly over how to interpret sources such as paintings, ceramics, and coins. Therefore, the descriptions that accompany the visual sources in this book are open to debate. They are designed primarily to show you *how* historians use visual materials—as unwritten evidence of what people in the past valued, thought, did, and found interesting.

Maps are a special kind of visual source. In this book, they are intended to shed light on relationships, such as the connections between geographical factors and political developments. As with other visual sources, the descriptions in the headnotes indicate some of the ways historians use maps.

With secondary sources, the authors (usually historians) often try to present a narrative of an event or era, or explain some social or political development. By its very nature, writing secondary sources means making decisions about what information to include. The author must make numerous judgment calls from among a huge amount of historical data. Therefore, read secondary sources with these questions in mind: What is the author's point or argument? What sort of evidence does he or she use to support the argument? Does the author's argument make sense to you? What political or ideological biases are revealed in the author's interpretation? How might somebody argue against the interpretation presented by the author?

All historical sources—whether primary, visual, or secondary—can only be so "objective." In fact, most evidence from the past omits important information about ordinary people's lives, children's lives, or particular ethnic groups. But good sources do reveal valuable information when you know what to look for and analyze them critically. In the hands of careful historians, they can offer a provocative glimpse into the hopes, the dreams, and the thoughts and actions of people from the past.

**5. What Connections and Comparisons Can Be Made?** In considering a source, ask yourself: Does this source relate in any way to another source in the chapter, to a broader topic covered in the chapter, or to any themes or developments covered in a textbook or classroom? Looking for connections and comparisons helps you stand back from the source and identify larger historical trends—perhaps even about yourself and your own society—beyond just the immediate message in the source.

To spot these links, read the chapter introductions. These list some of the broad question and themes around which the sources are organized. Sometimes the headnotes or "consider" points also suggest comparisons. In addition, the questions at the end of each chapter can help you make connections and comparisons. To answer these questions, you'll need to engage in analytical thought, look at several selections in the chapter together, and sometimes consider sources from several chapters.

**6. Employ the Models Presented in the "Using Primary Sources," "Using Visual Sources," and "Using Secondary Sources" Sections.** These provide examples of how a primary, a visual, and a secondary source might be read and studied. They appear at the beginning of the "Primary Sources," "Visual Sources," and "Secondary Sources" sections in the first chapter of this volume.

## Six-Point Checklist for Using This Book

- **Context.**
- **Kind of source** (primary, visual, secondary).
- **Message** (what does the source seem to be saying?).
- **Critical analysis** (who created the source, and why?).
- **Connections and comparisons.**
- **Models** (in the first chapter's "Using Primary Sources," "Using Visual Sources," and "Using Secondary Sources" sections).

# A Note on Chinese Romanization

From the first contacts of Europeans and Chinese there has been a problem in transliterating Chinese characters into the western alphabet. Many varied systems were developed. The romanization system most widely used in the English-speaking world was named after its 19th-century British creators, Wade and Giles.

In recent years there has been an attempt to develop a single transliteration that could be used universally. This system, adopted officially in the People's Republic of China in 1979, is known as pinyin. This system approximates the Chinese sounds more closely although it uses letters such as q and x in ways unfamiliar to most English speakers.

In this book we have used pinyin, but the first time a word appears, the Wade-Giles form will appear in parentheses except for particularly well-known names such as Sun Yat-sen, Chiang Kai-shek, Hong Kong, and Tibet.

# Chapter Thirteen

# Global Encounters and Cultures in Conflict, 1500–1700

Between the mid-15th and mid-16th centuries, much of Europe gained new political, economic, and technological strength. This enabled European states to support a new wave of expansion into the rest of the world. Led by Portugal and then Spain, these states sent explorers, missionaries, merchants, colonists, and armed forces throughout the world. In some cases, as for the civilizations of the Americas, the consequences of these encounters would be immediate and profound. In other cases, as in China and Japan, the effects would be more indirect. But in the long run, this European expansion would mark a turning point in world history.

In Asia, contacts between Westerners and peoples of south and east Asia extended back for centuries, long before Marco Polo, the most widely known European traveler, reached China in the 13th century. Organized by merchants, missionaries, adventurers, or explorers, caravans

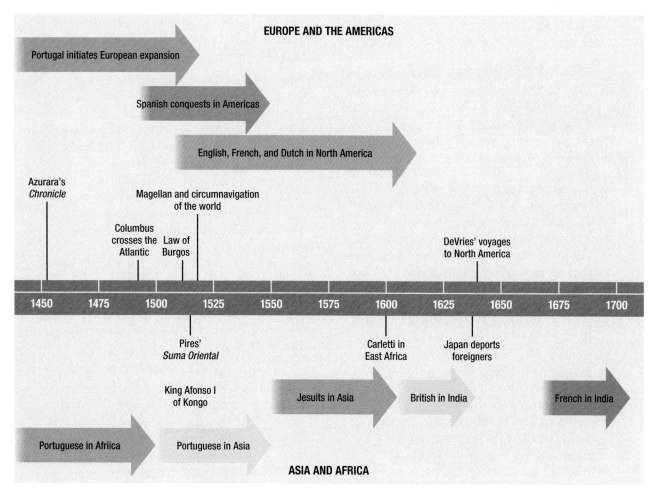

EUROPE AND THE AMERICAS

Portugal initiates European expansion

Spanish conquests in Americas

English, French, and Dutch in North America

Azurara's *Chronicle*

Magellan and circumnavigation of the world

Columbus crosses the Atlantic    Law of Burgos

DeVries' voyages to North America

| 1450 | 1475 | 1500 | 1525 | 1550 | 1575 | 1600 | 1625 | 1650 | 1675 | 1700 |

Pires' *Suma Oriental*

Carletti in East Africa    Japan deports foreigners

King Afonso I of Kongo

Jesuits in Asia    British in India    French in India

Portuguese in Afriica    Portuguese in Asia

ASIA AND AFRICA

crossed the vast plateaus of central Asia with the help of the local Turkic inhabitants. By the 15th century Arab-speaking merchants and bankers had developed a monopoly on the east and south Asia trade. This changed in the 15th, 16th, and 17th centuries as the Portuguese, Spanish, Dutch, British, and French moved in. During this same period the Russians were advancing eastward through Siberia, conquering as they went. A new Asian–European relationship had the potential of becoming a dialogue rewarding to all, but the relationship was marred from the beginning by ethnocentrism and the Europeans' propensity to force their will on the Asians. The long-established Asian societies were usually able to resist European efforts to establish control over them during this period.

In sub-Saharan Africa, the ability of Europeans to penetrate the continent beyond setting up coastal posts was limited by geographic factors, disease, and resistance from African kingdoms. However, this new contact with Europeans—particularly the development of the slave trade—would become important to both Africans and Europeans.

In the Americas, Christopher Columbus' arrival in 1492 has often been used as the starting point for discussion of American history. Recently, historians have acknowledged that the indigenous peoples of North, Central, and South America had a rich culture that predated Europeans' arrival but which has been neglected. As they established empires, Europeans from Spain, Portugal, France, Holland, and England had to adapt their own cultures to the existing environment of peoples and places in the western hemisphere. Europeans had to interact with the Native Americans they conquered and the Africans they brought to the Americas as slaves.

The sources in the chapter will examine three main topics. First, what were the motives for the European expansion? What did they have to gain? How did they justify

# PRIMARY SOURCES

## Using Primary Sources: The Chronicle of the Discovery and Conquest of Guinea

Primary sources have already been briefly defined and discussed in the Preface. What follows is a more specific guide to the use of primary sources. It focuses on the first primary source in this volume, *The Chronicle of the Discovery and Conquest of Guinea,* which appears on pages 3–4, as an example.

1. When reading primary sources such as the following selection from Azurara's *The Chronicle of the Discovery and Conquest of Guinea,* try to think of every line as evidence. Assume that you are a historian who knows little about the history of European expansion overseas during the 15th and 16th centuries and that this document falls into your hands. Your job is to use this document as evidence to support some conclusions about the Portuguese explorers, European expansion, and 15th-century encounters between Europeans and people in other areas of the world.

   Actually, you have a head start. You already know something about this subject from the chapter introduction, the time line, and the headnote preceding the source. You can use this information to better place the source in a historical context and to gain a sense of how the evidence in the source can be used. You also can

use information from the headnote to identify the general nature of the source, where it came from, and when it was written.

2. Think of questions as you read the source. These can keep you focused on how words, lines, and paragraphs of the source might be used as evidence. A general question to keep in mind is "What does this tell me about this civilization, about how people behaved, about how they thought, and about what they believed?" Try reading each line as a piece of evidence to answer part of this general question. More specific questions can be derived from the "consider" points in italics just before the beginning of the document. These points indicate that the source might be particularly useful for providing evidence about the causes, motives, and justifications for the early Portuguese expeditions and the importance of Portugal's (and Spain's) history of encounters with Islam.

3. There are several ways almost any of the paragraphs in this selection might be used as evidence. Read the first paragraph. It might be argued that Prince Henry's ("Lord Infant") first reason for sending ships south along the African coast was pride and stature (his "noble spirit . . . ever urging him both to begin and to carry out very great deeds"). There is also evidence in this

their actions? Second, what observations did the people involved in these cross-cultural contacts make? What do these observations tell us about the societies being observed? What do they reveal about the observer's own assumptions? Third, what were the consequences of these global encounters? What were the effects in Europe? What were the effects outside of Europe?

This last topic will bring us toward a more detailed examination of developments in various parts of the world, which will be the focus of later chapters.

## The Chronicle of the Discovery and Conquest of Guinea

*Azurara*

*The great geographic expansion and conquests of the 15th and 16th centuries were initiated by Prince Henry (the Navigator) of Portugal (1394–1460). Although he did not personally* participate in the explorations, he established a naval school and base of operations on the southwestern tip of Portugal from which he sent expeditions down the west coast of Africa. One of the clearest explanations of the motives for this effort has been provided by Gomes Eannes de Azurara, a friend of Prince Henry (referred to as "the Lord Infant"), who chronicled the voyages of 1452–53 at the request of King Alfonso V.

CONSIDER: *The explanations that sound more like rationalizations than reasons for explorations; whether economic, military, and religious motives are complementary or contradictory; how this document reflects the history of a country engaged with Islam.*

We imagine that we know a matter when we are acquainted with the doer of it and the end for which he

SOURCE: Gomes Eannes de Azurara, *The Chronicle of the Discovery and Conquest of Guinea,* vol. I, trans. Charles Raymond Beazley and Adgar Prestage (London: Hakluyt Society, 1896), pp. 27–29.

paragraph that Prince Henry was, in addition, after knowledge ("because he had also a wish to know the land that lay beyond"). But there is also evidence for two other possible motives in this paragraph: first, economic profit (so that his "mariners or merchants" would attempt voyages in "hope of profit"); and second, religion and conflict with Islam (Prince Henry kept his ships "well armed against the Infidel" and was "stirred up by his zeal for the service of God"). On the other hand, we must be careful not to read too many of our own assumptions into this article or take it at face value. For example, was Azurara (as revealed in the headnote, a friend of Prince Henry) only trying to flatter his patron? Are these "reasons" only justifications rather than motives for initiating the explorations? And are there more fundamental causes for the explorations underlying the reasons expressed by Azurara (such as a growing sense of power by the central government or the development of commercial capitalism) that might be hinted at by his words?

Read the second paragraph. Clearly this points to a hope to establish trade ("many kinds of merchandise might be brought to this realm, which would find a ready market") and reap economic profits ("products of this realm might be taken there, which traffic would bring great profit to our countrymen"). Again, care must be

taken to not read our own assumption back into this period of history. We live in a period in which many people think of economic motives as primary; this may lead us to assume that pursuit of economic profit (rather than stature, knowledge, or religion) was most important to the Portuguese in general and to Prince Henry and these explorers in particular.

Read the third, fourth, and fifth paragraphs. How can the information in these paragraphs be used to provide evidence about the motives, causes, or justifications for the Portuguese explorations? Go through the same process of questioning as you have with the first and second paragraphs.

4. After working on various parts of the source, pull back and consider the source as a whole. It can be used to provide evidence about how the Portuguese (and, perhaps, other Europeans) thought, about their religious beliefs, and about the history of their relations with Islamic peoples ("the Moors"). It can suggest what the Portuguese (and perhaps other Europeans who followed) might try to do when they encountered peoples further down the coast of Africa and elsewhere in the world. It can also hint at some of the conflicts that might occur when these different cultures came into contact.

did it. And since in former chapters we have set forth the Lord Infant as the chief actor in these things, giving as clear an understanding of him as we could, it is meet that in this present chapter we should know his purpose in doing them. And you should note well that the noble spirit of this Prince, by a sort of natural constraint, was ever urging him both to begin and to carry out very great deeds. For which reason, after the taking of Ceuta he always kept ships well armed against the Infidel, both for war, and because he had also a wish to know the land that lay beyond the isles of Canary and that Cape called Bojador, for that up to his time, neither by writings, nor by the memory of man, was known with any certainty the nature of the land beyond that Cape. Some said indeed that Saint Brandan had passed that way; and there was another tale of two galleys rounding the Cape, which never returned. But this doth not appear at all likely to be true, for it is not to be presumed that if the said galleys went there, some other ships would not have endeavoured to learn what voyage they had made. And because the said Lord Infant wished to know the truth of this—since it seemed to him that if he or some other lord did not endeavour to gain that knowledge, no mariners or merchants would ever dare to attempt it—(for it is clear that none of them ever trouble themselves to sail to a place where there is not a sure and certain hope of profit)—and seeing also that no other prince took any pains in this matter, he sent out his own ships against those parts, to have manifest certainty of them all. And to this he was stirred up by his zeal for the service of God and of the King Edward his Lord and brother, who then reigned. And this was the first reason of his action.

The second reason was that if there chanced to be in those lands some population of Christians, or some havens, into which it would be possible to sail without peril, many kinds of merchandise might be brought to this realm, which would find a ready market, and reasonably so, because no other people of these parts traded with them, nor yet people of any other that were known; and also the products of this realm might be taken there, which traffic would bring great profit to our countrymen.

The third reason was that, as it was said that the power of the Moors in that land of Africa was very much greater than was commonly supposed, and that there were no Christians among them, nor any other race of men; and because every wise man is obliged by natural prudence to wish for a knowledge of the power of his enemy; therefore the said Lord Infant exerted himself to cause this to be fully discovered, and to make it known determinately how far the power of those infidels extended.

The fourth reason was because during the one and thirty years that he had warred against the Moors, he had never found a Christian king, nor a lord outside this land, who for the love of our Lord Jesus Christ would aid him in the said war. Therefore he sought to know if

there were in those parts any Christian princes, in whom the charity and the love of Christ was so ingrained that they would aid him against those enemies of the faith.

The fifth reason was his great desire to make increase in the faith of our Lord Jesus Christ and to bring to him all the souls that should be saved,—understanding that all the mystery of the Incarnation, Death, and Passion of our Lord Jesus Christ was for this sole end—namely the salvation of lost souls—whom the said Lord Infant by his travail and spending would fain bring into the true path. For he perceived that no better offering could be made unto the Lord than this; for if God promised to return one hundred goods for one, we may justly believe that for such great benefits, that is to say for so many souls as were saved by the efforts of this Lord, he will have so many hundreds of guerdons in the kingdom of God, by which his spirit may be glorified after this life in the celestial realm. For I that wrote this history saw so many men and women of those parts turned to the holy faith, that even if the Infant had been a heathen, their prayers would have been enough to have obtained his salvation. And not only did I see the first captives, but their children and grandchildren as true Christians as if the Divine grace breathed in them and imparted to them a clear knowledge of itself.

## Africa and Europe: The Problems of Alliances
### Afonso I of Kongo

*The Kingdom of Kongo was the largest and most powerful state in west-central Africa before 1500. The Kongolese met Europeans for the first time when Portuguese sailors led by Diogo Cão reached their country in 1483. By 1491, the ruler (the Mani Kongo) had been baptized and accepted Christianity. King Afonso I, his son (ca. 1485–1543) was instrumental in making his state a Christian country, but often had to deal with a variety of problems, both with his own countrymen and with the Portuguese. Among the fruits of this contact were literacy, new building techniques, bureaucratic styles and titles, and a host of lesser cultural infusions. In his attempts to maintain Christianity, Afonso often turned to either Portugal or Rome for assistance. The following selection touches on the conflicts that emerged between various Portuguese factions who had different allies among the Kongolese nobility, and the relationship between the African king and his European ally.*

CONSIDER: *What the document reveals about the strengths and weaknesses of this African-European alliance; how relations between the Portuguese and Kongolese affected the propagation and growth of Christianity.*

SOURCE: William H. McNeill and Mitsuko Iriye, *Modern Asia and Africa* (Oxford: 1971), pp. 56–59.

Now we wish to tell your Highness about a certain Rui do Rego whom your Highness sent here to teach us and set an example for us, but as soon as he arrived here he wished to be treated like a nobleman and never wanted to teach a single boy. During the Lenten season he came to us and asked for an ox, and we ordered one to be given to him. Then he said he was dying of hunger, and we ordered two sheep to be given to him, but that he was to eat them secretly, so that our people would not see him. Yet he, disregarding this, went and killed the ox in the middle of Lent, in front of all our nobles, and even tempted us with the meat; so that when our people saw it, those who were young and had only been Christians a short time all fled to their lands, and the older ones who remained with us said things that are not to be repeated, stating that we had forbidden them to eat meat, while the white men had plenty of meat, and that we had deceived them and they wanted to kill us. Then we, with much patience and many gifts, were able to pacify them, telling them that they should save their souls and not look at what that man was doing, and that if he wished to go to Hell then they should let him go.

We were so disgusted with all this that we could not see Rui do Rego again and ordered him to go to Chela,[1] so that he could board the first ship that arrived—for he had not taught as your Highness had ordered him to, but had caused to return to idols those whom we, with much fatigue, had converted. So he went and stayed at Chela—and at this time Simão da Silva[2] arrived with two ships and found the said Rui do Rego, who told him so many evil things and so many lies that there is no reckoning them, and that he had been cheated. And then Simão da Silva believed him, through the wrongheadedness of Rui do Rego and what he had said—but Rego did not tell him of the wickedness and heresy that he had practiced here. So that Simão da Silva did not wish to come to where we were (as your Highness had ordered him to) and sent the [ship's] physician with your letters, whom we sheltered as if he had been our brother. A vicar from the island [of São Tomé], who was present here, asked us to let him take the physician to his house to stay with him—but that ecclesiastic spoke so evilly of us to the physician that the physician's mind was changed, and he became persuaded that Simão da Silva should not come [to the capital]. And your Highness will know that it was Fernão de Melo who had ordered all this, since your Highness has no trading station here, and he has tainted goods [to sell?] and always steals from us.

Yet notwithstanding this, Sire, the physician fell ill with fever and could not return to Simão da Silva with an answer, and he wrote him a letter advising him not to come here; that we were a "João Pires" [a "Mr. Nobody," a nonentity], and that we did not deserve any of the things sent by your Highness.[3] The which letter he gave to one of our servants, and it came into our hands and we showed it to all of your Highness' servants who had come in the fleet. When we saw those things we well understood that they had been done at the command of Fernão de Melo—and we gave thanks to our Lord God for having been called a "João Pires" for His love. And all these things, lord and brother, we have suffered with good judgement and prudence, crying many tears—and we have reported nothing to our nobles and people, so that they may not conspire against us.

Then we sent one of our cousins with a young nobleman and wrote to Simão da Silva that, for the love of God, he should come and comfort us, and punish the people who were here, for we would not send him to ask anything of your Highness, except to ask that everyone be treated justly. Because of our entreaties, and those of Dom João our cousin, he left to come, but halfway here the fevers afflicted him with such force that he died. When we heard the news it broke our feet and hands,[4] and we suffered so much vexation that never again, not until this day, have we ever had any pleasure, because of the great disorders and evils later done by the men who came with him.

## The Suma Oriental
### Tomé Pires

*Vasco da Gama's voyage around the southern tip of Africa to India in 1498, ending the Arab monopoly on Indian trade, initiated a massive European expansion into Asia. Soon the Portuguese established a string of outposts and colonies that stretched around much of the world. In Asia alone these posts included Goa, on the west coast of India in 1510, Malacca on the west coast of Malaya in 1511, Macao off the coast of China in 1514, Timor in the eastern tip of Indonesia in 1520, and Japan in 1543.*

*Portuguese travelers to trading posts and urban centers often wrote about the lands and peoples they encountered, providing us with much of our evidence about these early contacts. Tomé Pires was a Portuguese apothecary to his country's royal family. He was also an explorer and wandered to Asia, living in Goa and Malacca, but also traveling extensively from 1511 to 1517. In 1517 he was dispatched*

[1] A coastal region south of the Zaire River.
[2] In 1512 the king of Portugal sent Simão da Silva, with several ships and many men and supplies, as ambassador to the king of the Congo.

[3] The king of Portugal had sent an impressive diversity of supplies, animals, luxuries, plants, and seeds with his ambassador to the Kongo.
[4] A peculiar expression indicating great anguish.
SOURCE: Armando Cortesão, trans., *The Suma Oriental of Tomé Pires. An Account of the East, From the Red Sea to Japan, Written in Malacca and India in 1512–1515*, vol. II (London: Printed for the Hakluyt Society, 1944).

*as the Portuguese ambassador to China, where he was arrested after the Chinese authorities heard rumors that the Europeans were enslaving Chinese. He died in a Canton jail. In 1517 he submitted* The Suma Oriental (Account of the East) *to the King of Portugal as an account of the trade and political situations in Asia to aid future Portuguese exploitation of Asia. Excerpts from this work follow.*

CONSIDER: *The concerns and attitude of Tomé Pires; the flavor of the trading posts he describes; the mixture of people already present in Asian ports before the Europeans arrived.*

### CAMBAY

I now come to the trade of Cambay. . . . All the trade in Cambay is in the hands of the heathen. Their general designation is Gujaratees, and then they are divided into various races—Banians, Brahmans and Pattars. . . . They are men who understand merchandise; they are so properly steeped in the sound and harmony of it, that the Gujaratees say that any offence connected with merchandise is pardonable. . . . They are diligent, quick men in trade. They do their accounts with figures like ours and with our very writing. They are men who do not give away anything that belongs to them, nor do they want anything that belongs to anyone else; wherefore they have been esteemed in Cambay up to the present, practising their idolatry, because they enrich the kingdom greatly with the said trade. There are also some Cairo merchants settled in Cambay, and many Khorasans and Guilans from Aden and Ormuz, all of whom do a great trade in the seaport towns of Cambay. . . .

They trade with the kingdom of the Deccan and Goa and with Malabar, and they have factors everywhere, who live and set up business—as the Genoese do in our part [of the world]— . . . taking back to their own country the kind of merchandise which is valued there . . .

### SIAM

Through the cunning [of the Siamese] the foreign merchants who go to their land and kingdom leave their merchandise in the land and are ill paid; and this happens to them all—but less to the Chinese, on account of their friendship with the king of China. . . .

There are very few Moors in Siam. The Siamese do not like them. There are, however, Arabs, Persians, Bengalees, many Kling, Chinese and other nationalities. And all the Siamese trade is on the China side, and in Pase, Pedir and Bengal. The Moors are in the seaports.

### CHINA

They affirm that all those who take merchandise from Canton to the islands make a profit of three, four or five in every ten, and the Chinese have this custom so that the land shall not be taken from them, as well as in order to receive the dues on the merchandise exported as well as imported; and the chief [reason] is for fear lest the city be taken from them, because they say that the city of Canton is a rich one, and corsairs often come up to it. . . .

They say that the Chinese made this law about not being able to go to Canton for fear of the Javanese and Malays, for it is certain that one of these people's junks would rout twenty Chinese junks. They say that China has more than a thousand junks, and each of them trades where it sees fit; but the people are weak, and such is their fear of Malays and Javanese that it is quite certain that one [of our] ship[s] of four hundred tons could depopulate Canton, and this depopulation would bring great loss to China.

Not to rob any country of its glory, it certainly seems that China is an important, good and very wealthy country, and the Governor of Malacca would not need as much force as they say in order to bring it under our rule, because the people are very weak and easy to overcome. . . .

They say that there are people from Tartary (*Tartaria*) in the land of China . . . and these people are very white with red beards. They ride on horseback; they are warlike. And they say that they go from China to the land of the Tartars (*tartaros*) in two months, and that in Tartary they have horses shod with copper shoes, and this must be because China extends a long way on the northern side, and our bombardiers say that in Germany they heard tell of these people and of a city named by the Chinese *Quesechama*, and it seems to them that by this route they could go to their lands in a short time; but they say that by reason of the cold the land is uninhabited.

### JAVA

The king of Java is a heathen. . . . These kings of Java have a fantastic idea: they say that their nobility has no equal. The Javanese heathen lords are tall and handsome; they are lavishly adorned about their person, and have richly caparisoned horses. They use krises, swords, and lances of many kinds, all inlaid with gold. They are great hunters and horsemen—stirrups all inlaid with gold, inlaid saddles, such as are not to be found anywhere else in the world. The Javanese lords are so noble and exalted that there is certainly no nation to compare with them over a wide area in these parts. . . .

The lords of Java are revered like gods, with great respect and deep reverence. The land of Java is thickly peopled in the interior, with many cities, and very large ones, including the great city of *Dayo* where the king is in residence and where his court is. They say that the people who frequent the court are without number. The kings do not show themselves to the people except once or twice in the year. They stay in their palace . . . and there they are with all the pleasures and with feasts, with great quantities of wives and concubines. They say that the king of Java has a thousand eunuchs to wait on these women, and these eunuchs are dressed like women and wear their hair dressed in the form of diadems. . . .

MALACCA

Those from Cairo bring the merchandise brought by the galleasses of Venice, to wit, many arms, scarlet-in-grain, coloured woollen cloths, coral, copper, quicksilver, vermilion, nails, silver, glass and other beads, and golden glassware.

Those from Mecca bring a great quantity of opium, rosewater and such like merchandise, and much liquid storax.

Those from Aden bring to Gujarat a great quantity of opium, raisins, madder, indigo, rosewater, silver, seed-pearls, and other dyes, which are of value in Cambay.

In these companies go Parsees, Turks, Turkomans and Armenians, and they come and take up their companies for their cargo in Gujarat, and from there they embark in March and sail direct for Malacca; and on the return journey they call at the Maldive Islands.

## Women and Poverty in Japan
### Francesco Carletti

*The Asian–European relationship had the potential of becoming a dialogue rewarding to all sides, but in fact the relationship was marred from the beginning by each side lacking an understanding of the other's culture. The following selection is from the writings of Francesco Carletti, who was born in Florence in 1572. He spent several years traveling with his father around the world, including East Asia in 1597–98. Carletti is writing for an audience that has virtually no information about the Japanese and is relying on his accounts to formulate their own views. Here Carletti discusses poverty, women, and prostitution in Japan. Notice Carletti's hypocrisy since selling children and prostitution occurred in Europe as well.*

CONSIDER: *The image of Japanese civilization this account might produce in European readers' minds; whether this reveals more about European visions of Japanese women than about Japanese society; why the author might have chosen to write this account.*

[The Japanese] do not, however, hold in equal esteem the virtue of their daughters and sisters; or rather they take no account of this at all. Indeed it often happens that a girl's own father, mother, or brothers—without any feeling of shame on the part of any of those concerned—will without hesitation sell her as a prostitute before she is married, for a few pence, under the pressure of poverty, which is very severely felt throughout the whole country. And this poverty is the cause of the most shameless immorality—an immorality which is so gross and which takes such different and unusual forms, to pass belief.

But the Portuguese are my witnesses and cannot be gainsaid—especially those who come year by year from China, that is, from the island of Macao. . . . As soon as ever these Portuguese arrive and disembark, the pimps who control this traffic in women call on them in the houses in which they are quartered for the time of their stay, and enquire whether they would like to purchase, or acquire in any other method they please, a girl, for the period of their sojourn, or to keep her for so many months, or for a night, or for a day, or for an hour, a contract being first made with these brokers, or an agreement entered into with the girl's relations, and the money paid down. And if they prefer it they will take them to the girl's house, in order that they may see her first, or else they will take them to see her on their own premises, which are usually situated in certain hamlets or villages outside the city. And many of these Portuguese, upon whose testimony I am relying, fall in with this custom as the fancy takes them, driving the best bargain they can for a few pence. And so it often happens that they will get hold of a pretty little girl of fourteen or fifteen years of age, for three or four *scudi*, or a little more or less, according to the time during which they wish to have her at their disposal, with no other responsibility beyond that of sending her back home when done with. Nor does this practice in any way interfere with a girl's chances of marriage. Indeed many of them would never get married, if they had not by this means acquired a dowry, by accumulating 30 or 40 *scudi*, given to them from time to time by these Portuguese, who have kept them in their houses for seven or eight months on end, and who have in some cases married them themselves. And when these women are hired by the day, it is enough to give them the merest trifle, nor do they ever refuse to be hired on account of a variation in the price, which is hardly ever refused by their relations, or by those who keep them as a sort of stock in trade for these purposes in their houses, and to whom the money is paid—the women being in effect all slaves sold for these purposes. And there are, moreover, some of them who, by agreement with the brokers, ask for no more than their food and clothing—neither of which costs much—while the whole of their earnings go to the men who keep them.

To sum up, the country is more plentifully supplied than any other with these sort of means of gratifying the passion for sexual indulgence, just as it abounds in every

SOURCE: Bishop Trollope, trans., "The Carletti Discourse," published in *The Transactions of the Asiatic Society of Japan*, second series, vol. IX, 1932.

other sort of vice, in which it surpasses every other place in the world.

## The Aztec Account of the Conquest of Mexico

### Diego Munoz Camargo

*In contrast to Castillo's account, which emphasizes the technologically advanced nature of the Aztec empire, Spaniard Diego Munoz Camargo's view of this civilization spotlights its superstitions and spiritual side. Camargo married into the nobility of one of the groups who allied themselves with Cortez shortly after his arrival. This account suggests that superstition may have played a major role in the greatly outnumbered Spanish defeating the Aztec empire.*

CONSIDER: *The role of religion and superstition in the 15th and 16th centuries in Europe and Latin America.*

Ten years before the Spaniards came to this land, the people saw a strange wonder and took it to be an evil sign and portent. This wonder was a great column of flame which burned in the night, shooting out such brilliant sparks and flashes that it seemed to rain fire on the earth and to blaze like daybreak. It seemed to be fastened against the sky in the shape of a pyramid, its base set against the ground, where it was of vast width, and its bulk narrowing to a peak that reached up and touched the heavens. It appeared at midnight and could still be seen at dawn, but in the daytime it was quelled by the force and brilliance of the sun. This portent burned for a year, beginning in the year which the natives called 12-House—that is, 1517 in our Spanish reckoning.

When this sign and portent was first seen, the natives were overcome with terror, weeping and shouting and crying out, and beating the palms of their hands against their mouths, as is their custom. These shouts and cries were accompanied by sacrifices of blood and of human beings, for this was their practice wherever they thought they were endangered by some calamity.

This great marvel caused so much dread and wonder that they spoke of it constantly, trying to imagine what such a strange novelty could signify. They begged the seers and magicians to interpret its meaning, because no such thing had ever been seen or reported anywhere in the world. It should be noted that these signs began to appear ten years before the coming of the Spaniards, but that the year called 12-House in their reckoning was the year 1517, two years before the Spaniards reached this land.

. . . *The eighth wonder* and sign that appeared in Mexico: the natives saw two men merged into one

body—these they called *tlacantzolli* ("men-squeezed-together")—and others who had two heads but only one body. They were brought to the palace of the Black Hall to be shown to the great Motecuhzoma, but they vanished as soon as he had seen them, and all these signs and others became invisible. To the natives, these marvels augered their death and ruin, signifying that the end of the world was coming and that other peoples would be created to inhabit the earth. They were so frightened and grief-stricken that they could form no judgment about these things, so new and strange and never before seen or reported.

## Laws of the Burgos: The Spanish Colonize Central and South America

*As the first colonists in the New World, Spaniards sought to exploit the wealth of Central and South America through the use of forced labor. This encomienda system, a system of forced labor on extensive plantations, permitted Spanish settlers to compel native peoples to labor in gold and silver mines, agriculture, and the home. This excerpt is from a set of laws developed at Burgos, Spain, in 1512. They became the basis for the legal system for Spanish America in the early colonial period.*

CONSIDER: *Spanish assumptions and concerns about these native peoples; what these laws tell us about how the native population actually lived under Spanish domination.*

Whereas, the King, my Lord and Father, and the Queen, my Mistress and Mother (may she rest in glory!), always desired that the chiefs and Indians of the Island of Española be brought to a knowledge of our Holy Catholic Faith, and, . . .

Whereas, it has become evident through long experience that nothing has sufficed to bring the said chiefs and Indians to a knowledge of our Faith (necessary for their salvation), since by nature they are inclined to idleness and vice, and have no manner of virtue or doctrine (by which Our Lord is disserved), and that the principal obstacle in the way of correcting their vices and having them profit by and impressing them with the doctrine is that their dwellings are remote from the settlements of the Spaniards who go hence to reside in the said Island, because, although at the time the Indians go to serve them they are indoctrinated in and taught the things of our Faith, after serving they return to their dwellings where, because of the distance and their own evil inclinations, they immediately forget what they have been taught and go back to their customary idleness and vice, . . .

Whereas, this is contrary to our Faith, and,

---

SOURCE: Miguel Leon-Portilla, *The Broken Spears: The Aztec Account of the Conquest of Mexico* (Boston, Beacon Press, 1962), pp. 7, 11.

SOURCE: Lesley Byrd Simpson, trans., *The Laws of Burgos of 1512–1513* (Westport, Conn.: Greenwood Press).

Whereas, it is our duty to seek a remedy for it in every way possible, . . . the most beneficial thing that could be done at present would be to remove the said chiefs and Indians to the vicinity of the villages and communities of the Spaniards. . . .

First, since it is our determination to remove the said Indians and have them dwell near the Spaniards, we order and command that the persons to whom the said Indians are given, or shall be given, in encomienda, shall at once and forthwith build, for every fifty Indians, four lodges [bohìos] of thirty by fifteen feet, and have the Indians plant 5,000 hillocks (3,000 in cassava and 2,000 in yams), 250 pepper plants, and 50 cotton plants . . . and these shall be settled next to the estates of the Spaniards who have them in encomienda, well situated and housed, and under the eyes of you, our said Admiral and judges and officers . . . and the persons who have the said Indians in their charge [in encomienda] shall have them sow, in season, half a fanega of maize, and shall also give them a dozen hens and a cock to raise and enjoy the fruit thereof, the chickens as well as the eggs; and as soon as the Indians are brought to the estates they shall be given all the aforesaid as their own property. . . .

Also, we order and command that the citizen to whom the said Indians are given in encomienda shall, upon the land that is assigned to him, be obliged to erect a structure to be used for a church. . . . Every Sunday and obligatory feast day they may come there to pray and hear Mass, and also to hear the good advice that the priests who say Mass shall give them; and the priests who say Mass shall teach them the Commandments and the Articles of the Faith, and the other things of the Christian doctrine. Therefore, in order that they be instructed in the things of the Faith and become accustomed to pray and hear Mass, we command that the Spaniards who are on the estates with the said Indians and have charge of them shall be obliged to bring them all together to the said church in the morning and remain with them until after Mass is said; and after Mass they shall bring them back to the estates and give them their pots of cooked meat, in such wise that they eat on that day better than on any other day of the week. . . .

Also, we order and command that, after the Indians have been brought to the estates, all the founding [of gold] that henceforth is done on the said Island shall be done in the manner prescribed below: that is, the said persons who have Indians in encomienda shall extract gold with them for five months in the year and, at the end of these five months, the said Indians shall rest forty days, and the day they cease their labor of extracting gold shall be noted on a certificate, which shall be given to the miners who go to the mines. . . .

Also, we order and command that all those on the said Island who have Indians in encomienda, now or in the future, shall be obliged to give to each of them a hammock in which to sleep continually; and they shall not allow them to sleep on the ground, as hitherto they have been doing. . . .

## Voyages from Holland to America: The Dutch Colonize North America
### David Pietersz de Vries

*The Dutch were the first to colonize the area of the lower Hudson Valley in what are now the states of New York, New Jersey, and Connecticut in the United States. They established large estates and imported tenant farmers to work small parcels of land. Initially, Native Americans and the Dutch farmers traded together and lived in close proximity. Yet, new interests and new administrators led the Dutch to try to displace the Algonquins from their land. This document, about a massacre that took place in February 1643, reveals the harsh practices of colonists who had little respect for the rights or humanity of those they considered to be "uncivilized."*

CONSIDER: *The reasons for the author's opposition to the governor's actions; whether the governor's stand was based on self-interest or humanistic concerns.*

. . . So was this business begun between the 25th and 26th of February in the year 1643. I remained that night at the governor's, sitting up. I went and sat in the kitchen, when, about midnight, I heard a great shrieking, and I ran to the ramparts of the fort, and looked over to Pavonia. Saw nothing but firing, and heard the shrieks of the Indians murdered in their sleep. I returned again to the house by the fire. Having sat there awhile, there came an Indian with his squaw, whom I knew well, and who lived about an hour's walk from my house, and told me that they two had fled in a small skiff; that they had betaken themselves to Pavonia; that the Indians from Fort Orange had surprised them; and that they had come to conceal themselves in the fort. I told them that they must go away immediately; that there was no occasion for them to come to the fort to conceal themselves; that they who had killed their people at Pavonia were not Indians, but the Swannekens, as they call the Dutch, had done it. . . . When it was day, the soldiers returned to the fort, having massacred or murdered eighty Indians, and considering they had done a deed of Roman valour, in murdering so many in their sleep; where infants were torn from their mother's breasts, and hacked to pieces in the presence of the parents, and the pieces thrown into the fire and in the water, and other sucklings were bound to small boards, and then cut,

SOURCE: David Pietersz de Vries, *Voyages from Holland to America*, Henry C. Murphy, trans. (New York, 1853), pp. 167–71.

stuck, and pierced, and miserably massacred in a manner to move a heart of stone. . . . After this exploit, the soldiers were rewarded for their services, and Director Kieft thanked them by taking them by the hand and congratulating them. . . .

. . . As soon as the Indians understood that the Swannekens had so treated them, all the men whom they could surprise on the farm-lands, they killed; but we have never heard that they have ever permitted women or children to be killed. They burned all the houses, farms, barns, grain, haystacks, and destroyed everything they could get hold of. So there was an open destructive war begun. . . . When now the Indians had destroyed so many farms and men in revenge for their people, I went to Governor William Kieft, and asked him if it was not as I had said it would be, that he would only effect the spilling of Christian blood. Who would now compensate us for our losses? But he gave me no answer.

## A Voyage to South America: Caste and Race in Latin America

### Jorge Juan and Antonio de Ulloa

*Unlike English North America, which excluded Native Americans from any participation in colonial society and enslaved anyone who had any African ancestors, Spanish and Portuguese South America developed a much more complex social caste and racial system. While the English colonies enforced strict distinctions between blacks and whites, the Spanish developed a more varied set of racial categories, which some historians have argued led to less segregation and racial hostility. This excerpt was written by two Spanish officials after their inspection of the caste system of the Caribbean port, Carthagena.*

CONSIDER: *The ways that the South American system allowed for a relatively great degree of interaction among people of different racial backgrounds; how the caste system reinforced social and class distinctions.*

The inhabitants may be divided into different castes or tribes, who derive their origin from a coalition of Whites, Negroes, and Indians. Of each of these we shall treat particularly.

The Whites may be divided into two classes, the Europeans, and Creoles, or Whites born in the country. The former are commonly called Chapitones, but are not numerous; most of them either return into Spain after acquiring a competent fortune, or remove up into inland provinces in order to increase it. Those who are

SOURCE: Jorge Juan and Antonio de Ulloa, *A Voyage to South America*, vol. I (London, 1772), pp. 29–32.

settled at Carthagena carry on the whole trade of that place, and live in opulence; whilst the other inhabitants are indigent, and reduced to have recourse to mean and hard labor for subsistence. The families of the White Creoles compose the landed interest; some of them have large estates, and are highly respected. . . . Some of these families, in order to keep up their original dignity, have either married their children to their equals in the country, or sent them as officers on board the galleons, but others have greatly declined. Besides these, there are other Whites, in mean circumstances, who either owe their origin to Indian families, or at least to an intermarriage with them, so that there is some mixture in their blood; but when this is not discoverable by their color, the conceit of being White alleviates the pressure of every other calamity.

Among the other tribes which are derived from an intermarriage of the Whites with the Negroes, the first are the Mulattos. Next to these the Tercerones, produced from a White and a Mulatto, with some approximation to the former, but not so near as to obliterate their origin. After these follow the Quarterones, proceeding from a White and a Terceron. The last are the Quinterones, who owe their origin to a White and Quarteron. This is the last gradation, there being no visible difference between them and the Whites, either in color or features; nay, they are often fairer than the Spaniards. The children of a White and Quinteron are also called Spaniards, and consider themselves as free from all taint of the Negro race. Every person is so jealous of the order of their tribe or cast, that if, through inadvertence, you call them by a degree lower than what they actually are, they are highly offended, never suffering themselves to be deprived of so valuable a gift of fortune. . . .

These are the most known and common tribes or castes; there are indeed several others proceeding from their intermarriages; but, being so various, even they themselves cannot easily distinguish them. . . .

These castes, from the Mulattos, all affect the Spanish dress, but wear very slight stuffs on account of the heat of the climate. These are the mechanics of the city; the Whites, whether Creoles or Chapitones, disdaining such a mean occupation, follow nothing below merchandise. But it being impossible for all to succeed, great numbers not being able to procure sufficient credit, they become poor and miserable from their aversion to those trades they follow in Europe; and, instead of the riches which they flattered themselves with possessing in the Indies, they experience the most complicated wretchedness.

The class of Negroes is not the least numerous, and is divided into two parts; the free and the slaves. These are again subdivided into Creoles and Bozares, part of which are employed in the cultivation of the haciendas, or estancias. Those in the city are obliged to perform the most laborious services, and pay out of their wages a certain quota to their masters, subsisting themselves on the small remainder. The violence of the heat not permitting them to wear any clothes, their only covering is a small piece of cotton stuff about their waist; the female slaves go in the same manner. Some of these live at the estancias, being married to the slaves who work there; while those in the city sell in the markets all kind of eatables. . . .

# VISUAL SOURCES

## Using Visual Sources: Exploration, Global Encounters, and Politics

Visual sources have already been briefly defined and discussed. What follows is a more specific guide to their use. For example, the first visual source in this volume, Map 13–1 on page 12 in Chapter 13, shows some of the main routes taken by European overseas explorers and voyagers during the 15th and 16th centuries plus the prevailing ocean currents and winds they encountered.

1. Try to look at visual sources, whether they are maps, paintings, or photographs, as if they were written, primary documents. As with primary documents, assume that you are a historian who knows little about the overseas voyages made by Europeans during the 15th and 16th centuries and you discover this map. Your goal is to try to "read" it as evidence to support some conclusions about these voyages.

   Without some guidance, "reading" a visual source as historical evidence is more difficult than using a written source. The reproduction often makes the details hard to see, and most people are not used to looking at maps or pictures in this analytical way. Therefore, the first paragraph of the map's headnote gives the historical context of what is shown in the map—how technological discoveries and mapping of ocean currents and winds made the voyages by Europeans possible. The second paragraph describes and analyzes connections between ocean currents, prevailing winds, routes taken by voyagers, and the geopolitical results of this European expansion. Here, as with most visual sources, it is useful to go back and forth between the map and its accompanying written headnote.

2. As with primary documents think of questions as you look at the visual source and as you read the written guide to it. The general question to keep in mind is "What does this tell me about this civilization, about these historical developments, and about how people behaved, how they thought, or what they accomplished?" Other questions are suggested in the "consider" points, such as what information an artist might have been attempting to convey to the viewer of a picture or, here, what this map might reveal about patterns of exploration and global encounters during the 15th and 16th centuries.

3. This map shows the three main routes taken by European overseas voyagers across the Atlantic Ocean, the main ocean currents they encountered, and the prevailing winds. The headnote suggests some ways that the information derived from this map can be used as historical evidence to help explain why these routes were taken by European voyagers and what some of the geopolitical results of expansion were.

4. Now pull back and consider the map in the context of other sources in this chapter or other material you have looked at on the topic of exploration, global encounters, and politics during the 15th and 16th centuries. What might this tell us about the location of the commercial and colonial empires being established by Portugal, Spain, France, and England during this period? What geographic and political difficulties might these Europeans have encountered in trying to establish trade or control in different areas of the world? If one of the main motives for the voyages was trade with the East, why might these conditions have sailed west and south across the Atlantic instead of taking the shorter route across the Mediterranean Sea? What other information might be added to this map to make it more useful as a historical source? In what ways might this visual source complement or contradict material in written sources?

## Exploration, Expansion, and Politics

*Aside from the various motivations for the voyages of discovery during the 15th and 16th centuries, a number of factors combined to make those voyages physically possible when earlier they were not. Technological discoveries significantly improved shipbuilding and navigation. But also important was the understanding and mapping of prevailing ocean currents and winds in relation to land masses. It was much easier to sail with, rather than against, currents and winds, and sailors counted on finding land masses for supplies along the way.*

*The early voyages tended to take advantage of currents and winds as shown in this map. Thus, for example, early voyages to North America usually took a more southerly route westward across the Atlantic and returned on a more northerly route, while Portuguese ships headed east to the Indian Ocean by following winds and currents to Brazil and then crossed the Atlantic farther south. Prevailing currents and winds also explain the difficulty of westward voyages around the tip of South America. These patterns of voyages also shed light on some of the geopolitical results of expansion. For example, even though Portugal's efforts were directed toward an eastern route to the Far East, she acquired Brazil (her only territory in the New World) to the west since it was on a route favored by winds and currents.*

CONSIDER: *How this map helps explain the pattern of exploration and colonization by the various European powers.*

## A Buddhist Temple: European Views of Asia

*When the first European travelers returned from Asia, they brought with them tales of exotic lands and peoples that were so astonishing as to be barely believable. While Asian cultures were different enough from European cultures to elicit wonderment, travelers tended to exaggerate, and even distort, what they had seen. Europeans were interested in Asia as a source of precious goods (spice, tea, etc.), a market for excess European goods, and fertile ground for missionaries to proselytize. They rarely tried to understand what they were experiencing, and their contempt for non-European culture required distortion of their accounts lest anyone back home think these people were somehow equal to them. Illustration 13–1 is from the 1600s and depicts a Buddhist temple in China. The unknown European artist has seen fit to include two demons that look suspiciously European in origin on either side of the Buddha statue.*

CONSIDER: *The impression the artist was trying to create in European viewers' minds.*

## The Conquest of Mexico as Seen by the Aztecs

*With the exception of a few written documents, most accounts of Aztec culture, like that of Incan and Mayan cultures, come from pictographs, sculptures, and other artifacts.*

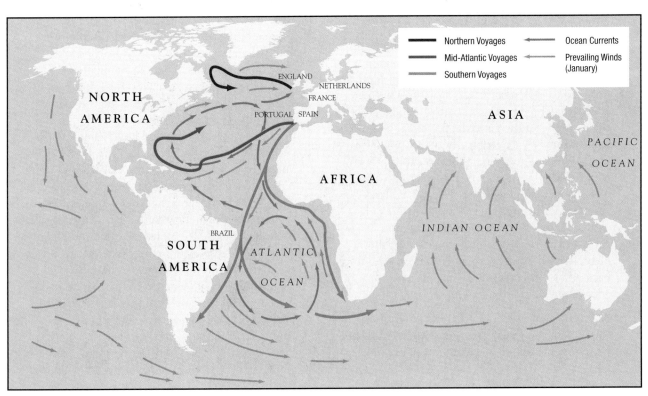

**Map 13–1** Overseas Explorations.

**Illustration 13–1** The Aldus Collection.

Historical events are often depicted from the point of view of the conqueror rather than the vanquished. Here we see one of the few depictions of the Spanish conquest of the Aztec from the perspective of the conquered people. In this Aztec manuscript from about 1519 to 1522 Illustration 13–2, shortly after Cortez entered Mexico in 1519, the bloody and brutal suppression of the Aztec is shown in all its horror. Notice the Aztec offering what appears to be a wreath to Cortez, holding a sword about to be swung.

CONSIDER: The symbols of conquest and destruction shown in the illustration.

**Illustration 13–2** Biblioteca Apostolica Vaticana, Rome.

# SECONDARY SOURCES

## Using Secondary Sources: the Expansion of Europe

Secondary sources have already been briefly defined and discussed. What follows is a more specific guide to the use of secondary sources, focusing on our first secondary source in this volume, *The Expansion of Europe*, which appears on pages 14–15 in Chapter 13.

1. Try to read a secondary source like *The Expansion of Europe* by Richard B. Reed not as historical evidence (as you would read a primary source) but as a set of conclusions—an interpretation of the evidence from primary sources—by a scholar (usually a historian). Your job is to try to understand what the writer's interpretation is, evaluate whether any arguments or evidence the writer presents seems to support it adequately, and decide in what ways you agree or disagree with that interpretation.

2. Try to think of questions as you read a secondary source. This process can keep you alert as to why the author selects and presents only certain

information and what conclusions the author is trying to convey to the reader. Perhaps the two most important questions to keep in mind are "What question is this author trying to answer?" and "What does all that the author had written add up to?" For each secondary source, guidance for these two questions and related questions is provided in the headnote to the source and in the "consider" points.

Here the headnote to this secondary source tells us that the author, Richard B. Reed, is trying to argue that the European expansion of the 15th and 16th centuries was a nationalistic phenomenon and that this explains why Portugal was an early leader in this expansion. The "consider" section alerts us to more specific aspects of what the author is trying to convince us of, such as why Portugal was in the best position to initiate the expansion and why Italy and Germany did not participate in this overseas expansion.

3. Try reading and summarizing in a few words what Reed is trying to say or argue in each paragraph. What conclusion is he reaching?

## The Expansion of Europe

*Richard B. Reed*

*In analyzing the overseas expansion of the 15th and 16th centuries, historians typically emphasize a combination of economic and religious factors to explain the motivation behind expansion while focusing on the establishment of adequate knowledge and technology as key conditions for its occurrence. In the following selection, Richard B. Reed argues that European expansion was a nationalistic phenomenon and that, because of this, Portugal was able to become the early leader.*

CONSIDER: *Why Italy and Germany did not participate in overseas expansion; how one might attack Reed's argument that Portugal was in a better position to initiate expansion than any other country; other factors that might help explain why Portugal led in overseas expansion.*

The expansion of Europe was an intensely nationalistic phenomenon. It was an aspect of the trend, most evident in the late fifteenth and early sixteenth centuries, toward

SOURCE: Richard B. Reed, "The Expansion of Europe," in *The Meaning of the Renaissance and Reformation*, ed. Richard L. DeMolen (Boston: Houghton Mifflin, 1974), p. 299. Reprinted by permission.

the establishment of strong centralized authority in the "new monarchies," as they have been called, and the emergence of the nation-state. A policy of overseas expansion required a degree of internal stability and national consciousness that only a powerful central government could command. Portugal achieved this position long before her eventual competitors, and under the leadership of the dynamic house of Avis became a consolidated kingdom comparatively free from feudal divisions before the end of the fifteenth century. While Spain was still divided into a number of conflicting political jurisdictions, England and France were preoccupied with their own and each other's affairs, and the Dutch were still an appendage of the Empire, the Portuguese combined the advantages of their natural geographic situation with their political and economic stability to initiate the age of discovery. Spain in the sixteenth century, and England, France, and the Netherlands in the seventeenth century, became active colonial powers only after each had matured into strong national entities, independent of feudal political and economic restrictions. . . .

The importance of the nation-state in Renaissance expansion is particularly apparent when the Italian city-states are considered. Venice and Genoa, cities that had

One could summarize the first paragraph by saying that Reed is trying to convince us that the expansion of Europe was a nationalistic phenomenon, occurring as part of the trend toward establishing strong centralized monarchies as nation-states emerged—first in 15th-century Portugal and only later in 16th-century Spain and 17th-century England, France, and the Netherlands. He adds that geographic location (on the southwestern edge of Europe) also helps us explain Portugal's lead in the expansion of Europe.

In the second paragraph Reed argues that the experience of Italian and German states supports the argument he is making in the first paragraph. He points out that while Italians and Germans played important roles in the expansion of Europe by supplying money, knowledge (particularly cartography and chronicles of new discoveries), and personnel (early voyagers like Columbus), they did not participate directly in Europe's overseas expansion because neither Italy nor Germany were united nations.

In the third paragraph Reed further supports his argument in his first paragraph by stating that expansion was not an international venture characterized by cooperation between nations; it was primarily a state enterprise.

4. Finally, pull back and consider a secondary source as a whole. Try to formulate the author's argument in a nutshell and consider what the author avoids.

Here you might say that while Reed argues, with supporting evidence, that European overseas expansion was a nationalistic phenomenon directly connected to the establishment of strong centralized governments in the nation-states of Europe, led by Portugal, he avoids other causes' importance to the expansion. For example, using evidence concerning the economic motives for expansion within some of the sources in this chapter and pointing to the development of commercial capitalism and long-distance trade just prior to and during the 15th century, one might argue that economic concerns were at least as important as nationalism.

contributed so many of the medieval travelers and early Renaissance geographers and mapmakers, did not participate directly in Europe's overseas expansion. Yet Italian names dominated the rolls of the early voyagers. Prince Henry employed Venetians and Florentines in his naval establishment, while Columbus, Vespucci, Verrazano, the Cabots, and many others sailed for Spain, France, and England. Italian cartography was the best in Europe until the second half of the sixteenth century, and a high proportion of the books and pamphlets that chronicled new discoveries emanated from the presses of Vicenza, Venice, Rome, and Florence. Italian bankers and merchants were also very active in the commercial life of the principal Iberian cities. A divided Italy was instrumental in making Renaissance expansion possible, but it could not take full advantage of its own endowments. Germans, too, figured prominently in the expansion of the sixteenth century, as the names of Federmann, Staden, Welser, and Fugger attest. But Germany, like Italy, was not united, and the emergence of these two nations as colonial powers had to wait until their respective consolidations in the nineteenth century.

While every nationality in Western Europe was represented in Renaissance expansion, it was by no means an international venture. On the contrary, it was very much an expression of that nationalistic fervor that characterized political developments in the fifteenth and sixteenth centuries. It was primarily a state enterprise, often financed privately but controlled and protected by the governments of the concerned powers. There was no cooperation between nations, and even after the upheaval of the Protestant Reformation, when political loyalties and alignments were conditioned by religious sympathies, there were no colonial alliances that provided for mutual Protestant or Catholic overseas policies.

## The Changing Ecology of New England
### William Cronon

*Along with new habits, technologies, and cultures, Europeans brought entirely new economic systems to New England. Together, these dramatically affected the environment of both the Native Americans and the colonists. We tend to think of ecological damage as being a product of 20th-century industrialism. In this excerpt, William Cronon summarizes the changes that New England underwent in the first 200 years of contact between colonists and Native Americans. Both groups changed the "natural" environment. Significantly, he does not see all these changes as being beneficial or even benign.*

CONSIDER: *Cronon's view that Americans, in addition to being "the people of plenty, were a people of waste"; the significance of ecological changes.*

New England in 1800 was far different from the land the earliest European visitors had described. By 1800, the Indians who had been its first human inhabitants were reduced to a small fraction of their former numbers, and had been forced onto less and less desirable agricultural lands. Their ability to move about the landscape in search of ecological abundance had become severely constrained, so that their earlier ways of interacting with the environment were no longer feasible and their earlier sources of food were less easy to find. Disease and malnutrition had become facts of life for them.

Large areas particularly of southern New England were now devoid of animals which had once been common: beaver, deer, bear, turkey, wolf, and others had vanished. In their place were hordes of European grazing animals which constituted a heavier burden on New England plants and soils. Their presence had brought hundreds of miles of fences. With fences had come the weeds: dandelion and rat alike joined alien grasses as they made their way across the landscape. New England's forests still exceeded its cleared land in 1800, but, especially near settled areas, the remaining forest had been significantly altered by grazing, burning, and cutting. The greatest of the oaks and white pines were gone, and cedar had become scarce. Hickory had been reduced because of its attractiveness as a fuel. Clear-cutting had shifted forest composition in favor of those trees that were capable of sprouting from stumps, with the result that the forests of 1800 were physically smaller than they had been at the time of European settlement. The cutting of upland species such as beech and maple, which were accustomed to moist sites, produced drying that encouraged species such as the oaks, which preferred drier soils.

Deforestation had in general affected the region by making local temperatures more erratic, soils drier, and drainage patterns less constant. A number of smaller streams and springs no longer flowed year-round, and some larger rivers were dammed and no longer accessible to the fish which had once spawned in them. Water and wind erosion were taking place with varying severity,

and flooding had become more common. Soil exhaustion was occurring in many areas as a result of poor husbandry, and the first of many European pests and crop diseases had already begun to appear. These changes had taken place primarily in the settled areas, and it was still possible to find extensive regions in the north where they did not apply. Nevertheless, they heralded the future. . . .

The implications of this . . . ecological contradiction stretched well beyond the colonial period. Although we often tend to associate ecological changes primarily with the cities and factories of the nineteenth and twentieth centuries, it should by now be clear that changes with similar roots took place just as profoundly in the farms and countrysides of the colonial period. The transition to capitalism alienated the products of the land as much as the products of human labor, and so transformed natural communities as profoundly as it did human ones. By integrating New England ecosystems into an ultimately global capitalist economy, colonists and Indians together began a dynamic and unstable process of ecological change which had in no way ended by 1800. We live with their legacy today. When the geographer Carl Sauer wrote in the twentieth century that Americans had "not yet learned the difference between yield and loot," he was describing one of the most longstanding tendencies of their way of life. Ecological abundance and economic prodigality went hand in hand: the people of plenty were a people of waste.

## Muslims in Ming China
*Morris Rossabi*

*Historically the Chinese were relatively inward looking, expressing little or no interest in the world outside their cultural boundaries. Yet, at the same time, they welcomed those who arrived within those boundaries as long as these outsiders adapted to the Chinese social and political systems and posed no threat to the Dragon Throne. Muslims (originally as Arab and Persian traders) arrived in China as early as the Tang Dynasty (618–906) and began to settle in various locales—especially in the northwest regions. They found the local people amenable to their presence and, particularly from the early years of the Ming Dynasty, they flourished. In this excerpt, Morris Rossabi discusses how the Muslims were treated by the Ming rulers and the people of China during the late 14th and 15th centuries.*

SOURCE: Morris Rossabi, "Muslims and Central Asian Revolts," in *From Ming to Ch'ing: Conquest, Region and Continuity in Seventeenth Century China,* Jonathan D. Spence and John E. Wills, Jr., eds. (New Haven and London: Yale University Press, 1979), pp. 170–85.

CONSIDER: *The difficulties of moving into a culture and society completely different from your own; the issues of acculturation and assimilation.*

The Chinese Muslims were a large and influential group and presented additional problems for the Ming Dynasty. . . .

Ming policy toward the Muslims who lived in nonstrategic areas was, in fact, fairly tolerant. The court employed them as astronomers, calendar makers, and diviners in the Directorate of Astronomy, all certainly critical occupations in an agricultural society. Muslims retained their preeminent positions in the directorate until the Jesuits successfully challenged their influence in the 1600s. Starting in the Yungluo reign (1403–24), the Ming also used Muslims as envoys, translators, and interpreters and occasionally accorded them prominent positions and offered them generous rewards. . . .

Two of the Ming emperors were attracted by Islam, and some Chinese Muslim accounts, which are not very trustworthy, report that they have become Muslim converts. . . . The Zhengde emperor (1506–21) was favorably disposed toward Muslims. He surrounded himself with several Muslim eunuchs and advisers; he authorized the production of bronzes and porcelains which contained Arabic inscriptions and were sold to Muslim patrons in China and Central Asia; and he invited to his court and was solicitous to a Muslim chieftain from Hami who had collaborated with China's Turfanese enemies, while he demoted some of his own officials who had imprisoned the chieftain. . . .

The Ming did not attempt to split up and disperse the large concentrations of Muslims living along the northwestern border, which is undoubtedly the most tangible proof of its policy of toleration. . . .

The Muslims, for their part, pursued a policy of peaceful coexistence in the early Ming. That is, they were not overly assertive in the practice or expression of their religious beliefs, though they attempted to live according to the fundamental injunctions of Islam. . . .

They retained their cohesion partly by living in separate quarters in the Chinese towns and partly by following the dictates of their religion discreetly. . . . They also built mosques and trained a few of their number in Persian and Arabic so that they had access to the original works of Islam. A few Muslims even traveled westward to carry out the cardinal responsibility of a pilgrimage to Mecca.

Yet the Muslims made some accommodations to Chinese society. They adopted Chinese dress, erected tablets near their mosques proclaiming their allegiance to the Chinese emperor, and learned to speak Chinese. . . . [M]ost began to assume Chinese names, and some inter-married with the Chinese. . . . Instead of decreasing as some of its members intermarried with the Chinese, the Muslim community in northwest China expanded and its devotion to Islam did not diminish. . . . Most of the intermarriages were between Muslim males and Chinese females, and the offspring were generally reared as Muslims. The Islamic community also increased through adoption. Wealthy Muslims on occasion adopted young Chinese boys, raised them as Muslims, and thus had marital partners for their daughters. . . .

[T]he Muslims in Ming China were in touch with the world Muslim community through Central Asia. During the Yuan, Chinese Muslims could travel, with scant if any interference from the government in Peking, to the Middle East. . . .

Their bonds were strengthened by the first type of work performed by the Chinese Muslims. Since several of the trade routes to Central Asia and Mongolia traversed northwest China, many Chinese Muslims had the opportunity to take part in commerce. Thus the Muslims served as merchants, interpreters, postal station attendants, and conveyors of goods, and held other commercial positions. By default, they tended to monopolize work that involves horses and camels. . . . The agrarian distress and the commercial restrictions confronting the Muslims inevitably resulted in clashes with the Ming government. According to late Ming sources, some Muslim merchants repeatedly and deliberately sought to circumvent Chinese commercial and tributary regulations, thus challenging and alienating the Ming court. Starting early in the sixteenth century, tensions between the court and the Muslims precipitated several insurrections.

## China's Response to the West
### *John K. Fairbank and Ssu-yu Teng*

*At first China welcomed Europeans. The Chinese view was that their civilization was superior and non-Chinese had been coming for centuries looking to acquire aspects of this superior culture. The Europeans, the Chinese believed, were just the latest of these visitors. What the Chinese discovered, however, was that these travelers were different. They believed their own civilization was better and brought technologically advanced goods to prove it. Moreover, they tried to convert the Chinese to Christianity, to Europeanize them, and to trade with them as equals. All this confused the Chinese court.*

SOURCE: John K. Fairbank and Ssu-yu Teng, *Response to the West,* Cambridge, Mass.: Harvard University Press, Copyright © 1954, 1979 by the President and Fellows of Harvard College, © renewed 1982. Reprinted by permission.

*While the earliest Portuguese arrivals did not endear themselves to the Chinese, the Jesuits (particularly Matteo Ricci, who became an advisor to the Emperor) respected and incorporated Confucian practices into Christian belief in a strategy designed to make conversion to Christianity appealing to the Chinese elite. Other orders (the Dominicans, for example) opposed any dilution of Christian beliefs and the opposing factions contested their views in the Vatican. This struggle came to be known as the Rites Controversy which the Jesuits ultimately lost, leading to the expulsion of all missionaries from China.*

*This reading is by two of the more prominent American historians of China, John K. Fairbank and Ssu-yu Teng. It explores how the Chinese officials met these early European challenges and what influences these Europeans left in their wake.*

CONSIDER: *What it was about these new Europeans that made the Chinese uncomfortable and why; how Westerners influenced China; why that influence was not greater.*

The first extensive cultural contact between China and Europe began near the end of the sixteenth century, when the Jesuit missionaries, in the wake of the Portuguese, reached China by sea. Their dual function is well known: they not only diffused Western ideas in China, including elements of mathematics, astronomy, geography, hydraulics, the calendar, and the manufacture of cannon, but they also introduced Chinese (particularly Confucian) ideas into Europe. The Jesuits found it easier to influence China's science than her religion. Perceiving this, they used their scientific knowledge as a means of approach to Chinese scholars. Although a small number of their Chinese converts took part in the translation and compilation of religious and scientific books, the majority of the native scholars, entrenched in their ethnocentric cultural tradition, were not seriously affected by the new elements of Western thought. . . .

. . . [T]he immediate Jesuit influence in China was through items of practical significance, such as cannon, the calendar, or Ricci's map of the world. Why is so little trace of Christian doctrine to be found in the writings of Chinese scholars in the subsequent century? If this is to be explained by the fact that government suppression cut off contact and the relatively few professed converts had few successors, we still face the question why the minds of the non-Christian scholars were not more permanently influenced by Western knowledge or ideas. . . .

Opposition to the Jesuits and other Western missionaries was motivated partly by the xenophobic suspicion that foreigners were spies; partly by ethical scruples against Christian religious ceremonies which seemed contrary to Chinese customs such as the veneration of Heaven, ancestors and Confucius; and partly by professional jealousy, on the assumption that if Catholicism were to become prevalent in China, the decline of the doctrines of Confucius, Buddha, and Lao-tzu would damage the position of their protagonists. . . .

The Chinese Buddhist leadership appears to have been vehemently anti-Catholic. Meanwhile most Chinese scholars remained dogmatically opposed to the Westerners' religion. Lacking enthusiasm for their religion, they also disliked their science. . . . The conservatives objected to Western scientific instruments, arguing that clocks were expensive but useless, that cannon could not annihilate enemies but usually burned the gunners first, and that on Ricci's map of the globe China was not in the very center and was not large enough. They also objected to Western painting because it lacked forceful strokes. . . .

Behind all this condemnation of Western learning lay the basic political fact that the Manchu rulers of China could not tolerate the propagation of a foreign religion which asserted the spiritual supremacy of Rome over Peking. By 1640 Japan, under the Tokugawa, had proscribed Christianity and foreign contact (except for the Dutch in Nagasaki) as politically dangerous. In China by the end of the seventeenth century there were Catholic congregations in all but two of the provinces; the Roman Catholic faith was banned in the Yongzheng (Yungcheng) period (1723–1735). . . .

All in all, the residual influence of the Western technology made available to China through the early missionaries seems to have been rather slight. Even when present, it was seldom acknowledged. Meanwhile an antiWestern political tradition had become well established.

## Europeans Arrive in Japan
### Jean-Pierre Lehmann

*In the 15th century, Europeans began to venture outside of their frontiers in search of new worlds. There had been contacts with East Asia much earlier, but for several centuries Europe had isolated itself. The Portuguese were the first to drive eastward, establishing colonies beginning with Goa (India) in 1510, then Malacca (Malaysia) and East Timor, and ending with Macao off the coast of China in 1557.*

*The Japanese, in turn, were ready to receive visitors. By that time Japan had become a major trading power, setting up bases all over East Asia as far as Thailand and Indonesia. In this passage, Japanologist Jean-Pierre Lehmann discusses the first European–Japanese contacts.*

SOURCE: Jean-Pierre Lehmann, *The Roots of Modern Japan* (New York: St. Martin's Press, 1982), pp. 36–42.

CONSIDER: *The consequences of Europeans' efforts to Christianize the Japanese; connections between religion and the rise of absolute monarchy according to Lehmann.*

It was in the course of the early/mid sixteenth century that one of the more convulsive events in Japanese history was to occur, namely the arrival of the Portuguese. The impact, both direct and indirect, on the course of Japanese history was substantial. . . . Portuguese presence mostly made itself felt and thereby influenced developments within Japan—warfare, medicine and the sciences in general, trade and navigation, religion and politics, and ultimately *sakoku* [closed country].

In 1542 the first Europeans to touch Japanese soil landed on the small island of Tanegashima off the southern coast of Kyushu; their arrival, however, was not predetermined, but the result of an accident, their ship having been diverted from their route to Macao by strong winds. A papal Bull of 1502 gave Portugal the exclusive right of proselytisation in the Far East; the propagation of Christianity by the two Iberian kingdoms was seen as an important element in their mercantile and political expansionism, thus missionaries operated under what was known as the *Padroado Real* (Royal Patronage) for Portugal and *Patronato Real* in Spanish. In 1564, as noted earlier, Spain undertook the conquest of the Philippines and thus sent her own missionaries eastwards. Generally speaking the Jesuit order (Society of Jesus) operated under the patronage of the Portuguese monarchy, while such medicant orders as the Franciscans were under the patronage of the Spanish monarchy. . . .

Although successful to begin with, as the century progressed the Jesuits incurred difficulties, some of which were attributable not to the Japanese but to missionaries operating from the Philippines. . . . Pope Gregory XIII (1502–85) had decreed in his *Ex pastolari officio* of 28 January 1585 that Japan was to remain a preserve of the Jesuits; Franciscans, Dominicans and Augustinians in the Philippines, however, resented and increasingly ignored the papal instructions and began sending their own missionaries to Japan, until Pope Paul V (1552–1621) in his *Sedis Apostolicae Providentia* of 11 June 1608 revoked the ban and permitted both Jesuits and mendicants to propagate the gospel in Japan. The incessant feuding between the Jesuits and the mendicant orders was by no means the sole cause of the eventual eclipse of Catholic missionary enterprise in Japan, but it certainly contributed to it.

By the late sixteenth century a number of anti-Christian edicts were passed and persecutions begun. . . . Finally in 1614 the conclusive edict banning Christianity was promulgated and all remaining missionaries expelled. Japanese Christians either abjured their foreign faith, or chose martyrdom, or . . . managed to go into exile. . . .

[T]raditionally the atmosphere in Japan has generally been reasonably tolerant in regard to religious matters. In early-seventeenth-century Japan, however, Christianity was perceived by the authorities not so much as a religion but as an ideology; this ideology was held to be inimical and subversive to the interests of the state, of what could be described as the nascent Tokugawa body-politic, and hence had to be routed out. . . .

[W]hat occurred in Japan also corresponds to a fairly universal pattern. A characteristic of the period lasting from roughly the late sixteenth to the early eighteenth centuries was the rise of absolutist monarchies—this was happening in the Ottoman Empire, also in Russia with the consolidation of Romanov rule, especially under Peter I (1672–1725), in France under a succession of Bourbon kings from Henry IV (1553–1610) to Louis XIV (1638–1715), in Mughal India under Akbar (1556–1605), in the foundations of the Ch'ing Empire in China, and so on.

The reestablishment of the Tokugawa dynasty by Ieyasu (1542–1616) was a Japanese variant of this fairly universal phenomenon. The advent of these absolutist monarchies in many parts of Europe and Asia was due to a multiplicity of factors, notably, for example, the changing technology of warfare and particularly the introduction and proliferation of firearms. . . .

[T]he consolidation of monarchical rule anywhere also required the consolidation of orthodox ideology; or, to put it another way, an absolutist monarchy required an absolutist doctrine. What was taking place in Japan was not in nature any different from what was happening in many other parts of the world undergoing similar political developments.

## The Effects of Expansion on the Non-European World
### M. L. Bush

*While the expansion of Europe was of great significance for European history, it was of even greater consequence for the non-European world touched by the explorers. However, its effects differed greatly in the New World, where the Spanish dominated, and the East, where the Portuguese were the leaders. In the following selection, M. L. Bush analyzes these differences.*

CONSIDER: *Internal factors in non-Western societies that help explain these differences; contrasts between Portugal and*

SOURCE: M. L. Bush, Renaissance, *Reformation and the Outer World* (New York: Harper & Row, 1967), pp. 143–45. London: Blanford Press, Ltd., 1967.

*Spain that help explain the different consequences for non-Western societies.*

The Castilian Empire in the West and the Portuguese Empire in the East had very different effects upon the world outside of Europe. In the first place, the Castilian expansion westwards precipitated a series of overseas migrations which were unparalleled in earlier times. For most of the sixteenth century, 1,000 or 2,000 Spaniards settled in the New World each year. Later this was followed by a large wave of emigrants from northwestern Europe, fleeing from persecution at home to the Atlantic sea-board of North America and the Caribbean, and a final wave of Africans forced into slavery in the West Indies and in Brazil. On the other hand, in the East, there was virtually no settlement in the sixteenth century. Europe impressed itself only by fort, factory and church, by colonial official, trader and missionary.

In the second place, the settlement of the New World had a severe effect upon native peoples, whereas in the East, European influence was very slight until much later times.

In the early 1520s, the conquistadors brought with them smallpox and typhoid. Between them these European diseases soon decimated the Indian population, particularly in the great epidemics of the 1520s, 1540s and 1570s. In central Mexico, for example, an Indian population which numbered 11,000,000 in 1519 numbered no more than 2,500,000 by the end of the century. In addition, the Indian was beset by enormous grazing herds of horned cattle which the white settler introduced. He escaped the herds by working for the white settler, but if this led him to the crowded labour settlements, as it quite often did, he stood less chance of escaping infection. Either through falling hopelessly in debt as a result of desiring the goods of the white man, or through entering the labour settlements on a permanent basis to avoid the herds and also the system of obligatory labour introduced by the Spaniard,[1] there was a strong tendency for the Indian to become europeanised. He became a wage-earner, a debtor and a Christian. The Indian was exploited. But in the law he remained free. Enslavement was practised, but it was not officially tolerated. Moreover, the Franciscan order, a powerful missionary force in the New World, did its best to save the Indian from the evil ways of the white man. In Bartholomew de Las Casas and Francisco de Vitoria, the Indian found influential defenders; and through their schemes for separate Indian Christian communities, he

found a partial escape from the white man. But the Indian mission towns, which were permitted by Charles V, were objected to by his successor, Philip II, and they only survived in remote areas.

With few exceptions, the way of life of the surviving Indians was basically changed by the coming of the white man. The outstanding exception was in Portuguese Brazil where the more primitive, nomadic Indians had a greater opportunity to retreat into the bush. There was also less settlement in Brazil, and generally less impression was made because of Portuguese preoccupations elsewhere, and also because of their lack of resources for empire-building on the Spanish scale. Furthermore, within the Spanish Empire, the European impressed himself less on the Incas in Peru than upon the Aztecs in Mexico. Because of the slow subjection of Peru, several Inca risings, the nature of the terrain, and the smallness of the Spanish community, the process of europeanisation was much slower, and in the long run much less complete. The remnants of the Inca aristocracy became Spanish in their habits and Catholic in their religion, but the peasantry tended to remain pagan. In contrast to these developments, the westernisation of the East was a development of more modern times.

The West impinged upon the East in the sixteenth century mainly through the missionary. With the arrival of St. Francis Xavier in 1542 in India, an impressive process of conversion was begun. Concentrating upon the poor fishermen of the Cape Comorin coast, within ten years he had secured, it was said, 60,000 converts. The Jesuits fixed their attention on the East, choosing Goa as their main headquarters outside of Rome. Little was accomplished in Malaya, Sumatra and China in the sixteenth century, and Christianity soon suffered setbacks in the Moluccas after a promising start, but in Ceylon the conversion of the young king of Kotte in 1557 was a signal triumph, and so were the conversions in Japan. In the 1580s Jesuit missionaries in Japan claimed to have converted 150,000, most of whom, however, were inhabitants of the island of Kyushu.

Christianity was not a new religion in the East. There were extensive communities of Nestorian Christians, but they were regarded as alien as the Muslim by the Europeans. The new Christians by 1583 were supposed to number 600,000. But compared with the expansion of Islam in the East—a process which was taking place at the same time—the expansion of Christianity was a minute achievement.

Finally, the Portuguese sea empire did little to transport Portuguese habits abroad. Their empire was essentially formed in response to local conditions. On the other hand, the Spanish land empire was to a much greater extent reflective of Castilian ways.

---

[1] This system depended upon every Indian village offering a proportion of its menfolk or labour service for a limited amount of time throughout the year.

In the New World a carefully developed and regulated system of government was established in which it was seen that the care taken to limit the independent power of feudal aristocrats in the Old World should also be applied to the New. There was a firm insistence upon government officials being royal servants. However, the government of the New World became much more regulated from the centre than that of the old. There was less respect for aristocratic privilege. Less power was unreservedly placed in the hands of the nobility. In the New World, in fact, the weaknesses of government, at first, did not lie in the powers and privileges of the nobility but rather in the cumbersome nature of the government machinery. Nevertheless, in spite of these precautions, the New World, by the early seventeenth century, had become a land of great feudal magnates enjoying, in practice, untrammelled power.

## Chapter Questions

1. Analyze the motives for the European expansion and the forces that stimulated and enabled the Europeans to carry out this expansion.

2. Compare the consequences of the new encounters in Asia, Africa, and the Americas. How do you explain the differences?

3. Drawing on the sources in this and the previous chapter, discuss what the observations made by Europeans tell us about the Europeans themselves and their own societies in addition to the societies they are observing.

## Chapter Fourteen

# Europe's Early Modern Era, 1500–1789

The Renaissance and the overseas expansion of Europe were two signs that Western civilization was emerging from the Middle Ages into a new era, stretching from the 16th to the 18th century, which Western historians have come to call Early Modern. There were several other signs. New monarchs created powerful national states that would endure for centuries. These states benefited from and took advantage of new economic developments such as the growth of commerce and the spread of capitalistic practices. The aristocracy, though still socially and culturally dominant, underwent internal changes and was challenged by a new middle class of merchants and entrepreneurs. The Roman Catholic Church, in decline during the last two centuries of

the Middle Ages, was split apart by the Protestant Reformation. New ideas and ways of thinking about the world and the human condition led to the intellectual revolutions known as the Scientific Revolution and the Enlightenment.

In this chapter we will focus on three of these developments. The first is the Reformation. Initiated in 1517 by Martin Luther's challenges to official Church doctrine and papal authority, the Reformation spread in Germany and other parts of Europe during the 16th century. The passion involved in the Reformation and the historical significance of this division in the western Christian Church have made the Reformation the object of intensive study. Here we will focus on the nature and appeal of the Protestant challenge

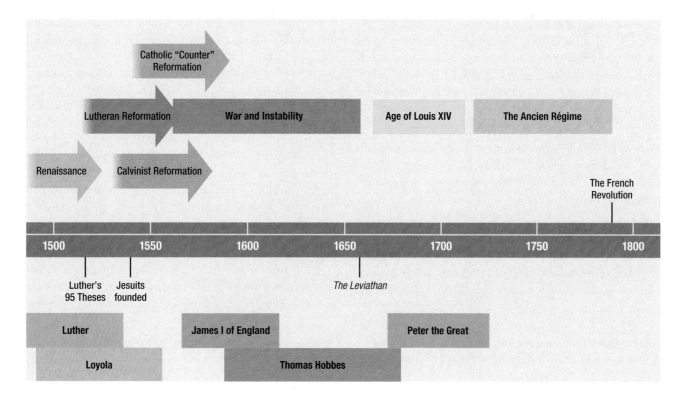

and the Catholic response, the much debated question of causes, and the possible significance of the Reformation.

The second development is the rise of early modern political institutions. Emphasis will be on the competition over the source and exercise of political power—both in theory and in practice. Here the conflict was usually between monarchs and the nobility or, particularly in England, between royal and parliamentary authority. This will lead us to examine connections between political struggle, economic policy, and religious conflict. Additionally, some developments in intellectual history will be touched on, particularly as they relate to political theory.

The third development is the nature of Early Modern society. Although wars, economic development, and urbanization were forces of change, the structure of society changed little during these centuries. At the base of society were commoners—mostly the peasantry—and at the top was the still dominant aristocracy. Sources in this chapter will examine these groups as well as the Early Modern family and the position of women.

# PRIMARY SOURCES

## Justification by Faith

*Martin Luther*

*The early leader of the Reformation was Martin Luther (1483–1546). Born in Germany to a wealthy peasant family, Luther became an Augustinian monk and a professor of theology at the University of Wittenberg. While at this post in 1517, he became concerned about the monk Tetzel's selling of indulgences and issued rather academic challenges in his 95 theses. News of this act quickly spread, and a major controversy developed. Although originally intending to stimulate only modest reforms within the Catholic Church, Luther soon found himself espousing doctrines markedly differing from those authorized by the Church and taking actions that eventually resulted in his expulsion from the Church.*

*Luther himself attributed his spiritual evolution to certain crucial experiences. The most important of these was his first formulation of the doctrines of "justification by faith," which constituted the core of his beliefs and much of the basis for Protestantism. In the following excerpts from his autobiographical writings, Luther describes this experience.*

CONSIDER: *What Luther meant by "justification by faith"; why this doctrine might have been so appealing to many Catholics; why this doctrine might have been threatening to the Catholic Church.*

I greatly longed to understand Paul's Epistle to the Romans and nothing stood in the way but that one expression, "the justice of God," because I took it to mean that justice whereby God is just and deals justly in punishing the unjust. My situation was that, although an impeccable monk, I stood before God as a sinner troubled in conscience, and I had no confidence that my merit would assuage him. Therefore I did not love a just and angry God, but rather hated and murmured against Him. Yet I clung to the dear Paul and had a great yearning to know what he meant.

Night and day I pondered until I saw the connection between the justice of God and the statement that "the just shall live by his faith." Then I grasped that the justice of God is that righteousness by which through grace and sheer mercy God justifies us through faith. Thereupon I felt myself to be reborn and to have gone through open doors into paradise. The whole of Scripture took on a new meaning, and whereas before the "justice of God" had filled me with hate, now it became to me inexpressibly sweet in greater love. This passage of Paul became to me a gate to heaven. . . .

If you have a true faith that Christ is your Saviour, then at once you have a gracious God, for faith leads you in and opens up God's heart and will, that you should see pure grace and overflowing love. This it is to behold God in faith that you should look upon His fatherly, friendly heart, in which there is no anger nor ungraciousness. He who sees God as angry does not see Him rightly but looks only on a curtain, as if a dark cloud had been drawn across his face.

## Constitution of the Society of Jesus

*The Catholic Church was not passive in the face of the challenges from Protestant reformers. In a variety of ways the Church reformed itself from within and took the offensive*

SOURCE: From Roland H. Bainton, *The Age of Reformation* (New York: D. Van Nostrand Co., Inc., 1956), pp. 97–98. Reprinted by permission.

SOURCE: James Harvey Robinson, ed., *Readings in European History*, vol. II (Boston: Ginn, 1904), pp. 162–63.

*against Protestants in doctrine and deed. Probably the most effective weapon of the Catholic Counterreformation was the Society of Jesus (the Jesuits) founded by Ignatius Loyola (1491–1556). Loyola, a soldier who had turned to the religious life while recovering from wounds, attracted a group of highly disciplined followers who offered their services to the pope. In 1540, the pope formally accepted their offer. The Jesuits became an arm of the Church in combating Protestantism, spreading Catholicism to foreign lands and gaining influence within Catholic areas of Europe. The following is an excerpt from the Constitution of the Society of Jesus, approved by Pope Paul III in 1540.*

CONSIDER: *The characteristics of this organization that help explain its success; how, in tone and content, this document differs from Luther's document.*

He who desires to fight for God under the banner of the cross in our society—which we wish to distinguish by the name of Jesus—and to serve God alone and the Roman pontiff, his vicar on earth, after a solemn vow of perpetual chastity, shall set this thought before his mind, that he is a part of a society founded for the especial purpose of providing for the advancement of souls in Christian life and doctrine and for the propagation of faith through public preaching and the ministry of the word of God, spiritual exercises and deeds of charity, and in particular through the training of the young and ignorant in Christianity and through the spiritual consolation of the faithful of Christ in hearing confessions; and he shall take care to keep first God and next the purpose of this organization always before his eyes. . . .

All the members shall realize, and shall recall daily, as long as they live, that this society as a whole and in every part is fighting for God under faithful obedience to one most holy lord, the pope, and to the other Roman pontiffs who succeed him. And although we are taught in the gospel and through the orthodox faith to recognize and steadfastly profess that all the faithful of Christ are subject to the Roman pontiff as their head and as the vicar of Jesus Christ, yet we have adjudged that, for the special promotion of greater humility in our society and the perfect mortification of every individual and the sacrifice of our own wills, we should each be bound by a peculiar vow, in addition to the general obligation, that whatever the present Roman pontiff, or any future one, may from time to time decree regarding the welfare of souls and the propagation of the faith, we are pledged to obey without evasion or excuse, instantly, so far as in us lies, whether he send us to the Turks or any other infidels, even to those who inhabit the regions men call the Indies; whether to heretics or schismatics, or, on the other hand, to certain of the faithful.

## The Powers of the Monarch in England
### James I

*Turmoil, instability, and war (often civil war) characterized much of the period between the mid-16th and mid-17th centuries. In England, friction between the monarchy and Parliament increased under the Stuart kings, starting with James I. Already the Scottish monarch, James became King of England on the death of Elizabeth in 1603. James had a scholarly background and a reputation for his strong views about the monarchy. One of his clearest presentations of these views was in a speech to Parliament in 1610. In it, he comments on the nature of the king's power, not simply in England but everywhere.*

CONSIDER: *How James justifies the high position and vast powers he feels should rightly belong to kings; the limits to monarchical powers.*

The state of Monarchy is the supremest thing upon earth; for kings are not only God's lieutenants upon earth and sit upon God's throne, but even by God himself they are called gods. There be three principal similitudes that illustrate the state of Monarchy: one taken out of the Word of God and the other two out of the grounds of policy and philosophy. In the Scriptures kings are called gods, and so their power after a certain relation compared to the Divine power. Kings are also compared to the fathers of families, for a king is truly *parens patriae*, the politic father of his people. And lastly, kings are compared to the head of his microcosm of the body of man.

Kings are justly called gods for that they exercise a manner or resemblance of Divine power upon earth; for if you will consider the attributes to God you shall see how they agree in the person of a king. God hath power to create or destroy, make or unmake, at his pleasure; to give life or send death; to judge all, and to be judged nor accomptable to none; to raise low things and to make high things low at his pleasure; and to God are both soul and body due. And the like power have kings; they make and unmake their subjects; they have power of raising and casting down; of life and death; judges over all their subjects and in all causes, and yet accomptable to none but God only. They have power to exalt low things and abase high things, and make of their subjects like men at the chess, a pawn to take a bishop or a knight, and to cry up or down any of their subjects as they do their money.

SOURCE: From J. R. Tanner, *Constitutional Documents of the Reign of James I, A.D. 1603–1625* (Cambridge, England: Cambridge University Press, 1930), pp. 15–16. Reprinted by permission.

And to the King is due both the affection of the soul and the service of the body of his subjects. . . .

As for the father of a family, they had of old under the Law of Nature *patriam potestatem*, which was *potestatem vitae et necis*, over their children or family (I mean such fathers of families as were the lineal heirs of those families whereof kings did originally come), for kings had their first original from them who planted and spread themselves in colonies through the world. Now a father may dispose of his inheritance to his children at his pleasure, yea, even disinherit the eldest upon just occasions and prefer the youngest, according to his liking; make them beggars or rich at his pleasure; restrain or banish out of his presence, as he finds them give cause of offence, or restore them in favour again with the penitent sinner. So may the King deal with his subjects.

And lastly, as for the head of the natural body, the head hath the power of directing all the members of the body to that use which the judgment in the head think most convenient. . . .

## The Powers of Parliament in England
### The House of Commons

*James's views on monarchical powers were not accepted by members of Parliament. Indeed, from the beginning of his reign through the reign of his son Charles I, king and Parliament struggled over their relative powers. Along with other problems, this struggle culminated in the 1640s with the outbreak of civil war and the eventual beheading of Charles I. The nature of this struggle is partially revealed in the following statements issued by the House of Commons in 1604 to the new king, James I.*

CONSIDER: *The powers over which the House of Commons and the king differed; the justifications used by James I and the House of Commons for their claims; any ways in which compromise was possible between these two positions.*

Now concerning the ancient rights of the subjects of this realm, chiefly consisting in the privileges of this House of Parliament, the misinformation openly delivered to your Majesty hath been in three things:

First, That we held not privileges of right, but of grace only, renewed every Parliament by way of donature upon petition, and so to be limited.

Second, That we are no Court of Record, nor yet a Court that can command view of records, but that our proceedings here are only to acts and memorials, and that the attendance with the records is courtesy, not duty.

SOURCE: From J. R. Tanner, *Constitutional Documents of the Reign of James I, A.D. 1603–1625* (Cambridge, England: Cambridge University Press, 1930), pp. 220–22. Reprinted by permission.

Thirdly and lastly, That the examination of the return of writs for knights and burgesses is without our compass, and due to the Chancery.

Against which assertions, most gracious Sovereign, tending directly and apparently to the utter overthrow of the very fundamental privileges of our House, and therein of the rights and liberties of the whole Commons of your realm of England which they and their ancestors from time immemorable have undoubtedly enjoyed under your Majesty's most noble progenitors, we, the knights, citizens, and burgesses of the House of Commons assembled in Parliament, and in the name of the whole commons of the realm of England, with uniform consent for ourselves and our posterity, do expressly protest, as being derogatory in the highest degree to the true dignity, liberty, and authority of your Majesty's High Court of Parliament, and consequently to the rights of all your Majesty's said subjects and the whole body of this your kingdom: And desire that this our protestation may be recorded to all posterity.

And contrariwise, with all humble and due respect to your Majesty our Sovereign Lord and Head, against those misinformations we most truly avouch,

First, That our privileges and liberties are our right and due inheritance, no less than our very lands and goods.

Secondly, That they cannot be withheld from us, denied, or impaired, but with apparent wrong to the whole state of the realm.

Thirdly, And that our making of request in the entrance of Parliament to enjoy our privilege is an act only of manners, and doth weaken our right no more than our suing to the King for our lands by petition. . . .

Fourthly, We avouch also, That our House is a Court of Record, and so ever esteemed.

Fifthly, That there is not the highest standing Court in this land that ought to enter into competency, either for dignity or authority, with this High Court of Parliament, which with your Majesty's royal assent gives laws to other Courts but from other Courts receives neither laws nor orders.

Sixthly and lastly, We avouch that the House of Commons is the sole proper judge of return of all such writs and of the election of all such members as belong to it, without which the freedom of election were not entire: And that the Chancery, though a standing Court under your Majesty, be to send out those writs and receive the returns and to preserve them, yet the same is done only for the use of the Parliament, over which neither the Chancery nor any other Court ever had or ought to have any manner of jurisdiction.

From these misinformed positions, most gracious Sovereign, the greatest part of our troubles, distrusts, and jealousies have risen. . . .

## Decree on the Invitation of Foreigners
*Peter the Great*

*Russia stood on the eastern edge of Europe and spread well into Asia. By the 16th century, Russia had expelled the Mongols and begun a vast expansion. A century later the Russian Empire extended to the Pacific, but ambitious tsars continued to feel thwarted in their efforts to expand Russia westward. Many people perceived Russia to be behind in technological and other developments occurring farther west in Europe. Tsar Peter the Great (1682–1725) was one of those who called for Russia to adopt certain western European institutions and practices. This is illustrated in the Decree on the Invitation of Foreigners, issued in 1702.*

CONSIDER: *How Peter is trying to promote changes in Russia; Peter's motives for the changes he wants; problems Peter anticipates in getting people to accept foreigners.*

It is sufficiently known in all the lands which the Almighty has placed under our rule, that since our accession to the throne all our efforts and intentions have tended to govern this realm in such a way that all of our subjects should, through our care for the general good, become more and more prosperous. For this end we have always tried to maintain internal order, to defend the State against invasion, and in every possible way to improve and to extend trade. With this purpose we have

been compelled to make some necessary and salutary changes in the administration, in order that our subjects might more easily gain a knowledge of matters of which they were before ignorant, and become more skillful in their commercial relations. We have therefore given orders, made dispositions, and founded institutions indispensable for increasing our trade with foreigners, and shall do the same in the future. Nevertheless, we fear that matters are not in such a good condition as we desire, and that our subjects cannot in perfect quietness enjoy the fruits of our labors, and we have therefore considered still other means to protect our frontier from the invasion of the enemy, and to preserve the rights and privileges of our State, and the general peace of all Christians, as is incumbent on a Christian monarch to do. To attain these worthy aims, we have endeavored to improve our military forces, which are the protection of our State, so that our troops may consist of well-drilled men, maintained in perfect order and discipline. In order to obtain greater improvement in this respect, and to encourage foreigners, who are able to assist us in this way, as well as artists and artisans profitable to the State, to come in numbers to our country, we have issued this manifesto, and have ordered printed copies of it to be sent throughout Europe. And as in our residence of Moscow, the free exercise of religion of all other sects, although not agreeing with our church, is already allowed, so shall this be hereby confirmed anew in such wise that we, by the power granted to us by the Almighty, shall exercise no compulsion over the consciences of men, and shall gladly allow every Christian to care for his own salvation at his own risk.

SOURCE: George Vernadsky, ed., *A Source Book for Russian History from Early Times to 1917* (New Haven: Yale University Press, 1972), p. 347 as excerpted.

# VISUAL SOURCES

## Luther and the New Testament

*The frontispiece of Luther's 1546 edition of the New Testament (Illustration 14–1) reveals much about the Protestant Reformation. First, most words are written in German, not Latin, thus reflecting the Protestant view that the Bible should be read by everyone. The place is Wittenberg, where Luther initiated the Reformation by posting his ninety-five theses in 1517. The year, 1546, was that of Luther's death. In the picture Christ on the cross is flanked by the praying Luther on the right and his patron, the elector of Saxony, on the left. This symbolizes the two unified in the central Protestant belief of justification by faith, the actual political-religious alliance of the two that was so important for the spread of Lutheranism in Germany, and the compatibility of Church and state according to Lutheranism. The general simplicity*

*and lack of ornamentation of this work reflect Lutheranism and part of what it rejected about Catholicism. The book itself, produced mechanically, indicates the importance of the recently invented printing press for the Reformation.*

CONSIDER: *How this frontispiece might explain or symbolize the causes of the Reformation.*

## Luther and the Catholic Clergy Debate
*Sebald Beham*

*Both Catholics and Protestants often used art to propogate their views in the Reformation debate. Nuremberg artist Sebald Beham's 1525 woodcut (Illustration 14–2) appeared in a broadsheet with a text by Hans Sachs entitled Luther and the Artisans. On the left are the "godless"—members* of trades, including a painter holding a stick and brush, a bell caster, and a fisherman with his net—all relying on religious commissions from the Catholic church. They complain that Luther has unjustly attacked the clergy for practices such as the sale of indulgences and rental of church lands. They are led by a nun and a priest, who points an accusing finger at Luther. On the right is a group of humble peasants—representing the "common man"—led by Martin Luther, who uses the Bible to answer charges against him and instruct his accusers to seek the kingdom of God. Christ, above in a cricle of clouds and holding orb and scepter as Lord of the world, casts his judgment against the clergy by including his scepter to Luther's side.

CONSIDER: What this painting reveals about the Reformation; how this painting compares to the previous illustration.

## Loyola and Catholic Reform

### Peter Paul Rubens

In this painting by Peter Paul Rubens (Illustration 14–3) commissioned by the Jesuits in 1619, Ignatius Loyola is shown preaching and casting out demons from the Church. In the center Loyola, with a halo and backed on his right by the clergy, preaches. He is supported above by angels. To the upper left the demons flee from their victims below, who are both overwhelmed and newly hopeful from the experience.

A comparison with (Illustration 14–1), the frontispiece of the 1546 edition of Luther's German translation of the New Testament, reveals part of the nature of Catholic reform. Here, the emphasis is on the Church's intervening between God and man, on the importance of the sacraments, and on the need for an ordained priesthood. The Catholic Church was willing to utilize the wealth and splendor available to it in its cause, as demonstrated not only by Loyola's robes and the grandeur of this Church interior, but in the commissioning of a leading artist like Rubens to paint in the new, elaborate, rich baroque style.

CONSIDER: If you view this picture and the previous two as propaganda pieces, in what ways might they be appealing, and to whom?

**Illustration 14–1**   Siftung Luthergedenksatatten in Sachsen-Anhalt

**Illustration 14–2**   Staatlichen Museen zu Berlin/Bildarchiv Preussischer Kulturbesitz 2003.

**Illustration 14–3**  Kunstnistorisches Museum Wien oder KHM, Wein.

## The Harvesters
*Pieter Brueghel the Elder*

*Illustration 14–4, a 1565 painting by Flemish artist Pieter Brueghel the Elder (ca. 1525–1569), shows a harvest taking place in Flanders. The scene reveal s much of everyday life of peasants in rural communities. In the foreground a group of peasants pause from their labors on a sun-drenched day for a noontime meal and a nap under a tree while others continue harvesting the wheat. Through a gap in the field a young man laboriously carries water pitchers to the group. To the right and in the distance are the churches and castles that represent and house many of the authorities of this society. Scarcely visible in the distance, wealthier members of this society, who probably rely on the labor of these peasants, are bathing in a pond and lawn bowling.*

CONSIDER: *The sense of community suggested by this painting; whether this painting seems to be a realistic or idealistic image of rural life.*

SOURCE: Pieter Brueghel the Elder, *The Harvesters,* 1565. New York, The Metropolitan Museum of Art.

**Illustration 14–4** *The Harvesters* (July–August) (1565) by Pieter Brueghal the Elder/The Metropolitan Museum of Art. Rogers Fund, 1919. (19.164) Photograph © 1988 The Metropolitan Museum of Art.

## The Leviathan: Political Order and Political Theory

### *Thomas Hobbes*

*Although England avoided the Thirty Years' War, she had her own experiences with passionate war and disruption of authority. Between 1640 and 1660 England endured the civil war, the trial and execution of her king, Charles I, the rise to power of Oliver Cromwell, and the return to power of the royal House of Stuart under King Charles II. These events stimulated Thomas Hobbes (1588–1679) to formulate one of the most important statements of political theory in history.*

*Hobbes supported the royalist cause during the civil war and served as tutor to the future Charles II. Applying some of the new philosophical and scientific concepts being developed during the 17th century, he presented a theory for the origins and proper functioning of the state and political authority. His main ideas appear in* Leviathan *(1651), the title page of*

*which appears here. It shows a giant monarchical figure, with symbols of power and authority, presiding over a well-ordered city and surrounding lands. On close examination one can see that the monarch's body is composed of the citizens of this commonwealth who, according to Hobbes's theory, have mutually agreed to give up their independence to an all-powerful sovereign who will keep order. This is explained in the following selection from Hobbes's book, in which he relates the reasons for the formation of a commonwealth to the nature of authority in that commonwealth.*

CONSIDER: *Why men form such a commonwealth and why they give such power to the sovereign; how Hobbes's argument compares with that of James I; why both those favoring more power for the House of Commons and those favoring increased monarchical power might criticize this argument.*

Whatsoever therefore is consequent to a time of war, where every man is enemy to every man; the same is consequent to the time, wherein men live without other security, than what their own strength, and their own invention shall furnish them withal. In such condition, there is no place for industry; because the fruit thereof is uncertain: and consequently no culture of the earth; no

SOURCE: Thomas Hobbes, *The Leviathan,* vol. III of *The English Works of Thomas Hobbes,* ed. Sir William Molesworth (London: John Bohn, 1889), pp. 113, 151–53, 157, 159.

**Illustration 14–5** Rare Book Division, New York Public Library, Astor, Lenox and Tilden Foundations.

navigation, nor use of the commodities that may be imported by sea; no commodious building; no instruments of moving, and removing, such things as require much force; no knowledge of the face of the earth; no account of time; no arts; no letters; no society; and which is worst of all, continual fear, and danger of violent death; and the life of man, solitary, poor, nasty, brutish, and short. . . .

The final cause, end, or design of men who naturally love liberty, and dominion over others, in the introduction of that restraint upon themselves, in which we see them live in commonwealths, is the foresight of their own preservation, and of a more contented life thereby; that is to say, of getting themselves out from that miserable condition of war, which is necessarily consequent . . . to the natural passions of men, when there is no visible power to keep them in awe, and tie them by fear of punishment to the performance of their covenants, and observation of those laws of nature set down. . . .

For the laws of nature, as *justice, equity, modesty, mercy*, and, in sum, doing to others as we would be done to, of themselves, without the terror of some power to cause them to be observed, are contrary to our natural passions, that carry us to partiality, pride, revenge, and the like. And covenants, without the sword, are but words, and of no strength to secure a man at all. . . .

The only way to erect such a common power, as may be able to defend them from the invasion of foreigners, and the injuries of one another, and thereby to secure them in such sort, as that by their own industry, and by the fruits of the earth, they may nourish themselves and live contentedly; is, to confer all their power and strength upon one man, or upon one assembly of men, that may reduce all their wills, by plurality of voices, unto one will: which is as much as to say, to appoint one man, or assembly of men, to bear their person; and every one to own, and acknowledge himself to be author of whatsoever he that so beareth their person, shall act, or cause to be acted, in those things which concern the common peace and safety; and therein to submit their wills, every one to his will, and their judgments to his judgment. This is more than consent, or concord; it is a real unity of them all, in one and the same person, made by covenant of every man with every man, in such manner, as if every man should say to every man, *I authorise and give up my right of governing myself, to this man, or to this assembly of men, on this condition, that thou give up thy right to him, and authorise all his actions in like manner.* This done, the multitude so united in one person, is called a COMMONWEALTH, . . . This is the generation of that great Leviathan, or rather, to speak more reverently, of that *mortal god*, to which we owe under the *immortal God*, our peace and defence. For by this authority, given him by every particular man in the commonwealth, he hath the use of so much power and strength conferred on him, that by terror thereof, he is enabled to perform the wills of them all, to peace at home, and mutual aid

against their enemies abroad. And in him consisteth the essence of the commonwealth; which to define it, is *one person, of whose acts a great multitude, by mutual covenants one with another, have made themselves every one the author, to the end he may use the strength and means of them all, as he shall think expedient, for their peace and common defence.*

And he that carrieth this person, is called SOVEREIGN, and said to have *sovereign power*; and every one besides, his SUBJECT.

## Happy Accidents of the Swing
### Jean-Honoré Fragonard

*The aristocracy remained dominant culturally during the Ancien Régime, commissioning most of the art of the period. It is not surprising, then, that the art reflected aristocratic values and tastes. Happy Accidents of the Swing by Jean-Honoré Fragonard exemplifies a type of painting quite popular among France's 18th-century aristocracy.*

*Fragonard was commissioned by Baron de Saint-Julien in 1767 to paint a picture of his mistress on a swing being pushed by a bishop who did not know that the woman was the baron's mistress, with the baron himself watching from a strategic place of hiding. In the picture the woman on the swing seems well aware of what is happening, flinging off her shoe toward a statue of the god of discretion in such a way as to cause her gown to billow out revealingly.*

*This painting reflects a certain religious irreverence on the part of the 18th-century aristocracy, for the joke is on the unknowing bishop. The significance of this irreverence is magnified by the fact that Saint-Julien had numerous dealings with the clergy, since he was at this time a government official responsible for overseeing clerical wealth.*

*The lush setting of the painting and the tenor of the scene suggest the love of romantic luxury and concern for sensual indulgence by this most privileged but soon to be declining part of society.*

CONSIDER: *The evidence in this picture of the attitudes and lifestyle of the 18th-century French aristocracy.*

**Illustration 14–3**   Reprinted by kind permission of the trustees of The Wallace Collection, London.

# SECONDARY SOURCES

## What Was the Reformation?

### Euan Cameron

*Historians usually agree that the Reformation comprised the general religious transformations in Europe during the 16th century. However, they often disagree on what exactly was at the core of the Reformation. In the following selection Euan Cameron argues that the essence of the Reformation was a combination of religious reformers' protests and laymen's political ambitions.*

CONSIDER: *How the protests by churchmen and scholars combined with the ambitions of politically active laymen to become the essence of the Reformation; what this interpretation implies about the causes for the Reformation.*

The Reformation, the movement which divided European Christianity into catholic and protestant traditions, is unique. No other movement of religious protest or reform since antiquity has been so widespread or lasting in its effects, so deep and searching in its criticism of received wisdom, so destructive in what it abolished or so fertile in what it created. . . .

The European Reformation was not a simple revolution, a protest movement with a single leader, a defined set of objectives, or a coherent organization. Yet neither was it a floppy or fragmented mess of anarchic or contradictory ambitions. It was a series of *parallel* movements; within *each* of which various sorts of people with differing perspectives for a crucial period in history combined forces to pursue objectives which they only partly understood.

First of all, the Reformation was a protest by churchmen and scholars, privileged classes in medieval society, against their own superiors. Those superiors, the Roman papacy and its agents, had attacked the teachings of a few sincere, respected academic churchmen which had seemed to threaten the prestige and privilege of clergy and papacy. Martin Luther, the first of those protesting clerics, had attacked 'the Pope's crown and the monks' bellies,' and they had fought back, to defend their status. The protesting churchmen—the 'reformers'—responded to the Roman counter-attack not by silence or furtive opposition, but by publicly denouncing their accusers in print. Not only that: they developed their teachings to make their protest more coherent, and to justify their disobedience.

Then the most surprising thing of all, in the context of medieval lay people's usual response to religious dissent, took place. Politically active laymen, not (at first) political rulers with axes to grind, but rather ordinary, moderately prosperous householders, took up the reformers' protests, identified them (perhaps mistakenly) as their own, and pressed them upon their governors. This blending and coalition—of reformers' protests and laymen's political ambitions—is the essence of the Reformation. It turned the reformers' movement into a new form of religious dissent: it became not a 'schism,' in which a section of the Catholic Church rose in political revolt against authority, without altering beliefs or practices; nor yet a 'heresy,' whereby a few people deviated from official belief or worship, but without respect, power, or authority. Rather it promoted a new pattern of worship and belief, publicly preached and acknowledged, which *also* formed the basis of new religious *institutions* for all of society, within the whole community, region, or nation concerned.

## Women in the Reformation

### Marilyn J. Boxer and Jean H. Quataert

*The great figures of the Reformation were men, and traditionally focus has been on their struggles and their doctrines. In recent years scholars have questioned what role women played in the Reformation and whether the Reformation benefited women socially or in any aspect of public life. These questions are addressed by Marilyn J. Boxer and Jean H. Quataert, both specializing in women's studies, in the following excerpt from their book* Connecting Spheres.

CONSIDER: *Ways women helped spread the Reformation; why the Reformation did not greatly change women's place in society.*

Defying stereotypes, women in good measure also were instrumental in spreading the ideas of the religious Reformation to the communities, towns, and provinces of Europe after 1517. In their roles as spouses and mothers they were often the ones to bring the early reform ideas to the families of Europe's aristocracy and to those of the common people in urban centers as well. The British theologian Richard Hooker (1553?–1600) typically explained the prominence of women in reform movements by reference to their "nature," to the "eagerness of their affection," not to their intelligence or ability to make conscious choices. Similarly, Catholic polemicists used notions about women's immature and frail "nature" to discredit Protestantism.

The important role played by women in the sixteenth-century Reformation should not surprise us, for they had been equally significant in supporting earlier heresies that challenged the established order and at times the gender hierarchy, too. Many medieval anticlerical movements that extolled the virtues of lay men praised lay women as well. . . .

Since the message of the Reformation, like that of the earlier religious movements, meant a loosening of hierarchies, it had a particular appeal to women. By stressing the individual's personal relationship with God and his or her own responsibility for behavior, it affirmed the ability of each to find truth by reading the original Scriptures. Thus, it offered a greater role for lay participation by women, as well as men, than was possible in Roman Catholicism. . . .

[Nevertheless], the Reformation did not markedly transform women's place in society, and the reformers had never intended to do so. To be sure, they called on men and women to read the Bible and participate in religious ceremonies together. But Bible-reading reinforced the Pauline view of woman as weak-minded and sinful. When such practice took a more radical turn in the direction of lay prophesy, as occurred in some Reform churches southwest of Paris, or in the coming together of women to discuss "unchristian pieces" as was recorded in Zwickau, reformers—Luther and Calvin alike—pulled back in horror. The radical or Anabaptist brand of reform generally offered women a more active role in religious life than did Lutheranism, even allowing them to preach. "Admonished to Christian righteousness" by more conservative Protestants, Anabaptists were charged with holding that "marriage and whoredom are one and the same thing." The women were even accused of having "dared to deny their husbands' marital rights." During an interrogation one woman explained that "she was wed to Christ and must therefore be chaste, for which she cited the saying, that no one can serve two masters."

The response of the magisterial Reformers was unequivocal. The equality of the Gospel was not to overturn the inequalities of social rank or the hierarchies of the sexual order. As the Frenchman Pierre Viret explained it in 1560, appealing to the old polarities again, the Protestant elect were equal as Christians and believers—as man and woman, master and servant, free and serf. Further, while the Reformation thus failed to elevate women's status, it deprived them of the emotionally

sustaining presence of female imagery, of saints and protectors who long had played a significant role at crucial points in their life cycles. The Reformers rejected the special powers of the saints and downplayed, for example, Saints Margaret and Ann, who had been faithful and succoring companions for women in childbirth and in widowhood. With the rejection of Mary as well as the saints, nuns, and abbesses, God the Father was more firmly in place.

## The World We Have Lost: The Early Modern Family
### Peter Laslett

*The family is a tremendously important institution in any society. Changes in its structure and functions occur very slowly and gradually. With the passage of centuries since Early Modern times, we can see some sharp differences between the family of that period and the family of today. In the following selection Peter Laslett, a social historian from Cambridge who has written extensively on the Early Modern period, points out the differences.*

CONSIDER: *The economic and social functions of the family revealed in this selection; how the structure of this family differs from that of a typical 20th-century family.*

In the year 1619 the bakers of London applied to the authorities for an increase in the price of bread. They sent in support of their claim a complete description of a bakery and an account of its weekly costs. There were thirteen or fourteen people in such an establishment; the baker and his wife, four paid employees who were called journeymen, two apprentices, two maidservants and the three or four children of the master baker himself. . . .

The only word used at that time to describe such a group of people was *family*. The man at the head of the group, the entrepreneur, the employer, or the manager, was then known as the master or head of the family. He was father to some of its members and in place of father to the rest. There was no sharp distinction between his domestic and his economic functions. His wife was both his partner and his subordinate, a partner because she ran the family, took charge of the food and managed the women-servants, a subordinate because she was woman and wife, mother and in place of mother to the rest.

The paid servants of both sexes had their specified and familiar position in the family, as much part of it as the children but not quite in the same position. At that time the family was not one society only but three societies fused together: the society of man and wife, of parents and children and of master and servant. But when they were young, and servants were, for the most part, young, unmarried people, they were very close to children in their status and their function. . . .

Apprentices, therefore, were workers who were also children, extra sons or extra daughters (for girls could be apprenticed too), clothed and educated as well as fed, obliged to obedience and forbidden to marry, unpaid and absolutely dependent until the age of twenty-one. If apprentices were workers in the position of sons and daughters, the sons and daughters of the house were workers too. John Locke laid it down in 1697 that the children of the poor must work for some part of the day when they reached the age of three. The sons and daughters of a London baker were not free to go to school for many years of their young lives, or even to play as they wished when they came back home. Soon they would find themselves doing what they could do in *bolting*, that is sieving flour, or in helping the maidservant with her panniers of loaves on the way to the market stall, or in playing their small parts in preparing the never-ending succession of meals for the whole household.

We may see at once, therefore, that the world we have lost, as I have chosen to call it, was no paradise or golden age of equality, tolerance or loving kindness. It is so important that I should not be misunderstood on this point that I will say at once that the coming of industry cannot be shown to have brought economic oppression and exploitation along with it. It was there already. The patriarchal arrangements which we have begun to explore were not new in the England of Shakespeare and Elizabeth. They were as old as the Greeks, as old as European history, and not confined to Europe. And it may well be that they abused and enslaved people quite as remorselessly as the economic arrangements which had replaced them in the England of Blake and Victoria. When people could expect to live for only thirty years in all, how must a man have felt when he realized that so much of his adult life, perhaps all, must go in working for his keep and very little more in someone's else's family?

## Lords and Peasants

*Jerome Blum*

*The aristocracy made up a small percentage of Europe's population. Some 80 to 90 percent of the people were still peasants.*

SOURCE: Jerome Blum, *The End of the Old Order in Rural Europe.* Copyright © 1978 Princeton University Press. Excerpt, pp. 29–31, 44–49, reprinted with permission of Princeton University Press.

*While peasants lived in a variety of different circumstances, most lived at not much more than a subsistence level. They were usually thought of as at the bottom of society. In the following selection, Jerome Blum analyzes attitudes held toward the peasants by seigniors (lords) and by peasants themselves.*

CONSIDER: *How lords viewed peasants in relation to themselves; how the lords' attitudes reflected actual social conditions; possible consequences of the negative attitudes held about peasants.*

With the ownership of land went power and authority over the peasants who lived on the land. There were a multitude of variations in the nature of that authority and in the nature of the peasants' subservience to their seigniors, in the compass of the seigniors' supervision and control, and in the obligations that the peasants had to pay their lords. The peasants themselves were known by many different names, and so, too, were the obligations they owed the seigniors. But, whatever the differences, the status of the peasant everywhere in the servile lands was associated with unfreedom and constraint. In the hierarchical ladder of the traditional order he stood on the bottom rung. He was "the stepchild of the age, the broad, patient back who bore the weight of the entire social pyramid . . . the clumsy lout who was deprived and mocked by court, noble and city." . . .

The subservience of the peasant and his dependence upon his lord were mirrored in the attitudes and opinions of the seigniors of east and west alike. They believed that the natural order of things had divided humankind into masters and servants, those who commanded and those who obeyed. They believed themselves to be naturally superior beings and looked upon those who they believed were destined to serve them as their natural inferiors. At best their attitude toward the peasantry was the condescension of paternalism. More often it was disdain and contempt. Contemporary expressions of opinion repeatedly stressed the ignorance, irresponsibility, laziness, and general worthlessness of the peasantry, and in the eastern lands the free use of the whip was recommended as the only way to get things done. The peasant was considered some lesser and sub-human form of life; "a hybrid between animal and human" was the way a Bavarian official put it in 1737. An eyewitness of a rural rising in Provence in 1752 described the peasant as "an evil animal, cunning, a ferocious half-civilized beast; he has neither heart nor honesty. . . . " The Moldavian Basil Balsch reported that the peasants of his land were "strangers to any discipline, order, economy or cleanliness . . . ; a thoroughly lazy, mendacious . . . people who are accustomed to do the little work that they do only under invectives or blows." A counselor of the duke of Mecklenburg in an official statement in 1750 described the peasant there as a "head of cattle" and declared that he must be treated accordingly. . . .

The conviction of their own superiority harbored by the seigniors was often compounded by ethnic and religious differences between lord and peasant. In many parts of central and eastern Europe the masters belonged to a conquering people who had established their domination over the native population. German seigniors ruled over Slavic peasants in Bohemia, Galicia, East Prussia and Silesia, and over Letts and Estonians in the Baltic lands; Polish lords were the masters of Ukrainian, Lithuanian, and White Russian peasants; Great Russians owned manors peopled by Ukrainians and Lithuanians and Poles; Magyars lorded it over Slovaks and Romanians and Slovenes—to list only some of the macroethnic differences. Few peoples of the rest of the world can match Europeans in their awareness of and, generally, contempt for or at least disdain for other ethnic and religious groups. . . . The dominant group, though greatly outnumbered, successfully maintained its cultural identity precisely because it considered the peasants over whom it ruled as lesser breeds of mankind, even pariahs. . . .

Schooling for most peasants was, at best, pitifully inadequate and usually entirely absent, even where laws declared elementary education compulsory. . . . [B]y far the greatest part of Europe's peasantry lived out their lives in darkest ignorance.

The peasants themselves, oppressed, condemned, and kept in ignorance by their social betters, accepted the stamp of inferiority pressed upon them. "I am only a serf" the peasant would reply when asked to identify himself. They seemed without pride or self-respect, dirty, lazy, crafty, and always suspicious of their masters and of the world that lay outside their village. Even friendly observers were put off by the way they looked and by their behavior. One commentator complained in the 1760's that "one would have more pity for them if their wild and brutish appearance did not seem to justify their hard lot."

## The Ancien Régime: Ideals and Realities
### John Roberts

It is difficult to look back at past societies with other than our own assumptions. However, people in the Ancien Régime—18th-century Europe—had their own beliefs, values, and perceptions about the world and their place in it. In the following selection John Roberts describes what most

SOURCE: From John Roberts, *Revolution and Improvement: The Western World, 1775–1847*, pp. 34–35. Copyright © 1976 John Roberts. Reprinted by permission of the Regents of the University of California Press, and the University of California Press.

18th-century Europeans would take for granted, emphasizing their mental conservatism.

CONSIDER: *The ways in which their assumptions differ from our own; the ways in which they are the same; why their view of innovation and the past is so important.*

What would be taken for granted by most continental Europeans in the eighteenth century and, to some extent, by Englishmen and English settlers abroad, would be assumptions which can be sketched briefly in such propositions as these: God made the world and gave it a moral and social structure; His revelation in Jesus Christ imposes a duty upon society to protect the Church, Christian truth and moral principles in a positive way by promoting sound behaviour and belief and harrying bad; Christianity teaches that the existing structure of society is in principle good and should be upheld; this structure is organized hierarchically and for the most part its hierarchies are hereditary, their apex usually being found in a monarch; privileges and duties are distributed in a manner which can be justified by reference to this hierarchy. It is also true (our list of assumptions could continue) that while the organization of society around hereditary units was a fundamental datum of society under the *ancien régime*, it took for granted respect for other groups in which men came together for religious, professional, economic or social purposes; corporations with these ends were thought the proper regulators of much of daily life—the practice of trade or the enjoyment of legal rights, for example—and the interests of individuals belonging to them came emphatically second to those of legal persons. . . .

It was also then assumed that much more of personal behaviour should be regulated by law and traditional practice than today. . . .

Social restraint reflected the pervasive anti-individualism of the *ancien régime*. Moreover, moral and ideological truth were thought indivisible and this left little room in theory for the vagaries of the individual. . . .

Across all these assumptions ran an overriding mental conservatism. One of the deepest differences between our own age and the *ancien régime* is the pervading conviction of those times that it was innovation which needed to be justified, not the past. A huge inertia generated by usage, tradition, prescription and the brutal fact of simple ignorance, lay heavily upon the institutions of the eighteenth century. As there had been for centuries, there was a self-evident justification for the ways of our fathers, for the forms and laws they had evolved and set down. One way in which this expressed itself was in an intense legalism, a fascination with old documents, judgments, lineage and inheritance. The higher classes were preoccupied with questions of blood, ancestry and family honour. Yet none of this preoccupation with the past was true historical-mindedness. Men were obsessed with the past as guidance, as precedent, even as spectacle, but not for its own sake. Few men had much sense that they were not looking at the same world as their ancestors. . . .

## Chapter Questions

1. Using the sources in this chapter, explain the Reformation and its spread in 16th-century Europe.

2. What arguments and tactics might someone supporting monarchical absolutism and someone opposing it use against each other?

3. How might sources in this chapter be used to compare the life of the aristocracy with that of commoners?

4. Speculate on how a history of Europe during this time might be written and understood by readers if historians drew primarily from sources dealing with the lives of commoners, such as some of the sources in this chapter.

# Chapter Fifteen

# Asia, 1500–1700

While these centuries marked major changes in the West and new encounters between East and West, it was not a period of major transformation in much of Asia. However, within the different Asian societies, important developments were taking place.

In China, the Ming Dynasty was characterized by relative stability and prosperity. Major building projects, such as the early 15th-century construction of the Forbidden City in Beijing (Peking), were undertaken. All cultural productions, and literature in particular, flourished—though more in quantity than in originality. The government fostered rigidity and remained relatively inward looking, apart from the vigilance needed against attack from Japanese pirates along the coast and from Mongols and Manchus from the north. By the mid-17th century, the Manchus were victorious and established their own dynasty. They

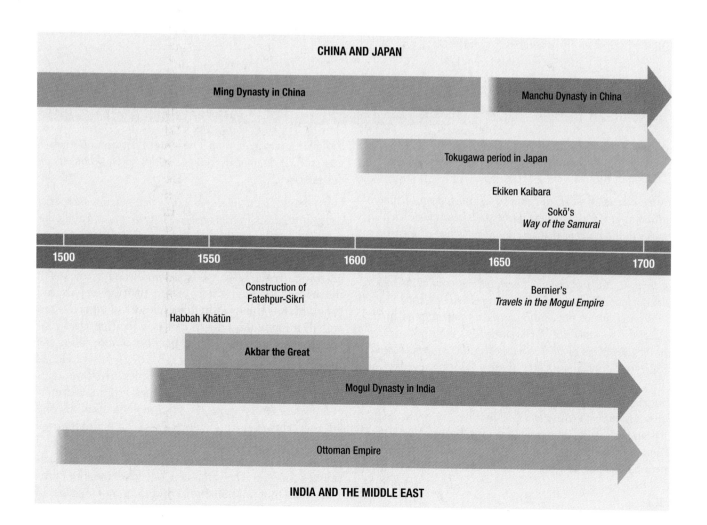

**CHINA AND JAPAN**

Ming Dynasty in China

Manchu Dynasty in China

Tokugawa period in Japan

Ekiken Kaibara

Sokō's
*Way of the Samurai*

| 1500 | 1550 | 1600 | 1650 | 1700 |

Construction of
Fatehpur-Sikri

Bernier's
*Travels in the Mogul Empire*

Habbah Khātūn

Akbar the Great

Mogul Dynasty in India

Ottoman Empire

**INDIA AND THE MIDDLE EAST**

adopted the Confucian bureaucracy and ways of governing, were generally accepted by the Chinese, and eventually extended Chinese rule as far as Tibet.

In contrast, this period was one of greater change for Japan. The 16th century witnessed the emergence of strong military leaders. By 1600, Japan was unified by the Tokugawa house that created the Shogunate in 1603 and would rule for the next 250 years. It outlawed Christianity, cut Japan off from the world, and established a centralized feudal state. Increasingly, through education, the samurai became government bureaucrats. And as the economy developed, a merchant class grew.

In India, the first Muslim rulers, the Delhi Sultanate (1211–1504), became ineffectual and were replaced by the Islamic Mogul (also Mughal—originally a Persian word for Mongols, but in the 16th century referring to the fierce Turkish tribe that conquered north India) Dynasty in 1526. Under Akbar, this rule was conciliatory toward the Hindus and encouraging of the arts. However, his 17th-century successors followed less tolerant policies and made costly attempts to expand their rule to the south, eventually leading to the collapse of Mogul power by the beginning of the 18th century and the spread of British power over India.

Finally, in the Middle East, Islamic powers not only remained strong but expanded their control. Most striking was the continued rise of the Ottoman Empire, which by the last decades of the 17th century included all the southern and eastern Mediterranean basin and extended well into eastern Europe. However, the Ottomans themselves were under pressure from the expanding Russian Empire to the north and from the rise of the Islamic Safavid state in Iran. By the 18th century these Islamic powers had already begun a long-term process of decline.

The sources in this chapter focus on three topics. The first is social and political life in China, Japan, and the Middle East. Here there is a particular focus on the role of women and the developing role of the samurai in Japan, as well as on family life in China. The second is Indian civilization, here also with some focus on women as well as the broader aspects of Indian culture. Finally, some sources will deal with Islamic civilizations, particularly the Ottoman Empire, which rose to heights during this period but also showed signs of long-term decline.

# PRIMARY SOURCES

## The Way of the Samurai

### Yamaga Sokō

*In the course of the 17th century, Confucianism became a greater influence as Japanese intellectuals began to develop an intellectual paradigm that was more reflective of their own culture. One of the first to do so was Yamaga Sokō (1622–85). A man of enormous intellect and independence of thought, Yamaga became interested not only in the major philosophies of his day, but in military science as well.*

*Worried about the continual inaction of samurai under peaceful Tokugawa rule, Yamaga tried to forge a new identity for these warriors. This was markedly different from China, where soldiers had very low status. Bringing together the ethics of Confucianism and the Japanese feudal tradition, Yamaga's writings are acknowledged as the beginnings of a creed known as bushido (the way of the warriors). Yamaga's writings on the samurai also symbolize the transformation of the samurai in this period from a military aristocracy to government bureaucrats and political and intellectual leaders. The*

SOURCE: Ryusaku Tsunoda et al., eds. *Sources of Japanese Tradition* (New York and London: Columbia University Press, 1961), pp. 398–401.

*following excerpts are from* The Way of the Samurai, *which was the first attempt by Yamaga to develop his thoughts on this subject.*

CONSIDER: *The nature of a society that requires such strict codes of behavior from its people; how Yamaga justifies this description of the samurai's duties.*

The master once said: The generation of all men and of all things in the universe is accomplished by means of the marvelous interaction of the two forces [yin and yang]. Man is the most highly endowed of all creatures, and all things culminate in man. Generation after generation men have taken their livelihood from tilling the soil, or devised and manufactured tools, or produced profit from mutual trade, so that peoples' needs were satisfied. Thus the occupations of farmer, artisan, and merchant necessarily grew up as complementary to one another. However, the samurai eats food without growing it, uses utensils without manufacturing them, and profits without buying or selling. What is the justification for this? . . . The samurai is one who does not cultivate, does not manufacture, and does not engage in trade, but it cannot be that he has no function at all as a samurai. He who satisfied his needs without performing any function at all would more properly be called an idler. Therefore one must devote all one's mind to the detailed examination of one's calling.

Human beings aside, does any creature in the land—bird or animal, lowly fish or insect, or insentient plant or tree—fulfill its nature by being idle? Birds and beasts fly and run to find their own food; fish and insects seek their food as they go about with one another; plants and trees put their roots ever deeper into the earth. . . . All things are thus. Among men, the farmers, artisans, and merchants also do the same. One who lives his whole life without working should be called a rebel against heaven. Hence we ask ourselves how it can be that the samurai should have no occupation; and it is only then as we inquire into the function of the samurai, that [the nature of] his calling becomes apparent. . . .

If one deeply fixes his attention on what I have said and examines closely one's own function, it will become clear what the business of the samurai is. The business of the samurai consists in reflecting on his own station in life, in discharging loyal service to his master if he has one, in deepening his fidelity in associations with friends, and, with due consideration of his own position, in devoting himself to duty above all. However, in one's own life, one becomes unavoidably involved in obligations between father and child, older and younger brother, and husband and wife. Though these are also the fundamental moral obligations of everyone in the land, the farmers, artisans, and merchants have no leisure from their occupations, and so they cannot constantly act in accordance with them and fully exemplify the Way. The samurai dispenses with the business of the farmer, artisan, and merchant and confines himself to practicing this Way; should there be someone in the three classes of the common people who transgresses against these moral principles, the samurai summarily punishes him and thus upholds proper moral principles in the land. It would not do for the samurai to know the martial and civil virtues without manifesting them. Since this is the case, outwardly he stands in physical readiness for any call to service and inwardly he strives to fulfill the Way of the lord and subject, friend and friend, father and son, older and younger brother, and husband and wife. Within his heart he keeps to the ways of peace, but without he keeps his weapons ready for use. The three classes of the common people make him their teacher and respect him. By following his teachings, they are enabled to understand what is fundamental and what is secondary.

Herein lies the Way of the samurai, the means by which he earns his clothing, food, and shelter; and by which his heart is put at ease, and he is enabled to pay back at length his obligation to his lord and the kindness of his parents. . . . But if perchance one should wish public service and desire to remain a samurai, he should sustain his life by performing menial functions, he should accept a small income, he should limit his obligation to his master, and he should do easy tasks [such as] gatekeeping and nightwatch duty. This then is [the samurai's] calling. The man who takes or seeks the pay of a samurai and is covetous of salary without in the slightest degree comprehending his function must feel shame in his heart. Therefore I say that that which the samurai should take as his fundamental aim is to know his own function.

## Greater Learning for Women
### Ekiken Kaibara

*There is some evidence that leads us to believe that in its earliest years, women enjoyed a fairly high status in Japanese society. With the introduction of feudalism and the emergence of a military society, along with the influence of Confucianism and Buddhism, that status deteriorated since militarization and both sets of beliefs denigrated women. Japan was soon emulating its neighbors and relegating women to a very low status.*

*The following excerpts are from the book* Greater Learning for Women *by a 17th-century intellectual, Ekiken Kaibara. Purporting to spell out the duties and functions of women in Japanese life, this book was widely used until late in the 19th century.*

CONSIDER: *Why these guidelines are so rigid; how men profit from these rules; what this reveals about Japanese society in general; the similarities with Ban Zhao's rules for women in China (Chapter 8).*

From her earliest youth a girl should observe the line of demarcation separating women from men, and never, even for an instant, should she be allowed to see or hear the least impropriety. The customs of antiquity did not allow men and women to sit in the same apartment, to keep their wearing apparel in the same place, to bathe in the same place, or to transmit to each other anything directly from hand to hand. . . . It is written likewise in the *Lesser Learning* that a woman must form no friendship and no intimacy except when ordered to do so by her parents or by middlemen. Even at the peril of her life must she harden her heart like rock or metal and observe the rules of propriety.

\*

SOURCE: Ekiken Kaibara, trans., *Women and Wisdom of Japan (Greater Learning for Women)* (London: John Murray, 1905), pp. 33–46.

In China marriage is called "returning," for the reason that a woman must consider her husband's home as her own, and that, when she marries, she is therefore returning to her own home. However low and needy her husband's position may be, she must find no fault with him, but consider the poverty of the household which it has pleased Heaven to give her as the ordering of an unpropitious fate. The sage of old taught that, once married, she must never leave her husband's house. Should she forsake the "way" and be divorced, shame shall cover her till her latest hour. With regard to this point, there are seven faults which are termed the "Seven Reasons for Divorce":

(i) A woman shall be divorced for disobedience to her father-in-law or mother-in-law. (ii) A woman shall be divorced if she fails to bear children, . . . (iii) Lewdness is a reason for divorce. (iv) Jealousy is a reason for divorce. (v) Leprosy or any like foul disease is a reason for divorce. (vi) A woman shall be divorced who, by talking over-much and prattling disrespectfully, disturbs the harmony of kinsmen and brings trouble on her household. (vii) A woman shall be divorced who is addicted to stealing. . . .

*

It is the chief duty of a girl living in the parental house to practise filial piety towards her father and mother. But after marriage her duty is to honour her father-in-law and mother-in-law, to honour them beyond her father and mother, to love and reverence them with all ardour, and to tend them with practice of every filial piety. . . .

*

A woman has no particular lord. She must look to her husband as her lord, and must serve him with all worship and reverence, not despising or thinking lightly of him. The great lifelong duty of a woman is obedience. In her dealings with her husband, both the expression of her countenance and style of her address should be courteous, humble, and conciliatory, never peevish and intractable, never rude and arrogant—that should be a woman's first and chiefest care. When the husband issues his instructions, the wife must never disobey them.

*

The five worst infirmities that afflict the female are indocility, discontent, slander, jealousy, and silliness. Without any doubt, these five infirmities are found in seven or eight out of every ten women, and it is from these that arises the inferiority of women to men. A woman should cure them by self-inspection and self-reproach.

## A Woman's Voice in India

### Habbah Khātūn

*Habbah Khātūn lived in India during the reign of Akbar in the mid-16th century. We know little of her life except that she was born into a well-to-do family and was married to a man in the same social class. She remained childless, which created difficulties in her marriage. The humiliation she felt in this situation was voiced in songs she sang while working with the other women in the field.*

*Her remarkable intelligence and talents led her to be ensconced in the palace of the ruling family of Kashmir. She developed her talents, giving a literary form to the Kashmiri language and developing a music system based on Persian and Indian styles. Her songs inspired much anti-Mogul feeling in northwest India. These are two of her songs, still sung today among the people of Kashmir.*

CONSIDER: *How women in a male-dominated society can emerge as prominent figures; what these songs reveal about Khātūn's and the life of other women in 16th-century India.*

He has pierced every fibre of my body with the
    lightning of love:
I, hapless one, am filled with longing for him.
He glanced at me from the top of the wall—
I wish I could tie a turban round his head.
Why did he then turn his back on me?
I, hapless one, am filled with longing for him.
He glanced at me through my door—

Who told him where I lived?
Why has he left me in such anguish?
I, hapless one, am filled with longing for him.
He glanced at me through my window,
He who is lovely like my ear-rings;
He has made my heart restless:
I, hapless one, am filled with longing for him.
He glanced at me through the crevice in my roof,
Sang like a bird that I may look at him,
Then, soft-footed, vanished from my sight:
I, hapless one, am filled with longing for him.
He glanced at me while I was drawing water,
I withered like a red rose,
My body and soul were ablaze with love:
I, hapless one, am longing for him.
He glanced at me in the waning moonlight of
    early dawn,
Stalked after me like one obsessed.
Why did he stoop so low?
I, hapless one, am filled with longing for him!

SOURCE: M. Mujeeb, *The Indian Muslims* (London: George Allen & Unwin, Ltd., 1967), pp. 328–29.

*
I thought I was indulging in play, and lost myself.
  Oh for the day that is dying!
At home I was secluded, unknown,
When I left home, my fame spread far and wide,
The pious laid all their merit at my feet.
  Oh for the day that is dying!
Me beauty was like a warehouse filled with rare
    merchandise,
Which drew men from all the four quarters;
Now my richness is gone, I have no worth:
  Oh for the day that is dying!
My father's people were of high standing,
I became known as Habbah Khātūn:
  Oh for the day that is dying!

## Travels in the Mogul Empire: Politics and Society in India

### François Bernier

*François Bernier (1620–88) was a French physician who traveled widely through the Middle East and India from 1654 to 1669. He spent about 12 years in Mogul [Mughal] India, including time traveling with and observing the court of the Mogul ruler, Aurangzeb. Upon his return to France, he published his writings and letters on his travels.*

*In this undated (1670?) letter to French Finance Minister Jean Baptiste Colbert, Bernier describes some of his adventures and observations while traveling with Aurangzeb. This excerpt attempts to explain one of the major problems the Mogul rulers had with social stratification and the consequences of allowing a small elite too much power.*

CONSIDER: *The connections between Indian politics, economics, and society revealed in this letter; how this letter might reflect Bernier's own concerns and assumptions.*

. . . The *King*, as proprietor of the land, makes over a certain quantity to military men, as an equivalent for their pay; and this grant is called *jah-ghir*, or, as in Turkey, *timar*; the word *jah-ghir* signifying the spot from which to draw, or the place of salary. Similar grants are made to governors, in lieu of their salary, and also for the support of their troops, on condition that they pay a certain sum annually to the King out of any surplus revenue that the land may yield. The lands not so granted are retained by the King as the peculiar domains of his house, and are seldom, if ever, given in the way of *jah-ghir*; and upon these domains he keeps contractors, who are also bound to pay him an annual rent.

SOURCE: François Bernier, *Travels in the Mogul Empire A.D. 1656–1668* (London: Oxford University Press, 1983), pp. 300–3.

The persons thus put in possession of the land, whether as *timariots*, governors, or contractors, have an authority almost absolute over the peasantry, and nearly as much over the artisans and merchants of the towns and villages within their district; and nothing can be imagined more cruel and oppressive than the manner in which it is exercised. There is no one before whom the injured peasant, artisan, or tradesman can pour out his just complaints; no great lords, parliaments, or judges of local courts exist, as in *France*, to restrain the wickedness of those merciless oppressors, and the *Kadis*, or judges, are not invested with sufficient power to redress the wrongs of these unhappy people. This sad abuse of the royal authority may not be felt in the same degree near capital cities such as *Dehly* and *Agra*, or in the vicinity of large towns and seaports, because in those places acts of gross injustice cannot easily be concealed from the court.

This debasing state of slavery obstructs the progress of trade and influences the manners and mode of life of every individual. There can be little encouragement to engage in commercial pursuits, when the success with which they may be attended, instead of adding to the enjoyments of life, provokes the cupidity of a neighbouring tyrant possessing both power and inclination to deprive any man of the fruits of his industry. When wealth is acquired, as must sometimes be the case, the possessor, so far from living with increased comfort and assuming an air of independence, studies the means by which he may appear indigent: his dress, lodging, and furniture continue to be mean, and he is careful, above all things, never to indulge in the pleasures of the table. In the meantime, his gold and silver remain buried at a great depth in the ground; agreeable to the general practice among the peasantry, artisans and merchants, whether *Mahomeians* or *Gentiles*, but especially among the latter, who possess almost exclusively the trade and wealth of the country, and who believe that the money concealed during life will prove beneficial to them after death. A few individuals alone who derive their income from the King or from the *Omrahs*, or who are protected by a powerful patron, are at no pains to counterfeit poverty, but partake of the comforts and luxuries of life.

I have no doubt that this habit of secretly burying the precious metals, and thus withdrawing them from circulation, is the principal cause of their apparent scarcity in *Hindoustan*.

## Village Life and Government in China

*Strong centralized rule, long a hallmark of Chinese government, remained intact during the Ming Dynasty (1368–1644). However, villages were given considerable self-government that allowed for the establishment and enforcement of local ordinances. The following three village ordinances told villagers what was expected of them as responsible citizens. Such ordinances were published in reference books such as* The Complete Compilation of Everything the Gentry and Commoners Need to Know *and* The Complete Book of Practical Information Convenient for the Use of Commoners.

CONSIDER: *How people were expected to behave; what sorts of problems faced village officials.*

## PROHIBITION ORDINANCE

In the imperial court there are laws; in the village there are ordinances. Laws rule the entire nation; ordinances control only one area. Although laws and ordinances differ in scope, the matters they deal with are equally significant.

Each year we set up ordinances for our village, and yet, to our deep regret, they are denigrated by the greedy and overturned by the influential. As a result, they are rendered ineffective, customs deteriorate, and incalcuable damage is done by our people and their animals.

The problem is not that ordinances cannot be enforced; rather, it is that those in charge of the ordinances are unequal to their posts, and those who design them are incompetent. Recently we have followed the suggestion of the villages and grouped all households into separate districts, each with a fixed number of members. On the first and the fifteenth of each month, each district will prepare wine and hold a meeting to awaken the conscience of its residents. In this manner, contact between the high and low will be established, and a cycle will be formed. Anyone who violates our village ordinances will be sentenced by the public; if he thinks the sentence is unfair, he can appeal to the village assembly. However, let it be known that no cover-up, bribery, blackmail, or frame-up will be tolerated; such evil doings will be exposed by Heaven and punished by thunder. We know that even in a small group there are good members as well as bad ones; how can there be a lack of honest people among our villagers?

From now on, our ordinances will be properly enforced and the morality of our people will be restored. The village as a whole as well as each individual will profit from such a situation, and there will be peace between the high and the low, their morality and custom having been unified. Thus, what is called an "ordinance" is nothing but the means to better ourselves.

SOURCE: Patricia Buckley Ebrey, ed. *Chinese Civilization and Society: A Sourcebook* (New York: The Free Press, 1981), pp. 136–37 as excerpted.

## ORDINANCE PROHIBITING GAMBLING

This concerns the prohibition of gambling. Those who are farmers devote their time to their work and certainly do not gamble. It is the unemployed vagrants who have the gambling disease—a disease which is detrimental to social customs and ruins family fortunes. Unfortunately in our village the population increases daily, and the proper behavior does not prevail. As a result vagrancy becomes the fashion. Among us there are homeless rovers who, lacking occupations, form gangs and occupy themselves solely with gambling. They either bet on card games or play with dice; vying to be the winner, they continue day and night, without food or sleep. They have nothing with which to support their parents or their wives and children. Thus, unlawful intents are born, and wicked schemes are hatched. In small offenses they dig holes or scale walls, using all the cunning they have to steal from others; in more serious cases they set fires and brandish weapons, stopping at nothing. If we fail to prohibit gambling, the situation will become impossible. This is why we are gathered here to enact an ordinance for the prohibition of gambling. From now on those in question should repent for their past sins and reform their souls; they should espouse duty and kindness; they should tend to their principal occupations. Should there be anyone who persists in this evil practice and fails to honor this ordinance, he will definitely be punished. The light offenders will be confined, upon the decision of our village assembly, and the serious ones will be brought to the officials for sentence.

Our purpose is clearly stated in the above, and this notice is not posted without good reason.

## PROHIBITION ON TRAVEL AT NIGHT

This ordinance is drawn up by so-and-so to prohibit travel at night, for the purpose of safeguarding our village.

In ancient times, night travel was strictly prohibited, and violaters were punished without exception. Robbers and thieves were prevented from climbing walls and boring holes in houses, to the benefit of all the inhabitants of the area.

Recently, however, night-wanderers, instead of resting at night, have dared to saunter around at will. Because of this we have prepared wine and called for this meeting to draw up a strict ordinance. As soon as the sun sets, no one will be allowed to walk about; not until the fifth drum will traffic be allowed to start again. We will take turns patrolling the streets, carrying a bell, and clapping the nightwatchman's rattle. He who sights a violator will sound his gong, and people in every household will come out with weapons to kill the violator on the spot. Should anyone fail to show up for roll call at the sound of the gong, he will be severely punished upon the decision of the village assembly.

We have made copies of this ordinance to be posted at various places so that night-wanderers will be warned and thieves and rogues will not prevail.

Duly enacted.

## The Ottoman Social Order

*Ghiselin de Busbecq*

*In 1555, Ghiselin de Busbecq (1522–90), a Flemish noble-man and diplomat, visited Istanbul on the instructions of his Habsburg ruler, Ferdinand I. Busbecq was much taken by what he saw and full of praise for the Ottoman Turks. The Ottomans had just taken over large parts of Hungary from the Habsburgs, and central Europeans were in awe of Ot-toman military might. Busbecq arrived at the height of the rule of Suleiman I, a skilled administrator and champion of the arts, who was known as "Suleiman the Magnificent." In this excerpt, Busbecq describes the Ottoman social order, particularly at the Ottoman court of Suleiman I.*

CONSIDER: *How one acquired status and rank in Ottoman society; how Busbecq compared the rules for acquiring social rank in his own society with those of the Ottomans.*

The Sultan's head-quarters were crowded by numerous attendants, including many high officials. All the cavalry of the guard were there . . . , and a large number of Janis-saries. In all that great assembly no single man owed his dignity to anything but his personal merits and bravery; no one is distinguished from the rest by his birth, and honour is paid to each man according to the nature of

SOURCE: tr. by Edward Seymour Forster, *The Turkish Letters of Ogier Ghiselin de Busbecq* (Oxford: The Clarendon Press, 1927), pp. 96–97.

the duty and offices which he discharges. Thus there is no struggle for precedence, every man having his place as-signed to him in virtue of the function which he per-forms. The Sultan himself assigns to all their duties and offices, and in doing so pays no attention to wealth or the empty claims of rank, and takes no account of any influ-ence or popularity which a candidate may possess; he only considers merit and scrutinizes the character, natural abil-ity, and disposition of each. Thus each man is rewarded according to his deserts, and offices are filled by men ca-pable of performing them. In Turkey every man has it in his power to make what he will of the position into which he is born and of his fortune in life. Those who hold the highest posts under the Sultan are very often the sons of shepherds and herdsmen, and, so far from being ashamed of their birth, they make it a subject of boasting, and the less they owe to their forefathers and to the accident of birth, the greater is the pride which they feel. They do not consider that good qualities can be conferred by birth or handed down by inheritance, but regard them partly as the gift of heaven and partly as the product of good train-ing and constant toil and zeal. Just as they consider that an aptitude for the arts, such as music or mathematics or geometry, is not transmitted to a son and heir, so they hold that character is not hereditary, and that a son does not necessarily resemble his father, but his qualities are divinely infused into his bodily frame. Thus, among the Turks, dignities, offices, and administrative posts are the rewards of ability and merit; those who were dishonest, lazy, and slothful never attain to distinction, but remain in obscurity and contempt. This is why the Turks succeed in all that they attempt and are a dominating race and daily extend the bounds of their rule. Our method is very different; there is no room for merit, but everything de-pends on birth; considerations of which alone open the way to high official position.

---

# VISUAL SOURCES

## Akbar Inspecting the Construction of Fatehpur-Sikri

*Tulsi the Elder, Bandi, and Madhu the Younger*

*After witnessing the death of two previous male offspring, In-dia's Mogul ruler Akbar had his most fervent wish fulfilled when, on August 30, 1569, a son and heir apparent was born. So inspired was he that a decision was made to build a grand edifice on the site of the birth just outside a town called Sikri. This magnificent structure, a classic example of Mogul architecture, became known as Fathabad, later Fatehpur*

*(City of Victory), and hence the name Fatehpur-Sikri. It be-came the Mogul capital. Construction took place from 1571–76 and consisted of palaces, pavilions for various ritu-als, grand mosques, bazaar areas, gardens, and courtyards.*

*Akbar was himself interested in architecture and had com-missioned many great building projects. This scene, painted in 1590, shows Akbar personally directing the building of the city and conferring with the stone masons while workers go about their business all around him.*

CONSIDER: *How people of different rank are distinguished; the role such building projects might play in a civilization.*

**Illustration 15–1** Victoria & Albert Museum, London/Art Resource.

## Architecture and the Imperial City

*Since Confucian thinking created a society of rules of behavior and etiquette, it is not surprising that the architecture would follow this same pattern. Those who could afford it built houses surrounded by high walls, with the buildings around the inside of the walls and the middle left to a courtyard, or several courtyards if the family was wealthy enough. This was not a random architecture but a design of specific purpose and intent. (See also the plan for the Chinese house in Chapter 3.) There were traditions as to where each family member resided.*

*The imperial family followed these designs and traditions as well. When the Ming Dynasty decided to move the capital of China to Beijing (Peking—northern capital) in the 15th century, it had built an Imperial City with an inner Forbidden City, thus named since only members of the court and those on official business could enter. The Ming rulers built themselves residential palaces and ceremonial halls surrounded by a high wall, with a door leading to each point on the compass. This Forbidden City was home to the court and thousands of imperial eunuchs. Outside the gates to the larger Imperial City stood the offices of the Chinese bureaucracy; each was designated a place according to its importance and status.*

CONSIDER: *The traditional ideas that influence the design of these buildings; how they are built specifically to the rules of Chinese society.*

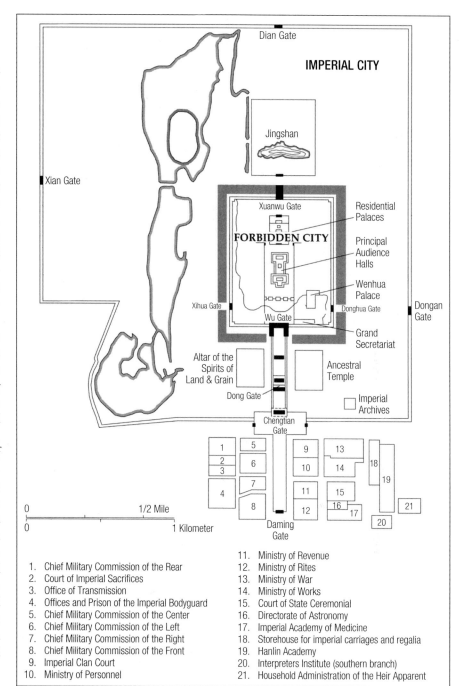

1. Chief Military Commission of the Rear
2. Court of Imperial Sacrifices
3. Office of Transmission
4. Offices and Prison of the Imperial Bodyguard
5. Chief Military Commission of the Center
6. Chief Military Commission of the Left
7. Chief Military Commission of the Right
8. Chief Military Commission of the Front
9. Imperial Clan Court
10. Ministry of Personnel
11. Ministry of Revenue
12. Ministry of Rites
13. Ministry of War
14. Ministry of Works
15. Court of State Ceremonial
16. Directorate of Astronomy
17. Imperial Academy of Medicine
18. Storehouse for imperial carriages and regalia
19. Hanlin Academy
20. Interpreters Institute (southern branch)
21. Household Administration of the Heir Apparent

**Map 15–1   THE IMPERIAL CITY.**

## Expansion of the Ottoman Empire, 1520–1639

*This map reveals the growing power of the Ottoman Empire during the 16th century. The greatest expansions were to the east and along the southern shore of the Mediterranean Sea.*

*The map also shows that the Ottomans launched many campaigns to the west, but with more mixed results. During the 17th century, the great period of Ottoman expansion ended.*

CONSIDER: *Who the Ottomans threatened the most; how the Ottomans served as links between different Western and non-Western civilizations.*

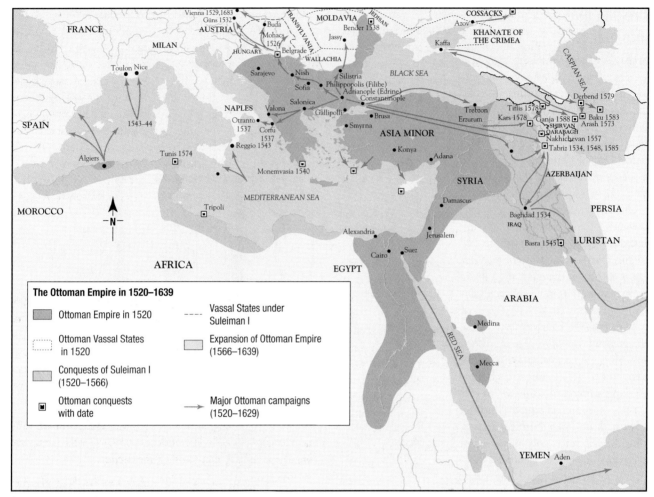

**Map 15–2**

# SECONDARY SOURCES

## Marriage, Caste, and Society in India
### V. P. S. Raghuvanshi

*Indian society was in great part structured by the caste system. Determined by birth, one's caste was lifelong, inherited, and unbending. For Hindus, it was universal. No aspect of the caste system was more rigid than the issues of intercaste sexual relations and marriage. They went to the heart of maintaining caste lines. The following excerpt, written by V. P. S. Raghuvanshi, a prominent social historian of India, analyzes the connections between sexual relations, marriage, caste, and society. His focus is on India during the 18th century, but his analysis applies to the 17th and 16th centuries almost as well.*

SOURCE: V. P. S. Raghuvanshi, *Indian Society in the 18th Century* (New Delhi: Associated Publishing House, 1969), pp. 53–56.

CONSIDER: *How and why marriage rules were so central to caste in Hindu society; the differences between functional castes and nonfunctional high castes.*

Caste governed the code of rules and conventions relating to marriage in Hindu society. In the 18th century, inter-caste matrimonial connections were beyond the comprehension of people and were liable to be visited by the sentence of excommunication. During the period we have evidence that the rules of caste, if violated in other respects, were leniently viewed but those in respect of marriage and sexual intercourse were rigorously enforced. . . . If a girl of high caste in Peshwas' dominions was detected in an act of adultery, she could be sold and treated as a slave. In this sense caste implied hereditary continuation of families in the same group and prevented wide inter-mixture of blood. Marriage in the same caste was a social maxim of almost universal applicability among the Hindus. . . . Elsewhere caste suffered from various distinctions of rank even within its own sub-groups and these, in their turn, influenced marriage. As a general rule, among castes whose people were not privileged to be reckoned as "twice-born," the sub-castes had become entirely distinct endogamous groups. In this sense anything like a *Sudra* caste was non-existent. The various artisan and professional castes, loosely termed *Sudra*, by the end of the 18th century had organized themselves into separate endogamous[1] units of society. Their sub-divisions had become distinct castes. So strict was the rule that even sexual connection of the woman with a man outside her caste invariably entailed her excommunication from her own. This rule was rigidly observed even by those castes which were considered "altogether vile."

If matrimony within the group be construed as the fundamental test of caste, then the Kayasthas of Northern India, who might have been one caste before, had ceased to be so by the end of the 18th century. Their various subdivisions like those of Srivastavas, Bhatnagars, Mathurs, Saxenas, Gaurs, etc., had formed themselves into separate matrimonial groups and had thus become separate castes. Similarly in South India, the Panchalars, including people of the trades of goldsmiths, black smiths, carpenters, masons, although reckoned as one caste, did not admit of inter-group matrimonial relationship.

The relationship between sub-caste and marriage was, however, not necessarily uniform in the upper castes. In Bengal, the Brahmans, as also the Kayasthas, constituted single castes as distinctions of sub-castes were not material in regulating marriages within the same group. Hence those of higher birth (Kulins) were coveted by all inferior to them. Here Kulinism, although it encouraged a nefarious traffic in women, prevented the formation of rigid endogamous sub-groups. But this was not the case in Northern India or Central India. In Bihar, the Brahmans claiming descent from Kanauj had split into various local sub-divisions like Shukla, Anturvedi, etc., and even among them there were no inter-matrimonial relations. The other Brahman sub-castes, too, were endogamous subgroups. In Central India, also, we find that there was nothing like a uniform Brahman caste. The Brahmans had frittered into endless, strictly endogamous sub-castes. The same was true of the *Vaisya* community in Northern India. It was divided into several sub-divisions which were endogamous. The Rajputs were a solid exception. There sub-groups arranged on clan basis were exogamous, and marriage was regulated primarily on the basis of "purity of descent." This, too, could be overruled as a serious consideration if the girl of the lower class or family belonged to a rich influential family. Marriage

outside the broad Rajput kin-group was, however, held in odium. Malcolm cites the degradation of the whole clan of Pamars in the social scale in Central India as their Chief, ruler of Dhar, married his daughter to a Maratha prince with whom "the poorest of the proud Rajput Chiefs" would refrain from eating together.

As such, we may say that caste was necessarily an endogamous group but among the functional castes, the sub-groups were also endogamous everywhere. In the non-functional high castes, the various sub-castes were not necessarily so everywhere, though in Northern India, among the Brahmans, *Vaisyas* and Kayasthas they had become so.

## The Ottoman Empire and Its Successors
### Peter Mansfield

*The Ottoman Empire grew rapidly during the 15th and 16th centuries, reaching its height during the second half of the 17th century. Nevertheless, there were already signs of decline in the 17th century. In the following excerpt from* The Ottoman Empire and Its Successors, *Peter Mansfield analyzes some of the causes for this long-term decline, here focusing on economic factors.*

CONSIDER: *The role of new trade routes and Ottoman taxation policies in the decline of the Empire; what the Ottoman Empire might have done to stem the decline.*

. . . The opening of a new trade route to Asia via the Cape by the Portuguese in the sixteenth century and the establishment of Dutch and British power in Asia in the 17th century "deprived Turkey of the greater part of her foreign commerce and left her, together with the countries over which she ruled, in a stagnant backwater through which the life-giving stream of world trade no longer flowed." At the same time the flood of cheap silver from the Spanish colonies in the New World caused a violent inflation, and disastrous devaluation of the currency of the Ottoman Empire. The consequent economic distress was compounded by the government's increasing demands for revenues from the already overtaxed peasantry for the swelling bureaucracy and armed forces. While the economies of the European powers made rapid progress in the 17th and 18th centuries, that of the Ottoman Empire actually declined. Agriculture deteriorated as the peasantry abandoned the countryside for the towns, but there was no compensating development of industry. Turkey's stagnant science and technology lagged increasingly behind the west, and it lacked any independent entrepreneurial class which might have led an industrial revolution. Western economic superiority was

---

[1] "Endogamous" refers to marriage within a particular caste or group in accordance with set custom or law.

SOURCE: Peter Mansfield, *The Ottoman Empire and Its Successors* (London: The Macmillan Press, Ltd., 1973), p. 7.

also manifested within the Ottoman Empire. In the sixteenth century, when the Empire was at the height of its powers, the Ottoman sultan granted special privileges to the French, English, Venetians and other non-Muslims, who had established themselves within the Empire to trade. These privileges—known as the Capitulations—exempted them from taxes imposed on Muslim Ottoman subjects and gave them the right to be tried in their own consular courts. As Ottoman power declined the privileges were reinforced. By the nineteenth century there were flourishing European business communities in many parts of the Empire which were virtually above the law.

## Hard Times and the Fall of China's Ming Dynasty

*Jonathan Spence*

*By the late 1500s, China's Ming dynasty (1368–1644) had begun its decline. Despite a strong and complex central government, Ming emperors were unable to adapt sufficiently to rapid changes in China. There were several signs of the approaching fall. In this selection, Jonathan Spence, a leading historian of China, focuses on rising problems for inhabitants of the cities as well as the countryside.*

CONSIDER: *The connections between problems for the poor and for the rich; how people tried to deal with hard times.*

For centuries, whether in the north or the south, the peasantry of China had shown their ability to work hard and to survive even when sudden natural calamities brought extreme deprivation. In times of drought or flood, there were various forms of mutual aid, loans, or relief grain supplies that could help to tide them and their families over. Perhaps some sort of part-time labor could be secured, as a porter, an irrigation worker, or barge puller. Children could be indentured, on short- or long-term contracts, for domestic service with the rich. Female children could be sold in the cities; and even if they ended up in brothels, at least they were alive and the family freed of an extra mouth to feed. But if, on top of all the other hardships, the whole fabric of law and order within the society began to unravel, then the situation became hopeless indeed. If the market towns closed their gates, if bands of desperate men began to roam the countryside, seizing the few stores that the rural families had laid in against the coming winter's cold, or stealing the last seed grain carefully hoarded for the next spring's planting, then the poor farmers had no choice but to abandon their fields—whether the land was rented or privately owned—and to swell the armies of the homeless marchers.

In the early 1600s, despite the apparent prosperity of the wealthier elite, there were signs that this dangerous unraveling might be at hand. Without state-sponsored work or relief for their own needy inhabitants, then the very towns that barred their gates to the rural poor might erupt from within. Driven to desperation by high taxes and uncertain labor prospects, thousands of silk weavers in the Yangzi delta city of Suzhou went on strike in 1601, burnt down houses, and lynched hated local tyrants. That same year, southwest of Suzhou, in the Jiangxi province porcelain-manufacturing city of Jingdezhen, thousands of workers rioted over low wages and the Ming court's demand that they meet heightened production quotas of the exquisite "dragon bowls" made for palace use. One potter threw himself into a blazing kiln and perished to underline his fellows' plight. A score of other cities and towns saw some kind of social and economic protest in the same period.

Instability in the urban world was matched by that in the countryside. There were incidents of rural protest in the late Ming, as in earlier periods, that can be seen as having elements of class struggle inherent in them. These incidents, often accompanied by violence, were of two main kinds: protests by indentured laborers or "bondservants" against their masters in attempts to regain their free status as farmers, and strikes by tenants who refused to pay their landlords what they regarded as unjust rents.

## Chapter Questions

1. Several sources in this chapter deal with the position of and problems facing women in China, Japan, and India during this period. Is it fair to make comparisons here? How might it be argued that these sources reveal similar circumstances facing women in these civilizations?

2. How might the sources in this chapter be used to support the argument that even though Western civilization was expanding during these two centuries, most Asian civilizations continued to develop in line with their own internal, rather than external, forces?

3. Drawing on sources from this chapter and the previous chapters on the West, how might it be argued that European societies were becoming increasingly dynamic and flexible at the same time that societies such as those in India, China, and the Ottoman Empire were becoming more rigid and tradition-bound? How might other sources be used to show that in many ways the lives of people in these civilizations and the problems they faced were similar?

SOURCE: Jonathan D. Spence. *The Search for Modern China* (New York: W. W. Norton, 1999), p. 15 as excerpted.

# Chapter Sixteen

# A World of Reason and Motion: The Scientific Revolution and the Enlightenment in the West, 1600–1800

One of the most important intellectual revolutions of Western civilization, an intellectual revolution that would eventually spread throughout the world, occurred in the 17th century. Building on some 16th-century breakthroughs and a more deeply rooted interest in the workings of the natural world, a small elite of thinkers and scientists—Descartes, Galileo, Newton, Kepler, Bacon, and Boyle—established the foundations for the modern sciences.

In the process of developing the modern sciences, these thinkers challenged the established conception of the universe as well as previous assumptions about knowledge. This ultimately successful challenge, now known as the Scientific Revolution, had a number of key elements. First, the view of the universe as being stable, fixed, and finite, with the earth at its center, gave way to a view of the universe as moving and almost infinite, with the earth

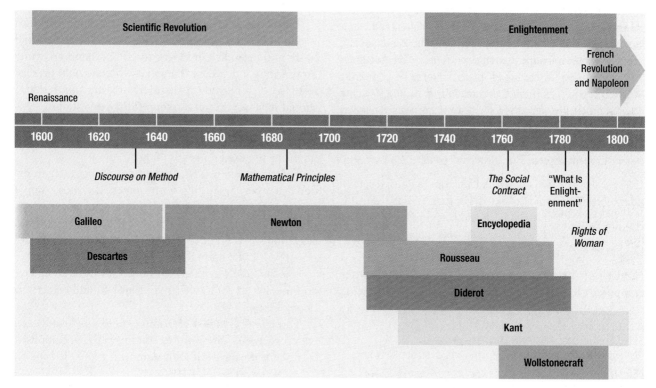

merely one of millions of bodies all subject to the laws of nature. Second, earlier methods for ascertaining the truth, which primarily involved referring to traditional authorities such as Aristotle, Ptolemy, and the Church, were replaced by methods that emphasized skepticism, rationalism, and rigorous reasoning based on observed facts and mathematical laws. Third, although these thinkers remained concerned with their own deeply held religious beliefs, the general scientific orientation shifted from theological questions to secular questions that focused on how things worked.

Most of these intellectual developments were known to only a few throughout Europe. In the 18th century these scientific ideas and methods became popularized as part of the intellectual ferment of the Enlightenment. A group of thinkers, called the *philosophes,* developed and popularized related sets of ideas that formed a basis for modern thought. Their methods emphasized skepticism, empirical reasoning, and satire. Most believed that Western civilization was on the verge of enlightenment, and that reasoning and education could quickly dispel the darkness of the past that

had kept people in a state of immaturity. The main objects of their criticisms were institutions (such as governments and the Church) and irrational customs that perpetuated old ways of thinking and thus hindered progress.

For the Scientific Revolution, the primary sources emphasize one broad question that faced these 17th-century scientists: how can one ascertain the truth? The secondary sources concentrate on the nature and causes of the Scientific Revolution as well as its importance for women.

For the Enlightenment, the primary and secondary sources concern two issues. First, what was the nature of Enlightenment thought? Second, how should we characterize the *philosophes?*

Together, the sources reveal an intellectual movement still tied to the traditional society of Early Modern Europe but with strikingly modern characteristics. Toward the end of the 18th century this movement would play an important role in the transition to Modern Europe, the subject of the following chapters. During the 19th and 20th centuries, the principles and ideas of this intellectual movement would spread throughout the world.

# PRIMARY SOURCES

## The Discourse on Method

### *René Descartes*

*Seventeenth-century science needed new philosophical and methodological standards for truth to replace those traditionally used to support scientific assumptions. These were forcefully provided by René Descartes (1596–1650) in his* Discourse on Method *(1637). Born and educated in France, but spending his most productive years in Holland, Descartes gained fame as a mathematician, physicist, and metaphysical philosopher. The following excerpt from his* Discourse *contains the best-known statement of his approach to discovering truth.*

CONSIDER: *The ways in which Descartes' approach constitutes a break with traditional ways of ascertaining the truth; the weaknesses of this approach and how a modern scientist might criticize this method; how this approach reflects Descartes' background as a mathematician.*

In place of the multitude of precepts of which logic is composed, I believed I should find the four following

SOURCE: René Descartes, "The Discourse on Method," in *The Philosophy of Descartes,* Henry A. P. Torrey, ed. and trans. (New York: Henry Holt, 1982), pp. 46–48.

rules quite sufficient, provided I should firmly and steadfastly resolve not to fail of observing them in a single instance.

The first rule was never to receive anything as a truth which I did not clearly know to be such; that is, to avoid haste and prejudice, and not to comprehend anything more in my judgments than that which should present itself so clearly and so distinctly to my mind that I should have no occasion to entertain a doubt of it.

The second rule was to divide every difficulty which I should examine into as many parts as possible, or as might be required for resolving it.

The third rule was to conduct my thoughts in an orderly manner, beginning with objects the most simple and the easiest to understand, in order to ascend as it were by steps to the knowledge of the most composite, assuming some order to exist even in things which did not appear to be naturally connected.

The last rule was to make enumerations so complete, and reviews so comprehensive, that I should be certain of omitting nothing.

Those long chains of reasoning, quite simple and easy, which geometers are wont to employ in the accomplishment of their most difficult demonstrations, led me to think that everything which might fall under the cognizance of the human mind might be connected together in a similar manner, and that, provided only one should take care not to receive anything as true which was not so, and if one were always careful to preserve the order necessary for deducing one truth from another, there would be none so remote at which he might not at last arrive, nor so concealed which he might not discover. And I had no great difficulty in finding those with which to make a beginning, for I knew already that these must be the simplest and easiest to apprehend; and considering that, among all those who had up to this time made discoveries in the sciences, it was the mathematicians alone who had been able to arrive at demonstrations—that is to say, at proofs certain and evident—I did not doubt that I should begin with the same truths which they investigated.

## Mathematical Principles of Natural Philosophy

*Sir Isaac Newton*

*The greatest scientific synthesis of the 17th century was made by England's Isaac Newton (1642–1727), a professor of mathematics at Cambridge University. Newton made his most important discoveries early in life. By the beginning of the 18th century he was the most admired scientific figure in Europe. He made fundamental discoveries concerning gravity, light, and differential calculus. Most important, he synthesized various scientific findings and methods into a description of the universe as working according to measurable, predictable mechanical laws. Newton's most famous work,* Mathematical Principles of Natural Philosophy *(1687), contains his theory of universal gravitation. In the following selection from that work, Newton describes his four rules for arriving at knowledge.*

CONSIDER: *Why Newton's rules might be particularly useful for the experimental sciences; ways these rules differ from those of Descartes.*

### RULE I

*We are to admit no more causes of natural things than such as are both true and sufficient to explain their appearances.*

To this purpose the philosophers say that Nature does nothing in vain, and more is in vain when less will serve;

for Nature is pleased with simplicity, and affects not the pomp of superfluous causes.

### RULE II

*Therefore to the same natural effects we must, as far as possible, assign the same causes.*

As to respiration in a man and in a beast; the descent of stones in *Europe* and in *America*; the light of our culinary fire and of the sun; the reflection of light in the earth, and in the planets.

### RULE III

*The qualities of bodies, which admit neither intensification nor remission of degrees, and which are found to belong to all bodies within the reach of our experiments, are to be esteemed the universal qualities of all bodies whatsoever.*

For since the qualities of bodies are only known to us by experiments, we are to hold for universal all such as universally agree with experiments; and such as are not liable to diminution can never be quite taken away.

### RULE IV

*In experimental philosophy we are to look upon propositions inferred by general induction from phenomena as accurately or very nearly true, notwithstanding any contrary hypotheses that may be imagined, till such time as other phenomena occur, by which they may either be made more accurate, or liable to exceptions.*

This rule we must follow, that the argument of induction may not be evaded by hypotheses.

## What Is Enlightenment?

*Immanuel Kant*

*One of the most pervasive themes among Enlightenment thinkers was a self-conscious sense of a spirit of Enlightenment. This is illustrated in the following excerpt from a short essay by Immanuel Kant (1724–1804) of Königsberg in East Prussia. Kant, one of the world's most profound philosophers, is particularly known for his analysis of the human mind and how it relates to nature, as set forth in his* Critique of Pure Reason *(1781). In the following essay, written in 1784, Kant defines the spirit of the Enlightenment and describes some of its implications.*

CONSIDER: *What Kant means by "freedom" and why he feels freedom is so central to the Enlightenment; how people*

SOURCE: Sir Isaac Newton, *Mathematical Principles of Natural Philosophy,* Andrew Motte, trans., revised by Florian Cajori (Berkeley: University of California Press, 1947), pp. 398, 400. Copyright © 1934 Renewed 1962 Regents of the University of California. Reprinted by permission of the University of California Press.

SOURCE: Immanuel Kant, "What Is Enlightenment?" in *The Philosophy of Kant,* Carl J. Friedrich, ed. Reprinted by permission of Random House, Inc. (New York, 1949), pp. 132–34, 138–39. Copyright © 1949 by Random House, Inc.

*can become enlightened and the appropriate environment to facilitate this enlightenment; what Kant would consider "mature"; how Kant relates enlightenment and politics.*

Enlightenment is man's leaving his self-caused immaturity. Immaturity is the incapacity to use one's intelligence without the guidance of another. Such immaturity is self-caused if it is not caused by lack of intelligence, but by lack of determination and courage to use one's intelligence without being guided by another. *Sapere Aude!* Have the courage to use your own intelligence! is therefore the motto of the enlightenment.

Through laziness and cowardice a large part of mankind, even after nature has freed them from alien guidance, gladly remain immature. It is because of laziness and cowardice that it is so easy for others to usurp the role of guardians. It is so comfortable to be a minor! If I have a book which provides meaning for me, a pastor who has conscience for me, a doctor who will judge my diet for me and so on, then I do not need to exert myself. I do not have any need to think; if I can pay, others will take over the tedious job for me. The guardians who have kindly undertaken the supervision will see to it that by far the largest part of mankind, including the entire "beautiful sex," should consider the step into maturity, not only as difficult but as very dangerous. . . .

But it is more nearly possible for a public to enlighten itself: this is even inescapable if only the public is given its freedom. . . .

All that is required for this enlightenment is *freedom*; and particularly the least harmful of all that may be called freedom, namely, the freedom for man to make *public use* of his reason in all matters. . . .

The question may now be put: Do we live at present in an enlightened age? The answer is: No, but in an age of enlightenment. Much still prevents men from being placed in a position or even being placed into position to use their own minds securely and well in matters of religion. But we do have very definite indications that this field of endeavor is being opened up for men to work freely and reduce gradually the hindrances preventing a general enlightenment and an escape from self-caused immaturity. In this sense, this age is the age of enlightenment and the age of Frederick (The Great). . . .

I have emphasized the main point of enlightenment, that is of man's release from his self-caused immaturity, primarily *in matters of religion*. I have done this because our rulers have no interest in playing the guardian of their subjects in matters of arts and sciences. Furthermore immaturity in matters of religion is not only most noxious but also most dishonorable. But the point of view of a head of state who favors freedom in the arts and sciences goes even further; for he understands that there is no danger in legislation permitting his subjects to make *public* use of their own reason and to submit *publicly* their thoughts regarding a better framing of such laws together with a frank criticism of existing *legislation*. We have a shining example of this; no prince excels him whom we admire. Only he who is himself enlightened does not fear spectres when he at the same time has a well-disciplined army at his disposal as a guarantee of public peace. Only he can say what (the ruler of a) free state dare not say: *Argue as much as you want and about whatever you want but obey!*

## Prospectus for the Encyclopedia of Arts and Sciences
### *Denis Diderot*

*More than any other work, the* Encyclopedia of Arts and Sciences, *edited by Denis Diderot (1713–84) and Jean-le-Rond d'Alembert (1717–83), epitomizes the Enlightenment. Written between 1745 and 1780, it presented to the public the sum of knowledge considered important by Enlightenment thinkers. The critical Enlightenment spirit underlying the En-cyclopedia led traditional authorities to condemn it and to suppress it more than once. The following is an excerpt from the* Prospectus *that appeared in 1750, announcing the forth-coming* Encyclopedia. *The* Prospectus *was written by Diderot, a philosopher, novelist, and playwright who had already been in trouble with the authorities for his writings. The* Prospectus *apparently aroused widespread expectations; even before the first volume of the* Encyclopedia *appeared, more than a thousand orders for it had been received.*

CONSIDER: *What a reader could hope to gain by purchasing the* Encyclopedia *and how these hopes themselves reflect the spirit of the Enlightenment; how this selection from the* Prospectus *reflects the same ideas expressed by Kant; how the Enlightenment as described here related to the scientific revolution of the 17th century.*

It cannot be denied that, since the revival of letters among us, we owe partly to dictionaries the general enlightenment that has spread in society and the germ of science that is gradually preparing men's minds for more profound knowledge. How valuable would it not be, then, to have a book of this kind that one could consult on all subjects and that would serve as much to guide those who have the courage to work at the instruction of others as to enlighten those who only instruct themselves!

SOURCE: Denis Diderot, *Prospectus à l'Encyclopèdie,* in Diderot, *Oeuvres complètes,* eds. Jules Assézat and Maurice Tourneux, 20 vols. (Paris, 1875–77), vol. XIII, pp. 129–31, in Richard W. Lyman and Lewis W. Spitz, eds., *Major Crises in Western Civilization,* vol. II, Nina B. Gunzenhauser, trans. (New York: Harcourt, Brace & World, 1965), pp. 11–12. Reprinted by permission of Harcourt Brace Jovanovich, Inc.

This is one advantage we thought of, but it is not the only one. In condensing to dictionary form all that concerns the arts and sciences, it remained necessary to make people aware of the assistance they lend each other; to make use of this assistance to render principles more certain and their consequences clearer; to indicate the distant and close relationships of the beings that make up nature, which have occupied men; to show, by showing the interlacing both of roots and of branches, the impossibility of understanding thoroughly some parts of the whole without exploring many others; to produce a general picture of the efforts of the human spirit in all areas and in all centuries; to present these matters with clarity; to give to each the proper scope, and to prove, if possible, our epigraph by our success. . . .

The majority of these works appeared during the last century and were not completely scorned. It was found that if they did not show much talent, they at least bore the marks of labor and of knowledge. But what would these encyclopedias mean to us? What progress have we not made since then in the arts and sciences? How many truths discovered today, which were not foreseen then? True philosophy was in its cradle; the geometry of infinity did not yet exist; experimental physics was just appearing; there was no dialectic at all; the laws of sound criticism were entirely unknown. Descartes, Boyle, Huyghens, Newton, Leibnitz, the Bernoullis, Locke, Bayle, Pascal, Corneille, Racine, Bourdaloue, Bossuet, etc., either had not yet been born or had not yet written. The spirit of research and competition did not motivate the scholars: another spirit, less fecund perhaps, but rarer, that of precision and method, had not yet conquered the various divisions of literature; and the academies, whose efforts have advanced the arts and sciences to such an extent, were not yet established. . . . At the end of this project you will find the tree of human knowledge, indicating the connection of ideas, which has directed us in this vast operation.

## A Vindication of the Rights of Woman
### Mary Wollstonecraft

*While the Enlightenment was dominated by men, there were possibilities for active involvement by women. Several women played particularly important roles as patrons and intellectual contributors to the gatherings of philosophes and members of the upper-middle-class and aristocratic elite held in the salons of Paris and elsewhere. It was, however, far more difficult for a woman to publish serious essays in the Enlightenment tradition. Indeed, Enlightenment thinkers did little to change basic attitudes about the inferiority of women. One person who managed to do both was Mary Wollstonecraft (1759–97), a British author who in 1792 published* A Vindication of the Rights of Woman. *The book was a sharply reasoned attack against the oppression of women and an argument for educational change. In the following excerpt, Wollstonecraft addresses the author of a proposed new constitution for France that, in her opinion, does not adequately deal with the rights of women.*

CONSIDER: *Why education is so central to her argument; how this argument reflects the methods and ideals of the Enlightenment.*

Contending for the rights of woman, my main argument is built on this simple principle, that if she be not prepared by education to become the companion of man, she will stop the progress of knowledge and virtue; for truth must be common to all, or it will be inefficacious with respect to its influence on general practice. And how can woman be expected to co-operate unless she knows why she ought to be virtuous? unless freedom strengthens her reason till she comprehends her duty, and see in what manner it is connected with her real good. If children are to be educated to understand the true principle of patriotism, their mother must be a patriot; and the love of mankind, from which an orderly train of virtues spring, can only be produced by considering the moral and civil interest of mankind; but the education and situation of woman at present shuts her out from such investigations.

In this work I have produced many arguments, which to me were conclusive, to prove that the prevailing notion respecting a sexual character was subversive of mortality, and I have contended, that to render the human body and mind more perfect, chastity must more universally prevail, and that chastity will never be respected in the male world till the person of a woman is not, as it were, idolised, when little virtue or sense embellish it with the grand traces of mental beauty, or the interesting simplicity of affection.

Consider, sir, dispassionately these observations, for a glimpse of this truth seemed to open before you when you observed, "that to see one-half of the human race excluded by the other from all participation of government was a political phenomenon, that, according to abstract principles, it was impossible to explain." If so, on what does your constitution rest? If the abstract rights of man will bear discussion and explanation, those of woman, by a parity of reasoning, will not shrink from the same test; though a different opinion prevails in this country, built on the very arguments which you use to justify the oppression of woman—prescription.

SOURCE: Mary Wollstonecraft, *The Rights of Woman* (London: J. M. Dent and Sons, Ltd., 1929), pp. 10–11.

Consider—I address you as a legislator—whether, when men contend for their freedom, and to be allowed to judge for themselves respecting their own happiness, it be not inconsistent and unjust to subjugate women, even though you firmly believe that you are acting in the manner best calculated to promote their happiness? Who made man the exclusive judge, if woman partake with him of the gift of reason?

## The Social Contract

### Jean Jacques Rousseau

*More than anyone else, Jean Jacques Rousseau (1712–78) tested the outer limits of Enlightenment thought and went on to criticize its very foundations. Born in Geneva, he spent much of his life in France (mainly in Paris), where he became one of the philosophes who contributed to the* Encyclopedia. *Yet he also undermined Enlightenment thought by holding that social institutions had corrupted people and that human beings were more pure, free, and happy in the state of nature than in modern civilization. This line of thought provided a foundation for the growth of Romanticism in the late 18th and early 19th centuries. Rousseau's most important political work,* The Social Contract *(1762), argued for popular sovereignty. In the following selection from that work, Rousseau focuses on what he considers the fundamental argument of the book—the passage from the state of nature to the civil state by means of the social contract.*

CONSIDER: *Rousseau's solution to the main problem of* The Social Contract; *the advantages and disadvantages of the social contract; what characteristics of Enlightenment thought are reflected in this selection.*

"The problem is to find a form of association which will defend and protect with the whole common force the person and goods of each associate, and in which each, while uniting himself with all, may still obey himself alone, and remain as free as before." This is the fundamental problem of which *The Social Contract* provides the solution.

The clauses of this contract are so determined by the nature of the act that the slightest modification would make them vain and ineffective; so that, although they have perhaps never been formally set forth, they are everywhere the same and everywhere tacitly admitted and recognised, until, on the violation of the social compact, each regains his original rights and resumes his natural liberty, while losing the conventional liberty in favour of which he renounced it.

SOURCE: Jean Jacques Rousseau, *The Social Contract and Discourses* (London: J. M. Dent, Everyman Library, 1913), pp. 14–15, 18–19.

These clauses, properly understood, may be reduced to one—the total alienation of each associate, together with all his rights, to the whole community; for, in the first place, as each gives himself absolutely, the conditions are the same for all; and, this being so, no one has any interest in making them burdensome to others.

Moreover, the alienation being without reserve, the union is as perfect as it can be, and no associate has anything more to demand: for, if the individuals retained certain rights, as there would be no common superior to decide between them and the public, each, being on one point his own judge, would ask to be so on all; the state of nature would thus continue, and the association would necessarily become inoperative or tyrannical.

Finally, each man, in giving himself to all, gives himself to nobody; and as there is no associate over whom he does not acquire the same right as he yields others over himself, he gains an equivalent for everything he loses, and an increase of force for the preservation of what he has.

If then we discard from the social compact what is not of its essence, we shall find that it reduces itself to the following terms—

Each of us puts his person and all his power in common under the supreme direction of the general will, and, in our corporate capacity, we receive each member as an indivisible part of the whole.

\*

The passage from the state of nature to the civil state produces a very remarkable change in man, by substituting justice for instinct in his conduct, and giving his actions the morality they had formerly lacked. Then only, when the voice of duty takes the place of physical impulses and right of appetite, does man, who so far had considered only himself, find that he is forced to act on different principles, and to consult his reason before listening to his inclinations. Although, in this state, he deprives himself of some advantages which he got from nature, he gains in return others so great, his faculties are so stimulated and developed, his ideas so extended, his feelings so ennobled, and his whole soul so uplifted, that, did not the abuses of this new condition often degrade him below that which he left, he would be bound to bless continually the happy moment which took him from it for ever, and, instead of a stupid and unimaginative animal, made him an intelligent being and a man.

Let us draw up the whole account in terms easily commensurable. What man loses by the social contract is his natural liberty and an unlimited right to everything he tries to get and succeeds in getting; what he gains is civil liberty and the proprietorship of all he possesses. If we are to avoid mistake in weighing one against the other, we must clearly distinguish natural liberty, which is bounded only by the strength of the individual, from civil liberty, which is limited by the general will; and possession, which is merely the effect of force or the right of the first occupier, from property, which can be founded only on a positive title.

We might, over and above all this, add, to what man acquires in the civil state, moral liberty, which alone makes him truly master of himself; for the mere impulse of appetite is slavery, while obedience to a law which we prescribe to ourselves is liberty. But I have already said too much on this head, and the philosophical meaning of the word liberty does not now concern us.

# VISUAL SOURCES

## Frontispiece to Marco Vincenzo Coronelli's Atlas, 1691

*In this frontispiece from a 1691 world atlas published by the accomplished Venetian mapmaker and mathematician Marco Coronelli (1650–1718) (Illustration 16–1), a globe and ship occupy center stage and represent the West's exploration of the world. Just above, the banner of a trumpeting angel reads, "Yet farther"—words that contrast sharply with the traditional medieval expression "No farther." Drawings of the numerous instruments that characterized the new age of exploration and science occupy the periphery of the image.*

CONSIDER: *The ways the entire illustration suggests a people proudly using science to fuel their growing power—over other peoples as well as nature itself; how this illustration reveals the underlying culture of the Renaissance, which stressed learning and exploration through reading and art.*

## Experiment with an Air Pump

### Joseph Wright

*Few paintings provide a better image of the Enlightenment than Experiment with an Air Pump (1768) by the British artist Joseph Wright (Illustration 16–2). The experiment takes place in the center of the picture; its apparent success is evidenced by the dying bird inside a closed glass bowl from which the air has been pumped out. The informally dressed experimenter is carefully observing his work. Around him are members of his family and some well-dressed friends.*

*The form and content of this picture symbolize the Enlightenment. A small source of light is sufficient to enlighten humanity and reveal the laws of nature. Science is not just for specialists but something amateurs can understand and practice to obtain practical results. That it is a British painting is particularly significant, for the English led in developing useful machines and were identified as having a more pragmatic approach to science and ideas than other peoples. The painting also reveals customary images of the sexes: the experimenter boldly forging on while to his left a friend or asso-*

*ciate calmly explains what is happening to a woman and her daughter, whose sensibilities are as appropriately fragile as the dying bird—the main object of their concern.*

CONSIDER: *Any common themes in this painting and the documents by Diderot and Kant.*

**Illustration 16–1** The Burndy Library, Dibner Institute for the History of Science and Technology, Cambridge, Massachusetts.

**Illustration 16–2** The National Gallery, London.

**Illustration 16–3** University Library, Istanbul, Turkey/The Bridgeman Art Library.

# SECONDARY SOURCES

## Islamic and Western Science
*Dick Teresi and An Ottoman Observatory*

*Between the 8th and 12th centuries—well before the Renaissance and Scientific Revolution in Europe—Islamic science and technology clearly surpassed that in Europe. During the 14th, 15th, and 16th centuries, European scholars forged ahead of their Muslim predecessors. Nevertheless, as suggested in the following excerpt by Dick Teresi, Europeans owed much to their Muslim counterparts and through them to discoveries made in Asian societies.*

*Moreover, Illustration 16–3, a painting depicting an observatory established by the Ottomans in 1575 at Istambul, suggests that the Ottoman Turks appreciated the importance of some 16th-century scholarship and scientific discoveries. In the top two rows of figures, Islamic scholars study astronomy and various navigational tools and methods. In the middle and the bottom row, scholars study geography and carefully record various observations.*

CONSIDER: *What debt Western scholars such as Copernicus might have owed to Islamic sources; whether Illustration 16–3 supports Teresi's argument about Western and Islamic scholarship.*

Many traditional Western historians believe that little original science was conducted after the collapse of the Greek civilization; that the Arabs copied the work of Euclid, Ptolemy, Apollonius, et al.; and that eventually Europe recouped its scientific heritage from the Islamic world. During the Middle Ages, Arab scholars sought out Greek manuscripts and set up centers of learning and translation at Jund-i-Shapur in Persia and Baghdad in Iraq. Western historians don't often like to admit that these same scholars also sought manuscripts from China and India, and created their own science.

Scholarship moved to Cairo and then to Cordoba and Toledo in Spain as the Muslim empire expanded into Europe. When the Christians recaptured Toledo in the twelfth century European scholars descended upon the documents. They were interested in all Arabic documents—translations of Greek works but also original Arabic writings and Arabic translations of other cultures' manuscripts. Much of the scientific knowledge of the ancient world—Greece as well as Babylonia, Egypt, India, and China—was funneled to the West through Spain. George Saliba has found that there was an intense traffic in Arabic manuscripts between Damascus

and Padua during the early 1500s, and more and more scientific documents, written in Arabic, are being rediscovered in European libraries. Saliba has documented that many European scholars in the Renaissance were literate in Arabic. They read the Islamic papers and shared the information with their less literate colleagues.

One example is Copernicus, who studied at Padua. Saliba points out that if Copernicus did borrow from Islamic astronomers—and the jury is still out—he had good reason not to acknowledge his intellectual debt. It would have been impolitic, says Saliba, to mention Islamic science when the Ottoman Empire was at the door of Europe.

## Women and the Scientific Revolution
*Bonnie S. Anderson and Judith P. Zinsser*

*Traditionally, historians have concluded that the Scientific Revolution was generally carried out by men. In recent years, however, some historians have pointed to women who did participate in it. In the following selection from their interpretive survey of women in European history, A History of Their Own, Bonnie S. Anderson and Judith P. Zinsser examine the extent to which women were drawn to the Scientific Revolution and whether the new science resulted in changing assumptions about women—particularly about female physiology.*

CONSIDER: *The ways women participated in the Scientific Revolution; the problems that faced women as potential scholars; what Anderson and Zinsser mean when they say that "for women, however, there was no Scientific Revolution."*

In the same way that women responded to and participated in Humanism, so they were drawn to the intellectual movement known as the Scientific Revolution. The excitement of the new discoveries of the seventeenth and eighteenth centuries, in particular, inspired a few gifted women scientists to formulate their own theories about the natural world, to perform their own experiments and to publish their findings. In contrast to those educated strictly and formally according to Humanist precepts, these women had little formal training, and chose for themselves what they read and studied. Rather than encouraging them, their families at best left them to their excitement with the wonders of the "Scientific Revolution"; at worst, parents criticized their daughters'

SOURCE: Dick Teresi, *Lost Discoveries: The Ancient Roots of Modern Science* (New York: Simon & Schuster, 2002), pp. 13–14.

SOURCE: Bonnie Anderson and Judith Zinsser, *A History of Their Own*, vol. II (New York: Harper & Row, Publishers, 1988), pp. 87–89, 96 as excerpted.

absorption in such inappropriate, inelegant, and unfeminine endeavors.

All across Europe from the sixteenth to the eighteenth centuries these women found fascination in the natural sciences. They corresponded and studied with the male scientists of their day. They observed, and they formulated practical applications from their new knowledge of botany, horticulture, and chemistry.

Mathematics, astronomy, and studies of the universe also interested these self-taught women scientists. . . .

From the fifteenth to the eighteenth centuries privileged women participated in the new intellectual movements. Like the men of their class, they became humanist scholars, naturalists, and scientists. Unfortunately, many of these women found themselves in conflict with their families and their society. A life devoted to scholarship conflicted with the roles that women, however learned, were still expected to fulfill. . . .

For women, however, there was no Scientific Revolution. When men studied female anatomy, when they spoke of female physiology, of women's reproductive organs, of the female role in procreation, they ceased to be scientific. They suspended reason and did not accept the evidence of their senses. Tradition, prejudice, and imagination, not scientific observation, governed their conclusions about women. The writings of the classical authors like Aristotle and Galen continued to carry the same authority as they had when first written, long after they had been discarded in other areas. Men spoke in the name of the new "science" but mouthed words and phrases from the old misogyny. In the name of "science" they gave a supposed physiological basis to the traditional views of women's nature, function, and role. Science affirmed what men had always known, what custom, law, and religion had postulated and justified. With the authority of their "objective," "rational" inquiry they restated ancient premises and arrived at the same traditional conclusions: the innate superiority of the male and the justifiable subordination of the female.

## The Age of Enlightenment

### Lester G. Crocker

*The Enlightenment owes its substance to the thought of a relatively small group of 18th-century philosophes who came from many countries but were centered in France. Although they often argued among themselves, there was a set of approaches and propositions upon which most of them agreed.*

*In the following selection Lester Crocker analyzes what unified the philosophes.*

CONSIDER: *How the primary documents support or contradict Crocker's interpretations; why the philosophes were so concerned with Christianity and the Church; the elements of this outlook that make the most sense to you for today's world.*

What we call the Enlightenment gradually took shape in individual minds, over several generations, before it became conscious of itself as a movement during the late 1740's. The principal galvanizing forces were Voltaire's ceaseless efforts in propagandizing and in whipping up "party" spirit, and the prolonged battle over the *Encyclopédie*, which served to unite many of the *philosophes*, as we call the writers who were engaged in furthering the goals of the Enlightenment. The *philosophes* were more often than not at odds among themselves on the answers they proposed to various questions or problems. Their solidarity lay in their awareness of a common foe—the *status quo*, and those who supported it, particularly Christianity and the Church. It lay also in their agreement on what the questions and problems were. The *philosophes* held certain ideas and aims in common. Among these were religious tolerance (belief in toleration of all ideas as well as personal tolerance was not universal among the *philosophes*); the conviction that human life can be improved through the improvement of society, since men are (more or less) shaped by laws and government; the idea that the enlightened group should influence those who govern, both directly and through public opinion. Their stance rested on a base of secularism and humanism. Regardless of their varying religious beliefs, all the *philosophes* held that the proper business (if there was any) of organized churches was the salvation of souls. Science, government, economic policy, even (many thought) moral values and personal morality had to be freed from the dead hand of Christian authority. The Enlightenment was for unfettered critical reason, for social experience to indicate what course men should take in meeting the challenges involved in ameliorating human affairs. God, if he existed, had no influence on these—Bayle had demonstrated that, before the end of the seventeenth century. To the *philosophes*, churches were what we would now call "power groups" and, like all such groups, interested primarily in themselves. Revealed religions were fantasies or downright frauds. Christianity, especially, was hostile to the demands of human nature and pretended (the critics claimed) to direct men away from their self-interest in this life to a mythical paradise in a nonexistent life beyond. Reaction against the Christian world view and religious control of thought had been the very origin of the freethinking (*libertin*) movement in the seventeenth century. The *philosophes* were united by the conviction, above all else, that man must control his own destiny for the sole purpose of a better life on earth and that he must do everything possible to enlarge that control.

## Chapter Questions

1. What were the main ways in which the science of the 17th century constituted a break from the past? What were some of the main problems facing 17th-century scientists in making this break?

2. What core of ideas and attitudes most clearly connects Enlightenment thinkers as revealed in these sources? How do these ideas relate to 18th-century society and institutions?

3. In what ways do the sources support the argument that together, the Scientific Revolution and the Enlightenment constitute a single intellectual revolution of great long-term significance?

# Chapter Seventeen

# Revolution, Nationalism, and the State in Europe, 1789–1914

In 1789, the French Revolution ended the relative political and social stability of the Ancien Régime and initiated the period Western historians usually call the Modern Era. Within a few tumultuous years, feudalism was abolished, liberal principles echoing Enlightenment thought were formally recognized, Church lands were confiscated, the monarchy was abolished, and government administration was reorganized.

A decade later the turmoil initiated in 1789 was far from over. Napoleon Bonaparte, rising with opportunities presented by the French Revolution, gained power not only in France, but directly and indirectly throughout much of continental Europe. His final fall in 1815 marked the end of a series of wars and the Age of Napoleon.

The European powers crafted a settlement at the Congress of Vienna (1814–15). Conservatism dominated, rejecting changes instituted during the revolutionary and Napoleonic periods, restoring traditional groups and governments to power, and resisting liberalism and nationalism. Nevertheless, movements for national liberation and liberal reform surfaced during the 1820s, 1830s, and 1840s. Liberalism, encompassing demands for greater freedom, constitutional government, and political rights, was particularly strong in western Europe. A climax came in 1848, when revolutions erupted across Europe—usually in the name of nationalism or liberalism. Victories proved short-lived and soon groups standing for authoritarian rule took advantage of the disunity to regain power.

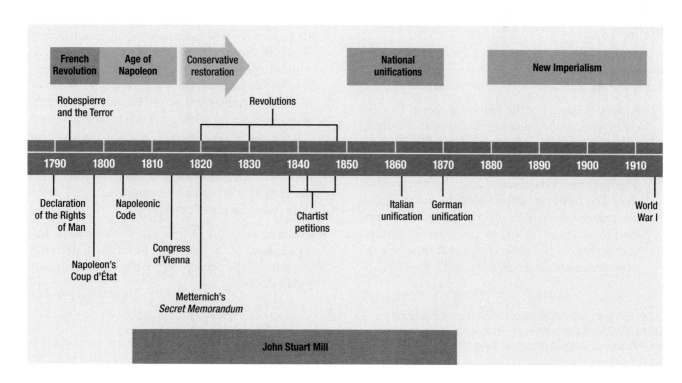

Between 1850 and 1914 politics in Europe became focused on increased governmental involvement in the economic and social life of the nation and the growth of nationalism. With its roots in the French Revolution and the Napoleonic period, nationalism was capitalized on by national governments and was at the core of the successful unification movements in Italy and Germany.

The sources in this chapter focus on three topics: revolution; conservatism and liberalism; and nationalism. Historians are fascinated by revolutions, through which change is unusually rapid and dramatic. Here several sources deal with the causes and significance of various revolutions dur-

ing the period, particularly the French Revolution of 1789. Included is an examination of Napoleon's appeal and the significance of his policies for women. The nature of conservatism and liberalism will be examined by looking at their doctrines and political policies. Nationalism will be analyzed by examining its tendency to become militant during the second half of the 19th century.

This focus on revolution and political developments in Europe between 1789 and 1914 sets the stage for an examination of the economic, social, and cultural changes that transformed the West during this same period.

# PRIMARY SOURCES

## The Cahiers: Discontents of the Third Estate

*Pressured by discontent and financial problems, Louis XVI called for a meeting of the Estates General in 1789. This representative institution, which had not met for 175 years, reflected the traditional formal divisions in French society: the First Estate, the clergy; the Second Estate, the nobility; and the Third Estate, all the rest from banker and lawyer to peasant. In anticipation of the meeting of the Estates General, the king requested and received cahiers, lists of grievances drawn up by local groups of each of the three Estates. These cahiers have provided historians with an unusually rich source of materials revealing what was bothering people just before the outbreak of the revolution in 1789. The following is an excerpt from a cahier from the Third Estate in Carcassonne.*

CONSIDER: *Why these grievances might be revolutionary; the ways in which these grievances are peculiar to the Third Estate and not shared by the First and Second Estates.*

8. Among these rights the following should be especially noted: the nation should hereafter be subject only to such laws and taxes as it shall itself freely ratify.

9. The meetings of the Estates General of the kingdom should be fixed for definite periods, and the subsidies judged necessary for the support of the state and the public service should be noted for no longer a period than to the close of the year in which the next meeting of the Estates General is to occur.

10. In order to assure to the third estate the influence to which it is entitled in view of the number of its members, the amount of its contributions to the public treasury, and the manifold interests which it has to defend or promote in the national assemblies, its votes in the assembly should be taken and counted by head.

11. No order, corporation, or individual citizen may lay claim to any pecuniary exemptions. . . . All taxes should be assessed on the same system throughout the nation.

12. The due exacted from commoners holding fiefs should be abolished, and also the general or particular regulations which exclude members of the third estate from certain positions, offices, and ranks which have hitherto been bestowed on nobles either for life or hereditarily. A law should be passed declaring members of the third estate qualified to fill all such offices for which they are judged to be personally fitted.

13. Since individual liberty is intimately associated with national liberty, his Majesty is hereby petitioned not to permit that it be hereafter interfered with by arbitrary orders for imprisonment. . . .

14. Freedom should be granted also to the press, which should however be subjected, by means of strict regulations, to the principles of religion, morality, and public decency. . . .

SOURCE: "Cahier of the Grievances, Complaints, and Protests of the Electoral District of Carcassone . . ." From James Harvey Robinson, ed., *Readings in European History,* vol. II (Boston: Ginn, 1904), pp. 399–400.

## Women of the Third Estate

*The vast majority of 18th-century Europeans were not members of the aristocracy. Over 90 percent were peasants, artisans, domestics, and laborers—often referred to in France as members of the Third Estate. While both men and women of the Third Estate shared much, women's positions and grievances often differed from those of men. Articulate records of these women's grievances are difficult to find, but the flood of formal petitions preceding the French Revolution of 1789 provides us with some rich sources. The following is a "Petition of the Women of the Third Estate to the King," dated several months prior to the outbreak of the French Revolution.*

CONSIDER: *What options seem available to women; the problems identified and solutions proposed; ways in which men's interests and women's interests might clash.*

1 January 1789. Almost all women of the Third Estate are born poor. Their education is either neglected or misconceived, for it consists in sending them to learn from teachers who do not themselves know the first word of the language they are supposed to be teaching. . . . At the age of fifteen or sixteen, girls can earn five or six sous a day. If nature has not granted them good looks, they get married, without a dowry, to unfortunate artisans and drag out a grueling existence in the depths of the provinces, producing children whom they are unable to bring up. If, on the other hand, they are born pretty, being without culture, principles, or any notion of morality, they fall prey to the first seducer, make one slip, come to Paris to conceal it, go totally to the bad here, and end up dying as victims of debauchery.

Today, when the difficulty of earning a living forces thousands of women to offer themselves to the highest bidder and men prefer buying them for a spell to winning them for good, any woman drawn to virtue, eager to educate herself, and with natural taste . . . is faced with the choice either of casting herself into a cloister which will accept a modest dowry or of going into domestic service. . . .

If old age overtakes unmarried women, they spend it in tears and as objects of contempt for their nearest relatives.

To counter such misfortunes, Sire, we ask that men be excluded from practicing those crafts that are women's prerogative, such as dressmaking, embroidery, milinery, etc. Let them leave us the needle and the spindle and we pledge our word never to handle the compass or the set-square.

We ask, Sire . . . to be instructed and given jobs, not that we may usurp men's authority but so that we may have a means of livelihood, and so that the weaker

among us who are dazzled by luxury and led astray by example should not be forced to join the ranks of the wretched who encumber the streets and whose lewd audacity disgraces both our sex and the men who frequent them.

## The Declaration of the Rights of Man and Citizen

*No document better summarizes the ideals underlying the French Revolution than The Declaration of the Rights of Man and Citizen. After an extended discussion, this document was passed by the National Assembly on August 27, 1789; later a revised version of it was incorporated into the Constitution of 1791. Its provisions are a combination of general statements about human rights and specific statements about what the government should and should not do. This document corresponds to the American Declaration of Independence. It is also viewed more broadly as containing the general principles for democratic revolutions in the 18th and 19th centuries.*

CONSIDER: *How this document reflects ideals of the Enlightenment; at which social groups this document was aimed; who would suffer most from or be most infuriated by its provisions; the ways in which this document is inconsistent with monarchical government; how a monarch might retain meaningful powers while still conforming to this document.*

The representatives of the French people, organized as a National Assembly, believing that the ignorance, neglect or contempt of the rights of man are the sole cause of public calamities and of the corruption of governments, have determined to set forth in a solemn declaration the natural, inalienable and sacred rights of man, in order that this declaration, being constantly before all the members of the social body, shall remind them continually of their rights and duties; in order that the acts of the legislative power, as well as those of the executive power, may be compared at any moment with the ends of all political institutions and may thus be more respected; and, lastly, in order that the grievances of the citizens, based hereafter upon simple and incontestable principles, shall tend to the maintenance of the constitution and redound to the happiness of all. Therefore the National Assembly recognizes and proclaims, in the presence and under the auspices of the Supreme Being, the following rights of man and of the citizen:—

SOURCE: Excerpts from *Not In God's Image* by Julia O'Faolain and Lauro Martines. Copyright © 1973 by Julia O'Faolain and Lauro Martines. Reprinted by permission of Harper & Row, Publishers, Inc.

SOURCE: James Harvey Robinson, ed., "The French Revolution, 1789–1791," in *Translations and Reprints from the Original Sources of European History*, vol. I, no. 5, Department of History of the University of Pennsylvania, ed. (Philadelphia: University of Pennsylvania Press, 1898), pp. 6–8.

Article 1. Men are born and remain free and equal in rights. Social distinctions may only be founded upon the general good.

2. The aim of all political association is the preservation of the natural and imprescriptible rights of man. These rights are liberty, property, security and resistance to oppression.

3. The principle of all sovereignty resides essentially in the nation. No body nor individual may exercise any authority which does not proceed directly from the nation.

4. Liberty consists in the freedom to do everything which injures no one else; hence the exercise of the natural rights of each man has no limits except those which assure to the other members of the society the enjoyment of the same rights. These limits can only be determined by law.

5. Law can only prohibit such actions as are hurtful to society. Nothing may be prevented which is not forbidden by law, and no one may be forced to do anything not provided for by law.

6. Law is the expression of the general will. Every citizen has a right to participate personally or through his representative in its formation. It must be the same for all, whether it protects or punishes. All citizens, being equal in the eyes of the law, are equally eligible to all dignities and to all public positions and occupations, according to their abilities, and without distinction except that of their virtues and talents.

7. No person shall be accused, arrested or imprisoned except in the cases and according to the forms prescribed by law. Any one soliciting, transmitting, executing or causing to be executed any arbitrary order shall be punished. But any citizen summoned or arrested in virtue of the law shall submit without delay, as resistance constitutes an offence.

8. The law shall provide for such punishments only as are strictly and obviously necessary, and no one shall suffer punishment except it be legally inflicted in virtue of a law passed and promulgated before the commission of the offence.

9. As all persons are held innocent until they shall have been declared guilty, if arrest shall be deemed indispensable, all harshness not essential to the securing of the prisoner's person shall be severely repressed by law.

10. No one shall be disquieted on account of his opinions, including his religious views, provided their manifestation does not disturb the public order established by law.

11. The free communication of ideas and opinions is one of the most precious of the rights of man. Every citizen may, accordingly, speak, write and print with freedom, but shall be responsible for such abuses of this freedom as shall be defined by law.

12. The security of the rights of man and of the citizen requires public military force. These forces are, therefore, established for the good of all and not for the personal advantage of those to whom they shall be entrusted.

13. A common contribution is essential for the maintenance of the public forces and for the cost of administration. This should be equitably distributed among all the citizens in proportion to their means.

14. All the citizens have a right to decide, either personally or by their representatives, as to the necessity of the public contribution; to grant this freely; to know to what uses it is put; and to fix the proportion, the mode of assessment, and of collection, and the duration of the taxes.

15. Society has the right to require of every public agent an account of his administration.

16. A society in which the observance of the law is not assured, nor the separation of powers defined, has no constitution at all.

17. Since property is an inviolable and sacred right, no one shall be deprived thereof except where public necessity, legally determined, shall clearly demand it, and then only on condition that the owner shall have been previously and equitably indemnified.

## Speech to the National Convention— February 5, 1794: The Terror Justified
### Maximilien Robespierre

*Between 1793 and 1794, France experienced the most radical phase of the revolution, known as the Reign of Terror. During this period France was essentially ruled by the 12-member Committee of Public Safety elected by the National Convention every month. The outstanding member of this committee was Maximilien Robespierre (1758–94), a provincial lawyer who rose within the Jacobin Club and*

SOURCE: Raymond P. Stearns, ed., *Pageant of Europe.* Copyright 1947 by Harcourt Brace Jovanovich, Inc., and renewed by Josephine B. Stearns. Reprinted by permission of Harcourt Brace Jovanovich, Inc. (New York, 1947), pp. 404–5.

*gained a reputation for incorruptibility and superb oratory. Historians have argued over Robespierre, some singling him out as a bloodthirsty individual with the major responsibility for the executions during the Reign of Terror, others seeing him as a sincere, idealistic, effective revolutionary leader called to the fore by events of the time. In the following speech to the National Convention on February 5, 1794, Robespierre defines the revolution and justifies extreme actions, including terror, in its defense.*

CONSIDER: *What Robespierre means when he argues that terror flows from virtue; how the use of terror relates to the essence of the revolution; how this speech might be interpreted as an Enlightenment attack on the Ancien Régime carried to its logical conclusion.*

It is time to mark clearly the aim of the Revolution and the end toward which we wish to move; it is time to take stock of ourselves, of the obstacles which we still face, and of the means which we ought to adopt to attain our objectives. . . .

What is the goal for which we strive? A peaceful enjoyment of liberty and equality, the rule of that eternal justice whose laws are engraved, not upon marble or stone, but in the hearts of all men.

We wish an order of things where all low and cruel passions are enchained by the laws, all beneficent and generous feelings aroused; where ambition is the desire to merit glory and to serve one's fatherland; where distinctions are born only of equality itself; where the citizen is subject to the magistrate, the magistrate to the people, the people to justice; where the nation safeguards the welfare of each individual, and each individual proudly enjoys the prosperity and glory of his fatherland; where all spirits are enlarged by the constant exchange of republican sentiments and by the need of earning the respect of a great people; where the arts are the adornment of liberty, which ennobles them; and where commerce is the source of public wealth, not simply of monstrous opulence for a few families.

In our country we wish to substitute morality for egotism, probity for honor, principles for conventions, duties for etiquette, the empire of reason for the tyranny of customs, contempt for vice for contempt for misfortune, pride for insolence, the love of honor for the love of money . . . that is to say, all the virtues and miracles of the Republic for all the vices and snobbishness of the monarchy.

We wish in a word to fulfill the requirements of nature, to accomplish the destiny of mankind, to make good the promises of philosophy . . . that France, hitherto illustrious among slave states, may eclipse the glory of all free peoples that have existed, become the model of all nations. . . . That is our ambition; that is our aim.

What kind of government can realize these marvels? Only a democratic government. . . . But to found and to consolidate among us this democracy, to realize the peaceable rule of constitutional laws, it is necessary to conclude the war of liberty against tyranny and to pass successfully through the storms of revolution. Such is the aim of the revolutionary system which you have set up. . . .

Now what is the fundamental principle of democratic, or popular government—that is to say, the essential mainspring upon which it depends and which makes it function? It is virtue: I mean public virtue . . . that virtue which is nothing else but love of fatherland and its laws. . . .

The splendor of the goal of the French Revolution is simultaneously the source of our strength and of our weakness: our strength, because it gives us an ascendancy of truth over falsehood, and of public rights over private interests; our weakness, because it rallies against us all vicious men, all those who in their hearts seek to despoil the people. . . . It is necessary to stifle the domestic and foreign enemies of the Republic or perish with them. Now in these circumstances, the first maxim of our politics ought to be to lead the people by means of reason and the enemies of the people by terror.

If the basis of popular government in time of peace is virtue, the basis of popular government in time of revolution is both virtue and terror: virtue without which terror is murderous, terror without which virtue is powerless. Terror is nothing else than swift, severe, indomitable justice; it flows, then, from virtue.

## Memoirs: Napoleon's Appeal
### Madame de Remusat

*Napoleon was the candidate neither of those longing to turn France to a more revolutionary course nor of those who wanted to return France to the legitimacy of the Ancien Régime. He came to power promising to uphold both revolutionary principles and order. Scholars have analyzed the question of why he was able to rise to power. Some see him as a military and political genius; others argue that he was an opportunist who took advantage of circumstances as they arose. One of the earliest analyses of Napoleon's rise to power was written by Madame de Remusat (1780–1821). As a lady-in-waiting to Empress Josephine and wife of a Napoleonic official, she observed Napoleon firsthand and described him in her* Memoirs.

SOURCE: From James Harvey Robinson, ed., *Readings in European History,* vol. II (Boston: Ginn, 1904), pp. 491–92.

CONSIDER: *Why, according to Remusat, Napoleon was so appealing to the French; the means Napoleon used to secure his power.*

I can understand how it was that men worn out by the turmoil of the Revolution, and afraid of that liberty which had long been associated with death, looked for repose under the dominion of an able ruler on whom fortune was seemingly resolved to smile. I can conceive that they regarded his elevation as a decree of destiny and fondly believed that in the irrevocable they should find peace. I may confidently assert that those persons believed quite sincerely that Bonaparte, whether as consul or emperor, would exert his authority to oppose the intrigue of faction and would save us from the perils of anarchy.

None dared to utter the word "republic," so deeply had the Terror stained that name; and the government of the Directory had perished in the contempt with which its chiefs were regarded. The return of the Bourbons could only be brought about by the aid of a revolution; and the slightest disturbance terrified the French people, in whom enthusiasm of every kind seemed dead. Besides, the men in whom they had trusted had one after the other deceived them; and as, this time, they were yielding to force, they were at least certain that they were not deceiving themselves.

The belief, or rather the error, that only despotism could at that epoch maintain order in France was very widespread. It became the mainstay of Bonaparte; and it is due to him to say that he also believed it. The factions played into his hands by imprudent attempts which he turned to his own advantage. He had some grounds for his belief that he was necessary; France believed it, too; and he even succeeded in persuading foreign sovereigns that he constituted a barrier against republican influences, which, but for him, might spread widely. At the moment when Bonaparte placed the imperial crown upon his head there was not a king in Europe who did not believe that he wore his own crown more securely because of that event. Had the new emperor granted a liberal constitution, the peace of nations and of kings might really have been forever secured.

## Secret Memorandum to Tsar Alexander I, 1820: Conservative Principles
### Prince Klemens von Metternich

*The outstanding leader of the conservative tide that rose with the fall of Napoleon was Prince Klemens von Metternich (1773–1859). From his post as Austrian minister of foreign affairs, Metternich hosted the Congress of Vienna and played a dominating role within Austria and among the conservative states of Europe between 1815 and 1848. Both in principle and in practice, he represented a conservatism that rejected the changes wrought by the French Revolution and stood against liberalism and nationalism. The following is an excerpt from a secret memorandum that Metternich sent to Tsar Alexander I of Russia in 1820, explaining his political principles. While not a sophisticated statement of political theory, it does reflect key elements of conservative attitudes and ideas.*

CONSIDER: *What threats Metternich perceives; how Metternich connects "presumption" with the middle class; how this document reflects the experience of the revolutionary and Napoleonic periods; the kinds of policies that would logically flow from these attitudes.*

"L'Europe," a celebrated writer has recently said, "*fait aujourd' hui pitié à l'homme d'esprit et horreur à l'homme vertueux.*"[1]

It would be difficult to comprise in a few words a more exact picture of the situation at the time we are writing these lines!

Kings have to calculate the chances of their very existence in the immediate future; passions are let loose, and league together to overthrow everything which society respects as the basis of its existence; religion, public morality, laws, customs, rights, and duties, all are attacked, confounded, overthrown, or called in question. The great mass of the people are tranquil spectators of these attacks and revolutions, and of the absolute want of all means of defense. A few are carried off by the torrent, but the wishes of the immense majority are to maintain a repose which exists no longer, and of which even the first elements seem to be lost. . . .

Having now thrown a rapid glance over the first causes of the present state of society, it is necessary to point out in a more particular manner the evil which threatens to deprive it, at one blow, of the real blessings, the fruits of genuine civilisation, and to disturb it in the midst of its enjoyments. This evil may be described in one word—presumption; the natural effect of the rapid progression of the human mind towards the perfecting of so many things. This it is which at the present day leads so many individuals astray, for it has become an almost universal sentiment.

Religion, morality, legislation, economy, politics, administration, all have become common and accessible to everyone. Knowledge seems to come by inspiration; experience has no value for the presumptuous man; faith is nothing to him; he substitutes for it a pretended individual conviction, and to arrive at this conviction dispenses

SOURCE: Prince Richard Metternich, ed., *Memoirs of Prince Metternich, 1815–1829*, vol. III, Mrs. Alexander Napier, trans. (New York: Charles Scribner's Sons, 1881), pp. 454–55, 458–60, 468–69.

[1]Europe . . . is pitied by men of spirit and abhorred by men of virtue.

with all inquiry and with all study; for these means appear too trivial to a mind which believes itself strong enough to embrace at one glance all questions and all facts. Laws have no value for him, because he has not contributed to make them, and it would be beneath a man of his parts to recognise the limits traced by rude and ignorant generations. Power resides in himself; why should he submit himself to that which was only useful for the man deprived of light and knowledge? That which, according to him, was required in an age of weakness cannot be suitable in an age of reason and vigour amounting to universal perfection, which the German innovators designate by the idea, absurd in itself, of the Emancipation of the People! Morality itself he does not attack openly, for without it he could not be sure for a single instant of his own existence; but he interprets its essence after his own fashion, and allows every other person to do so likewise, provided that other person neither kills nor robs him.

In thus tracing the character of the presumptuous man, we believe we have traced that of the society of the day, composed of like elements, if the denomination of society is applicable to an order of things which only tends in principle towards individualising all the elements of which society is composed. Presumption makes every man the guide of his own belief, the arbiter of laws according to which he is pleased to govern himself, or to allow some one else to govern him and his neighbours; it makes him, in short, the sole judge of his own faith, his own actions, and the principles according to which he guides them. . . .

The Governments, having lost their balance, are frightened, intimidated, and thrown into confusion by the cries of the intermediary class of society, which, placed between the Kings and their subjects, breaks the sceptre of the monarch, and usurps the cry of the people—the class so often disowned by the people, and nevertheless too much listened to, caressed and feared by those who could with one word reduce it again to nothingness.

We see this intermediary class abandon itself with a blind fury and animosity which proves much more its own fears than any confidence in the success of its enterprises, to all the means which seem proper to assuage its thirst for power, applying itself to the task of persuading Kings that their rights are confined to sitting upon a throne, while those of the people are to govern, and to attack all that centuries have bequeathed as holy and worthy of man's respect—denying, in fact, the value of the past, and declaring themselves the masters of the future. We see this class take all sorts of disguises, uniting and subdividing as occasion offers, helping each other in the hour of danger, and the next day depriving each other of all their conquests. It takes possession of the press, and employs it to promote impiety, disobedience to the laws of religion and the State, and goes so far as to preach murder as a duty for those who desire what is good.

## On Liberty

### John Stuart Mill

*During the second half of the 19th century, liberalism in theory and practice started to change. In general it became less wedded to laissez-faire policies and less optimistic than it was during the first half of the 19th century. This change is reflected in the thought of John Stuart Mill (1806–73), the most influential British thinker of the mid-19th century and probably the leading liberal theorist of the period. When he was young he favored the early liberalism of his father, James Mill, a well-known philosopher, and Jeremy Bentham, the author of utilitarianism. Over time he perceived difficulties with this early liberalism, and new dangers. He modified his liberal ideas, a change that would later be reflected in liberal political policies of the late 19th and early 20th centuries. In the following selection from* On Liberty *(1859), his most famous work, Mill analyzes this evolution of liberalism starting with the aims of liberals during the first half of the 19th century.*

CONSIDER: *What Mill feels was the essence of early liberalism; what crucial changes occurred to transform liberalism; what Mill means by tyranny of the majority.*

The aim, therefore, of patriots was to set limits to the power which the ruler should be suffered to exercise over the community; and this limitation was what they meant by liberty. It was attempted in two ways. First, by obtaining a recognition of certain immunities, called political liberties or rights, which it was to be regarded as a breach of duty in the ruler to infringe; and which if he did infringe, specific resistance, or general rebellion, was held to be justifiable. A second, and generally a later expedient, was the establishment of constitutional checks, by which the consent of the community, or of a body of some sort, supposed to represent its interests, was made a necessary condition to some of the more important acts of the governing power. To the first of these modes of limitation, the ruling power, in most European countries, was compelled, more or less, to submit. It was not so with the second; and, to attain this, or when already in some degree possessed, to attain it more completely, became everywhere the principal object of the lovers of liberty. And so long as mankind were content to combat one enemy by another, and to be ruled by a master, on condition of being guaranteed more or less efficaciously

SOURCE: John Stuart Mill, *Utilitarianism, Liberty, and Representative Government* (London: J. M. Dent and Sons Ltd., Everyman Liberty, 1910), pp. 66–68.

against his tyranny, they did not carry their aspirations beyond this point.

A time, however, came, in the progress of human affairs, when men ceased to think it a necessity of nature that their governors should be an independent power, opposed in interest to themselves. It appeared to them much better that the various magistrates of the State should be their tenants or delegates, revocable at their pleasure. In that way alone, it seemed, could they have complete security that the powers of government would never be abused to their disadvantage. By degrees this new demand for elective and temporary rulers became the prominent object of the exertions of the popular party, wherever any such party existed; and superseded, to a considerable extent, the previous efforts to limit the power of rulers. As the struggle proceeded for making the ruling power emanate from the periodical choice of the ruled, some persons began to think that too much importance had been attached to the limitation of the power itself. *That* (it might seem) was a resource against rulers whose interests were habitually opposed to those of the people. What was now wanted was, that the rulers should be identified with the people; that their interest and will should be the interest and will of the nation. The nation did not need to be protected against its own will. There was no fear of its tyrannising over itself. Let the rulers be effectually responsible to it, promptly removable by it, and it could afford to trust them with power of which it could itself dictate the use to be made. Their power was but the nation's own power, concentrated, and in a form convenient for exercise. This mode of thought, or rather perhaps of feeling, was common among the last generation of European liberalism, in the Continental section of which it still apparently predominates. . . .

In time, however, a democratic republic came to occupy a large portion of the earth's surface, and made itself felt as one of the most powerful members of the community of nations; and elective and responsible government became subject to the observations and criticisms which wait upon a great existing fact. It was now perceived that such phrases as "self-government" and "the power of the people over themselves" do not express the true state of the case. The "people" who exercise the power are not always the same people with those over whom it is exercised; and the "self-government" spoken of is not the government of each by himself, but of each by all the rest. The will of the people, moreover, practically means the will of the most numerous or the most active *part* of the people; the majority, or those who succeed in making themselves accepted as the majority; the people, consequently *may* desire to oppress a part of their number; and precautions are as much needed against this as against any other abuse of power. The limitation, therefore, of the power of government over individuals loses none of its importance when the holders of power are regularly accountable to the community, that is, to the strongest party therein. This view of things, recommending itself equally to the intelligence of thinkers and to the inclination of those important classes in European society to whose real or supposed interests democracy is adverse, has had no difficulty in establishing itself; and in political speculations "the tyranny of the majority" is now generally included among the evils against which society requires to be on its guard.

Like other tyrannies, the tyranny of the majority was at first, and is still vulgarly, held in dread, chiefly as operating through the acts of the public authorities. But reflecting persons perceived that when society is itself the tyrant—society collectively over the separate individuals who compose it—its means of tyrannising are not restricted to the acts which it may do by the hands of its political functionaries. Society can and does execute its own mandates: and if it issues wrong mandates instead of right, or any mandates at all in things with which it ought not to meddle, it practises a social tyranny more formidable than many kinds of political oppression, since, though not usually upheld by such extreme penalties, it leaves fewer means of escape, penetrating much more deeply into the details of life, and enslaving the soul itself. Protection, therefore, against the tyranny of the magistrate is not enough: there needs protection also against the tyranny of the prevailing opinion and feeling; against the tendency of society to impose, by other means than civil penalties, its own ideas and practices as rules of conduct on those who dissent from them; to fetter the development, and, if possible, prevent the formation, of any individuality not in harmony with its ways, and compel all characters to fashion themselves upon the model of its own. There is a limit to the legitimate interference of collective opinion with individual independence: and to find that limit, and maintain it against encroachment, is as indispensable to a good condition of human affairs, as protection against political despotism.

## The First Chartist Petition: Demands for Change in England

*Movements for reform occurred throughout Europe between 1815 and 1848 despite the efforts of conservatives to quash them. Eventually almost all countries in Europe experienced the revolutions conservatives feared so much. One exception was England, but even there, political movements threatened to turn into violent revolts against the failure of the government to change. The most important of these was the*

*Chartist movement, made up primarily of members of the working class who wanted reforms for themselves. The following is an excerpt from the first charter presented to the House of Commons in 1838. Subsequent charters were presented in 1842 and 1848. In each case the potential existed for a mass movement to turn into a violent revolt, and in each case Parliament rejected the Chartist demands. Only later in the century were most of these demands met.*

CONSIDER: *The nature of the Chartists' demands; by what means the Chartists hoped to achieve their ends; how Metternich might analyze these demands.*

Required, as we are universally, to support and obey the laws, nature and reason entitle us to demand that in the making of the laws the universal voice shall be implicitly listened to. We perform the duties of freemen; we must have the privileges of freemen. Therefore, we demand universal suffrage. The suffrage, to be exempt from the corruption of the wealthy and the violence of the powerful, must be secret. The assertion of our right necessarily involves the power of our uncontrolled exercise. We ask for the reality of a good, not for its semblance, therefore we demand the ballot. The connection between the representatives and the people, to be beneficial, must be intimate. The legislative and constituent powers, for correction and for instruction, ought to be brought into frequent contact. Errors which are comparatively light, when susceptible of a speedy popular remedy, may produce the most disastrous effects when permitted to grow inveterate through years of compulsory endurance. To public safety, as well as public confidence, frequent elections are essential. Therefore, we demand annual parliaments. With power to choose, and freedom in choosing, the range of our choice must be unrestricted. We are compelled, by the existing laws, to take for our representatives men who are incapable of appreciating our difficulties, or have little sympathy with them; merchants who have retired from trade and no longer feel its harrassings; proprietors of land who are alike ignorant of its evils and its cure; lawyers by whom the notoriety of the senate is courted only as a means of obtaining notice in the courts. The labours of a representative who is sedulous in the discharge of his duty are numerous and burdensome. It is neither just, nor reasonable, nor safe, that they should continue to be gratuitously rendered. We demand that in the future election of members of your honourable house, the approbation of the constituency shall be the sole qualification, and that to every representative so chosen, shall be assigned out of the public

taxes, a fair and adequate remunerative for the time which he is called upon to devote to the public service. The management of his mighty kingdom has hitherto been a subject for contending factions to try their selfish experiments upon. We have felt the consequences in our sorrowful experience. Short glimmerings of uncertain enjoyment, swallowed up by long and dark seasons of suffering. If the self-government of the people should not remove their distresses, it will, at least, remove their repinings. Universal suffrage will, and it alone can, bring true and lasting peace to the nation; we firmly believe that it will also bring prosperity. May it therefore please your honourable house, to take this our petition into your most serious consideration, and to use your utmost endeavours, by all constitutional means, to have a law passed, granting to every male of lawful age, sane mind, and unconvicted of crime, the right of voting for members of parliament, and directing all future elections of members of parliament to be in the way of secret ballot, and ordaining that the duration of parliament, so chosen, shall in no case exceed one year, and abolishing all property qualifications in the members, and providing for their due remuneration while in attendance on their parliamentary duties.

"And your petitioners shall ever pray."

## Militant Nationalism
### *Heinrich von Treitschke*

*The idea of nationalism and nationalistic movements gained great power throughout the 19th century. While favored by a variety of liberal and conservative thinkers and groups during the first half of the century, nationalism became more militant, extreme, and racist in the second half of the century, particularly in central Europe. One of the most influential proponents of this militant nationalism in Germany was Heinrich von Treitschke (1834–96), a historian at the University of Berlin. In the following selections from his works, Treitschke puts forth his views on national character, the state, war, and Jews.*

CONSIDER: *What might be appealing about these views; possible reasons for Treitschke's views of the English and Jews; what policies might logically flow from these ideas.*

ON THE GERMAN CHARACTER

Depth of thought, idealism, cosmopolitan views; a transcendent philosophy which boldly oversteps (or freely looks over) the separating barriers of finite existence;

SOURCE: From R. G. Gammage, *History of the Chartist Movement*, 2d ed. (Newcastle-on-Tyne, England: Browne and Browne, 1894), pp. 88–90.

SOURCE: Louis L. Snyder, ed., *Documents of German History* (New Brunswick, NJ: Rutgers University Press, 1958), pp. 259–62.

familiarity with every human thought and feeling, the desire to traverse the worldwide realm of ideas in common with the foremost intellects of all nations and all times. All that has at all times been held to be characteristic of the Germans and has always been praised as the essence of German character and breeding. . . .

## ON THE STATE

The state is a moral community, which is called upon to educate the human race by positive achievement. Its ultimate object is that a nation should develop in it, a nation distinguished by a real national character. To achieve this state is the highest moral duty for nation and individual alike. All private quarrels must be forgotten when the state is in danger.

At the moment when the state cries out that its very life is at stake, social selfishness must cease and party hatred be hushed. The individual must forget his egoism, and feel that he is a member of the whole body.

The most important possession of a state, its be-all and end-all, is power. He who is not man enough to look this truth in the face should not meddle in politics. The state is not physical power as an end in itself, it is power to protect and promote the higher interests. Power must justify itself by being applied for the greatest good of mankind. It is the highest moral duty of the state to increase its power.

The true greatness of the state is that it links the past with the present and future; consequently, the individual has no right to regard the state as a means for attaining his own ambitions in life. Every extension of the activities of the state is beneficial and wise if it arouses, promotes, and purifies the independence of free and reasoning men; it is evil when it kills and stunts the independence of free men. It is men who make history. . . .

Only the truly great and powerful states ought to exist. Small states are unable to protect their subjects against external enemies; moreover, they are incapable of *Kultar* in great dimensions. Weimar produced a Goethe and a Schiller; still these poets would have been greater had they been citizens of a German national state. . . .

## ON WAR

The idea of perpetual peace is an illusion supported only by those of weak character. It has always been the weary, spiritless, and exhausted ages which have played with the dream of perpetual peace. A thousand touching portraits testify to the sacred power of the love which a righteous war awakes in noble nations. It is altogether impossible that peace be maintained in a world bristling with arms, and even God will see to it that war always recurs as a drastic medicine for the human race. Among great states the greatest political sin and the most contemptible is feebleness. It is the political sin against the Holy Ghost.

War is elevating because the individual disappears before the great conception of the state. The devotion of the members of a community to each other is nowhere so splendidly conspicuous as in war.

Modern wars are not waged for the sake of goods and chattels. What is at stake is the sublime moral good of national honor, which has something in the nature of unconditional sanctity, and compels the individual to sacrifice himself for it.

## ON THE ENGLISH

The hypocritical Englishman, with the Bible in one hand and a pipe of opium in the other, possesses no redeeming qualities. The nation was an ancient robber-knight, in full armor, lance in hand, on every one of the world's trade routes.

The English possess a commercial spirit, a love of money which has killed every sentiment of honor and every distinction of right and wrong. English cowardice and sensuality are hidden behind unctuous, theological fine talk which is to us free-thinking German heretics among all the sins of English nature the most repugnant. In England all notions of honor and class prejudices vanish before the power of money, whereas the German nobility has remained poor but chivalrous. That last indispensable bulwark against the brutalization of society—the duel—has gone out of fashion in England and soon disappeared, to be supplanted by the riding whip. This was a triumph of vulgarity. The newspapers, in their accounts of aristocratic weddings, record in exact detail how much each wedding guest has contributed in the form of presents or in cash; even the youth of the nation have turned their sports into a business, and contend for valuable prizes, whereas the German students wrought havoc on their countenances for the sake of a real or imaginary honor.

## ON JEWS

The Jews at one time played a necessary role in German history, because of their ability in the management of money. But now that the Aryans have become accustomed to the idiosyncrasies of finance, the Jews are no longer necessary. The international Jew, hidden in the mask of different nationalities, is a disintegrating influence; he can be of no further use to the world. It is necessary to speak openly about the Jews, undisturbed by the fact that the Jewish press befouls what is purely historical truth.

# VISUAL SOURCES

## Allegory of the Revolution
### Jeaurat de Bertray

Jeaurat de Bertray's "Allegory of the Revolution" is literally a jumble of historical and revolutionary symbols. At the top is a portrait of Jean Jacques Rousseau, whom at the time many considered to be the spiritual and intellectual father of the French Revolution even though he never advocated revolution and died 11 years before it began. Below him are the new flags of the French Republic, the one on the left with the nationalistic words "love of country." Farther to the left is a triangular monument to Equality; below it two maidens representing Goodness and Good Faith, and in the center a bundle of rods and arms topped by a red liberty cap, all symbolizing a fair, forceful republican government. Just below is paper money, the assignats, that helped finance the revolution and pay off debts, and in the center right grows a liberty tree. To the right are two unfinished pillars, the first dedicated to the regeneration of morals and The Declaration of the Rights of Man and Citizen, the second to the French Revolution. Just below them and in the background are symbols of forceful determination to uphold and defend the revolution: a guillotine, a cannon, and a soldier. In the right foreground is a peasant wearing a liberty cap and sowing a field. This painting pulls together many symbols and elements of the revolutionary ideology. It was painted in 1794, the time of the most radical phase of the revolution.

**Illustration 17–1**   Musée de la Ville de Paris, Musée Carnavalet, Paris/Art Resource, NY.

CONSIDER: Connections between this picture, The Declaration of the Rights of Man and Citizen, and the Enlightenment; the ways in which the Ancien Régime is rejected symbolically in this picture.

## Internal Disturbances and the Reign of Terror

Understanding of the Reign of Terror has often been distorted by an image of random and purposeless brutality. One way to gain clearer insights into the Terror is through the use of maps and statistics, which reveal where the Terror occurred, how intensive it was, and who its victims were. These two maps compare by region the amount of civil disturbance facing government officials and the number of executions occurring in the various departments of France during the Terror. The first pie chart shows the estimated percentages of France's population belonging to the various classes in 1789. For comparison, the second shows the social classes of people executed during the Terror from March 1793 to August 1794.

## Bonaparte Visiting the Plague Victims at Jaffa

### Antoine-Jean Gros

*Despite the British victory at Aboukir Bay in Egypt, which annihilated French sea power, Napoleon retained hopes of conquering the Near East by land. In February 1799, French forces moved northeast from Cairo to Gaza and Nazareth. Despite some victories, the campaign failed to establish French control over the area. Nevertheless, Napoleon tried to transform these disappointments by promoting paintings that created images of success in this campaign.*

*In 1804 Antoine-Jean Gros (1771–1835) presented a scene from the Near Eastern campaigns of 1799 that showed the heroic Napoleon displaying humanism, charity, and nobility Illustration 17–2. The painting records Napoleon, after the battle of Jaffa, entering the mosque courtyard (with its horseshoe arches and pointed arcades) of a pest house (plague hospital) at the Palestinian city of Jaffa in the Holy Land on March 11, 1799. Within lay victims of the bubonic plague, which had recently broken out among Arab defenders of the city and spread to the French. When the plague struck, Napoleon at first had his chief medical officer Desgenettes (just behind and to the right of Napoleon, who stands at the center of the painting) deny the presence of the sickness. Here Napoleon tries to stop the panic and inspire his troops by showing that he is not afraid of contamination and that the victims will be well cared for. At this moment the apparently immune and clearly fearless Napoleon reaches out and even touches the dreaded buboes (an inflamed swelling of the lymphatic glands that usually preceded death) of a French victim, perhaps conveying a sense that his touch might miraculously heal the*

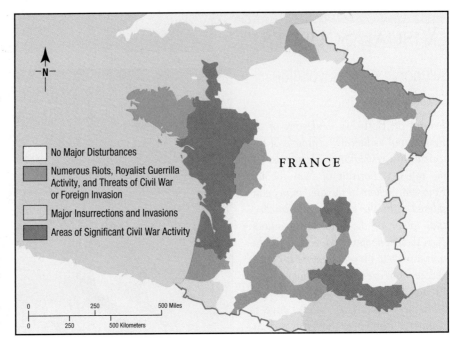

**Map 17–1   Internal Disturbances.**

Legend:
- No Major Disturbances
- Numerous Riots, Royalist Guerrilla Activity, and Threats of Civil War or Foreign Invasion
- Major Insurrections and Invasions
- Areas of Significant Civil War Activity

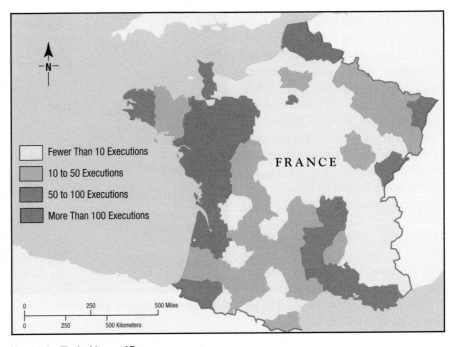

**Map 17–2   The Incidence of Terror.**

Legend:
- Fewer Than 10 Executions
- 10 to 50 Executions
- 50 to 100 Executions
- More Than 100 Executions

*stricken man. Just behind Napoleon, to the left, a more cautious officer holds a handkerchief to his face to ward off the stench of disease and death. In the foreground lay the dead and the agonized dying. At the left, an Arab physician in white robes attends the sick and an assistant carries bread for distribution to the needy. To the right, a blind man, leaning against a column, tries to approach Napoleon, and on the extreme bottom right a doctor, while caring for a soldier, succumbs himself. In the background are the white cubic houses and rising*

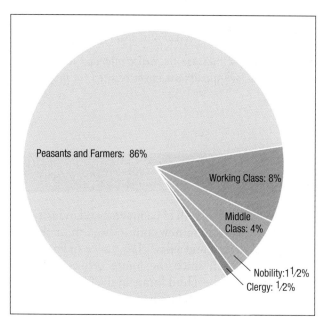

Chart 17–1  Classes in France.

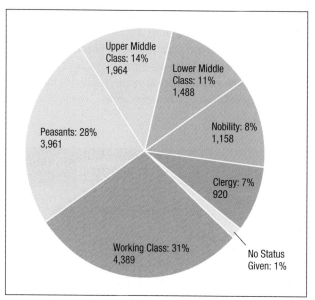

Chart 17–2  Executions during the Reign of Terror.

Illustration 17–2  Réunion des Musées Nationaux/Art Resource, NY.

*minarets of Jaffa. High in the center from the top of a Franciscan monastery flies triumphantly the French tricolor.*

*The surrounding facts differ from the historical image presented by this painting. During the battle of Jaffa, Napoleon had agreed to protect the lives of enemy soldiers if they capitulated. But upon laying down their arms, Napoleon ordered*

*the 3000 prisoners massacred and plundered the town. By May 1799, French forces had retreated back to Egypt.*

CONSIDER: *The message the artist intended to convey to viewers; how high-quality art might be used for propaganda purposes.*

# SECONDARY SOURCES

## The Coming of the French Revolution
### Georges Lefebvre

*Probably no event in modern history has been interpreted at greater length and with greater passion than the French Revolution. The historiographic tradition related to this event is so extensive that numerous books and articles have been written on this historiography itself. A central controversy involves the cause or causes of the revolution and is dealt with in the following selection from* The Coming of the French Revolution *by Georges Lefebvre. Lefebvre held the prestigious chair of French revolutionary history at the Sorbonne until his death in 1959. His work on the French Revolution continues to be highly respected among historians, many of whom differ greatly among themselves.*

CONSIDER: *The most important cause of the French Revolution, according to Lefebvre; how this interpretation relates the revolution in France to areas outside of France; how social, economic, and political factors are linked in this interpretation of the French Revolution; how this view is supported by the primary documents.*

The ultimate cause of the French Revolution of 1789 goes deep into the history of France and of the western world. At the end of the eighteenth century, the social structure of France was aristocratic. It showed the traces of having originated at a time when land was almost the only form of wealth, and when the possessors of land were the masters of those who needed it to work and to live. It is true that in the course of age-old struggles (of which the Fronde, the last revolt of the aristocracy, was as recent as the seventeenth century) the king had been able gradually to deprive the lords of their political power and subject nobles and clergy to his authority. But he had left them the first place in the social hierarchy. Still restless at being merely his "subjects," they remained privileged persons.

Meanwhile the growth of commerce and industry had created, step by step, a new form of wealth, mobile or commercial wealth, and a new class, called in France the bourgeoisie, which since the fourteenth century had taken its place as the Third Estate in the General Estates of the kingdom. This class had grown much stronger with the maritime discoveries of the fifteenth and sixteenth centuries and the ensuing exploitation of new worlds, and also because it proved highly useful to the monarchical state in supplying it with money and competent officials. In the eighteenth century commerce, industry and finance occupied an increasingly important place in the national economy. It was the bourgeoisie that rescued the royal treasury in moments of crisis. From its ranks were recruited most members of the liberal professions and most public employees. It had developed a new ideology which the "philosophers" and "economists" of the time had simply put into definite form. The role of the nobility had correspondingly declined; and the clergy, as the ideal which it proclaimed lost prestige, found its authority growing weaker. These groups preserved the highest rank in the legal structure of the country, but in reality economic power, personal abilities and confidence in the future had passed largely to the bourgeoisie. Such a discrepancy never lasts forever. The Revolution of 1789 restored the harmony between fact and law. This transformation spread in the nineteenth century throughout the west and then to the whole globe, and in this sense the ideas of 1789 toured the world.

## The Revolution of the Notables
### Donald M. G. Sutherland

*Georges Lefebvre's interpretation for the causes of the French Revolution became part of what has been called the "classical view" of the origins of the revolution. In recent years this*

SOURCE: Georges Lefebvre, *The Coming of the French Revolution,* R. R. Palmer, trans. (Princeton, NJ: Princeton University Press, 1947), pp. 1–3.

SOURCE: From Donald Sutherland, *France, 1789–1815,* pp. 15–18, © 1986 Oxford University Press. Reprinted by permission of HarperCollins Publishers, Ltd, and Oxford University Press.

*view has been strongly criticized by increasing numbers of historians, most of whom reject Lefebvre's social-economic view in favor of a more political analysis. In the following selection Donald M. G. Sutherland reviews this controversy.*

CONSIDER: *The basis for the attack on the classical view; why "exclusivism" is so important for these interpretations; how a representative of the classical view might respond.*

There was a time when historians could be fairly confident in describing the origins of the French Revolution. The operative concept was 'aristocratic reaction.' It meant several things at once. Politically, it referred to the undermining of the absolutism of Louis XIV which was thought to have subverted the independence and privileges of the aristocracy. The parliaments, the regional sovereign and appeal courts of which that of Paris was by far the most important, were the driving forces behind the noble offensive. They were able to transform their right of registering laws and edicts into a veto on progressive royal legislation. The Crown was consequently much weaker. This had implications in the social sphere as well. In the course of the eighteenth century, the aristocracy ended up monopolizing the highest offices in government, the military, the Church and judiciary. This in turn had its effects on the bourgeoisie. No longer able to advance to the top of the major social and political institutions of the day, the bourgeoisie became increasingly alienated from the state and from respectable society. Frustrated from achieving its highest ambitions, its loyalties strained, ever open to suggestive criticisms of the system, it was well placed to take advantage of the political crisis of 1788–9 to overthrow the old order altogether. One of the many crises of the Old Regime was a crisis of social mobility.

The argument was irresistibly attractive, partly because of its internal elegance and partly because it explained so much. It made sense of the reign of Louis XIV, the eighteenth century and the Revolution too. The struggle between revolution and counterrevolution could be reduced to two actors, the bourgeoisie and the aristocracy, who had first come to blows in the closing years of the reign of Louis XIV. The aristocracy lost, of course, and specialists of the nineteenth century could move on to the next round, the struggle between the bourgeoisie and the working class.

Unfortunately, research and reflective criticism over the past twenty years have rendered the classical view of the origins of the Revolution utterly untenable. In the first place, it assumes rather than demonstrates the aristocracy's progressive monopoly of high posts. It assumes, too, that the society of the seventeenth century was more open than its successor but relies on incomplete evidence and a limited range of contemporary complaints. The Duc de Saint-Simon's famous observation that Louis XIV raised up the 'vile bourgeoisie' turns out to be untrue in the case of the episcopate, partially true but grossly misleading of the ministry and unknown in the case of the officer corps of the army. . . .

Closer examination of some of the major signs of noble exclusivism shows that restrictions were often aimed at excluding the rich parvenu nobles, not a rising bourgeoisie. . . . The Old Regime aristocracy was thus comparatively young and was in a constant process of renewal.

The doors of the Second Estate were well oiled to men of talent but above all to those with money. Society was therefore capable of absorbing the most thrusting, entrepreneurial and ambitious men of the plutocracy. . . .

The effect of the revisionist critique of the classical interpretation has been to reassert the importance of the political origins of the Revolution. If the nobility had always been a dominant class, if whatever trends there were towards exclusivism are problematic to interpret, if opportunities for advancement were far greater than was ever suspected, and if nobles and bourgeois shared similar economic functions and interests, the notion that the Revolution originated in a struggle between two distinct classes has to be abandoned. Politics remains. Both groups could agree to unite to overthrow absolutism in favour of a liberal constitution but, according to which revisionist historian one follows, they fell out either over means or because of a failure of political leadership or the form the political crisis took, or even over something as amorphous as 'style.'

## An Evaluation of the French Revolution
*William Doyle*

*Although most would say that rapid and vast changes occurred during the French Revolution, it is difficult to evaluate the extent to which these changes were more apparent than real. Many historians have concluded that while the revolution stood for much, most of the promises made by the revolution were not carried out. Others argue that much that has been attributed to the revolution would probably have come about anyway. In the following selection William Doyle attempts to strike a balance between what was and was not accomplished by the revolution.*

CONSIDER: *How Doyle determines what changes would in all probability have come about in any case; what Doyle*

SOURCE: From William Doyle, *The Oxford History of the French Revolution*, pp. 423–25. Copyright 1989. Reprinted by permission of Oxford University Press.

*attributes directly to the revolution; how Doyle's argument might be used by those opposing revolutions in general.*

The shadow of the Revolution, therefore, fell across the whole of the nineteenth century and beyond. Until 1917 few would have disputed that it was the greatest revolution in the history of the world; and even after that its claims to primacy remain strong. It was the first modern revolution, the archetypal one. After it, nothing in the European world remained the same, and we are all heirs to its influence. And yet, it can be argued, much that was attributed to it would in all probability have come about in any case. Before 1789 there were plenty of signs that the structure of French society was evolving towards domination by a single élite in which property counted for more than birth. The century-long expansion of the bourgeoise which underlay this trend already looked irreversible; and greater participation by men of property in government, as constant experiments with provincial assemblies showed, seemed bound to come. Meanwhile many of the reforms the Revolution brought in were already being tried or thought about by the absolute monarchy—law codification, fiscal rationalization, dimunition of venality, free trade, religious toleration. With all these changes under way or in contemplation, the power of government looked set for steady growth, too—which ironically was one of the complaints of the despotism-obsessed men of 1789. In the Church, the monastic ideal was already shrivelling and the status of parish priests commanding more and more public sympathy. Economically, the colonial trade had already peaked, and failure to compete industrially with Great Britain was increasingly manifest. In other structural areas, meanwhile, the great upheaval appears to have made no difference at all. Conservative investment habits still characterized the early nineteenth century, agricultural inertia and unentrepreneurial business likewise. And in international affairs, it is hard to believe that Great Britain would not have dominated the world's seas and trade throughout the nineteenth century, that Austro-Prussian rivalry would not have run much the course it did, or that Latin America would not have asserted its independence in some form or other, if the French Revolution had never happened. In all these fields, the effect was to accelerate or retard certain trends, but not to change their general drift.

Against all this, it is equally hard to believe that the specifically anti-aristocratic, anti-feudal revolutionary ideology of the Rights of Man would have emerged as it did without the jumble of accident, miscalculation, and misunderstanding which coalesced into a revolution in specifically French circumstances. It is equally hard to believe that anything as extraordinary as dechristianiza-

tion would have occurred without the monumental misjudgment which produced the Revolution's quarrel with the Catholic Church. Without that quarrel, the dramatic revival in the authority of the papacy also seems inconceivable. Representative government may well have been on the horizon, but how long would the ideal of popular democracy have taken to establish itself without the example of the sansculotte movement? It certainly transformed and widened out of all recognition the cause of parliamentary reform in England—although the blood-stained figure of the sansculotte probably galvanized conservative resistance on the other side. Above all, the revolutionaries' decision to go to war, which all historians agree revolutionized the Revolution, destroyed an established pattern of warfare in a way no old regime government would otherwise have promoted. Arming the people was the last thing they would have dreamed of. The emergencies of that war in turn produced the scenes which have indelibly marked our memory of the Revolution: the Terror. Massacres were nothing new, and the worst ones of the 1790s occurred outside France. But there was something horribly new and unimaginable in the prospect of a government systematically executing its opponents by the cartload for months on end, and by a device which, however humane in concept, made the streets run with blood. And this occurred in what had passed for the most civilized country in Europe, whose writers had taught the eighteenth century to pride itself on its increasing mildness, good sense, and humanity. This great drama transformed the whole meaning of political change, and the contemporary world would be inconceivable if it had not happened.

In other words it transformed men's outlook.

## Women and the Napoleonic Code
*Bonnie G. Smith*

*However they evaluate Napoleon and his rule, most historians point to the set of rationally organized laws—the Napoleonic Code—as one of Napoleon's most important and lasting legacies. The Code embodied many principles of the Enlightenment and French Revolution, and the Code was modified and adopted outside of France in Europe and the western hemisphere. While it has been generally considered a progressive legal system, historians now point out that it may have represented a step back for women. In the following selection from her Changing Lives: Women in European*

SOURCE: From *Changing Lives: Women in European History since 1700* by Bonnie G. Smith. Copyright © 1989 by D. C. Heath and Company. Reprinted by permission of the publisher.

History since 1700, *Bonnie G. Smith analyzes the significance of the Napoleonic Code for women.*

CONSIDER: *Ways the Code made women legally and economically dependent on men; what concept of woman's proper role the Code supported; what concept of man's proper role the Code supported.*

First, women acquired the nationality of their husbands upon marriage. This made a woman's relationship to the state an indirect one because it was dependent on her husband's. Second, a woman had to reside where her husband desired. Women could not participate in lawsuits or serve as witnesses in court or as witnesses to civil acts such as births, deaths, and marriages. Such a reduction in woman's civil status enhanced that of the individual male. Moreover, the code reduced, if not eliminated, male accountability for sexual acts and thrust it squarely on women. For example, men were no longer susceptible to paternity suits or legally responsible for the support of illegitimate children. Women were weakened economically if they bore illegitimate children, whereas men were not so affected if they fathered them. Finally, female adultery was punished by imprisonment and fines unless the husband relented and took his wife back. Men, however, suffered no such sanctions unless they brought their sexual partner into the home. The sexual behavior of women was open to scrutiny and prescribed by law, whereas that of men, almost without exception, had no criminal aspect attached to it. Thus male sexuality was accepted with few limitations, but women's was only acceptable if it remained within strict domestic boundaries. The Napoleonic Code institutionalized the republican responsibility of women to generate virtue—a term that began to acquire sexual overtones to its civic definition.

The Napoleonic Code also defined the space women would occupy in the new regime as marital, maternal, and domestic—all public matters would be determined by men. This circumscription was made more effective by the way the property law undercut the possibilities for women's economic independence and existence in a world beyond the home. In general, a woman had no control over property. Even if she was married under a contract that ensured a separate accounting of her dowry, her husband still had administrative control of funds. This administrative power of the husband and father replaced arbitrary patriarchal rule and was more in tune with modern ideas of government. Instead of serving the king's whim, governmental officials served the best interests of the nation just as the father increased the well-being of the family. This kind of economic control of women held in all classes. Women's wages went to their husbands, and market women and others engaged in business could not do so without permission from their husbands. Once a woman gained permission she did acquire some kind of legal status, in that a business woman could be sued. On the other hand, she had no control of her profits—these always passed to her husband, and court records demonstrate the continuing enforcement of this kind of control. Moreover, the husband's right to a businesswoman's property meant that the property passed to his descendants rather than hers. All of these provisions meant that, in the strictest sense, women could not act freely or independently.

The Napoleonic Code influenced many legal systems in Europe and the New World and set the terms for the treatment of women on a widespread basis. Establishing male power by transferring autonomy and economic goods from women to men, the Code organized gender roles for more than a century. "From the way the Code treats women, you can tell it was written by men," so older women reacted to the new decree. Women's publications protested the sudden repression after a decade of more equitable laws. Even in the 1820s, books explaining the Code to women always recognized their anger. The justification for the Code's provisions involved reminders about men's chivalrous character and women's weakness. Arguments were based on nature both to invoke the equality of all men and to reinforce the consequences of women's supposed physical inferiority. Looking at nature, one writer saw in terms of gender man's "greater strength, his propensity to be active and assertive in comparison to woman's weakness, lack of vigor and natural modesty." At the time the Code was written, the codifiers were looking at nature in two ways. In theorizing about men alone, nature was redolent of abstract rights. As far as women were concerned, however, nature became empirical in that women had less physical stature than men. Although short men were equal to tall men, women were simply smaller than men and thus were unequal.

According to jurists, therefore, women needed protection, and this protection was to be found within the domicile. The law, they maintained, still offered women protection from individual male brutality, in the rare cases when that might occur. Legislators thus used the law officially to carve out a private space for women in which they had no rights. At the same time, law codes were supposed to protect women from the abuses allowed in the first place. The small number of abuses that might result were not seen as significant drawbacks by the jurists. They saw the Code as "insuring the safety of patrimonies and restoring order in families." It mattered little to them that the old regime carried over for women in the form of an "estate"—a term that indicated an unchangeable lifetime situation into which people were born and would always remain. Estates had been abolished for men in favor of mobility, but it continued for women.

By the time the Napoleonic Code went into effect, little remained of liberal revolutionary programs for women except the provision for equal inheritance by sisters and brothers. The Code cleared the way for the rule of property and for individual triumph. It ushered in an age of mobility, marked by the rise of the energetic and heroic. The Code gave women little room for that kind of acquisitiveness or for heroism. Instead, women's realm was to encompass virtue, reproduction, and family.

## The Revolutions of 1848

### John Weiss

*The revolutions of 1848 have been at the center of historical debate for a long time. To some, 1848 represents the end of the system set up by the Congress of Vienna; to others, it represents the great battle between the forces of liberalism and conservatism; and to still others, it represents the point at which liberalism, nationalism, socialism, and romanticism met. Perhaps the most persistent historiographical tradition views 1848 as a point at which history made a "wrong" turn. Aspects of this historical debate are reflected in the following interpretation of 1848 by John Weiss. Here he de-emphasizes the role of liberalism, stressing instead the role played by artisans and peasants in the revolution.*

CONSIDER: *According to Weiss, the social and economic causes of the revolutions; how Weiss supports his conclusion that it is misleading to label these revolutions liberal.*

The revolutions of 1848 were the last in Europe, excluding those caused by defeat in war. Their suppression also marked the last triumph of the semi-feudal varieties of conservatism discussed previously. It is misleading to label these revolutions liberal, as is usually done. The revolutions were started and maintained by artisans and peasants who were either fighting to maintain some elements of the traditional order, or whose status had been dislocated by the intrusion of liberal commercial capitalism. It is true that liberals assumed leadership once the

SOURCE: From John Weiss, *Conservatism in Europe*, p. 56. Reprinted by permission of Thames & Hudson, Ltd.

outbreaks had started, but they wanted reform, not revolution. Moreover, the liberals did not represent the middle class as a whole, but only the politically aware professional groups—lawyers, civil servants, educators and students. There was no mass following for liberal reforms in Europe, and the middle classes in general had no clearly perceived class enemy blocking their social mobility as in 1789. Consequently they were much more wary of the potential for social upheaval from below.

The liberal leaders of the revolutions were isolated from their own class and, as it turned out, had little to offer the artisans and peasants in revolt that could not as easily have been granted by conservatives. Only in Hungary and Italy, where nationalism incited mass risings against Austrians, were the revolutions truly violent and sweeping. Elsewhere, we find only urban revolts accompanied by sporadic peasant uprisings. Excluding France, frightened conservative élites were never overthrown; they merely made paper concessions and withdrew temporarily until the weakness of the revolutionaries was evident, whereupon they returned in force. East of France traditionalists could still dominate the forms of social upheaval characteristic of pre-industrial society. In 1848 the industrial proletariat played almost no role whatsoever, and the outbreaks had familiar traditional causes: 1846 and 1847 were the years of the most terrible crop failures of nineteenth-century Europe, from which stemmed famine, inflation, shrinking markets and unemployment.

## Chapter Questions

1. Utilizing the material in the sources, what best explains the causes and the general nature of the French Revolution?

2. Analyze liberalism and conservatism as alternative ways of dealing with the issues raised by the French Revolution. What policies would logically follow from each?

3. What connections might there be between nationalism and the French Revolution of 1789? In what ways might both liberals and conservatives have used nationalism to their own advantage during this period?

## Chapter Eighteen

# Industrialism, Social Change, and Culture in the West, 1700s–1914

The Industrial Revolution, which transformed economic life in the West during the 19th century and throughout the world in the 20th century, began in England toward the end of the 18th century. After the Napoleonic period it spread to western Europe, and by the end of the 19th century it had touched most of Western civilization. The Industrial Revolution was characterized by unprecedented economic growth, the factory system of production, and the use of new, artificially powered machines for transportation and mechanical operations. The potential was tremendous; for the first time, human beings had the ability to produce far more than was needed to sustain a large percentage of the population. Whether that potential would be realized, and at what cost, remained to be seen.

In the wake of industrialization came great social changes. The middle and working classes were most affected by industrialization, and both grew in number and social influence, as did the urban areas in which they worked and lived. But it was the middle class that benefited most, enjoying a rising standard of living, increased

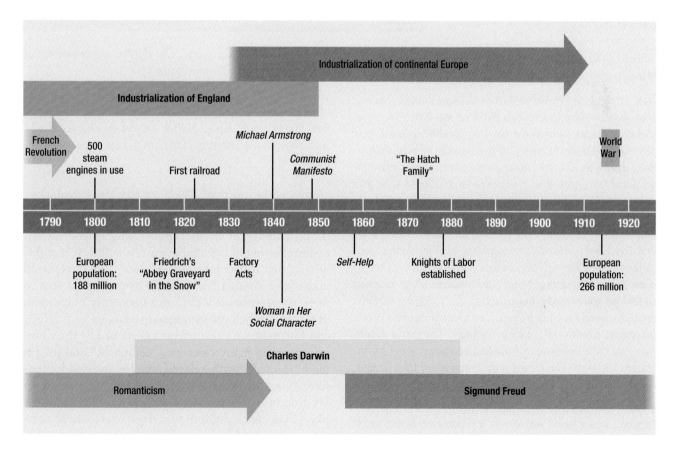

prestige, and growing political influence. Whether the working class benefited from industrialization during the early decades is a matter for debate among historians. Clearly it was this class that bore the burdens of urban social problems: overcrowded slums, poor sanitation, insufficient social services, and a host of related problems. The aristocracy, the peasantry, and the artisans—classes tied to the traditional agricultural economy and older means of production—slowly diminished in numbers and social importance as industrialization spread.

This period of industrialization and social change was also one of great intellectual and cultural ferment. Part of this ferment was the reaction of thinkers, artists, and writers to industrialization itself and accompanying developments such as urbanization. Perhaps an even more important element of the intellectual and cultural ferment was the growth in numbers, wealth, power, and prestige of the urban middle class. This class increasingly asserted its own values and assumptions, which were reflected in the ideas and creative productions that appealed to it. At the same time, this growing influence of the middle class in thought and culture was being challenged on all sides, particularly by those more sensitive to the problems of the working class and those asserting more conservative views.

The sources in this chapter deal with these economic, social, and cultural changes. For industrialization, the focus will be on the origins and spread of the Industrial Revolution, particularly in England. For the social changes of the period, the focus will be on those affecting the working and middle classes, who were most tied to industrialization. Here, particular attention is given to women's attitudes and the significance of economic and social changes for women during the period. For cultural changes, emphasis will be on, first, some of the major intellectual and cultural trends of the period, such as Darwinism, Marxism, and Freudianism, and second, Romanticism, one of the most important cultural styles during the first half of this period.

The sources in this and the previous chapter provide insights into the nature of European civilization during the 19th century, a period in which this civilization was in many ways at its height. The following chapters will focus on the Americas, Asia, and Africa, areas of the world developing according to both their own internal dynamics and the growing impact of European civilization.

# PRIMARY SOURCES

## Testimony for the Factory Act of 1833: Working Conditions in England

*Industrialization carried with it broad social and economic changes that were quickly felt by those involved. The most striking changes were in the working conditions in the new factories and mines. During the first decades of industrialization, there was little government control over working conditions and few effective labor organizations; laborers were thus at the mercy of factory owners who were pursuing profit in a competitive world. Investigations into conditions in factories and mines conducted by the British Parliament in the 1830s and 1840s led eventually to the enactment of legislation, such as the Factory Act of 1833. These parliamentary investigations provide us with extensive information about working conditions and attitudes toward them. The following selection contains three excerpts from a parliamentary commission's investigations into child labor in factories. The first is a summary by the commission of medical examiners from northeastern England. The second is the testimony of John Wright,*

SOURCE: Commission for Inquiry into the Employment of Children in Factories, *Second Report, with Minutes of Evidence and Reports by the Medical Commissioners,* vol. V, Session 29 January–20 August, 1833 (London: His Majesty's Printing Office, 1833), pp. 5, 26–28.

*a steward in a silk factory. The third is the testimony of William Harter, a silk manufacturer.*

CONSIDER: *What these people perceived as the worst abuses of factory labor; the causes of the poor working conditions; how Harter might defend himself against the charges that he was abusing the working class; what biases the witnesses might hold.*

### TESTIMONY OF THE COMMISSION OF MEDICAL EXAMINERS

The account of the physical condition of the manufacturing population in the large towns in the Northeastern District of England is less favourable. It is of this district that the Commissioners state, "We have found undoubted instances of children five years old sent to work thirteen hours a day; and frequently of children nine, ten, and eleven consigned to labour for fourteen and fifteen hours." The effects ascertained by the Commissioners in many cases are, "deformity," and in still more "stunted growth, relaxed muscles, and slender conformation:" "twisting of the ends of the long bones, relaxation of the ligaments of the knees, ankles, and the like." "The representation that these effects are so common and universal as to enable some persons invariably to distinguish factory children from other children is, I have no hesitation in saying, an exaggerated and unfaithful picture of their general condition; at the same time it must be said, that the individual instances in which some one or other of those effects of severe labour are discernible are rather frequent than rare. . . .

"Upon the whole, there remains no doubt upon my mind, that under the system pursued in many of the factories, the children of the labouring classes stand in need of, and ought to have, legislative protection against the conspiracy insensibly formed between their masters and parents, to tax them to a degree of toil beyond their strength.

"In conclusion, I think it has been clearly proved that children have been worked a most unreasonable and cruel length of time daily, and that even adults have been expected to do a certain quantity of labour which scarcely any human being is able to endure. I am of opinion no child under fourteen years of age should work in a factory of any description for more than eight hours a day. From fourteen upwards I would recommend that no individual should, under any circumstances, work more than twelve hours a day; although if practicable, as a physician, I would prefer the limitation of ten hours, for all persons who earn their bread by their industry."

TESTIMONY OF JOHN WRIGHT

How long have you been employed in a silk-mill?—More than thirty years.

Did you enter it as a child?—Yes, betwixt five and six.

How many hours a day did you work then?—The same thirty years ago as now.

What are those hours?—Eleven hours per day and two over-hours: over-hours are working after six in the evening till eight. The regular hours are from six in the morning to six in the evening, and two others are two over-hours: about fifty years ago they began working over-hours. . . .

Why, then, are those employed in them said to be in such a wretched condition?—In the first place, the great number of hands congregated together, in some rooms forty, in some fifty, in some sixty, and I have known some as many as 100, which must be injurious to both health and growing. In the second place, the privy is in the factory, which frequently emits an unwholesome smell; and it would be worth while to notice in the future erection of mills, that there be betwixt the privy door and the factory wall a kind of a lobby of cage-work. 3dly, The tediousness and the everlasting sameness in the first process preys much on the spirits, and makes the hands spiritless. 4thly, the extravagant number of hours a child is compelled to labour and confinement, which for one week is seventy-six hours. . . . 5thly, About six months in the year we are obliged to use either gas, candles, or lamps, for the longest portion of that time, nearly six

hours a day, being obliged to work amid the smoke and soot of the same; and also a large portion of oil and grease is used in the mills.

What are the effects of the present system of labour?—From my earliest recollections, I have found the effects to be awfully detrimental to the well-being of the operative; I have observed frequently children carried to factories, unable to walk, and that entirely owing to excessive labour and confinement. The degradation of the workpeople baffles all description: frequently have two of my sisters been obliged to be assisted to the factory and home again, until by-and-by they could go no longer, being totally crippled in their legs. And in the next place, I remember some ten or twelve years ago working in one of the largest firms in Macclesfield, (Messrs. Baker and Pearson,) with about twenty-five men, where they were scarce one half fit for His Majesty's service. Those that are straight in their limbs are stunted in their growth; much inferior to their fathers in point of strength. 3dly, Through excessive labour and confinement there is often a total loss of appetite; a kind of langour steals over the whole frame—enters to the very core—saps the foundation of the best constitution—and lays our strength prostrate in the dust. In the 4th place, by protracted labour there is an alarming increase of cripples in various parts of this town, which has come under my own observation and knowledge. . . .

Are all these cripples made in the silk factories?—Yes, they are, I believe. . . .

TESTIMONY OF WILLIAM HARTER

What effect would it have on your manufacture to reduce the hours of labour to ten?—It would instantly much reduce the value of my mill and machinery, and consequently of far prejudice my manufacture.

How so?—They are calculated to produce a certain quantity of work in a given time. Every machine is valuable in proportion to the quantity of work which it will turn off in a given time. It is impossible that the machinery could produce as much work in ten hours as in twelve. If the tending of the machines were a laborious occupation, the difference in the quantity of work might not always be in exact proportion to the difference of working time; but in my mill, and silk-mills in general, the work requires the least imaginable labour; therefore it is perfectly impossible that the machines could produce as much work in ten hours as in twelve. The produce would vary in about the same ratio as the working time.

## The Knights of Labor: Unionization

*As industrialization spread across Europe and North America, workers found that they were constantly attacked on a number of fronts. Skilled labor in particular found their position eroding as mechanization undermined their ability to control the pace of work and output. Workers—once independent artisans working out of their own homes and workshops—found themselves drawn into factories where they faced long hours, horrid work conditions, and low pay. Although in the United States workers did not organize socialist parties, they did organize unions that sought to protect their position as skilled independent workers. The Knights of Labor was among the first national, cross-industry organizations in the United States that addressed the problems created by industrialization. It was at the center of nationwide strikes and was succeeded by the American Federation of Labor, which chose to organize only skilled craftsmen. This selection is the preamble to the Constitution adopted by the Knights of Labor meeting in Pennsylvania, January 3, 1878.*

CONSIDER: *The problems facing workers as reflected in this document; how they justify their demands; the goals of the Knights of Labor; how their goals compare with those of labor unions today.*

The recent alarming development and aggression of aggregated wealth, which, unless checked, will inevitably lead to the pauperization and hopeless degradation of the toiling masses, render it imperative, if we desire to enjoy the blessings of life, that a check should be placed upon its power and upon unjust accumulation, and a system adopted which will secure to the laborer the fruits of his toil; and as this much-desired object can only be accomplished by the thorough unification of labor, and the united efforts of those who obey the divine injunction that "In the sweat of thy brow shalt thou eat bread," we have formed the * * * * * with a view of securing the organization and direction, by co-operative effort, of the power of the industrial classes; and we submit to the world the objects sought to be accomplished by our organization, calling upon all who believe in securing "the greatest good to the greatest number" to aid and assist us: . . .

II. To secure to the toilers a proper share of the wealth that they create; more of the leisure that rightfully belongs to them; more societary advantages; more of the benefits, privileges and emoluments of the world; in a word, all those rights and privileges necessary to make them capable of enjoying, appreciating, defending and perpetuating the blessings of good government. . . .

IV. The establishment of co-operative institutions, productive and distributive.

V. The reserving of the public lands—the heritage of the people—for the actual settler; not another acre for railroads or speculators.

VI. The abrogation of all laws that do not bear equally upon capital and labor, the removal of unjust technicalities, delays and discriminations in the administration of justice, and the adopting of measures providing for the health and safety of those engaged in mining, manufacturing or building pursuits.

VII. The enactment of laws to compel chartered corporations to pay their employees weekly, in full, for labor performed during the preceding week, in the lawful money of the country. . . .

X. The substitution of arbitration for strikes, whenever and wherever employers and employees are willing to meet on equitable grounds.

XI. The prohibition of the employment of children in workshops, mines and factories before attaining their fourteenth year.

XII. To abolish the system of letting out by contract the labor of convicts in our prisons and reformatory institutions.

XIII. To secure for both sexes equal pay for equal work.

XIV. The reduction of the hours of labor to eight per day, so that the laborers may have more time for social enjoyment and intellectual improvement, and be enabled to reap the advantages conferred by the labor-saving machinery which their brains have created.

## The Communist Manifesto

*Karl Marx and Friedrich Engels*

*Although initially only one of many radical doctrines, Marxism proved to be the most dynamic and influential challenge to industrial capitalism and middle-class civilization in general. Its most succinct and popular statement is contained in the* Communist Manifesto, *written by Karl Marx (1818–83) and Friedrich Engels (1820–95) and first published in 1848. Karl Marx was born in Germany, studied history and philosophy, and entered a career as a journalist, writer, and revolutionary. For most of his life he lived in exile in London. His collaborator, Friedrich Engels, was also born in Germany and lived in England, but there he helped manage his family's cotton business in Manchester. Their doctrines directly attacked the middle class and industrial capitalism, presenting communism as a philosophically, historically, and scientifically justified alternative that would inevitably replace capitalism. They saw themselves as revolutionary leaders of the*

SOURCE: Terrence V. Powderly, *Thirty Years of Labor* (Philadelphia, 1890), pp. 128–30.

SOURCE: Karl Marx and Friedrich Engels, *Manifesto of the Communist Party,* 2d ed. (New York: National Executive Committee of the Socialist Labor Party, 1898), pp. 30–32, 41–43, 60.

*growing proletariat (the working class). The following is a selection from the* Communist Manifesto.

CONSIDER: *The appeal of the ideas presented here; the concrete policies advocated by Marx and Engels; the historical and intellectual trends reflected in the Manifesto.*

A specter is haunting Europe—the specter of Communism. All the powers of old Europe have entered into a holy alliance to exorcise this specter; Pope and Czar, Metternich and Guizot, French radicals and German police spies.

Where is the party in opposition that has not been decried as Communistic by its opponents in power? Where the opposition that has not hurled back the branding reproach of Communism, against the more advanced opposition parties, as well as against its reactionary adversaries?

Two things result from this fact.

I. Communism is already acknowledged by all European powers to be in itself a power.

II. It is high time that Communists should openly, in the face of the whole world, publish their views, their aims, their tendencies, and meet this nursery tale of the Specter of Communism with a Manifesto of the party itself.

To this end the Communists of various nationalities have assembled in London, and sketched the following manifesto to be published in the English, French, German, Italian, Flemish and Danish languages.

\*

In what relation do the Communists stand to the proletarians as a whole?

The Communists do not form a separate party opposed to other working class parties.

They have no interests separate and apart from those of the proletariat as a whole.

They do not set up any sectarian principles of their own by which to shape and mould the proletarian movement.

The Communists are distinguished from the other working class parties by this only: 1. In the national struggles of the proletarians of the different countries, they point out and bring to the front the common interests of the entire proletariat, independently of all nationality. 2. In the various stages of development which the struggle of the working class against the bourgeoisie has to pass through, they always and everywhere represent the interests of the movement as a whole.

The Communists, therefore, are on the one hand, practically, the most advanced and resolute section of the working class parties of every country, that section which pushes forward all others; on the other hand, the-

oretically, they have over the great mass of the proletariat the advantage of clearly understanding the line of march, the conditions, and the ultimate general results of the proletarian movement.

The immediate aim of the Communists is the same as that of all the other proletarian parties: formation of the proletariat into a class, overthrow of the bourgeois supremacy, conquest of political power by the proletariat.

The theoretical conclusions of the Communists are in no way based on ideas or principles that have been invented, or discovered, by this or that would-be universal reformer.

They merely express, in general terms, actual relations springing from an existing class struggle, from a historical movement going on under our very eyes. The abolition of existing property relations is not at all a distinctive feature of Communism.

All property relations in the past have continually been subject to historical change, consequent upon the change in historical conditions.

The French revolution, for example, abolished feudal property in favor of bourgeois property.

The distinguishing feature of Communism is not the abolition of property generally, but the abolition of bourgeois property. But modern bourgeois private property is the final and most complete expression of the system of producing and appropriating products, that is based on class antagonisms, on the exploitation of the many by the few.

In this sense the theory of the Communists may be summed up in the single sentence: Abolition of private property.

We have seen above that the first step in the revolution by the working class is to raise the proletariat to the position of the ruling class; to win the battle of democracy.

The proletariat will use its political supremacy to wrest, by degrees, all capital from the bourgeoisie; to centralize all instruments of production in the hands of the State, i.e., of the proletariat organized as the ruling class; and to increase the total of productive forces as rapidly as possible.

Of course, in the beginning this cannot be effected except by means of despotic inroads on the rights of property and on the conditions of bourgeois production; by means of measures, therefore, which appear economically insufficient and untenable, but which, in the course of the movement, outstrip themselves, necessitate further inroads upon the old social order and are unavoidable as a means of entirely revolutionizing the mode of production.

These measures will, of course, be different in different countries.

Nevertheless in the most advanced countries the following will be pretty generally applicable:

1. Abolition of property in land and application of all rents of land to public purposes.

2. A heavy progressive or graduated income tax.

3. Abolition of all right of inheritance.

4. Confiscation of the property of all emigrants and rebels.

5. Centralization of credit in the hands of the State, by means of a national bank with State capital and an exclusive monopoly.

6. Centralization of the means of communication and transport in the hands of the State.

7. Extension of factories and instruments of production owned by the State; the bringing into cultivation of waste lands, and the improvement of the soil generally in accordance with a common plan.

8. Equal liability of all to labor. Establishment of industrial armies, especially for agriculture.

9. Combination of agriculture with manufacturing industries: gradual abolition of the distinction between town and country, by a more equitable distribution of the population over the country.

10. Free education for all children in public schools. Abolition of children's factory labor in its present form. Combination of education with industrial production, etc., etc.

When, in the course of development, class distinctions have disappeared and all production has been concentrated in the hands of a vast association of the whole nation, the public power will lose its political character. Political power, properly so called, is merely the organized power of one class for oppressing another. If the proletariat during its contest with the bourgeoisie is compelled, by the force of circumstances, to organize itself as a class, if, by means of a revolution, it makes itself the ruling class, and, as such, sweeps away by force the old conditions of production, then it will, along with these conditions, have swept away the conditions for the existence of class antagonisms, and of classes generally, and will thereby have abolished its own supremacy as a class.

In place of the old bourgeois society with its classes and class antagonisms we shall have an association in which the free development of each is the condition for the free development of all.

## Self-Help: Middle-Class Attitudes
### Samuel Smiles

*Middle-class liberals were not totally unaware of the consequences of industrialization for society. Doctrines were developed that reflected and appealed to their attitudes. Such doctrines served to justify the position of the middle class, to support policies it usually favored, and to rationalize the poor state of the working class. Many of these doctrines appeared in* Self-Help, *the popular book by Samuel Smiles, a physician, editor, secretary of two railroads, and author. First published in 1859,* Self-Help *became a best seller in England and was translated into many languages. The following excerpt is a good example of the individualism and moral tone that appear throughout the book.*

CONSIDER: *How Smiles justifies his assertion that self-help is the only answer to problems; how Smiles would analyze the situation of the working class and how he would react to the testimony presented to the parliamentary commission on child labor.*

"Heaven helps those who help themselves" is a well tried maxim, embodying in a small compass the results of vast human experience. The spirit of self-help is the root of all genuine growth in the individual; and, exhibited in the lives of many, it constitutes the true source of national vigor and strength. Help from without is often enfeebling in its effects, but help from within invariably invigorates. Whatever is done for men or classes, to a certain extent takes away the stimulus and necessity of doing for themselves; and where men are subjected to over-guidance and over-government, the inevitable tendency is to render them comparatively helpless.

Even the best institutions can give a man no active help. Perhaps the most they can do is, to leave him free to develop himself and improve his individual condition. But in all times men have been prone to believe that their happiness and well-being were to be secured by means of institutions rather than by their own conduct. Hence the value of legislation as an agent in human advancement has usually been much overestimated. To constitute the millionth part of a Legislature, by voting for one or two men once in three or five years, however conscientiously this duty may be performed, can exercise but little active influence upon any man's life and character. Moreover, it is every day becoming more clearly understood, that the function of Government is negative and restrictive, rather than positive and active; being resolvable principally into protection—protection of life, liberty, and property. Laws, wisely administered, will secure men in the enjoyment of the fruits of their labor, whether of mind or body, at a comparatively small personal sacrifice; but no laws, however stringent, can make the idle industrious, the shiftless provident, or the drunken sober. Such reforms can only be effected by means of individual action, economy, and self-denial; by better habits, rather than by greater rights. . . .

SOURCE: Samuel Smiles, *Self-Help* (Chicago: Belford, Clarke, 1881), pp. 21–23, 48–49.

Indeed, all experience serves to prove that the worth and strength of a State depend far less upon the form of its institutions than upon the character of its men. For the nation is only an aggregate of individual conditions, and civilization itself is but a question of the personal improvement of the men, women, and children of whom society is composed.

National progress is the sum of individual industry, energy, and uprightness, as national decay is of individual idleness, selfishness, and vice. What we are accustomed to decry as great social evils, will for the most part be found to be but the outgrowth of man's own perverted life; and though we may endeavor to cut them down and extirpate them by means of Law, they will only spring up again with fresh luxuriance in some other form, unless the conditions of personal life and character are radically improved. If this view be correct, then it follows that the highest patriotism and philanthropy consist, not so much in altering laws and modifying institutions, as in helping and stimulating men to elevate and improve themselves by their own free and independent individual action.

One of the most strongly marked features of the English people is their spirit of industry, standing out prominent and distinct in their past history, and as strikingly characteristic of them now as at any former period. It is this spirit, displayed by the commons of England, which has laid the foundations and built up the industrial greatness of the empire. This vigorous growth of the nation has been mainly the result of the free energy of individuals, and it has been contingent upon the number of hands and minds from time to time actively employed within it, whether as cultivators of the soil, producers of articles of utility, contrivers of tools and machines, writers of books, or creators of works of art. And while this spirit of active industry has been the vital principle of the nation, it has also been its saving and remedial one, counteracting from time to time the effects of errors in our laws and imperfections in our constitution.

The career of industry which the nation has pursued, has also proved its best education. As steady application to work is the healthiest training for every individual, so is it the best discipline of a state. Honorable industry travels the same road with duty; and Providence has closely linked both with happiness. The gods, says the poet, have placed labor and toil on the way leading to the Elysian fields. Certain it is that no bread eaten by man is so sweet as that earned by his own labor, whether bodily or mental. By labor the earth has been subdued, and man redeemed from barbarism; nor has a single step in civilization been made without it. Labor is not only a necessity and a duty, but a blessing: only the idler feels it to be a curse. The duty of work is written on the thews and muscles of the limbs, the mechanism of the hand, the nerves and lobes of the brain—the sum of whose healthy action is satisfaction and enjoyment. In the

school of labor is taught the best practical wisdom; nor is a life of manual employment, as we shall hereafter find, incompatible with high mental culture.

## Woman in Her Social and Domestic Character

### Elizabeth Poole Sandford

*Industrialization also had its effects on middle-class women. As the wealth and position of these women rose in a changing economic environment, previous models of behavior no longer applied. A variety of books and manuals appeared to counsel middle-class women on their proper role and behavior. The following is an excerpt from one of these,* Woman in Her Social and Domestic Character *(1842), written by Mrs. John Sandford.*

CONSIDER: *Woman's ideal function in relation to her husband, according to this document; by implication, the role of the middle-class man in relation to his wife; possible explanations for this view of women.*

The changes wrought by Time are many. It influences the opinions of men as familiarity does their feelings; it has a tendency to do away with superstition, and to reduce every thing to its real worth.

It is thus that the sentiment for woman has undergone a change. The romantic passion which once almost deified her is on the decline; and it is by intrinsic qualities that she must now inspire respect. She is no longer the queen of song and the star of chivalry. But if there is less of enthusiasm entertained for her, the sentiment is more rational, and, perhaps, equally sincere; for it is in relation to happiness that she is chiefly appreciated.

And in this respect it is, we must confess, that she is most useful and most important. Domestic life is the chief source of her influence; and the greatest debt society can owe to her is domestic comfort: for her happiness is almost an element of virtue; and nothing conduces more to improve the character of men than domestic peace. A woman may make a man's home delightful, and may thus increase his motives for virtuous exertion. She may refine and tranquillize his mind—may turn away his anger or allay his grief. Her smile may be the happy influence to gladden his heart, and to disperse the cloud that gathers on his brow. And in proportion to her endeavors to make those around her happy, she will be esteemed and loved. She will secure by her excellence that interest and regard which she might formerly claim as the privilege of her sex, and will really merit the deference which was then conceded to her as a matter of course. . . .

SOURCE: Mrs. John Sandford (Elizabeth Poole Sandford), *Woman in Her Social and Domestic Character* (Boston: Otis, Broaders and Co., 1842), pp. 5–7, 15–16.

Perhaps one of the first secrets of her influence is adaptation to the tastes, and sympathy in the feelings, of those around her. This holds true in lesser as well as in graver points. It is in the former, indeed, that the absence of interest in a companion is frequently most disappointing. Where want of congeniality impairs domestic comfort, the fault is generally chargeable on the female side. It is for woman, not for man, to make the sacrifice, especially in indifferent matters. She must, in a certain degree, be plastic herself if she would mould others. . . .

To be useful, a woman must have feeling. It is this which suggests the thousand nameless amenities which fix her empire in the heart, and render her so agreeable, and almost so necessary, that she imperceptibly rises in the domestic circle, and becomes at once its cement and its charm.

*

Nothing is so likely to conciliate the affections of the other sex as a feeling that woman looks to them for support and guidance. In proportion as men are themselves superior, they are accessible to this appeal. On the contrary, they never feel interested in one who seems disposed rather to offer than to ask assistance. There is, indeed, something unfeminine in independence. It is contrary to nature, and therefore it offends. We do not like to see a woman affecting tremors, but still less do we like to see her acting the amazon. A really sensible woman feels her dependence. She does what she can; but she is conscious of inferiority, and therefore grateful for support. She knows that she is the weaker vessel, and that as such she should receive honor. In this view, her weakness is an attraction, not a blemish.

In every thing, therefore, that women attempt, they should show their consciousness of dependence. If they are learners, let them evince a teachable spirit; if they give an opinion, let them do it in an unassuming manner. There is something so unpleasant in female self-sufficiency that it not unfrequently deters instead of persuading, and prevents the adoption of advice which the judgment even approves.

## Why We Are Militant
### Emmeline Pankhurst

*The movement for female suffrage had deep roots in the 19th century, but gained force toward the end of the century. Various women's organizations in the West circulated petitions, led marches, and held demonstrations to support their demands for the right to vote. In the years before World War I, women's groups became more militant in the face of refusals by governmental officials to act. In Britain, Emmeline Pankhurst (1858–1928) helped organize the Women's Social and Political Union, which conducted assaults on private property and hunger strikes to promote the cause of women's suffrage. In the following excerpt from a 1913 speech, Pankhurst explains why her group is so militant.*

CONSIDER: *The problems facing women who wanted to gain the right to vote; how Pankhurst explains why it became necessary for women to revolt; what arguments government officials might use to oppose Pankhurst.*

I know that in your minds there are questions like these; you are saying, 'Woman Suffrage is sure to come; the emancipation of humanity is an evolutionary process, and how is it that some women, instead of trusting to that evolution, instead of educating the masses of people of their country, instead of educating their own sex to prepare them for citizenship, how is it that these militant women are using violence and upsetting the business arrangements of the country in their undue impatience to attain their end?' . . .

Meanwhile, during the '80's, women, like men, were asking for the franchise. Appeals, larger and more numerous than for any other reform, were presented in support of Woman's Suffrage. Meetings of the great corporations, great town councils, and city councils, passed resolutions asking that women should have the vote. More meetings were held, and larger, for Woman Suffrage than were held for votes for men, and yet the women did not get it. Men got the vote because they were and would be violent. The women did not get it because they were constitutional and law-abiding. Why, is it not evident to everyone that people who are patient where mis-government is concerned may go on being patient! Why should anyone trouble to help them? I take to myself some shame that through all those years, at any rate from the early '80's, when I first came into the Suffrage movement, I did not learn my political lessons.

I believed, as many women still in England believe, that women could get their way in some mysterious manner, by purely peaceful methods. We have been so accustomed, we women, to accept one standard for men and another standard for women, that we have even applied that variation of standard to the injury of our political welfare.

Having had better opportunities of education, and having had some training in politics, having in political life come so near to the 'superior' being as to see that he was not altogether such a fount of wisdom as they had supposed, that he had his human weaknesses as we had, the twentieth century women began to say to themselves. 'Is it not time, since our methods have failed and

SOURCE: Jane Marcus, ed., *Suffrage and the Pankhursts* (New York: Routledge and Kegan Paul, 1987), pp. 153–56.

the men's have succeeded, that we should take a leaf out of their political book?' . . .

Well, I say the time is long past when it became necessary for women to revolt in order to maintain their self respect in Great Britain. The women who are waging this war are women who would fight, if it were only for the idea of liberty—if it were only that they might be free citizens of a free country—I myself would fight for that idea alone. But we have, in addition to this love of freedom, intolerable grievances to redress. . . .

Well, in Great Britain, we have tried persuasion, we have tried the plan of showing (by going upon public bodies, where they allowed us to do work they hadn't much time to do themselves) that we are capable people. We did it in the hope that we should convince them and persuade them to do the right and proper thing. But we had all our labour for our pains, and now we are fighting for our rights, and we are growing stronger and better women in the process. We are getting more fit to use our rights because we have such difficulty in getting them.

## The Origin of Species *and* The Descent of Man

*Charles Darwin*

*The 19th century was a period of great scientific ideas and discoveries. Perhaps the most important, and certainly the most controversial, was Darwin's theory of evolution. Charles Darwin (1809–82), a British naturalist, gathered data while on voyages in the southern Pacific. He used that data to develop his theory of evolution by natural selection. This theory of evolution, particularly as applied to human beings, challenged biblical accounts of creation. He argued that all life, including human life, evolved from lower forms. Evolution was slow and extended over a much longer period than had been assumed. Natural selection, or survival of the fittest, determined how species evolved. Darwin first formulated his findings and theory in an 1844 essay. However, it was only after 1859, when he published* The Origin of Species by Means of Natural Selection, *that his ideas became well known and widely controversial. The first of two selections below is from that book. The second is from* The Descent of Man, *which he published in 1871.*

CONSIDER: *Why his ideas might be so welcome by some and so disturbing to others; the possible psychological impact of his ideas; how those favoring biblical accounts might respond.*

### THE ORIGIN OF SPECIES

. . . [C]an we doubt (remembering that many more individuals are born than can possibly survive) that individuals having any advantage, however slight, over others, would have the best chance of surviving and of procre-

ating their kind? On the other hand, we may feel sure that any variation in the least degree injurious would be rigidly destroyed. This preservation of favourable individual differences and variations, and the destruction of those which are injurious, I have called Natural Selection, or the Survival of the Fittest. . . .

Natural selection acts solely through the preservation of variations in some way advantageous, which consequently endure. Owing to the high geometrical rate of increase of all organic beings, each area is already fully stocked with inhabitants; and it follows from this, that as the favored forms increase in number, so, generally, will the less favored decrease and become rare. Rarity, as geology tells us, is the precursor to extinction.

### THE DESCENT OF MAN

The main conclusion here arrived at, and now held by many naturalists who are well competent to form a sound judgment, is that man is descended from some less highly organized form. The grounds upon which this conclusion rests will never be shaken, for the close similarity between man and the lower animals in embryonic development, as well as in innumerable points of structure and constitution, both of high and of the most trifling importance—the rudiments which he retains, and the abnormal reversions to which he is occasionally liable—are facts which cannot be disputed. They have long been known, but until recently they told us nothing with respect to the origin of man. Now when viewed by the light of our knowledge of the whole organic world, their meaning is unmistakable. The great principle of evolution stands up clear and firm, when these groups of facts are considered in connection with others, such as the mutual affinities of the members of the same group, their geographical distribution in past and present times, and their geological succession. It is incredible that all these facts should speak falsely. He who is not content to look, like a savage, at the phenomena of nature as disconnected, cannot any longer believe that man is the work of a separate act of creation. . . .

We have seen that man incessantly presents individual differences in all parts of his body and in his mental faculties. These differences or variations seem to be induced by the same general causes, and to obey the same laws as with the lower animals. In both cases similar laws of inheritance prevail. Man tends to increase at a greater rate than his means of subsistence; consequently he is occasionally subjected to a severe struggle for existence, and

SOURCE: Charles Darwin, *The Origin of Species by Means of Natural Selection,* 6th ed. (London: John Murray, 1872), pp. 63, 85. Charles Darwin, *The Descent of Man* (New York: D. Appleton and Co., 1883), pp. 606–7, 619.

natural selection will have effected whatever lies within its scope. A succession of strongly-marked variations of a similar nature is by no means requisite; slight fluctuating differences in the individual suffice for the work of natural selection. . . .

[M]an with all his noble qualities, with sympathy which feels for the most debased, with benevolence which extends not only to other men but to the humblest living creature, with his god-like intellect which has penetrated into the movements and constitution of the solar system—with all these exalted powers—Man still bears in his bodily frame the indelible stamp of his lowly origin.

# VISUAL SOURCES

## Industrialization and Demographic Change

*A comparison of the first two maps, which show the population density of England in 1801 and 1851, reveals the relatively rapid increase in population and urbanization in certain areas during this period. The third map shows where industry (mainly textiles, metallurgy, and mining) was concentrated in 1851. A comparison of all three maps reveals the connections between shifting population density, urbanization, and industrialization during this period of early, rapid modernization of England's economy.*

CONSIDER: *What some of the geopolitical consequences of these connections between demographic and economic changes might be; what some of the social consequences might be.*

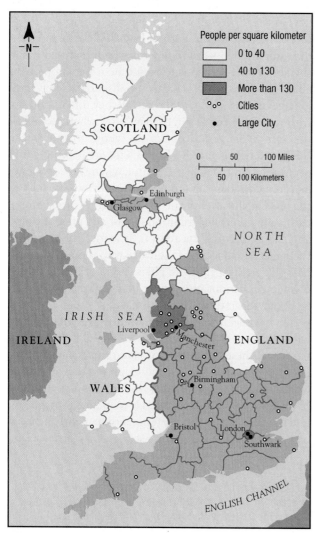

**Map 18–1    *England's Population Density, 1801.***

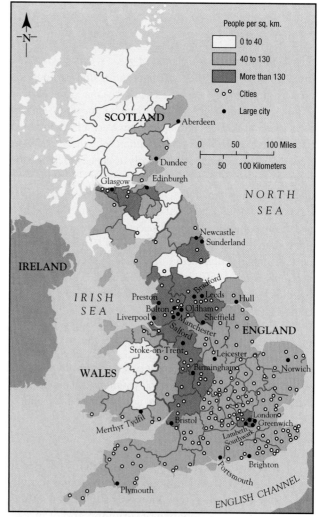

**Map 18–2    *England's Population Density, 1851.***

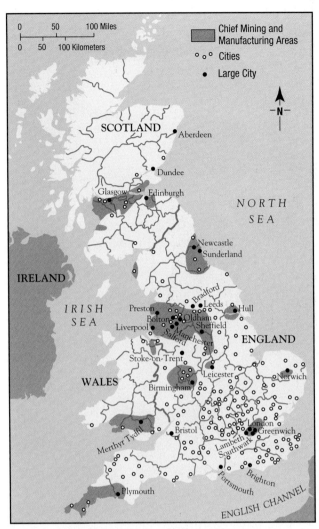

**Map 18–3   England's Concentration of Industry, 1851.**

**Illustration 18–1**   Bettmann/Corbis.

## Illustration from Life and Adventures of Michael Armstrong

This is an illustration from a novel, Life and Adventures of Michael Armstrong (1840), by the well-known British author, Mrs. Frances Trollope. The illustration depicts several main elements of the Industrial Revolution in England. It shows the inside of a textile factory—a factory in the most advanced of the new industries. Thanks to mechanization and artificial power, a few workers can now do the work of many. The workers—men, women, and children—are obviously poor. In the background stands the stern middle-class owner talking with others of his class while in the foreground a child worker embraces his middle-class counterpart for some kindness he has displayed. The scene is reflective of the typical middle-class view of the poor and poverty—as problems of morals, to be treated with pity and philanthropic concern but not yet requiring substantial social or economic change.

CONSIDER: The ways in which this illustration reflects aspects of industrialization touched on by other documents in this chapter.

## Iron and Coal

*William Bell Scott*

In the caption to his 1860 painting of industrial activity in Tyneside, England (Illustration 18–2), British artist William Bell Scott (1811–1891) proudly proclaims: "In the Nineteenth Century the Northumbrians show the World what can be done with Iron and Coal." He may have painted the picture in response to a plea in a publication complaining that in most paintings "we miss . . . the poetry of the things about us; our railways, factories, mines, roaring cities, steam vessels, and the endless novelties and wonders produced everyday." Certainly this mid-nineteenth century painting celebrates these industrial "things." The foreground setting is an engineering workshop. In the center, three muscular workers hammer out molten iron. On the right is a drawing of a steam engine built by Robert Stephenson and Co., and indeed an example of that steam engine is crossing Stephenson's High Level Bridge in the background to the right. In the left foreground, a girl sits on an Armstrong gun with her father's lunch and an arithmetic book in her lap. In the shop are other industrial objects made of iron: an anchor, a marine air pump, and a heavy chain with a pulley. In back of the three workers a boy who works in the mines stands with a Davy safety lamp and looks down on the docks below. On the river a coal barge passes.

**Illustration 18–2** National Trust Photographic Library/Derrick E. Witty.

CONSIDER: *What image of industrial activity this painting presents to the viewer; what other images of industrial activity might an artist present.*

## Gare St.-Lazare

*Claude Monet*

*Great railroad stations became the buildings that most glorified the new industrial civilization, as revealed in Illustration 18–3, a painting of the Saint-Lazare train station, located in the heart of 19th-century Paris, by the French Impressionist*

*Claude Monet (1840–1926). This station served as the arrival and departure point for cities and villages to the north and west of Paris. The great glass-and-iron shed housing the trains and passengers allows sunlight to penetrate the steam and smoke; street lamps such as those hanging on the right help light the station for night trains. Iron—so pliable, durable, strong, and inexpensive—is everywhere, from the train itself to the rails and beams. On the right, people wait to board the scheduled Normandy train, its steam engine already fired and belching smoke. On the left another train, monitored by workers, is leaving the busy station. Beyond the*

**Illustration 18–3** *The Gare Saint-Lazare: Arrival of a Train,* 1877 by Claude Monet. Courtesy of the Fogg Art Museum, Harvard University Art Museums, Bequest from the collection of Maurice Wertheim, Class of 1906. Photo by David Matthews. © President and Fellows of Harvard College.

opening of the shed, the buildings of Paris rise into a broad sky scarcely distinguishable from the smoke rising from steam engines. Railroad stations such as this became centers in cities, structures to visit and admire like great cathedrals.

CONSIDER: *The associations that a 19th-century viewer might have upon viewing this painting.*

## The Hatch Family: The Upper Middle Class
### Eastman Johnson

This 1871 portrait of the Hatch family by the American artist Eastman Johnson shows a number of elements of the condition, lifestyle, and values of the upper middle class. Both the quality and quantity of the furnishings and the clothes indicate how materially well-to-do this family is. The clothes and demeanor convey the strong sense of propriety; yet the activities of the children and the position of their toys denote how child-centered this family is. The appropriate sexual roles are suggested: the father at center right in an authoritative pose, with pen in hand sitting at his desk, the grandfather on the left, keeping up on the news by reading a paper, the mother on the right, generally surveying her children, and the grandmother on the left, knitting. The large painting on the left as well as the sculptures on the right show this family to be properly supportive and appreciative of the arts. The large bookcase on the right indicates a respect for literature and

learning. Heavy curtains largely block out the outside world; values of domesticity and privacy are evident.

CONSIDER: *What lessons the 19th-century viewer might learn from this portrait.*

## The Stages of a Worker's Life
### Léon Frédéric

Léon Frédéric (1856–1940), for a time Belgium's most famous painter, tried to encompass all stages of a worker's life in this large 1895 triptych (Illustration 18–5). In the foreground of the central panel, children on the right play cards while on the left they carry and nibble bread. Their parents and young couples stand just behind them; in the background are the aged members of the working class whose ultimate fate is marked by the distant but approaching funeral coach. The left side panel depicts the man's work world, where men of all ages, from adolescence to old age, engage in manual labor or observe it. In the foreground they are digging while in the middle ground they struggle with heavy beams. Behind them are the factories where they work. The right side panel shows women's world, all mothering and nurturing with babies in their arms and at their breasts. Behind them are market stalls where they shop. Here is a vision of workers' lives in a nutshell: hard manual labor for men, childrearing and food preparation for women, and at the end old age and death for all.

**Illustration 18–4**    The Metropolitan Museum of Art, Gift of Frederick H. Hatch, 1926 (26.97).

**Illustration 18–5**    Musée d'Orsay, Paris, France/Réunion des Musées Nationaux/Art Resource, NY.

CONSIDER: *Whether this seems like a realistic depiction of workers' lives; how, in content and tone, a corresponding depiction of middle-class lives might look.*

## Abbey Graveyard in the Snow: Visual Romanticism

*Caspar David Friedrich*

Abbey Graveyard in the Snow (1819) *was painted by the well-known north German artist Caspar David Friedrich. In the center are the ruins of a Gothic choir of a monastic church* surrounded by a snow-covered graveyard and leafless winter forest. To the left a procession of monks follows a coffin into the ruins.

This painting exemplifies many elements typical of Romanticism, particularly German Romanticism. The scene, while visually accurate, goes beyond realism: The light is too perfectly placed, the church remains are too majestic, the surrounding forest is too symmetrical a frame, and the funeral procession is out of place (funerals did not take place in ruins). By implication, this painting rejects the limits of Enlightenment rationalism and the reality of 19th-century urban life. Instead, a Romantic version of the Middle Ages, the

**Illustration 18–6**  Bildarchiv Preussischer Kulturbesitz.

spirituality of nature, and the glories of Christianity are evoked. The Romantic longing to be overwhelmed by eternal nature is suggested particularly by the rendering of small human figures in a large landscape. Romanticism typically exalted the emotional over the rational, even if it was a melancholy sensitivity that was being displayed.

CONSIDER: The ways in which this painting is consistent with typical traits of Romanticism; the feelings Friedrich sought to evoke in the viewer.

## SECONDARY SOURCES

### The Making of Economic Society: England, the First to Industrialize

*Robert Heilbroner*

*Although it is clear that industrialization occurred first in England, it is not apparent why this was so. During the 18th century, France was prosperous and economically advanced. Other countries such as Belgium and the Netherlands possessed certain economic advantages over England and might have industrialized earlier but did not. In the following selection, Robert Heilbroner, an economist and economic historian, addresses the question of why England was first.*

CONSIDER: *Why Heilbroner stresses the role of the "New Men" over the other factors he lists; any disadvantages England had to overcome; whether it was simply the circumstances that gave rise to the "New Men" or whether it was the "New Men" who took advantage of the circumstances when most men in most other nations would not have.*

Why did the Industrial Revolution originally take place in England and not on the continent? To answer the

SOURCE: Robert L. Heilbroner, *The Making of Economic Society.* Reprinted by permission of Prentice-Hall, Inc. (Englewood Cliffs, NJ, 1980), pp. 76–77, 80–81.

question we must look at the background factors which distinguished England from most other European nations in the eighteenth century.

The first of these factors was simply that England was relatively wealthy. In fact, a century of successful exploration, slave-trading, piracy, war, and commerce had made her the richest nation in the world. Even more important, her riches had accrued not merely to a few nobles, but to a large upper-middle stratum of commercial bourgeoisie. England was thus one of the first nations to develop, albeit on a small scale, a prime requisite of an industrial economy: a "mass" consumer market. As a result, a rising pressure of demand inspired a search for new techniques.

Second, England was the scene of the most successful and thoroughgoing transformation of feudal society into commercial society. A succession of strong kings had effectively broken the power of the local nobility and had made England into a single unified state. As part of this process, we also find in England the strongest encouragement to the rising mercantile classes. Then too, as we have seen, the enclosure movement, which gained in tempo in the seventeenth and eighteenth centuries, expelled an army of laborers to man her new industrial establishments.

Third, England was the locus of a unique enthusiasm for science and engineering. The famous Royal Academy, of which Newton was an early president, was founded in 1660 and was the immediate source of much intellectual excitement. Indeed, a popular interest in gadgets, machines, and devices of all sorts soon became a mild national obsession: *Gentlemen's Magazine*, a kind of *New Yorker* of the period, announced in 1729 that it would henceforth keep its readers "abreast of every invention"—a task which the mounting flow of inventions soon rendered quite impossible. No less important was an enthusiasm of the British landed aristocracy for scientific farming: English landlords displayed an interest in matters of crop rotation and fertilizer which their French counterparts would have found quite beneath their dignity.

Then there were a host of other background causes, some as fortuitous as the immense resources of coal and iron ore on which the British sat; others as purposeful as the development of a national patent system which deliberately sought to stimulate and protect the act of invention itself. In many ways, England was "ready" for an Industrial Revolution. But perhaps what finally translated the potentiality into an actuality was the emergence of a group of new men who seized upon the latent opportunities of history as a vehicle for their own rise to fame and fortune. . . .

Pleasant or unpleasant, the personal characteristics fade beside one overriding quality. These were all men interested in expansion, in growth, in investment for investment's sake. All of them were identified with technological progress, and none of them disdained the productive process. An employee of Maudslay's once remarked, "It was a pleasure to see him handle a tool of any kind, but he was *quite splendid* with an 18-inch file." Watt was tireless in experimenting with his machines; Wedgwood stomped about his factory on his wooden leg scrawling, "This won't do for Jos. Wedgwood," wherever he saw evidence of careless work. Richard Arkwright was a bundle of ceaseless energy in promoting his interests, jouncing about England over execrable roads in a post chaise driven by four horses, pursuing his correspondence as he traveled.

"With us," wrote a French visitor to a calico works in 1788, "a man rich enough to set up and run a factory like this would not care to remain in a position which he would deem unworthy of his wealth." This was an attitude entirely foreign to the rising English industrial capitalist. His work was its own dignity and reward; the wealth it brought was quite aside. Boswell, on being shown Watt and Boulton's great engine works at Soho, declared that he never forgot Boulton's expression as the latter declared, "I sell here, sir, what all the world desires to have—Power."

The New Men were first and last *entrepreneurs*—enterprisers. They brought with them a new energy, as restless as it proved to be inexhaustible. In an economic, if not a political, sense, they deserve the epithet "revolutionaries," for the change they ushered in was nothing short of total, sweeping, and irreversible.

## The Industrial Revolution in Russia
*Peter N. Stearns*

*Before 1850 the industrial revolution was confined to Britain and a few limited areas in the West. Between 1850 and 1870, the coal mines, iron foundries, textile factories, steam engines, and railroads that had made Britain an industrial giant spread broadly into western and central Europe and North America. However, outside of these areas, no industrial revolution occurred until after the 1870s. Many historians have suggested reasons for this disparity between these areas of the West and elsewhere. In the following selection, Peter Stearns suggests reasons why Russia was slow to industrialize.*

CONSIDER: *What opportunities were available for industrial development in Russia; why, nevertheless, Russia did not industrialize sooner.*

Russia began to receive an industrial outreach from the West within a few decades of the advent of the industrial revolution. British textile machinery was imported beginning in 1843. Ernst Knoop, a German immigrant to Britain who had clerked in a Manchester cotton factory, set himself up as export agent to the Russians. He also sponsored British workers who installed the machinery in Russia and told any Russian entrepreneur brash enough to ask not simply for British models but for alterations or adaptations: "That is not your affair; in England they know better than you." Despite the snobbism, a number of Russian entrepreneurs set up small factories to produce cotton, aware that even in Russia's small urban market they could make a substantial profit by underselling traditional manufactured cloth. Other factories were established directly by Britons.

Europeans and Americans were particularly active in responding to calls by the tsar's government for assistance in establishing railway and steamship lines. The first steamship appeared in Russia in 1815, and by 1820 a regular service ran on the Volga River. The first public railroad, joining St. Petersburg to the imperial residence in the suburbs, opened in 1837. In 1851 the first major line connected St. Petersburg and Moscow, along a remarkably straight route desired by Tsar Nicholas I himself. American engineers were brought in, again by the government, to set up a railroad industry so that Rus-

SOURCE: Peter N. Stearns, *The Industrial Revolution in World History* (Boulder, CO: Westview Press, 1993), pp. 72–73.

sians could build their own locomotives and cars. . . .

But Russia did not then industrialize. Modern industrial operations did not sufficiently dent established economic practices. The nation remained overwhelmingly agricultural. High percentage increases in manufacturing proceeded from such a low base that they had little general impact. Several structural barriers impeded a genuine industrial revolution. Russia's cities had never boasted a manufacturing tradition; there were few artisans skilled even in preindustrial methods. Only by the 1860s and 1870s had cities grown enough for an artisan core to take shape—in printing, for example—and even then large numbers of foreigners (particularly Germans) had to be imported. Even more serious was the system of serfdom that kept most Russians bound to agricultural estates. While some free laborers could be found, most rural Russians could not legally leave their land, and their obligation to devote extensive work service to their lords' estates reduced their incentive even for agricultural production. Peter the Great had managed to adapt serfdom to a preindustrial metallurgical industry by allowing landlords to sell villages and the labor therein for expansion of ironworks. But this mongrel system was not suitable for change on a grander scale, which is precisely what the industrial revolution entailed.

Furthermore, the West's industrial revolution, while it provided tangible examples for Russia to imitate, also produced pressures to develop more traditional sectors in lieu of structural change. The West's growing cities and rising prosperity claimed rising levels of Russian timber, hemp, tallow, and, increasingly, grain. These were export goods that could be produced without new technology and without altering the existing labor system. Indeed, many landlords boosted the work-service obligations of the serfs in order to generate more grain production for sale to the West. The obvious temptation was to lock in an older economy—to respond to new opportunity by incremental changes within the traditional system and to maintain serfdom and the rural preponderance rather than to risk fundamental internal transformation.

## Europe and the People without History: Labor Migrations

*Eric R. Wolf*

*A large variety of social changes accompanied industrialization. One of the most important was the migration of large numbers of people. Part of this was the movement of people from the countryside to the cities and new industrial centers within Europe. Another part was the wave of labor migration from Europe overseas. In the following selection, Eric Wolf analyzes the waves of labor migrations related to industrialization occurring during the 19th and 20th centuries.*

CONSIDER: *The differences between the three waves of migration Wolf describes; the possible economic and social consequences of these labor migrations within and outside of Europe.*

People may move for religious, political, ecological, or other reasons; but the migrations of the nineteenth and twentieth centuries were largely labor migrations, movements of the bearers of labor power. These labor migrations, of course, carried with them newspaper editors to publish papers for Polish miners or German metalworkers, shopkeepers to supply their fellow migrants with pasta or red beans, religious specialists to minister to Catholic or Buddhist souls, and others. Each migration involved the transfer to the new geographical location not only of manpower but also of services and resources. Each migratory wave generated, in turn, supplies of services at the point of arrival, whether these were labor agents, merchants, lawyers, or players of percussion instruments.

In the development of capitalism, three waves of migration stand out, each a response to critical changes in the demand for labor, each creating new working classes. The first of these waves was associated with the initial period of European industrialization. Beginning in England, these initial movements toward capitalist industry covered only short distances, since industrial development was itself still localized and limited. Thus, in the cotton town of Preston in Lancashire, where roughly half the population consisted of immigrants in 1851, over 40 percent had come less than ten miles from their birthplaces and only about 30 percent had come more than thirty miles. Fourteen percent of all immigrants had been born in Ireland, however, and came to Preston as part of the rising tide of Irish immigration in the 1840s. Localized as such movements were, they made Lancashire the most urbanized county in Britain by the middle of the nineteenth century, with more than half the people of the county living in fourteen towns with populations of more than 10,000.

Belgium followed Britain in the movement of workers from the countryside, as the industrial towns of the Walloon-speaking southern provinces burgeoned in the 1820s. In the 1830s the Prussian provinces of Westphalia, Rhine, Berlin, and Brandenburg initiated their industrial expansion, attracting a large-scale flow of population from Prussia's eastern agricultural regions. This flow intensified greatly in the last quarter of the century, as dependent cultivators were displaced by the consolidation and mechanization of the large Junker estates.

SOURCE: Eric Wolf, *Europe and the People without History* (Berkeley: University of California Press), copyright © 1983 by the Regents of the University of California, University of California Press.

While the first wave of labor migration under capitalism carried people toward the industrial centers within the European peninsula, a second flow sent Europeans overseas. An estimated 50 million people left Europe permanently between 1800 and 1914. The most important destination of this movement was the United States, which between 1820 and 1915 absorbed about 32 million immigrants, most of them of European origins. This influx of people provided the labor power that underwrote the industrialization of the United States.

A third wave of migration carried contract laborers of diverse origins to the expanding mines and plantations of the tropics. This flow represents a number of developments, such as the establishment of a migratory labor force for the South African mines, the growth of the trade in Indian and Chinese contract labor, and the sponsored migration of Italian laborers to the coffee regions of Brazil. These movements not only laid the basis for a large increase in tropical production but also played a major part in creating an infrastructure of transport and communication, prerequisites for a further acceleration of capitalist development.

## The Family and Industrialization in Western Europe

### Michael Anderson

*The tremendous growth of interest in social history has stimulated scholars from other disciplines to address historical questions. A number of sociologists have applied methods from their discipline to social aspects of 19th-century industrialization. In the following selection, Michael Anderson, a sociologist from the University of Edinburgh, discusses the effects of industrialization on the working-class family.*

CONSIDER: *The specific ways in which the process of industrialization affected working-class families; how Anderson's interpretation might support the "optimists" or the "pessimists" in their debate over the effects of the Industrial Revolution on the working class; how the effects on middle-class families might differ.*

In industrial areas, then, the close interdependence of parents and children which was so important in peasant societies gave way, and this was reflected in changes in family relationships. The early stages of industrialization, however, probably changed relationships between husbands and wives much less, though freedom from such close supervision and a more private domestic situation

SOURCE: Michael Anderson, "The Family and Industrialization in Western Europe," *The Forum Series.* Reprinted by permission of Forum Press (St. Louis, MO., 1978), p. 14. Copyright © 1978 by Forum Press.

may have allowed rather more affection to develop between them than had been the case in pre-industrial peasant families. Husband and wife were no longer co-operating in the same productive task, but this had never been universal anyway. There was, however, a continued need and possibility for both husbands and wives to work as producers to keep the family above the subsistence line. In a few areas wives actually left the house to work in the factories. More usually, as women had always done, the wives of factory workers worked at home producing small items of clothing, processing some kind of food or drink, taking in the middle class's washing, or running a small shop or lodging house. The manifold needs of an industrial community were thus met in a way which contributed to working class family solidarity while allowing mothers to supervise and care (perhaps rather better than before) for small children during the lengthening period before they were able to enter the labor force themselves.

Initially, then, it was only in a few areas, especially those specializing in mining, machine-making, metal manufacturing, shipbuilding and sawmilling, that a change occurred in the economic status of women and with it in their family situation. In these areas there were not enough openings for female wage employment and, in consequence, many women were forced into the almost totally new situation of full-time housewife. However, as more and more traditional tasks were taken over by the application of factory production methods to clothing and food preparation, the home increasingly became confined to consumption. Only then did the distinction between male productive work outside the home and female consumption-oriented work inside the home become common among the working class.

Though the evidence is patchy, it seems that, at least in some areas, this had an effect on relationships between husbands and wives. Since the husband became the only income producer, the rest of the family became more dependent on him than he was on them. Whatever the husband did, the wife had little power to resist. While the family as a whole relied materially on the father, he needed them only to the extent that he could obtain from them emotional or other rewards which he could not obtain elsewhere or to the extent to which public opinion in the neighbourhood was effective in controlling his behavior (and with the weakened community control of large industrial cities, neighborhood control was often weak). Thus, in the working class, the idea that a woman's place was in the home and that her role was essentially an inferior domestic one is not of great antiquity. Rather it seems only to have developed as a response to a major shift in the power balance between husbands and wives which reflected the new employment situation of late nineteenth and early twentieth century industrial society.

## European Women

*Eleanor S. Riemer and John C. Fout*

*In recent years, many historians have pointed out the limitations facing middle-class women between 1850 and 1914. As investigations into women's history have multiplied and deepened, new interpretations have been made. In the following selection, historians Eleanor S. Riemer and John C. Fout argue that middle-class women during this period increasingly questioned their roles and often expanded their activities into new, important areas.*

CONSIDER: *How middle-class women's maternal and housewifely roles were justified; ways in which middle-class women expanded their roles; how middle-class women's new roles affected their attitudes.*

Middle-class women, too, faced new situations and challenges in the nineteenth and twentieth centuries. Although some lower-middle-class women continued to work alongside their shopkeeper husbands as they had in the past, most married middle-class women did not, and never expected to have to work for wages. Their lives were centered on caring for their children and homes. But most middle-class women did not lead leisured existences. Indeed, they found that the demands on their time and energy increased as modernization progressed, and middle-class families' standards for cleanliness, food preparation, and physical comfort were upgraded.

Middle-class women's maternal and housewifely roles were justified in the nineteenth century by a twofold conception of women's nature and capabilities. On the one hand, women were considered passive creatures who were physically and intellectually inferior to men. Thus, women needed protection and direction from their fathers and husbands. On the other hand, women, because they were nonaggressive and sexually passive and were removed from the contamination of the competitive workaday world, were deemed morally superior to men and were to be respected for that. A woman's unique capability and greatest responsibility in life was caring for the moral and spiritual needs of her family.

The contradictions within this ideal and women's attempts to reconcile or dispel them are recurring and ma-

jor themes in the documents. From the middle of the nineteenth century large numbers of middle-class women consciously and methodically expanded their maternal and moral roles—and thus their sphere of competence—outside their homes to society at large. One way they accomplished this was by transforming middle- and upper-class women's traditional, and often haphazard, charitable work into organized movements for social reform. These women became increasingly interested in the problems of poor women and children. They believed they understood and shared many of the concerns of working-class mothers and considered these women and their children the primary victims of the economic and social dislocations caused by urbanization and the new industrial order.

Through their social welfare and reform work, middle-class women gained a sense of both their own competence and their limitations in a world controlled by men. Many also realized that although women of their class expected to be dependent wives, economic and social realities were such that there was no guarantee women would be supported by men throughout their lives. Many came to believe that their own limited educations and the restrictions placed on them by the law and the ideals of ladylike conduct left women ill-equipped for the roles they might have to—or want to—play in life. Thus, the reform of society and reforms for women became closely identified and often were confronted simultaneously by organized women all over Europe.

## Chapter Questions

1. Drawing from the sources in the chapter, what social developments might be related to industrialization?

2. How might it be argued that industrialization should be considered a great boon, a mixed blessing, or a disaster for 19th-century Europeans?

3. Analyze the social roles of women during this period. In what ways might these roles be connected to the economic and social developments that accompanied industrialization?

4. In what ways was the rise of Marxism connected to industrialization and related social changes?

5. How might the sources be used to analyze Romanticism in art as a reaction to some of the developments occurring in late-18th and early-19th–century Europe?

SOURCE: From *European Women: A Documentary History, 1789–1945,* edited by Eleanor S. Riemer and John C. Fout. Copyright © 1980 by Schocken Books, Inc. Reprinted by permission of Schocken Books, published by Pantheon Books, a division of Random House, Inc.

# Chapter Nineteen

# The Americas, 1700s–1914

In 1700, the enormous land mass that we now call North, Central, and South America was under the colonial control of European powers. By 1914, however, virtually all the countries of this hemisphere were independent republics. Despite the great differences in culture, politics, economies, peoples, and values, they all shared in a common experience of seeking means by which to free themselves of foreign control. Yet, this general process obscures both the enormous price that different peoples paid for gaining liberation as well as the continuing legacies and influences of foreign domination in new and unexpected forms. While the North American nations of the United States and Canada developed urban, industrial economies that were self-sustaining and largely under indigenous control, the economies of Mexico and Central and South America remained largely rural and agricultural and were constantly threatened by dominance from the outside.

The United States, between 1776 and 1914, is a great success story in world history. Initially 13 colonies of the British Empire, dependent socially and economically on an island 3,000 miles away, the United States emerged as the dominant economic power on earth. Furthermore, its Revolution, built around principles of equality and liberty among men, provided a model of political reform emulated by scores of nations since.

Yet, the tremendous political revolution did not solve all of the problems of inequality that developed during the Colonial Period. Slavery, an institution begun before the revolution, continued for nearly 90 years after and was an underlying cause of one of the bloodiest civil wars in the world's history. Similarly, while the nation was organized to protect the liberty of men, it was not until after the first World War that women were even allowed the vote.

Historians have focused on the nation's important successes. Yet, in these documents, we see that the historical drive toward greater and greater freedom and equality was far from over by the time of the Great War. These documents deal with three basic issues. First, they address the

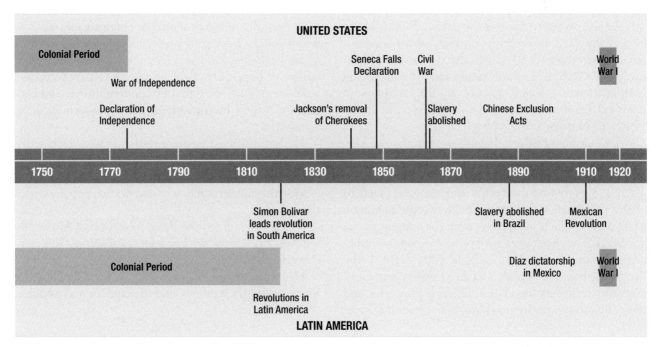

**UNITED STATES**

Colonial Period

War of Independence

Declaration of Independence

Jackson's removal of Cherokees

Seneca Falls Declaration

Civil War

Slavery abolished

Chinese Exclusion Acts

World War I

1750    1770    1790    1810    1830    1850    1870    1890    1910    1920

Simon Bolivar leads revolution in South America

Slavery abolished in Brazil

Mexican Revolution

Colonial Period

Diaz dictatorship in Mexico

World War I

Revolutions in Latin America

**LATIN AMERICA**

apparent goals of equality, liberty, and democracy that were at the heart of the New World's political movements during this period. The second issue involves the various ways in which resistance to these ideals remained strong and became integral to the economic and political lives of the new nations. Third, these selections look at continuing contradictory impulses, such as slavery and nativism, denial of women's equal rights, and political subjugation of Native American and African American rights.

# PRIMARY SOURCES

## The Declaration of Independence

*By the middle decades of the 18th century, relationships between England and the Colonies had deteriorated. Although the Colonies were divided among themselves over a host of issues such as slavery, regional interests, and the relative power of a central government over local government, they were united in their belief that they had little to gain from continuing the traditional colonial relationship. Even so, many colonists, perhaps as many as one-third, rejected outright rebellion and remained loyal to the Crown. The Declaration of Independence, written in 1776 at the outset of the Revolutionary War, was perhaps the most radical statement of the growing Enlightenment philosophies of the era and would become the model for other revolutionary documents from the French Revolution onward. Written primarily by Thomas Jefferson, it originally contained passages condemning slavery. But, in light of the southern states' dependence on slavery, antislavery passages were removed.*

CONSIDER: *Who in the Colonies might have been in favor of the Revolution; who might have been opposed; how useful this standard is for evaluating the legitimacy of a revolution.*

When in the Course of human events, it becomes necessary for one people to dissolve the political bonds which have connected them with another, and to assume among the Powers of the earth, the separate and equal station to which the Laws of Nature and of Nature's God entitle them, a decent respect to the opinions of mankind requires that they should declare the causes which impel them to the separation.

We hold these truths to be self-evident, that all men are created equal, that they are endowed by their Creator with certain unalienable Rights, that among these are Life, Liberty and the pursuit of Happiness. That to secure these rights, Governments are instituted among Men, deriving their just powers from the consent of the governed, That whenever any Form of Government becomes destructive of these ends, it is the Right of the People to alter or to abolish it, and to institute new Government, laying its foundation on such principles and organizing its powers in such form, as to them shall seem most likely to effect their Safety and Happiness. Prudence, indeed, will dictate that Governments long established should not be changed for light and transient causes; and accordingly all experience hath shown, that mankind are more disposed to suffer, while evils are sufferable, than to right themselves by abolishing the forms to which they are accustomed. But when a long train of abuses and usurpations, pursuing invariably the same Object evinces a design to reduce them under absolute Despotism, it is their right, it is their duty, to throw off such Government, and to provide new Guards for their future security.—Such has been the patient sufferance of these Colonies; and such is now the necessity which constrains them to alter their former Systems of Government. The history of the present King of Great Britain is a history of repeated injuries and usurpations, all having in direct object the establishment of an absolute Tyranny over these States. To prove this, let Facts be submitted to a candid world.

He has refused his Assent to Laws, the most wholesome and necessary for the public good.

He has forbidden his Governors to pass Laws of immediate and pressing importance, unless suspended in their operation till his Assent should be obtained; and when so suspended, he has utterly neglected to attend to them.

He has refused to pass other Laws for the accommodation of large districts of people, unless those people would relinquish the right of Representation in the Legislature, a right inestimable to them and formidable to tyrants only.

He has dissolved Representative Houses repeatedly, for opposing with manly firmness his invasions on the rights of the people. . . .

He has endeavoured to prevent the population of these States; . . .

He has obstructed the Administration of Justice, by refusing his Assent to Laws for establishing Judiciary Powers.

He has made Judges dependent on his Will alone, for the tenure of their offices, and the amount and payment of their salaries. . . .

He has kept among us, in times of peace, Standing Armies without the Consent of our legislature.

He has affected to render the Military independent of and superior to the Civil Power. . . .

For quartering large bodies of armed troops among us:

For protecting them, by a mock Trial, from Punishment for any Murders which they should commit on the Inhabitants of these States:

For cutting off our Trade with all parts of the world:

For imposing taxes on us without our Consent:

For depriving us in many cases, of the benefits of Trial by Jury:

For transporting us beyond Seas to be tried for pretended offences: . . .

For taking away our Charters, abolishing our most valuable Laws, and altering fundamentally the Forms of our Governments:

For suspending our own Legislature, and declaring themselves invested with Power to legislate for us in all cases whatsoever.

## Independence in South America

*Simon Bolivar*

*Simon Bolivar (1783–1830) was the great liberator of South America. Together with José de San Martin, he led successful revolts against the Spanish crown in South American territories during the first three decades of the 19th century. This excerpt is taken from Bolivar's "Message to the Congress of Angostura" (1819). It explains his ideas about a new constitution for the newly independent Republic of Venezuela. Bolivar worried about handing power to the uneducated and proposed, instead, to centralize political control in the hands of elite intellectuals and propertied classes.*

CONSIDER: *Why Bolivar favors a hereditary senate and a strong executive; why he hesitated at advocating full democracy; how ideas such as Bolivar's may have affected the future political course in Latin America.*

Venezuela had, has, and should have a republican government. Its principles should be the sovereignty of the people, division of powers, civil liberty, proscription of slavery, and the abolition of monarchy and privileges. We need equality to recast, so to speak, into a unified nation, the classes of men, political opinions, and public customs. . . .

A hereditary senate will be the fundamental basis of the legislative power, and therefore the foundation of

the entire government. It will also serve as a counterweight to both government and people; and as a neutral power it will weaken the mutual attacks of these two eternally rival powers. In all conflicts the calm reasoning of a third party will serve as the means of reconciliation. Thus the Venezuelan senate will give strength to this delicate political structure, so sensitive to violent repercussions; it will be the mediator that will lull the storms and it will maintain harmony between the head and the other parts of the political body. . . .

Although the authority of the executive power in England may appear to be extreme, it would, perhaps, not be excessive in the Republic of Venezuela. Here the Congress has tied the hands and even the heads of its men of state. This deliberative assembly has assumed a part of the executive functions, contrary to the maxim of Montesquieu, to wit: A representative assembly should exercise no active function. It should only make laws and determine whether or not those laws are enforced. Nothing is as disturbing to harmony among the powers of government as their intermixture. Nothing is more dangerous with respect to the people than a weak executive; and if a kingdom has deemed it necessary to grant the executive so many powers, then in a republic these powers are infinitely more indispensable. . . .

The people of Venezuela already enjoy the rights that they may legitimately and easily exercise. Let us now, therefore, restrain the growth of immoderate pretensions which, perhaps, a form of government unsuited to our people might excite. Let us abandon the federal forms of government unsuited to us; let us put aside the triumvirate which holds the executive power and center it in a president. We must grant him sufficient authority to enable him to continue the struggle against the obstacles inherent in our recent situation, our present state of war, and every variety of foe, foreign and domestic, whom we must battle for some time to come. Let the legislature relinquish the powers that rightly belong to the executive.

## Travels in Brazil: Religion and Slavery in Brazil

*Henry Koster*

*Slavery in Brazil was extremely important to the economy and social structure of the country until its abolition in 1889. Slaves accounted for fully one-third of the entire population and worked at most of the productive jobs in the country. In this excerpt, Henry Koster, a British traveler, recounts the important role religion and the church played in establishing*

SOURCE: *The Selective Writings of Bolivar,* vol. I, compiled by Vincente Lecuna, edited by Harold A. Bierck, Jr. (Colonial Press, 1951), pp. 175–91.

SOURCE: Henry Koster, *Travels in Brazil* (London: 2 vols., 1816), II, 238–43.

*control over Africans and ameliorating some of the harsh conditions of plantation life.*

CONSIDER: *The biases in Koster's account that make the reader sympathetic to the Church; how an account by an African slave might have differed.*

All slaves in Brazil follow the religion of their masters; and notwithstanding the impure state in which the Christian church exists in that country, still such are the beneficent effects of the Christian religion, that these, its adopted children, are improved by it to an infinite degree; and the slave who attends to the strict observance of religious ceremonies, invariably proves to be a good servant. The Africans, who are imported from Angola, are baptized in lots before they leave their own shores: and on their arrival in Brazil they are to learn the doctrines of the church, and the duties of the religion into which they have entered. These bear the mark of the royal crown upon their breasts, which denotes that they have undergone the ceremony of baptism, and likewise that the king's duty has been paid upon them. The slaves which are imported from other parts of the coast of Africa, arrive in Brazil unbaptized, and before the ceremony of making them Christians can be performed upon them, they must be taught certain prayers, for the acquirement of which one year is allowed to the master, before he is obliged to present the slave at the parish church. The law is not always strictly adhered to as to the time, but it is never evaded altogether. The religion of the master teaches him that it would be extremely sinful to allow his slave to remain a heathen: and indeed the Portuguese and Brazilians have too much religious feeling to let them neglect any of the ordinances of their church. The slave himself likewise wishes to be made a Christian; for his fellow-bondmen will, otherwise, in every squabble or trifling disagreement with him, close their string of opprobrious epithets with the name of *pagão* (pagan). The unbaptized negro feels that he is considered as an inferior being: and although he may not be aware of the value which the whites place upon baptism, still he knows that the stigma for which he is upbraided will be removed by it; and therefore he is desirous of being made equal to his companions. The Africans who have been long imported, imbibe a Catholic feeling; and appear to forget that they were once in the same situation themselves. The slaves are not asked whether they will be baptized or not. Their entrance into the Catholic church is treated as a thing of course: and indeed they are not considered as members of society, but rather as brute animals, until they can lawfully go to mass, confess their sins, and receive the sacrament.

The slaves have their religious brotherhoods as well as the free persons: and the ambition of the slave very generally aims at being admitted into one of these, and at being made one of the officers and directors of the concerns of the brotherhood. Even some of the money which the industrious slave is collecting for the purpose of purchasing his freedom, will oftentimes be brought out of its concealment for the decoration of a saint, that the donor may become of importance in the society to which he belongs. The negroes have one invocation of the Virgin (or I might almost say one virgin) which is peculiarly their own. Our Lady of the Rosary is even sometimes painted with a black face and hands. It is in this manner that the slaves are led to place their attention upon an object in which they soon take an interest, but from which no injury can proceed towards themselves, nor can any through its means be by them inflicted upon their masters. Their ideas are removed from any thought of the customs of their own country; and are guided into a channel of a totally different nature, and completely unconnected with what is practised there. The election of a King of Congo by the individuals who come from that part of Africa, seems indeed as if it would give them a bias towards the customs of their native soil. But the Brazilian Kings of Congo worship Our Lady of the Rosary; and are dressed in the dress of white men. They and their subjects dance, it is true, after the manner of their creole blacks, and mulattos, all of whom dance after the same manner: and these dances are now as much the national dances of Brazil, as they are of Africa. The Portuguese language is spoken by the slaves: and their own dialects are allowed to lie dormant until they are by many of them quite forgotten. No compulsion is resorted to, to make them embrace the habits of their masters: but their ideas are insensibly led to imitate and adopt them. The masters at the same time imbibe some of the customs of their slaves; and thus the superior and his dependent are brought nearer to each other. I doubt not that the system of baptizing the newly imported negroes, proceeded rather from the bigotry of the Portuguese in former times than from any political plan: but it has had the most beneficial effects. The slaves are rendered more tractable. Besides being better men and women, they become more obedient servants. They are brought under the control of the priesthood: and even if this was the only additional hold which was gained by their entrance into the church, it is a great engine of power which is thus brought into action.

## Call to Revolution in Canada
### William Lyon Mackenzie

*William Lyon Mackenzie, a radical politician who had emigrated to Canada from Scotland, was elected the first mayor of Toronto. But after his defeat in 1836, he supported a group who encouraged open rebellion against British rule. Agricultural crises, combined with a worldwide economic depression, further undermined British control of this huge country. In this excerpt Mackenzie calls for a revolution against what he calls "European tyranny."*

CONSIDER: *Mackenzie's use of religion as a rallying cry for rebellion; similarities and differences in the rhetoric of rebellion of the Canadians and of the colonists in the United States.*

Brave Canadians! God has put into the bold and honest hearts of our brethren in Lower Canada to revolt—not against "lawful" but against "unlawful authority." The law says we shall not be taxed without our consent by the voices of the men of our choice, but a wicked and tyrannical government has trampled upon that law—robbed the exchequer—divided the plunder—and declared that, regardless of justice they will continue to roll their splendid carriages, and riot in their palaces, at our expense—that we are poor spiritless ignorant peasants, who were born to toil for our betters. But the peasants are beginning to open their eyes and to feel their strength. . . .

Canadians! Do you love freedom? I know you do. Do you hate oppression? Who dare deny it? Do you wish perpetual peace, and a government founded upon the eternal heaven-born principle of the Lord Jesus Christ—a government bound to enforce the law to do to each other as you would be done by? Then buckle on your armour, and put down the villains who oppress and enslave our country. . . .

If we move now, as one man, to crush the tyrant's power, to establish free institutions founded on God's law, we will prosper, for He who commands the winds and waves will be with us—but if we are cowardly and mean-spirited, a woeful and dark day is surely before us. . . .

Canadians! It is the design of the Friends of Liberty to give several hundred acres to every Volunteer—to root up the unlawful Canada Company, and give *free deeds* to all settlers who live on their lands—to give gifts of the Clergy Reserve lots, to good citizens who have settled on them—and the like to settlers on Church of England Glebe Lots, so that the yeomanry may feel independent, and be able to improve the country, instead of sending the fruit of their labour to foreign lands. . . .

[T]he prize is a splendid one. A country larger than France or England; natural resources equal to our most boundless wishes—a government of equal laws—religion pure and undefiled—perpetual peace—education to all—millions of acres of lands for revenue—freedom from British tribute—free trade with all the world—but stop—I never could enumerate all the blessings attendant on independence!

Up then, brave Canadians! Get ready your rifles, and make short work of it; a connection with England would involve us in all her wars, undertaken for her own advantage, never for ours; with governors from England, we will have bribery at elections, corruption, villainy and perpetual discord in every township, but Independence would give us the means of enjoying many blessings. Our enemies in Toronto are in terror and dismay—they know their wickedness and dread our vengeance . . . now's the day and the hour! Woe be to those who oppose us, for "In God is our trust."

## The Removal of Native Americans in the United States

### *Andrew Jackson*

*Throughout the 19th century, the United States expanded westward, displacing Native American populations to reservations. These reservations undermined the health and destroyed the culture of the numerous tribes whose livelihoods had depended on open ranges and free migration. In the early part of the century, the Cherokees of Florida and Georgia adopted white agricultural practices and established a written language and even a constitution. Despite these attempts to adapt to white customs, laws, and values, in the winter of 1835–36 they were forced to abandon their homes and move westward to Oklahoma, then known as the Indian Territory. This trek became known as the Trail of Tears in light of the high death rates and terrible sacrifice. It is estimated that more than 100 Indians per day died from exposure, starvation, and disease. On December 7, 1835, President Andrew Jackson (1828–36), who gained national renown as an "Indian fighter," presented to Congress his rationale for uprooting thousands of people from their traditional homes and forcing them to march to unfamiliar and unknown territory.*

CONSIDER: *How Jackson justifies his policy; what this reveals about attitudes toward Native Americans; alternative resolutions to the conflicts that arose between white and Native American populations.*

SOURCE: Margaret Fairly, ed., *The Selected Writings of William Lyon Mackenzie* (Toronto: Oxford University Press, 1960), in J. M. Bliss, *Canadian History in Documents, 1763–1966* (Toronto: The Ryerson Press, 1966), pp. 46–48.

SOURCE: James D. Richardson, ed., *A Compilation of the Messages and Pages of the Presidents 1787–1897* (Washington DC: Government Printing Office, 1896–1899), vol. 3, pp. 171–72.

. . . The plan of removing the aboriginal people who yet remain within the settled portions of the United States to the country west of the Mississippi River approaches its consummation. . . . All preceding experiments for the improvement of the Indians have failed. It seems now to be an established fact that they can not live in contact with a civilized community and prosper. Ages of fruitless endeavors have at length brought us to a knowledge of this principle of intercommunication with them. The past we can not recall, but the future we can provide for. . . . [N]o one can doubt the moral duty of the Government of the United States to protect and if possible to preserve and perpetuate the scattered remnants of this race which are left within our borders. In the discharge of this duty an extensive region in the West has been assigned for their permanent residence. . . .

The plan for their removal and reëstablishment is founded upon the knowledge we have gained of their character and habits, and has been dictated by a spirit of enlarged liberality. A territory exceeding in extent that relinquished has been granted to each tribe. Of its climate, fertility, and capacity to support an Indian population the representations are highly favorable. To these districts the Indians are removed at the expense of the United States, and with certain supplies of clothing, arms, ammunition, and other indispensable articles; they are also furnished gratuitously with provisions for the period of a year after their arrival at their new homes. In that time, from the nature of the country and of the products raised by them, they can subsist themselves by agricultural labor, if they choose to resort to that mode of life; if they do not they are upon the skirts of the great prairies, where countless herds of buffalo roam, and a short time suffices to adapt their own habits to the changes which a change of the animals destined for their food may require. Ample arrangements have also been made for the support of schools; in some instances council houses and churches are to be erected, dwellings constructed for the chiefs, and mills for common use. Funds have been set apart for the maintenance of the poor; the most necessary mechanical arts have been introduced, and blacksmiths, gunsmiths, wheelwrights, millwrights, etc., are supported among them. Steel and iron, and sometimes salt, are purchased for them, and plows and other farming utensils, domestic animals, looms, spinning wheels, cards, etc., are presented to them. And besides these beneficial arrangements, annuities are in all cases paid, amounting in some instances to more than $30 for each individual of the tribe, and in all cases sufficiently great, if justly divided and prudently expended, to enable them, in addition to their own exertions, to live comfortably.

## Declaration of Sentiments: Women's Rights in the United States
### Seneca Falls Convention

*The rhetoric of democracy and freedom that had emerged as a bedrock of American ideology highlighted the innumerable inequities that existed. In addition to the enormous abolitionist movement then overtaking the nation, women began to demand equality. The Seneca Falls Convention of 1848 was the first dedicated to gaining women's rights. More than 100 men and women gathered in the small upstate New York community and drafted this declaration demanding not only political, but social, religious, and economic equality for the sexes. Self-consciously modeled on the Declaration of Independence, the statement presaged the movement in the early 20th century that finally gained women the right to vote in 1920.*

CONSIDER: *The difficulties, according to this document, facing women at this time; the reasons for the parallels and differences between this statement and the Declaration of Independence; why it took so long for women to gain the vote.*

We hold these truths to be self-evident: that all men and women are created equal; that they are endowed by their Creator with certain inalienable rights; that among these are life, liberty, and the pursuit of happiness; that to secure these rights governments are instituted, deriving their just powers from the consent of the governed. Whenever any form of government becomes destructive of these ends, it is the right of those who suffer from it to refuse allegiance to it, and to insist upon the institution of a new government, laying its foundation on such principles, and organizing its powers in such form, as to them shall seem most likely to effect their safety and happiness. . . . Such has been the patient sufferance of the women under this government, and such is now the necessity which constrains them to demand the equal station to which they are entitled.

The history of mankind is a history of repeated injuries and usurpations on the part of man toward woman, having in direct object the establishment of an absolute tyranny over her. To prove this, let facts be submitted to a candid world.

He has never permitted her to exercise her inalienable right to the elective franchise. . . .

He has made her, if married, in the eye of the law, civilly dead.

He has taken from her all right in property, even to the wages she earns.

SOURCE: Elizabeth Cady Stanton, Susan B. Anthony, and Matilda J. Gage, eds., *History of Woman Suffrage*, vol. I, pp. 70–71.

He has made her, morally, an irresponsible being, as she can commit many crimes with impunity, provided they be done in the presence of her husband. In the covenant of marriage, she is compelled to promise obedience to her husband, he becoming, to all intents and purposes, her master—the law giving him power to deprive her of her liberty, and to administer chastisement.

He has so framed the laws of divorce . . . upon a false supposition of the supremacy of man, and giving all power into his hands. . . .

He has monopolized nearly all the profitable employments, and from those she is permitted to follow, she receives but a scanty remuneration. . . .

He has denied her the facilities for obtaining a thorough education, all colleges being closed against her.

He allows her in Church, as well as State, but a subordinate position, claiming Apostolic authority for her exclusion from the ministry, and, with some exceptions, from any public participation in the affairs of the Church.

He has created a false public sentiment by giving to the world a different code of morals for men and women, by which moral delinquencies which exclude women from society, are not only tolerated, but deemed of little account in man. . . .

He has endeavored, in every way that he could, to destroy her confidence in her own powers, to lessen her self-respect, and to make her willing to lead a dependent and abject life.

Now, in view of this entire disfranchisement of one-half the people of this country, their social and religious degradation—in view of the unjust laws above mentioned, and because women do feel themselves aggrieved, oppressed, and fraudulently deprived of their most sacred rights, we insist that they have immediate admission to all the rights and privileges which belong to them as citizens of the United States.

## For Land and Liberty
*Emiliano Zapata*

*Throughout the 19th century, Latin America struggled first to gain its independence from Spain and Portugal and then to establish popular democracies. The United States had always provided inspiration for these independence and democratic struggles. But, in the wake of the Spanish American War in 1898, the United States assumed an imperialist role for some of the Central American and Caribbean nations. In Mexico, Emiliano Zapata led a popular revolution that culminated in the establishment of an agrarian reform program for Mexico's peasants. He was assassinated in 1919 but remained a symbol of popular resistance to oppression for millions in his country and around the world. In this selection, the plan of Ayala, Emiliano Zapata calls for radical reform of the economic as well as the political system.*

CONSIDER: *Why Zapata adopted the slogan* Tierra y Libertad *(land and liberty) rather than simply calling for political democracy; what this reveals about the discontents of the peasantry and urban poor.*

We, the undersigned, constituted as a Revolutionary Junta, in order to maintain and achieve the fulfillment of the promises made by the revolution of November 29, 1910, declare to the civilized world which judges us and before the Nation to which we belong and love, the principles that we have formulated in order to end the tyranny that oppresses us. . . .

1. . . . Considering that the President of the Republic, Señor Don Francisco I. Madero, had made a bloody mockery of Effective Suffrage by . . . entering into an infamous alliance with the *cientificos*, the *haciendos*, the feudalists, and oppressive *caciques*, enemies of the Revolution that he proclaimed, in order to forge the chains of a new dictatorship more hateful and terrible than that of Porfirio Dìaz . . . : For these reasons we declare the said Francisco I. Madero unfit to carry out the promises of the Revolution of which he was the author . . . for having betrayed the principles and mocked the faith of the people . . . and from today onward we continue the Revolution begun by him, until we overthrow the dictatorship which exists. . . .

5. The Revolutionary Junta of the State of Morales will not conduct regular business until the dictatorial elements of Porfirio Dìaz and Francisco Madero are overthrown. The country is tired of false men and traitors who make promises as liberators but when they get to power, they forget their promises. . . .

6. As an additional part of the plan which we are invoking, we proclaim that the lands, woods, and waters usurped by the *haciendos*, *cientificos*, or *caciques* through tyranny and venal justice henceforth belong to the towns or citizens who have corresponding titles to these properties, of which they were despoiled by the bad faith of our oppressors. They shall retain possession of the said properties at all costs, arms in hand. The usurpers who think they have a right to the said lands may state their claims before special tribunals to be established upon the triumph of the Revolution.

SOURCE: Gilberto Magana, *Emiliano Zapata y el Agrarismo en Mexico* (Mexico: 1934–37), vol. II, pp. 126–29 (excerpt translated by Andrea Vasquez).

7. Since the immense majority of the Mexican towns and citizens own nothing but the ground on which they stand and suffer the horrors of a miserable existence, without the opportunity to improve their social condition or to dedicate themselves to industry or agriculture because a few individuals monopolize the lands, woods, and waters—for these reasons the great estates shall be expropriated, with indemnification to the owners of one third of such monopolies so that the towns and citizens of Mexico may obtain colonies, towns, sites and arable lands. Thus the lack of prosperity and welfare of all the Mexican people can improve.

## Banning Chinese Immigration to the United States

### United States House of Representatives

*The American nation contained vast natural resources such as coal, iron, oil, water, and wood. Yet, the relative scarcity of workers raised the costs of labor and forced industrialists to encourage immigration. Vast numbers of Irish, German, Italian, Jewish, and Eastern European immigrants came to the east coast in the last decades of the century. On the west coast, Asians and Mexicans were recruited to provide a ready supply of labor in railroads, mining, fishing, and agriculture. This led to enormous tensions as native-born workers and earlier immigrants competed for jobs at reduced pay. Race and racism were potent issues in defining the conflicts on the west coast and led to political movements to restrict immigration. The Chinese Restriction Act of 1882 was the first measure specifically aimed at a particular ethnic group. It was renewed and broadened in 1892 and was not finally repealed until World War II. This selection is from a report by the United States Congress, House Committee on Immigration and Naturalization, in 1892 that strongly recommended the passage of a bill renewing restrictions on Chinese immigration.*

CONSIDER: *The attitudes exhibited toward the Chinese in this document; the justifications and motivations for this legislation.*

There is urgent necessity for prompt legislation on the subject of Chinese immigration. The exclusion act approved May 6, 1882, and its supplement expires by limitation of time on May 6, 1892, and after that time there will be no law to prevent the Chinese hordes from invading our country in number so vast, as soon to outnumber the present population of our flourishing States on the Pacific slope. . . .

The popular demand for legislation excluding the Chinese from this country is urgent and imperative and almost universal. Their presence here is inimical to our institutions and is deemed injurious and a source of danger. They are a distinct race, saving from their earnings a few hundred dollars and returning to China. This they succeed in doing in from five to ten years by living in the most miserable manner, when in cities and towns in crowded tenement house, surrounded by dirt, filth, corruption, pollution, and prostitution; and gambling houses and opium joints abound. When used as cooks, farm-hands, servants, and gardeners they are more cleanly in habits and manners. They, as a rule, have no families here; all are men, save a few women, usually prostitutes. They have no attachment to our country, its laws or its institutions, nor are they interested in its prosperity. They never assimilate with our people, our manners, tastes, religion, or ideas. With us they have nothing in common.

Living on the cheapest diet (mostly vegetable), wearing the poorest clothing, with no family to support, they enter the field of labor in competition with the American workman. In San Francisco, and in fact throughout the whole Pacific slope, we learn from the testimony heretofore alluded to, that the Chinamen have invaded almost every branch of industry; manufacturers of cigars, cigar boxes, brooms, tailors, laundrymen, cooks, servants, farm-hands, fishermen, miners and all departments of manual labor, for wages and prices at which white men and women could not support themselves and those dependent upon them. Recently this was a new country, and the Chinese may have been a necessity at one time, but now our own people are fast filling up and developing this rich and highly favored land, and American citizens will not and can not afford to stand idly by and see this undesirable race carry away the fruits of the labor which justly belongs to them. A war of races would soon be inaugurated; several times it has broken out, and bloodshed has followed. The town of Tacoma, in 1887, banished some 3,000 Chinamen on twenty-four hours' notice, and no Chinaman has ever been permitted to return.

Our people are willing, however, that those now here may remain, protected by the laws which they do not appreciate or obey, provided strong provision be made that no more shall be allowed to come.

SOURCE: U.S. Congress, House of Representatives, Report #225, February 10, 1892, pp. 1–4.

# VISUAL SOURCES

## Manifest Destiny

*John Gast*

The painting *Manifest Destiny* by John Gast reveals the idealized myth of westward expansion that prevailed in the United States during the 19th century. Moving from the Atlantic coast cities of the east across the plains and mountains toward the Pacific, the goddess of Destiny carries a schoolbook in one hand and a telegraph wire in the other. Below, here come white male hunters and settlers, pushing Indians and buffalo farther west in retreat. In Destiny's wake follows the railroad.

CONSIDER: The impressions a 19th-century person might have gotten on viewing this; the meaning and justification of westward expansion according to this image.

## The Mexican Revolution

*Diego Rivera*

The Mexican Revolution stands out as Latin America's first successful revolt against dictatorship and foreign domination during the 20th century. This illustration is from a vast mural that the great Mexican artist Diego Rivera (1886–1957) painted in the National Palace to depict the history of Mexico. Here he shows the ways that foreigners have dominated and destroyed so much of indigenous Mexican culture over the centuries. The Spanish Conquistadors are shown at the bottom of the mural killing Aztec warriors. In the middle, the Church is shown as a force of oppression, executing heretics. At the top, Rivera shows the widespread support that the Revolution enjoyed among peasants, workers, and the middle class. Note particularly, in the very center, the phrase

**Illustration 19–1**   The Library of Congress.

"Tierra, Libertad y Pan" (Land, Liberty and Bread)—the slogan of the Revolution. At the very top of the painting are the latest foreign interests that were seen as destroying Mexican freedoms: British and U.S. oil interests.

CONSIDER: *What the viewer might conclude from this painting; whether Rivera considers this a hopeful view of Mexican history or a warning of the dangers that lie ahead.*

## The Western Hemisphere, 1770 and 1830

*In 1770 most of the Western Hemisphere was governed by the European powers. The Native American populations of North and South America maintained some autonomy in remote areas, but, for the most part, their populations had been decimated by disease and conquest. Yet, 60 years later, wars of independence by former Spanish, French, English, and Portuguese colonies had virtually ended European colonialism.*

*These two maps illustrate the rapid decolonization that occurred during this period. The first map shows the extent of European control in the late 18th century, before the wars of independence. The second map illustrates the new independent nation-states established at the beginning of the 19th century. By 1830, only the Caribbean region, Guyana, Alaska, and Canada were still ruled by the original colonial powers. Together, these maps show the rapid disintegration of the European colonial systems in both North and South America and the rise of independent states that still maintained close economic and political ties to their former colonial masters.*

**Illustration 19–2**   Diego Rivera/Instituto Nacional de Bellas Artes, Mexico City.

CONSIDER: *How these maps illustrate the anticolonial sentiments of the peoples of the Western Hemisphere; what you might use as indicators of continuing cultural and linguistic ties to the Old World.*

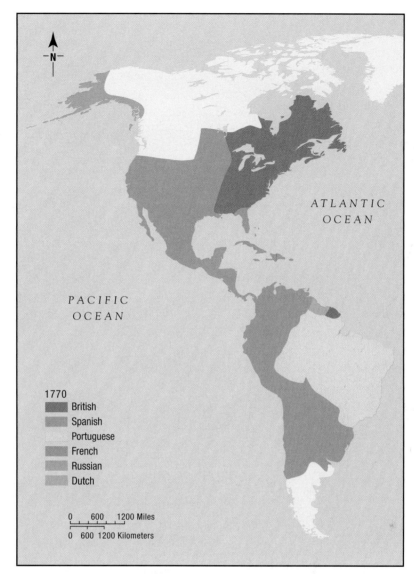

**Map 19–1**

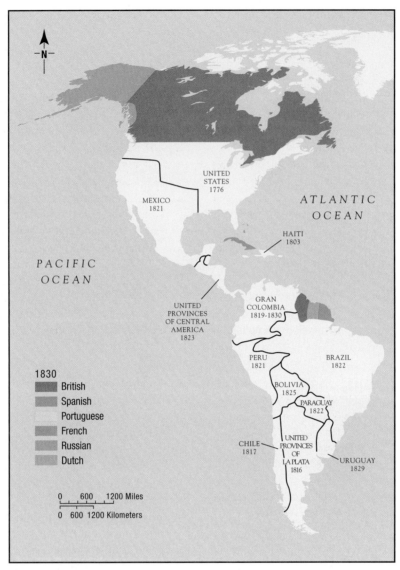

**Map 19–2**

# SECONDARY SOURCES

## Democracy and the American Revolution
### Merrill Jensen

The American Revolution is usually viewed as a revolt by the Colonists against England. But historians have also argued that the rhetoric of the revolution led many of the poor farmers and artisans to demand greater social and economic

SOURCE: Merrill Jensen, "Democracy and the American Revolution," *The Huntington Library Quarterly* 20 (August 1957), pp. 338–41. Reprinted with the permission of the Henry E. Huntington Library.

equality as well. In this excerpt, Merrill Jensen, a noted historian of the revolutionary era, argues that the War of Independence in the United States was also an internal revolution that sought a greater degree of democracy and freedom for the less well-to-do segments of American society.

CONSIDER: The revolutionary changes resulting from the break from Great Britain, according to Jensen; the evidence Jensen uses to support this thesis.

[B]y 1776 there were people in America demanding the establishment of democratic state governments, by which they meant legislatures controlled by a majority of the voters, and with none of the checks upon their actions such as had existed in the colonies. At the same time there were many Americans who were determined that there should be no changes except those made inevitable by separation from Great Britain. . . .

The significant thing is not the continuity of governmental structure, but the alteration of the balance of power within the structure, and in the political situation resulting from the break away from the supervising power of a central government—that of Great Britain.

The first and most revolutionary change was in the field of basic theory. In May 1776, to help bring about the overthrow of the Pennsylvania assembly, the chief stumbling block in the way of independence, Congress resolved that all governments exercising authority under the crown of Great Britain should be suppressed, and that "all the powers of government [be] exerted under the authority of the people of the colonies. . . . " John Adams described it as "the most important resolution that ever was taken in America." The Declaration of Independence spelled it out in terms of the equality of men, the sovereignty of the people, and the right of a people to change their governments as they pleased.

Second: the Revolution ended the power of a sovereign central government over the colonies. Britain had had the power to appoint and remove governors, members of upper houses of legislatures, judges, and other officials. It had the power to veto colonial legislation, to review cases appealed from colonial supreme courts, and to use armed force. All of this superintending power was wiped out by independence.

Third: the new central government created in America by the Articles of Confederation was, in a negative sense at least, a democratic government. The Congress of the United States had no power over either the states or their citizens. Hence, each state could govern itself as it pleased, and as a result of some of the new state constitutions, this often meant by a majority of the voters within a state.

Fourth: in writing the state constitutions, change was inevitable. The hierarchy of appointed legislative, executive, and judicial officials which had served as a check upon the elective legislatures was gone. The elective legislature became the supreme power in every state, and the lower houses, representing people however inadequately, became the dominant branch. The appointive houses of colonial times were replaced by elective senates, which in theory were supposed to represent property. They were expected to, and sometimes did, act as a check upon the lower houses, but their power was far less than that of pre-war councils.

Fifth: the office of governor underwent a real revolution. The governors of the royal colonies had, in theory at least, vast powers, including an absolute veto. In the new constitutions, most Americans united in shearing the office of governor of virtually all power.

Sixth: state supreme courts underwent a similar revolution. Under the state constitutions they were elected by the legislatures or appointed by governors who were elected officials. And woe betide a supreme court that tried to interfere with the actions of a legislature.

What such changes meant in terms of political realities was that a majority of voters within a state, if agreed upon a program and persistent enough, could do what it wanted, unchecked by governors or courts or appeals to a higher power outside the state. . . .

. . . The American Revolution was a democratic movement, not in origin, but in result. Certainly the political leaders of the eighteenth century thought the results were democratic. Whether they thought the results were good or bad is another story.

## By Reasonable Force: Power Politics and International Relations in South America
### Robert N. Burr

*When the peoples of the New World achieved their independence from the various European powers, some leaders believed that the newly freed states should reject Old World values and ways of relating to each other. But as Robert N. Burr explains in the following selection, most of the elites in South America accepted the prevailing European model of international relations and this led to constant conflict within the continent. Burr also shows how, even though colonialism was defeated in most of Latin America, European powers and nationals found new ways to exert their influence and control during the 19th century.*

CONSIDER: *Why the European powers were able to exert such a dominant influence in South America after independence; what alternatives there were to the European system of power politics.*

South American nations tended early to focus their political interests on one another, if only because of their confinement to a continent separated from the rest of the world by wide expanses of ocean. Moreover, rivalries and conflicts over elements of national power, and

SOURCE: Robert N. Burr, *By Reason or Force: Chile and the Balancing of Power in South America* (Berkeley: University of California Press). Copyright © 1966 The Regents of the University of California.

fluctuations in the power structure of the continent, produced interactions among South American nations. . . .

[An] early component of a system of power politics in South America was acceptance by its leaders of the axioms and techniques of power politics. The culture and education of the ruling elite were of European derivation; European values and forms in literature, fashions, and politics tended to be accepted and imitated, along with the European state system. To be sure, some voices in the wilderness cried out against the transplantation to the New World of European-style power politics, damning them as decadent, corrupt, and un-American. But those who gained power did not seriously question the concept of a community of competing sovereign states, each with the duty to defend itself and to expand its interests, preferably by peaceful means but by force if "necessary," even at the expense of other states. The Great Powers of Europe, those leading practitioners of the art of power politics, were the specific models for the international behavior of the South American nations. And because South American culture was largely derivative, and because South Americans suffered from a sense of inferiority bequeathed by their former colonial status and by the relative weakness of their respective nations, high prestige was attached to the imitation of European models. . . .

Difficulties in regularization of relations with the Great Powers . . . [diverted] the attention of the new states from intra-South American matters. Upon independence, recognition and expanded commerce had been sought from the Great Powers. South Americans wished, moreover, to borrow funds for both public and private purposes and to import the more highly developed technology and the skillful nationals of Europe and the United States. South America's attraction of money, people, and technology from Europe and the United States was indispensable to its fulfillment of urgent material and cultural aspirations. The more highly developed nations responded with alacrity to such an opportunity to exploit markets and resources, which Spain had so long denied them. But difficulties soon arose concerning the protection of the interests of Great Power nationals. Poverty often prevented South American governments from fulfilling their financial commitments; instability imperiled the persons and the interests of foreign nationals; the attitudes of the parties to resultant disputes made solution difficult. Xenophobia was prevalent among the Spanish-speaking peoples of South America to whom both the Spanish economic system and the Inquisition had for centuries denied contact with and knowledge of the outside world. In turn, immigrants from the Great Powers regarded the "backward" peoples of South America with contempt. They tended to enlist the superior coercive strength of their home governments to resolve conflicts of interest rather than to negotiate upon a basis of theoretical equality.

## The Mansions and the Shanties: The Making of Modern Brazil

### Gilberto Freyre

*During the 19th century, urban areas grew in South America. In these new environments, the social classes built their own institutions. In the process, they created new social relationships in which both rich and poor were forced to coexist. In the following selection, Gilberto Freyre, a noted Brazilian historian, analyzes the relationships between elites and the poor in 19th-century Brazil. Here he focuses on the changing functions of "the street"—the place where the poor and rich came into direct contact with each other.*

CONSIDER: *The different circumstances for the rich and poor in new urban communities; the different ways the street served these two classes and how they viewed its purpose.*

It was when our social environment began to change in the sense that the plantation manors became city mansions more after the European manner, and the slave quarters were reduced practically to servants' rooms, that adjustment disintegrated, and new forms of subordination, new social barriers began to develop between rich and poor, white and colored, between the big house and the little. Settlements of shanties and slums sprang up alongside the mansions, but with almost no communication between them, and African cults, diverging more from Catholicism than had been the case on plantations and ranches. A new distribution of power came about, but still resting for the most part in the hands of white landowners. Sharper antagonisms arose between the rulers and the ruled, between white children brought up in the house and colored children brought up in the street, without the old zone of fraternization between the two that was common on the plantations, and between the mistress of the mansion and the women of the street. There was a greater economic gap between the two extremes.

Only gradually did there begin to emerge moments of fraternization between these social extremes: the religious procession, the church festival, carnival revelries. For the parks, the so-called public promenades, the squares shaded by spreading *gameleira* trees and, for many years, encircled by iron railings similar to those which were taking the place of walls around the most fashion-

SOURCE: Gilberto Freyre, *The Mansions and the Shanties: The Making of Modern Brazil* (Berkeley: University of California Press, 1963, 1986), pp. xxiv–xxix. Reprinted by permission of the Gilberto Freyre Foundation.

able houses, were limited to the use and enjoyment of the wearers of high shoes, silk hat, cravat, sunshade—insignia of race, but principally of class. They were for the use and enjoyment of the man of a certain social position, but only for the man. The women and children stayed inside the house, or in the grounds to the rear—at most, on the verandah, at the gate, by the hitching rail, by the garden wall. The boy who went out to fly his kite or spin his top in the street was looked upon as a vagabond. A lady who went into the street to shop ran the risk of being taken for a streetwalker. . . .

By the beginning of the nineteenth century the street was ceasing to be the drain for the dirty water of the city houses, through which the well-shod foot of the respectable citizen had to pick its way, and was taking on dignity and social importance. By night it was no longer a dark passage which citizens crossed, preceded by a slave bearing a lantern, but was lighted by street lamps burning fish oil and hung from wires on high posts. This was the beginning of public lighting, the first gleam of dignity of the street, previously so neglected that it depended for its illumination on that of private houses and the candles burning in the saints' niches.

At about this time the municipality began to defend the street against the abuses of the mansion, which had moved into the cities bringing with it the same high-handed ways, almost the same arrogance of its plantation and ranch days, making of the street a place to chop wood, a dump for dead animals, refuse, dirty water, at times even chamber pots. The very architecture of the town mansion developed on the basis of the street as its adjunct: the drain pipes emptying their flood of rain water into the streets; doors and shutters opening on to the street; and windows—when windows came to take the place of jalousies—which made it convenient for men to expectorate into the street.

City ordinances at the beginning of the nineteenth century were for the most part directed toward restraining these abuses and toward establishing the importance, dignity, rights of the street which had been so disregarded and flouted. . . .

The Negro shanty dwellers were forbidden by ordinance to wash clothes at the public fountain in the middle of the city, and were ordered to do this in the streams outside the gates.

Other restrictions on individual liberties followed, such as forbidding the mansion owners to whip their slaves after the church bell, which played such an important role in the domestic and even the public life of Brazilian cities before clocks became common, had solemnly rung nine at night.

Still other ordinances were designed to make the street respected by the backwoodsman who came down from the hills, the backlands, or the plantations, riding high in the saddle or in his oxcart. He was ordered to dismount and lead his animal by bridle or reins, failure to do so carrying a penalty of twenty-four hours in jail; in the case of Negro slaves, two dozen lashes. And nobody was any longer to show such disrespect as to enter the city in shirt and drawers, or cantering or galloping through the streets down which, since the end of the eighteenth century, vehicles had begun to roll, coaches, chaises, buggies, at first, then cabriolets, cabs, tilburies, gigs, all jolting over cobblestones and potholes.

The builders and owners of urban property were also being made to respect the street. They had to build their houses in a straight line along it and not at random or hit-or-miss as before. They had to fill in the holes and mud puddles in front of them. They had to observe a similar alignment in the promenades and sidewalks, doing away with the constant ups-and-downs from one strip of pavement to another, laid when each houseowner followed his own whim and thought only of what suited him best.

Thus the street was becoming emancipated from the absolute dominion of the "villa," the "manor," the mansion. The street urchin—that vivid expression of the Brazilian street—was showing a growing lack of respect for the great house as he defaced walls and fences with scrawls that were often obscene. Not to mention relieving himself on the doorstep of illustrious portals and even on the stair landing in the halls of the mansion itself.

Yet, though losing face to the street and diminished in its patriarchal functions (which it preserved even in the heart of certain cities) by the cathedral, the factory, the school, the hotel, the laboratory, the drugstore, the house of the nineteenth century continued to exert more influence than any other factor on the social formation of the urban Brazilian. The mansion, more European, produced one social type; the shanty, more African or Indian, produced another. And the street, the square, the church festival, the market, the school, the carnival, all contributed to the communication between classes, the intermingling of races, and the working out of a Brazilian solution for coming to terms with different ways of life, different cultural patterns.

## The Cult of True Womanhood
### Barbara Welter

*During the 19th century, an ideology was being developed calling for American women to return to the home and family.*

SOURCE: Barbara Welter, "The Cult of True Womanhood: 1820–1860," *American Quarterly* 18 (Summer 1966), pp. 151–53, 173–74.
Copyright © 1966 American Studies Association.

*Femininity was idealized in literature, popular imagery, and professional journals and was linked to leisure and domesticity. Some have suggested that the "cult of true womanhood" was, in fact, an attack on the professional and political ambitions of a rising group of middle-class women. Others have suggested that it was an attempt to distinguish between middle-class and working-class women, thereby splitting a potentially powerful new force in American society and culture. The following article by Barbara Welter was crucial in identifying for historians the subtle ways in which culture was used to create separate spheres for women and men and to relegate women to a position below men.*

CONSIDER: *How "putting women on a pedestal" led to their degradation and dependence on men.*

The nineteenth-century American man was a busy builder of bridges and railroads, at work long hours in a materialistic society. The religious values of his forebears were neglected in practice if not in intent, and he occasionally felt some guilt that he had turned this new land, this temple of the chosen people, into one vast countinghouse. But he could salve his conscience by reflecting that he had left behind a hostage, not only to fortune, but to all the values which he held so dear and treated so lightly. Woman, in the cult of True Womanhood presented by the women's magazines, gift annuals and religious literature of the nineteenth century, was the hostage in the home. In a society where values changed frequently, where fortunes rose and fell with frightening rapidity, where social and economic mobility provided instability as well as hope, one thing at least remained the same—a true woman was a true woman, wherever she was found. If anyone, male or female, dared to tamper with the complex of virtues which made up True Womanhood, he was damned immediately as an enemy of God, of civilization and of the Republic. It was a fearful obligation, a solemn responsibility, which the nineteenth-century American woman had—to uphold the pillars of the temple with her frail white hand.

The attributes of True Womanhood, by which a woman judged herself and was judged by her husband, her neighbors and society could be divided into four cardinal virtues—piety, purity, submissiveness and domesticity. Put them all together and they spelled mother, daughter, sister, wife—woman. Without them, no matter whether there was fame, achievement or wealth, all was ashes. With them she was promised happiness and power. . . .

The American woman had her choice—she could define her rights in the way of the women's magazines and insure them by the practice of the requisite virtues, or she could go outside the home, seeking other rewards than love. It was a decision on which, she was told, everything in her world depended. "Yours it is to determine," the Rev. Mr. Stearns solemnly warned from the pulpit, "whether the beautiful order of society . . . shall continue as it has been" or whether "society shall break up and become a chaos of disjointed and unsightly elements." If she chose to listen to other voices than those of her proper mentors, sought other rooms than those of her home, she lost both her happiness and her power, "that almost magic power, which, in her proper sphere, she now wields over the destinies of the world."

But even while the women's magazines and related literature encouraged this ideal of the perfect woman, forces were at work in the nineteenth century which impelled woman herself to change, to play a more creative role in society. The movements for social reform, westward migration, missionary activity, utopian communities, industrialism, the Civil War—all called forth responses from woman which differed from those she was trained to believe were hers by nature and divine decree. The very perfection of True Womanhood, moreover, carried within itself the seeds of its own destruction. For if woman was so very little less than the angels, she should surely take a more active part in running the world, especially since men were making such a hash of things.

## Chapter Questions

1. What were some of the common issues behind the revolutions, rebellions, and protests that marked this period of history in the western hemisphere?

2. In what ways were ideals established when nations gained their independence and carried out thereafter, and in what ways were these ideals not firmly established and not carried out?

3. What methods were used by governments and powerful groups to maintain the status quo and hinder others from either joining the mainstream of society or moving to positions of equality with white, middle-, or upper-class males?

4. Drawing on the sources in this and previous chapters, in what ways should the Americas be most usefully thought of as part of Western civilization during this period? In what ways should the Americas be most usefully thought of as separate from European civilization?

# Chapter Twenty

# Africa, 1500–1880

From the 16th century on, Africa would be increasingly affected by trade and contact with Europeans. However, except for the coastal regions and certain limited areas in South Africa, Angola, and Mozambique much of sub-Saharan Africa would remain dominated by internal developments during the 16th and 17th centuries. By the end of the 17th century, the issue of how the states were to be governed was being worked out. In some cases this led to civil wars (in Benin and Kongo, for example); in others (the Gold Coast, for example) larger and more autocratically governed states evolved; while in others (Senegambia, for example) there was a combination of both processes. In areas such as North Africa and parts of East Africa, changes in the Islamic world were of great consequence. The Ottoman Empire extended its control over large areas of North Africa during the 16th century, and during the 17th century Arabs from Oman gained some control in coastal areas of East Africa. Meanwhile, Islam had fused with African religious traditions and a distinctly local variant of Islam had emerged and was spreading.

The 18th and 19th centuries were crucial both for Africa's relationship to Europe and for the major internal changes that the continent underwent. To outsiders, Africa was a primary supplier of labor and raw materials for European and Muslim markets. European possessions in the Americas alone received some 7 million slaves from 1700 to 1810. After 1810, in the period generally referred to as the period of free trade, Africa supplied a variety of raw materials—hardwoods, palm products, ivory, rubber, and the like—to the expanding industrial centers of Europe and America. Even more fundamental than this external trade were the major political and economic transformations occurring within Africa. In many regions new and strong states were emerging (the Sotho and Asante, for example), while in other regions (Kongo and Zimbabwe, for example) older state systems were consolidating different kinds of constitutional arrangements. But during the second half of the 19th century—particularly after the 1880s—most of Africa would succumb to colonial conquest by European powers.

The sources in this chapter focus on two main topics. The first topic is the internal developments within Africa during these centuries. What was the political nature of these states? What sorts of societies developed, particularly in West Africa? How did individual states interact with others? The second topic involves the growing presence of

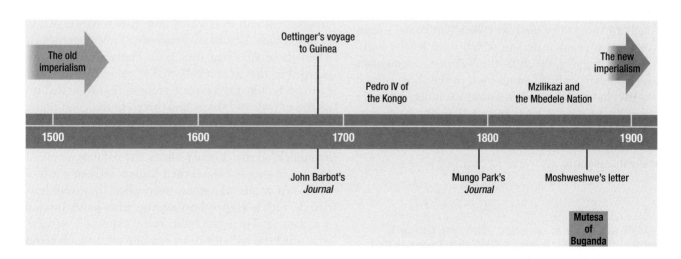

The old imperialism

Oettinger's voyage to Guinea

Pedro IV of the Kongo

Mzilikazi and the Mbedele Nation

The new imperialism

1500    1600    1700    1800    1900

John Barbot's *Journal*

Mungo Park's *Journal*

Moshweshwe's letter

Mutesa of Buganda

foreigners in Africa. How did Africans attempt to deal with Western influence? What were some of the attitudes of African leaders toward Europeans? This second topic will bring us to the last decades of the 19th century, when Africa would be overwhelmed by a new wave of imperialism—a subject that will be explored in Chapter 22.

# PRIMARY SOURCES

## Voyage to Guinea: The European Slave Trade in Africa

*Johann Peter Oettinger*

*Johann Peter Oettinger was a surgeon who took a position with the Brandenburg (Prussia) Africa Company and made the voyage described in this journal in 1692–93. His comments highlight the trading system between Europeans and Africans that had developed on the west African coast since the first European contact in the 1440s. The slaves purchased from this area would be sent to European possessions in the New World, where the sugar boom of the late 17th century created a huge demand for labor. Commerce in slaves was fast becoming the most significant aspect of Euro–African relations from this period until the 19th century.*

CONSIDER: *How international the business aspect of slaving on the African coast was, with agents from many different countries involved; the treatment of the slaves as if they were commodities; the author's attitudes toward Africans; the efforts the Africans made to resist.*

[A]rrangements were made on that ship for accommodating slaves. Large cauldrons were fitted into the upper deck, to prepare food for seven to eight hundred mouths. Water vats in considerable numbers were taken on board, and on top of the ballast another sort of deck was laid, to accommodate the black cargo in several tiers.

Communication between the ships and the shore was maintained by our own boats or, when the sea was too rough for these to be used, so-called "surf boats"—light vessels of a peculiar design, which were locally built. When occupied on the ships, the Negroes . . . sometimes jumped overboard and swam back to the shore, which was in some circumstances a dangerous undertaking. On one such occasion it happened that a young Negro boy had both his legs torn off up to the knees by a shark, and only the mutilated corpse could be brought back to the miserable parents. . . .

SOURCE: Adam Jones, ed. and trans., "Johann Peter Oettinger's Account of His Voyage to Guinea," in *Brandenburg Sources for West African History, 1680–1700* (Stuttgart, Germany: Franz Steiner, 1985), pp. 187, 189, 195–96 as excerpted.

Accra was occupied by the English, Danes and Dutch, and the fortifications formed a belt around the landing place. It is no more favoured with a harbour than any of the other places on the Gold Coast. The land there is even less accessible than elsewhere, as the surfboats must be particularly on their guard against the rocks, against which the rolling waves of the ocean break. To our right, half a mile further east, lay Fort Christiansborg, on a high shore covered with beautiful vegetation and shaded by palm trees. In the distance a wooded chain of hills stood out against the horizon. An extremely colourful, picturesquely higgledy-piggledy crowd of naked children and several hundred dirty Negroes, wearing cotton garments which shone in every colour of the rainbow, received us as soon as we had been safely dragged . . . ashore and made our entry. During our stay at Accra a lively, friendly relationship developed between our captain and the Commandant. Our chief factor Hoffmann made use of the time to land silk goods, linen, gunpowder, glass beads, etc. and exchange them for gold and slaves. A male slave cost about 25 thaler, a female 20 to 22, a boy 12 to 14 and a girl about 10. . . .

. . . As soon as a sufficient number of the unfortunate victims were collected, they were examined by me: the healthy and strong ones were bought, whereas the *magrones*—those who had fingers or teeth missing or were disabled—were rejected. The slaves who had been bought then had to kneel down, twenty or thirty at a time; their right shoulder was smeared with palm oil and branded with an iron which bore the initials C AB C (*Churfürstlich-Afrikanisch-Brandenburgische Compagnie*). Then those who had thus been marked were strictly guarded in the quarters allotted to them. When about fifty or a hundred slaves were present, they were tied together in twos and threes and driven to the coast under escort. The task of guarding the transport was given to me, and for that purpose I was carried in the rear in a hammock, so that I could survey the column. Some of these poor people obeyed their leaders without a will of their own or any resistance, even when they were hurried on with a whip; others, on the other hand, howled and danced. There were also many, especially women, who filled the air with heart-rending cries which could hardly be drowned by the drums or other noisy instruments and often cut me to the quick. But it did not lie in my power to alter the fate of these unfortunates. When we reached the coast, a pre-arranged signal was given and the ship's boats came ashore to take the black cargo on board.

On the way back, the negro escorts, numbering about a hundred, were employed to carry the merchandize landed from the ship. I again had the duty of leading and supervising them, which, given the thievish . . . character of these wretched scoundrels, involved difficulties of many kinds. Not only did the carriers have to be induced by kindness or strictness to walk faster, but often, either on purpose or accidentally, they dropped those barrels which they suspected to contain the dainty little shells, or damaged them in other ways, whereby a portion of the contents which fell out found its way into their large straw hats.

On one of these trips I caught the thieves in the act and wanted to flog them with my sword. But I only made things worse; for the fellows threw the barrel down and fled, so that I had trouble getting it carried to its destination by other carriers.

On 4 April the ship was at last loaded with 738 slaves, male and female, so that we could take our leave of the king and return to the ships. As on our arrival, we were carried back to the beach in palanquins. Then we treated our carriers and attendants with brandy and climbed into the boat.

## Government, Taxes, and War in Benin

### John Barbot

*During the 17th century, Benin, on the coast of West Africa, became one of the most powerful and wealthy states in the region. In the last quarter of the 17th century, John Barbot, a private trader, traveled to West Africa. The following are excerpts from a combination of two journals, including material by others, containing information collected between the 1630s and 1700. Here he describes Benin's political system, its taxation policies, and its conflicts with neighboring states.*

CONSIDER: *The nature of this political system and its complexity; how the social system is reflected in the system of taxation; how power is maintained by military means.*

The government of Benin is principally vested in the king, and three chief ministers, call'd great *Veadors*; that is, intendants, or overseers; besides the great marshall of the crown, who is intrusted with the affairs relating to war, as the three others are with the administration of justice, and the management of the revenue; and all four are obliged to take their circuits throughout the several

provinces, from time to time, to inspect into the condition of the country, and the administration of the governors and justices in each district, that peace and good order may be kept as much as possible. Those chief ministers of state have under them each his own particular officers and assistants in the discharge of their posts and places. They call the first of the three aforemention'd ministers of state, the *Onegwa*, and second *Ossade*, and the third *Arribon*.

They reside constantly at court, as being the king's privy council, to advise him on all emergencies and affairs of the nation; and any person that wants to apply to the prince, must address himself first to them, and they acquaint the king with the petitioner's business, and return his answer accordingly: but commonly, as in other countries, they will only inform the king with what they please themselves; and so in his name, act very arbitrarily over the subjects. Whence it may well be inferr'd, that the government is entirely in their hands; for it is very seldom they will favour a person so far as to admit him to the king's presence, to represent his own affairs to that prince: and every body knowing their great authority, endeavours on all occasions to gain their favour as much as possible, by large gratifications and presents, in order to succeed in their affairs at court, for which reason their offices and posts are of very great profit to them.

Besides these four chief ministers of state, there are two other inferior ranks about the king: the first is composed of those they call *Reis de Ruas*, signifying in *Portuguese*, kings of streets, some of whom preside over the commonalty, and others over the slaves; some again over military affairs; others over affairs relating to cattle and the fruits of the earth, &c. there being supervisors or intendants over every thing that can be thought of, in order to keep all things in a due regular way.

*

The king's income is very great, his dominions being so large, and having such a number of governors, and other inferior officers, each of whom is obliged, according to his post, to pay into the king's treasury so many bags of *Boejies*, some more some less, which all together amount to a prodigious sum; and other officers of inferior rank are to pay in their taxes in cattle, chicken, fruits, roots and cloths, or any other things that can be useful to the king's household; which is so great a quantity, that it doth not cost the king a penny throughout the year to maintain and subsist his family; so that there is yearly a considerable increase of money in his treasury. Add to all this, the duties and tolls on imported or exported goods, paid in all trading places, to the respective *Veadors* and other officers, which are also partly convey'd to the treasury; and were the collectors thereof just and honest,

SOURCE: Awnsham and John Churchill eds., *A Collection of Voyages*, vol. V (London: J. Walthoe, 1732), pp. 355–75 *passim*.

so as not to defraud the prince of a considerable part, these would amount to an incredible sum.

*

This prince is perpetually at war with one nation or other that borders on the northern part of his dominions, and sometimes with another north-west of his kingdom, which are all potent people, but little or not at all known to *Europeans*, over whom he obtains from time to time considerable advantages, subduing large portions of those unknown countries, and raising great contributions, which are partly paid him in jasper, and other valuable goods of the product of those countries. Wherewith, together with his own plentiful revenue, he is able, upon occasion, to maintain an army of an hundred thousand horse and foot; but, for the most part, he doth not keep above thirty thousand men, which renders him more formidable to his neighbours than any other *Guinea* king: nor is there any other throughout all *Guinea*, that has so many vassals and tributary kings under him; as for instance, those of *Istanna, Forcado, Jaboe, Issabo* and *Oedoba*, from whom he receives considerable yearly tributes, except from him of *Issabo*, who, though much more potent than all the others, yet pays the least.

## Travels in the Interior Districts of Africa: Urban Life and Women in West Africa
### *Mungo Park*

*Beginning in the 11th century, some Arabs had established themselves in urban and commercial centers of West Africa. But it was not until the late 18th and early 19th centuries that many Europeans penetrated beyond the coast into the interior of West Africa. Mungo Park, a Scottish doctor, was one of the earliest of these. He reached the long-sought Niger River at Segu (Sego), the capital of Bambarra, in 1796. In the following excerpts from his journal he describes Sego, where the King of Bambarra resided, and then his interactions with women in a nearby village.*

CONSIDER: *The qualities of the urban areas Mungo Park describes; the significance of the presence of Moorish mosques; the involvement of the king in the slave trade; the role and independence of women.*

Sego, the capital of Bambarra, at which I had now arrived, consists, properly speaking, of four distinct towns; two on the northern bank of the Niger, called Sego Korro and Sego Boo; and two on the southern bank, called Sego Soo Korro and Sego See Korro. They are all surrounded with high mud-walls; the houses are built of

SOURCE: Mungo Park, *Travels in the Interior Districts of Africa* (London, 1799), pp. 195–98.

clay, of a square form, with flat roofs; some of them have two stories, and many of them are whitewashed. Besides these buildings, Moorish mosques are seen in every quarter; and the streets, though narrow, are broad enough for every useful purpose, in a country where wheel carriages are entirely unknown. From the best inquiries I could make, I have reason to believe that Sego contains altogether about thirty thousand inhabitants. The King of Bambarra constantly resides at Sego See Korro; he employs a great many slaves in conveying people over the river, and the money they receive (though the fare is only ten Kowrie shells for each individual) furnishes a considerable revenue to the king, in the course of a year. . . .

. . . The view of this extensive city; the numerous canoes upon the river; the crowded population, and the cultivated state of the surrounding country, formed altogether a prospect of civilization and magnificence, which I little expected to find in the bosom of Africa.

I waited more than two hours, without having an opportunity of crossing the river; during which time the people who had crossed, carried information to Mansong the King, that a white man was waiting for a passage, and was coming to see him. He immediately sent over one of his chief men, who informed me that the king could not possibly see me, until he knew what had brought me into his country; and that I must not presume to cross the river without the king's permission. He therefore advised me to lodge at a distant village, to which he pointed, for the night; and said that in the morning he would give me further instructions how to conduct myself. This was very discouraging. However, as there was no remedy, I set off for the village; where I found, to my great mortification, that no person would admit me into his house. I was regarded with astonishment and fear, and was obliged to sit all day without victuals, in the shade of a tree; and the night threatened to be very uncomfortable, for the wind rose, and there was great appearance of a heavy rain; and the wild beasts are so very numerous in the neighbourhood, that I should have been under the necessity of climbing up the tree, and resting amongst the branches. About sunset, however, as I was preparing to pass the night in this manner, and had turned my horse loose, that he might graze at liberty, a woman, returning from the labours of the field, stopped to observe me, and perceiving that I was weary and dejected, inquired into my situation, which I briefly explained to her; whereupon, with looks of great compassion, she took up my saddle and bridle, and told me to follow her. Having conducted me into her hut, she lighted up a lamp, spread a mat on the floor, and told me I might remain there for the night. Finding that I was very hungry, she said she would procure me something to eat. She accordingly went out, and returned in a short time with a very fine fish; which, having caused to be half boiled upon some embers, she gave me for supper. The rites of hospitality being thus performed towards a stranger in distress; my worthy benefactress (pointing to the mat, and telling me I might sleep there without apprehension) called to the female part of her family, who had stood gazing on me all the while in fixed astonishment, to resume their task of spinning cotton; in which they continued to employ themselves great part of the night. They lightened their labour by songs, one of which was composed extempore; for I was myself the subject of it. It was sung by one of the young women, the rest joining in a sort of chorus. The air was sweet and plaintive, and the words, literally translated, were these. "The winds roared, and the rains fell. The poor white man, faint and weary, came and sat under our tree. He has no mother to bring him milk; no wife to grind his corn. *Chorus.* Let us pity the white man; no mother has he, &c. &c." Trifling as this recital may appear to the reader, to a person in my situation, the circumstance was affecting in the highest degree. I was oppressed by such unexpected kindness; and sleep fled from my eyes. In the morning I presented my compassionate landlady with two of the four brass buttons which remained on my waistcoat; the only recompence I could make her.

## The Ndebele Nation in Central Africa
*Robert Moffat*

*The Ndebele nation was a military state that rose to power in Southern Africa after the 1820s when its ruler, Mzilikazi, broke away from Shaka, the founder of the great Zulu military state in South Africa. The autocratic Mzilikazi enjoyed success in wars against various Central and South African peoples but was defeated by a combination of Boer (Afrikaner) and African allies in 1837–38. He moved north with his followers to the Rhodesian uplands, where he ruled, supported by a strong army and centralized political control, until 1868. The following selection is by Robert Moffat, a British missionary who developed a close relationship with Mzilikazi. Here Moffat records the trial and judgment of a noble warrior accused of a crime and brought before Mzilikazi.*

CONSIDER: *Factors involved in this system of justice; the importance of class and rank in Ndebele society.*

He [the accused] was a man of rank, and what was called an Entuna (an officer), who wore on his head the usual badge of dignity. He was brought to head-quarters. His arm bore no shield, nor his hand a spear; he had been divested of these, which had been his glory. He was brought into the presence of the king, and his chief council, charged with a crime, for which it was in vain to expect pardon, even at the hands of a more humane gov-

ernment. He bowed his fine elastic figure, and kneeled before the judge. The case was investigated silently, which gave solemnity to the scene. Not a whisper was heard among the listening audience, and the voices of the council were only audible to each other, and the nearest spectators. The prisoner, though on his knees, had something dignified and noble in his mien. Not a muscle of his countenance moved, but his bright black eyes indicated a feeling of intense interest, which the moving balance between life and death only could produce. The case required little investigation; the charges were clearly substantiated, and the culprit pleaded guilty. But, alas! he knew it was at a bar where none ever heard the heart-reviving sound of pardon, even for offences small compared with his. A pause ensued, during which the silence of death pervaded the assembly. At length the monarch spoke, and, addressing the prisoner, said, "You are a dead man, but I shall do to-day what I never did before; I spare your life for the sake of my friend and father"—pointing to the spot where I . . . stood. "I know his heart weeps at the shedding of blood; for his sake I spare your life; he has travelled from a far country to see me, and he has made my heart white; but he tells me that to take away life is an awful thing, and never can be undone again. He has pleaded with me not to go to war, nor destroy life. I wish him, when he returns to his own home again, to return with a heart as white as he has made mine. I spare you for his sake, for I love him, and he has saved the lives of my people. But," continued the king, "you must be degraded for life; you must no more associate with the nobles of the land, nor enter the towns of the princes of the people; nor ever again mingle in the dance of the mighty. Go to the poor of the field, and let your companions be the inhabitants of the desert." The sentence passed, the pardoned man was expected to bow in grateful adoration to him whom he was wont to look upon and exalt in songs applicable only to One to whom belongs universal sway and the destinies of man. But, no! holding his hands clasped on his bosom, he replied, "O king, afflict not my heart! I have merited thy displeasure; let me be slain like the warrior; I cannot live with the poor." And, raising his hand to the ring he wore on his brow, he continued, "How can I live among the dogs of the king, and disgrace these badges of honour which I won among the spears and shields of the mighty? No, I cannot live! Let me die, O Pezoolu!" His request was granted.

## Letter to Sir George Grey: Conflict and Diplomacy in South Africa
*Moshweshewe*

*In the interior regions of South Africa, Africans had effectively blocked European expansion from the Cape Coast and*

SOURCE: Robert Moffat, *Missionary Labours and Scenes in Southern Africa* (London: J. Snow, 1842), pp. 539–41.

*Natal settlements for most of the 18th century. However, from the early 1800s onward, the original Dutch settlers (now known as Afrikaners) moved inward to avoid exactions from the new British overlords. There were increasing clashes between the newcomers and the African populations as they attempted to protect their land from being expropriated by the Afrikaners. The Sothos [Basutos], led by their king Moshweshewe, used skillful diplomacy to exploit the conflicts between the British and the Afrikaners. They were among the few African peoples in South Africa to maintain some territorial integrity in the wake of later European takeover. The lands eventually became the independent state of Lesotho in 1966. The following letter from Moshweshewe to Sir George Grey, written in 1858, is an excellent demonstration of Moshweshewe's diplomatic skill.*

CONSIDER: *How much the letter reveals about black–white relations in South Africa at the time; how the king achieved his aim of preserving his people's independence against European aggression; how much the letter reveals about internal African political organization at the time.*

Thaba Bosigo, June, 1858.

Your Excellency,—it may scarcely appear necessary to lay before Your Excellency any lengthened details of what has taken place between the Orange Free State and myself. I know that you have followed with interest the transactions which have led to the commencement of hostilities, and you have heard with pain of the horrors occasioned by the war, at present suspended in the hopes that peace may be restored by Your Excellency's mediation.

Allow me, however, to bring to your remembrance the following circumstances:—About twenty-five years ago my knowledge of the White men and their laws was very limited. I knew merely that mighty nations existed, and among them was the English. These, the blacks who were acquainted with them, praised for their justice. Unfortunately it was not with the English Government that my first intercourse with the whites commenced. People who had come from the Colony first presented themselves to us, they called themselves Boers. I thought all white men were honest. Some of these Boers asked permission to live upon our borders. I was led to believe they would live with me as my own people lived, that is, looking to me as to a father and a friend.

About sixteen years since, one of the Governors of the Colony, Sir George Napier, marked down my limits on a treaty he made with me. I was to be ruler within those limits. A short time after, another Governor came, it was Sir P. Maitland. The Boers then began to talk of *their right* to places I had then lent to them. Sir P. Mait-

land told me those people were subjects of the Queen, and should be kept under proper control; he did not tell me that he recognised any right they had to land within my country, but as it was difficult to take them away, it was proposed that all desiring to be under the British rule should live in that part near the meeting of the Orange and Caledon rivers.

Then came Sir Harry Smith, and he told me not to deprive any chief of their lands or their rights, he would see justice done to all, but in order to do so, he would make the Queen's Laws extend over every white man. He said the Whites and Blacks were to live together in peace. I could not understand what he would do. I thought it would be something very just, and that he was to keep the Boers in my land under proper control, and that I should hear no more of their claiming the places they lived on as their exclusive property. But instead of this, I now heard that the Boers consider all those farms as their own, and were buying and selling them one to the other, and driving out by one means or another my own people.

In vain I remonstrated. Sir Harry Smith had sent Warden to govern in the Sovereignty. He listened to the Boers, and he proposed that all the land in which those Boers' farms were should be taken from me. I was at that time in trouble, for Sikonyela and the Korannas were tormenting me and my people by stealing and killing; they said openly the Major gave them orders to do so, and I have proof he did so. One day he sent me a map and said, sign that, and I will tell those people (Mantatis and Korannas) to leave off fighting: if you do not sign the map, I cannot help you in any way. I thought the Major was doing very improperly and unjustly. I was told to appeal to the Queen to put an end to this injustice. I did not wish to grieve Her Majesty by causing a war with her people. I was told if I did not sign the map, it would be the beginning of a great war. I signed, but soon after I sent my cry to the Queen. I begged Her to investigate my case and remove 'the line,' as it was called, by which my land was ruined. I thought justice would soon be done, and Warden put to rights. . . .

I tried my utmost to satisfy them and avert war. I punished thieves, and sent my son Nehemiah and others to watch the part of the country near the Boers, and thus check stealing. In this he was successful, thieving did cease. We were at peace for a time. In the commencement of the present year (1858) my people living near farmers received orders to remove from their places. This again caused the fire to burn, still we tried to keep all quiet, but the Boers went further and further day by day in troubling the Basutos and threatening war. The President (Boshof) spoke of Warden's line, this was as though he had really fired upon us with his guns. Still I tried to avert war.

It was not possible, it was commenced by the Boers in massacring my people of Beersheba, and ruining that

SOURCE: G. McC. Theal, ed., *The Basutoland Records* II (Capetown: Government of Capetown, 1883), pp. 384–88.

station, against the people of which there was not a shadow of a complaint ever brought forward. Poor people, they thought their honesty and love for Christianity would be a shield for them, and that the white people would attack in the first place, if they attacked at all, those who they said were thieves. I ordered my people then all to retreat towards my residence, and let the fury of the Boers be spent upon an empty land; unfortunately some skirmishes took place, some Boers were killed, some of my people also. We need not wonder at this, such is war! But I will speak of many Basutos who were taken prisoners by the Whites and then killed, most cruelly. If you require me to bring forward these cases, I will do so. I will however speak of the horrible doings of the Boers at Morija, they there burnt down the Missionary's house, carried off much goods belonging to the Mission, and pillaged and shamefully defiled the Church Buildings.

I had given orders that no farms should be burnt, and my orders were obeyed till my people saw village after village burnt off, and the corn destroyed, they then carried destruction among the enemy's homes.

On coming to my mountain, the Boers found I was prepared to check their progress, and they consequently retired. My intention was then to have followed them up, and to have shewn them that my people could also carry on offensive operations, believing that having once experienced the horrors of war in their midst, I should not soon be troubled by them again.

My bands were getting ready to make a descent upon them, when the Boers thought proper to make request for a cessation of hostilities. I knew what misery I should bring upon the country by leaving the Basutos to ravage the Boer places, and therefore I have agreed to the proposal of Mr. J. P. Hoffman. I cannot say that I do so with the consent of my people, for many of those who suffered by the enemy were anxious to recover their losses.

If they have remained quiet, it has been owing to my persuasions and my promises that they might have good hope of justice,—Your Excellency having consented to act as arbitrator between the Boers and Basutos. With the expectation of soon meeting you, I remain, etc.,

Mark ✕ of Moshesh. Chief of the Basutos.

## Culture and Imperialism in East Africa
### Ernest Linant de Fellefonds

*From the 1830s to 1885, European missionaries reopened the cultural and religious exchanges that the Portuguese and Africans had initiated in the 16th century. These new openings were happening at a time when in many parts of Africa rulers were increasingly willing to welcome European trade as well as ideas.*

*Kabaka Mutesa (M'Tesa) of Buganda in the interior of East Africa was one such ruler. Born around 1838, Mutesa* *made Buganda a major power in East Africa through wars against neighboring states. He entertained both Christians and Muslims, seeking to play them against each other to preserve his kingdom's independence in an era of growing imperialism. His meetings with European missionaries illustrate his attempts to come to terms with the new knowledge, which he realized was necessary to maintain his country's independence. Ernest Linant de Fellefonds, a Roman Catholic missionary of French ancestry, wrote the following observation of Kabaka Mutesa (M'Tesa) I in 1875.*

CONSIDER: *Fellefonds' perspective of the European as teacher, his disdain for both African and Islamic knowledge, and his reaction to Mutesa's intelligence; the king's concern that his closest advisers be exposed to the new knowledge; the existence of a group of Africans already literate in European languages.*

*21, 22, 23 April*—I have had many different discussions with M'Tesa during the last three days. Our conversation had dwelled on all the different powerful forces of the world in turn: America, England, France, Germany, Russia, the Ottoman Empire, constitutions, government, military might, production, industry and religion.

The King's sister was present at these sessions. The daughters and sisters of the King never go on foot; they are always carried by their slaves.

*25th April*—M'Tesa summoned me at eleven o'clock at the same time as the Fakir of the Xoderia.[1] Our talk therefore was exclusively about the Koran. The poor Fakir was at a loss as to how to answer all the King's questions. I had to give him some help.

I informed the King of the system of trade by means of money. The value of all goods is based on the tallari. This system makes trade and transactions easier.

*27th April*—In answer to all M'Tesa's questions concerning the earth, the sun, the moon, the stars and the sky and in order to make him understand the movements of the heavenly bodies, I had to make shapes on a board, the heavenly bodies being represented by little glass balls. The lecture took place today. The gathering was not very large: the two viziers Katikiro and Chambarango, four leading officers, the two scribes and a few favourites. The four cardinal points, the rotation of the earth, its movement round the sun, night and day, the seasons, the movement of the moon round the earth and its phases (which I did by means of a mirror) and the general movement of our system in space.

M'Tesa grasped everything perfectly. We were seated on the ground in a circle and there was a very friendly atmosphere. I have never seen M'Tesa so happy. It was the first time that we had spoken to each other directly

SOURCE: D. A. Low, *Mind of Buganda: Documents of the Modern History of an African Kingdom* (Berkeley: University of California Press), pp. 2–3.
[1]A Muslim cleric from the upper Nile region.

without using interpreters, and this is against all the laws of etiquette. M'Tesa himself explained afterwards to the wonder-struck gathering. What was so surprising was that M'Tesa was able to inspire in his associates and in many of his people this quest for understanding, for self-instruction and for knowledge. There is great rivalry among them and they are very eager to improve. They are an inquiring, observant, intelligent people with minds longing for the learning of white people whose superiority they recognize; and with the help of a mission having farmers, carpenters and smiths amongst them,

these Gandas will soon become an industrial people. This being so, Ganda would be the centre of civilization of all this part of Africa. . . .

I left the King at two o'clock after we had arranged to meet again at four. The same people were there as in the morning. The talk was of Genesis. M'Tesa had the story of Genesis from the Creation to the Flood taken down on a writing-tablet. We parted at nightfall. M'Tesa is spellbound and I shall be able to obtain all I want from him. . . .

# VISUAL SOURCES

## The Oba of Benin

*The West Africans were skilled sculptors and carvers of metal, terra-cotta, and ivory. Perhaps the most famous of their metal-works were the elaborate Benin bronzes, of which this is a striking example. Probably dating from the 16th, 17th, or 18th century, when Benin was at its height of wealth and power, this shows the Oba (king) of Benin mounted on a horse and surrounded protectively by his subordinates. The cords or necklaces around his neck as well as his size and position reveal his status as monarch.*

CONSIDER: *The possible meanings of this image to contemporary viewers; the qualities of the society that produced this.*

**Illustration 20–1**   The Metropolitan Museum of Art, The Michael C. Rockefeller Memorial Collection, Gift of Nelson A. Rockefeller, 1965. (1978.412.309) Photograph © 1983.

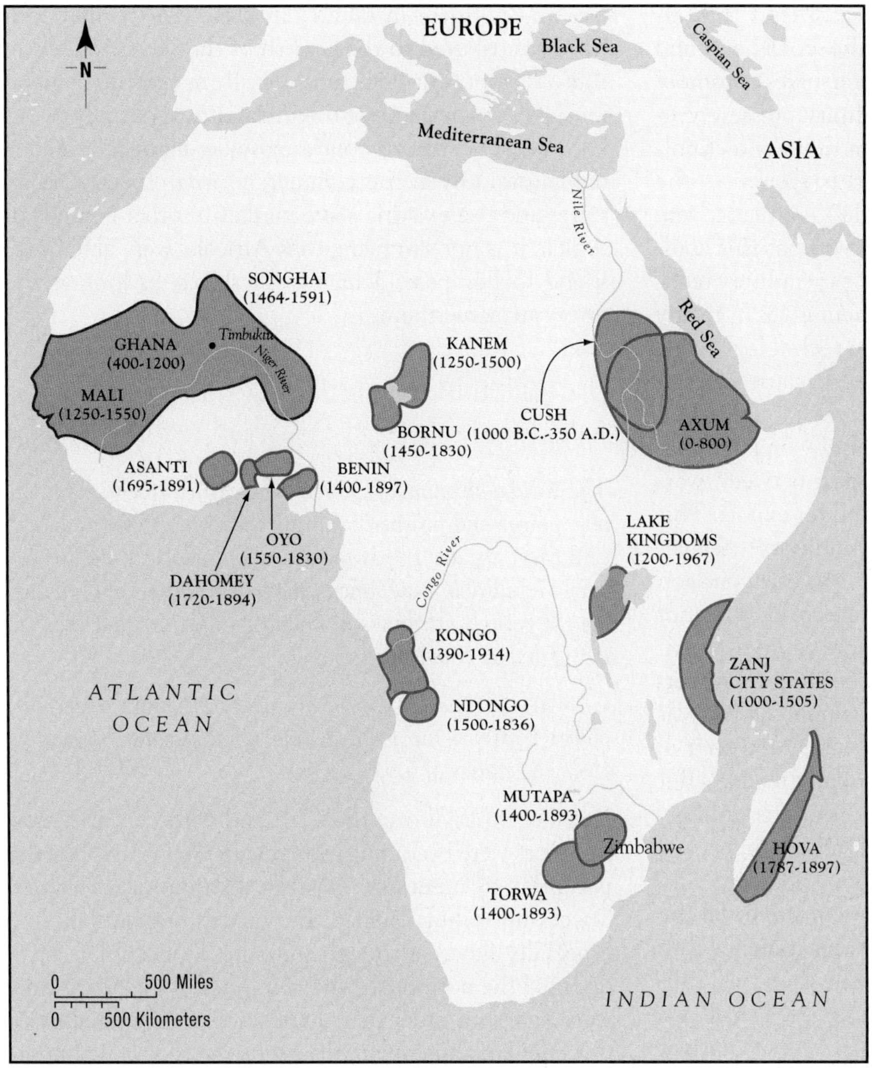

## Indigenous States in Sub-Saharan Africa to the Nineteenth Century

*This map shows some of the major states of sub-Saharan Africa to the 19th century. Though it's far from complete, it indicates the long and varied history of civilizations throughout Africa. (The presence of many small political units precludes including them on the map.) It also reveals how dynamic the political history of some areas, such as West Africa, was, with various states competing with and succeeding each other over time. When viewed with the maps in Chapter 22 on the new imperialism, it allows a fuller understanding of the significance of the late-19th-century conquests and partitions of Africa by Europeans.*

CONSIDER: *The relationship between states and their location near rivers; the size of states and changing political boundaries over time.*

**Map 20–1**

# SECONDARY SOURCES

## Africa and Africans in the Making of the Atlantic World, 1400–1680: The Atlantic Slave Trade

*John K. Thornton*

Europeans began arriving along the Atlantic coast of Africa in the 15th and 16th centuries. They were drawn there mainly for the trade in gold, spices, and other products, among them slaves. However, Europeans had no military success against African states as they were later to achieve against various American peoples. In the following excerpt, John Thornton

SOURCE: John K. Thornton, *Africa and Africans in the Making of the Atlantic World, 1400–1680* (New York: Cambridge University Press, 1992), pp. 98–99, 125, as excerpted.

shows why African leaders and merchants were willing and able to sell as many as 15 million people to European and American merchants over the next four centuries.

CONSIDER: *How the political and economic situation in Atlantic Africa both was conducive to entry by European slave merchants and averted possible conquest; what factors made African decision makers continue the trade for so long.*

Africans were not under any direct commercial or economic pressure to deal in slaves. Furthermore, we have seen not only that Africans accepted the institution of slavery in their own societies, but that the special place of slaves as private productive property made slavery widespread. At the beginning, at least, Europeans were only tapping existing slave markets. Nevertheless, one need not accept that these factors alone can explain the slave trade. There are scholars who contend that although Europeans did not invade the continent and take slaves themselves, they did nevertheless promote the slave trade through indirect military pressure created by European control of important military technology, such as horses and guns. In this scenario—the "gun–slave cycle" or "horse–slave cycle"—Africans were compelled to trade in slaves, because without this commerce they could not obtain the necessary military technology (guns and horses) to defend themselves from any enemy. Furthermore, possession of the technology made them more capable of obtaining slaves, because successful war guaranteed large supplies of slaves. . . .

The contemporary evidence strongly supports the idea that there was a direct connection between wars and slavery, both for domestic work and for export. This did not mean that there was no nonmilitary enslavement, of course. Judicial enslavement was one common way of obtaining slaves, and judges, moreover, were not above distorting the law to provide more captives or enslaving distant relatives of guilty parties. Jesuit observers believed that this was common in Ndongo as early as 1600, and missionary travelers often commented on it in the seventeenth-century Upper Guinea region. But however scandalous this may have been, it is unlikely that judicial enslavement accounted for more than a few percent of the total exports from Africa.

Thus the fact that military enslavement was by far the most significant method is important, for it means that rulers were not, for the most part, selling their own subjects but people whom they, at least, regarded as aliens. The fact that many exported slaves were recent captives means that they were drawn from those captured in the course of warfare who had not yet been given an alternative employment within Africa. In these cases, rulers were deciding to forgo the potential future use of these slaves. Some of the exports were slaves whom local masters wished to dispose of for one reason or another and those who had been captured locally by brigands or judicially enslaved. . . .

In conclusion, then, we must accept that African participation in the slave trade was voluntary and under the control of African decision makers. This was not just at the surface level of daily exchange but even at deeper levels. Europeans possessed no means, either economic or military, to compel African leaders to sell slaves.

The willingness of Africa's commercial and political elite to supply slaves should be sought in their own internal dynamics and history. Institutional factors predisposed African societies to hold slaves, and the development of Africa's domestic economy encouraged large-scale trading and possession of slaves long before Europeans visited African shores. The increase in warfare and political instability in some regions may well have contributed to the growth of the slave trade from those regions, but one cannot easily assign the demand for slaves as the cause of the instability, especially as our knowledge of African politics provides many more internal causes. Given the commercial interests of African states and the existing slave market in private hands in Africa, it is not surprising that Africans were able to respond to European demands for slaves, as long as the prices attracted them.

## Disruption in the Yoruba Kingdom of Oyo
### Robin Law

*The Yoruba kingdom of Oyo in West Africa rose to considerable power and prosperity during the 16th, 17th, and 18th centuries. By the 1830s the kingdom collapsed due to civil war. Here Robin Law, one of the few historians of Oyo during the period, attributes its collapse to factors that arose in the 17th and 18th centuries.*

CONSIDER: *The economic and military factors underlying power in Oyo; the political and administrative system of Oyo; the causes of Oyo's decline.*

It is clear that during the 17th and 18th centuries new resources were becoming available in Oyo which had the potential to upset the existing distribution of power. Successful military expansion yielded booty, including especially slaves: although some modern scholars have disputed the notion that in precolonial West Africa wars were fought in order to acquire slaves, oral testimony in Oyo regularly and explicitly asserts the economic importance of war as a source of captives. The territorial expansion of Oyo, effected by these military successes, also increased the amount of tribute coming into the capital city: tribute appears to have been exacted principally in money (cowries), trade goods, and slaves. The expansion of the Atlantic slave trade, in which the Oyo sold not only their own war captives but also slaves purchased from the countries further north, likewise presented new opportunities for enrichment. It seems a reasonable inference that some light can be thrown on the background to the political tensions in Oyo by looking at what was happening to these newly available resources.

With regard to the booty derived from successful warfare, much depends upon the details of the military organization of Oyo, which unfortunately are very unclear. Although in principle all adult males were liable

SOURCE: Robin Law, "Making Sense of a Traditional Narrative: Political Disintegration in the Kingdom of Oyo," in *Cahiers d'études Africaines*, vol. 23 (1982), pp. 397–98.

for military service, this in practice operated only in time of crisis. Warfare was normally the business of a small group of specialists, the war chiefs and their trained warriors, recruited largely from the slaves and junior relatives of their households: as Clapperton observed in 1826, 'the military force consists of the caboceers [chiefs] and their own immediate retainers.' The *alafin* had his own private army, recruited from among the slaves of the palace. It appears, however, that the principal military force in the capital consisted of seventy war chiefs called the *eso*, who lived in the non-royal wards of the city and came under the authority of the *Oyo mesi*. The army of the capital was thus controlled mainly by the *Oyo mesi*, and was normally commanded by the *basorun*. (That the balance of military power in the capital lay with the *Oyo mesi* rather than with the *alafin* is confirmed by the fact that *alafin* Abiodun in 1774 had to call in military assistance from outside the city, under the *are ona kakamfo*, to overthrow *basorun* Gaha.) Although the *alafin* was entitled to receive a share of the slaves and other booty taken by the army, the direct proceeds of warfare probably went predominantly to the non-royal chiefs.

The situation with regard to tribute is more complicated. Within the Oyo kingdom, that of the subordinate towns was normally delivered to the *alafin* through titleholders of the capital, who kept a share of it. In other smaller Yoruba kingdoms in the 19th century, the collection was controlled entirely by the non-royal chiefs, and it seems likely that in Oyo also the *Oyo mesi* originally monopolized this function. By the 19th century, however, the *alafin* was making extensive use of women and slave officials of the palace as intermediaries in the transmission of tribute, and the *Oyo mesi* did not control all the subordinate towns. Moreover, it appears that the tribute paid by dependencies of Oyo outside the boundaries of the kingdom proper, such as the Egba and Dahomey, was collected directly by the *alafin's* slave officials. It thus appears that the *alafin* was the principal beneficiary from the territorial expansion of the Oyo empire.

The development of commerce, in slaves and other commodities, offered opportunities of enrichment to both the palace and the non-royal wards. There was no royal monopoly of trade in Oyo, and both the *alafin* and the *Oyo mesi* could employ their agents in trade. Both, moreover, had ready access to supplies of the most important commodity, slaves, the *Oyo mesi* principally as booty from their military activities, the *alafin* probably mainly through tribute. The *alafin* did, however, ensure competitive advantages for his agents by exempting them from the payment of market dues and road tolls throughout the kingdom and requiring provincial rulers to provide them with free lodgings.

# Beyond Decline: The Kingdom of the Kongo in the Eighteenth and Nineteenth Centuries
*Susan Herlin Broadhead*

*The kingdom of the Kongo, located on the west coast of central Africa, had been a relatively strong, centralized state by the time the Portuguese arrived in the 15th century. Despite periods of difficulties, both with the Portuguese and internally, the kingdom remained powerful until its collapse during the second part of the 17th century. In 1709, when the kingdom was restored under king Pedro IV after more than half a century of civil war, it was much less centralized and the major ruling families continued to compete. Over the following century and a half, no ruler was able to assert control over all parts of the country or to defeat completely the rival families. It was this weakness in the political system that laid the foundations for the Portuguese takeover at the end of the 19th century. In the following selection, Susan Broadhead analyzes the political beliefs of the Bakongo (Kongo) people and the structure of the Kongo state that help explain Portuguese conquest.*

CONSIDER: *The Kongo conception of political order and social hierarchy; the effects of this political ideology on the integrity of the state; how this political perspective compares to those in non-African societies during the same period.*

Before we can proceed with their history, it is necessary to consider something of what the Bakongo people believed about politics and right government. What were the basic elements of the political system from the point of view of those principles of political theory and action generally accepted by the public? By what models did they form their organizations, judge their leaders and settle their quarrels? The outline of these principles can be inferred by carefully reading historical data in the light of modern political theory.

The first principle, understood by all, was (and is) that politics—the exercise of power in this world—is not a purely secular activity. On the contrary, it is intrinsically sacred, and sacred power can be controlled only by the appropriate ritual means. This is clearly demonstrated by the overlapping functions and insignia of the major spiritual specialists of the Bakongo—chief, magician, witch and prophet—all of whom share the ability to see things supernaturally and to participate in the power of darkness, that is, of death.

Building on this fundamental premise, two sets of organizing principles can be identified—one hierarchical

SOURCE: Susan Herlin Broadhead, "Beyond Decline: The Kingdom of the Kongo in the Eighteenth and Nineteenth Centuries," in *International Journal of African Historical Studies*, 1980, pp. 623–27, as excerpted.

and ideal, the other egalitarian and pragmatic. There were two kinds of hierarchical structures: one based in the ritually powerful institution of sacred chief and the other on the more generalized idea of hierarchical relationships between elder and junior (fathers–sons, patrons–clients, masters–slaves) which operated at all levels of society. In the kingdom hierarchy was, of course, associated with the activities of a political elite. In practice, however, these groups did not always have the resources to impose their authority; they had to attract followers through patronage, prestige or purchase.

The apex of the Bakongo political hierarchy was occupied in theory by the king at Mbanza Kongo, who embodied the ideal combination of sacred power and secular authority. Conceptually this was paralleled in the role of all invested chiefs, that is, political leaders whose investiture confirmed in them the sacred power of life and death. Investiture required not only personal qualification, but also hierarchy. Investment was performed by a superior on an inferior. It further required wealth since regalia were only conferred on those who could pay the required fees and who might reasonably be expected to contribute periodic tribute and military assistance. In the centralized structure of the seventeenth century, the king was elected by a committee, but subordinate titles were appointed from the center. The structure of investiture remained in the eighteenth and nineteenth centuries, although the power to select officials devolved upon the localities. . . .

However, invested chiefs, of whom the king at Mbanza Kongo was the senior, had ritual powers. . . . The supernatural powers of the invested chiefs in eighteenth and nineteenth century Kongo derived from at least two sources: the ritual strength of the ancient cult of the local priests of the land and the powers of the Christian cult built up as a counterweight by the ruling aristocrats in their earlier struggles for control with the local officials. Both elements were represented in the installation of titleholders or chiefs. With the disappearance of the strong concentration of economic, military and ritual power represented by mid-seventeenth century San Salvador, the nobility faced a problem. How could they maintain their preeminence in society and the kingdom without giving up too much to any central authority? Their answer appears to have been to continue their campaign to strengthen the Christian cult, which was already closely associated with the aristocracy. Thus their introduction of a Christian founding hero into the traditions of Kongo, the emphasis on a central Christian ancestor cult dedicated to that hero, Afonso I, and the consequent continuation of their interest—and especially that of a king—in Catholic priests, practices and artifacts.

## Chapter Questions

1. Drawing on the materials in this chapter, what were some of the most important sources of political power of African states during these centuries?

2. Using sources from this and previous chapters on European history, in what ways might it be argued that African societies were similar to European societies during the 16th, 17th, and 18th centuries? In what ways might it be argued that they differed?

3. In what ways did African civilizations respond to the increasing presence and demands of Westerners? What do these responses reveal about the politics and cultures of these civilizations? How are these responses similar to or different from the responses to the West by other non-Western civilizations?

# Chapter Twenty-One

# Asia, 1700–1914

Throughout most of Asia, the 18th and 19th centuries were a period of transition from independence and concern with internal affairs to increasing intervention by Europeans and response to that external threat.

During the 18th century, China (which had been ruled by the Manchus since 1644) was at the height of its geographic expansion. It maintained its worldview of itself as the center of civilization surrounded by lesser civilizations.

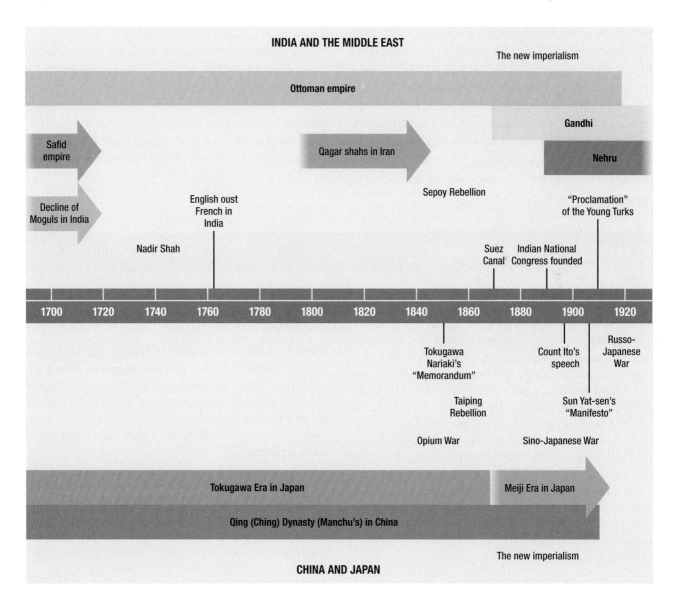

**INDIA AND THE MIDDLE EAST**

The new imperialism

Ottoman empire

Gandhi

Safid empire

Qagar shahs in Iran

Nehru

Decline of Moguls in India

English oust French in India

Sepoy Rebellion

"Proclamation" of the Young Turks

Nadir Shah

Suez Canal

Indian National Congress founded

| 1700 | 1720 | 1740 | 1760 | 1780 | 1800 | 1820 | 1840 | 1860 | 1880 | 1900 | 1920 |

Tokugawa Nariaki's "Memorandum"

Count Ito's speech

Russo-Japanese War

Taiping Rebellion

Sun Yat-sen's "Manifesto"

Opium War

Sino-Japanese War

Tokugawa Era in Japan

Meiji Era in Japan

Qing (Ching) Dynasty (Manchu's) in China

The new imperialism

**CHINA AND JAPAN**

By the end of that century Europeans were beginning to make inroads into Chinese affairs. By the middle of the 19th century, the British and others had forced trade and unequal treaties on the Chinese, seriously weakening the Chinese throne. The Manchus also had to contend with a population explosion (140 million in 1700 to 420 million in 1850) with only a 10 percent increase in arable land—a problem that persists to this day. These events contributed to internal problems and revolts, further weakening the throne. However, China remained too large and powerful to entirely lose its independence.

Japan had cut itself off from the West and limited its contact with its neighbors in the early 1600s, enjoying its isolation until the early 1800s, when British, Russian, and American ships began to probe its shores. Soon the Japanese were facing the same dilemmas as the Chinese, but (unlike the Chinese) quickly resolved them by launching a social and political revolution from the top down. Borrowing heavily from the European and American models, they created a melding of Western institutions, technology, and Japanese culture. By the end of the 19th century, Japan was acquiring an empire and bidding for equality with the Western powers.

The nations of southeast Asia, weaker and distracted by rivalries of their own, were less able to withstand the Europeans. During the 18th and 19th centuries, the British (in Burma, Malaya, and Singapore) and the French (in Cambodia, Laos, and Vietnam) gained control.

In India, the Moguls were losing power. Europeans quickly stepped into the vacuum, the British winning in their competition with the Portuguese and French. By the 19th century, the British had brought together a hodgepodge of princely states, territories, and tribal groups to create the Indian state under British control. British rule resulted in important economic, social, and cultural changes in India as well as development of a growing feeling of anti-British nationalism.

Finally, Islamic powers such as the Ottomans in the Middle East were in decline but still in control of their heartland. This empire increasingly faced internal problems from peoples with conflicting loyalties and external pressure from European powers, particularly Russia, who were well aware of the Empire's weaknesses.

The sources in this chapter focus on changes facing these Asian civilizations and how they responded to the changes. Perhaps the most pressing question was how to deal with Western influence that was growing so dramatically, particularly during the second half of this period. Developments in these areas connected with the rise of the new imperialism at the end of the 19th century will be examined in Chapter 22.

## PRIMARY SOURCES

### Confessions of Taiping Rebels: The Chinese People Rebel

*The importation of opium, the arrival of Western businesses, and the resulting weakening of the Chinese government (including a loss of face due to their inability to repel the foreigners) created in China conditions that severely speeded up the demise of the Qing (Ch'ing) Dynasty. Rebellions broke out widely. One group of rebels in particular, the Taipings, seriously threatened the Manchus when they conquered more than half of the country. Internal squabbles among the Taiping leaders, the ability of the Manchus to regroup their forces, and the aid of a Western mercenary army all led to the demise of the Taipings. This reading is a confession, after their capture sometime in the 1850s, by three Chinese rebels associated with the Taipings.*

CONSIDER: *Their reasons for joining the rebels; the social, political, and economic problems facing China that are revealed here.*

We were born in a time of prosperity and were good people. We lived in towns and were taught to distinguish right from wrong. But because of continuous flooding in our area, we could not get a grain of rice to eat even if we worked hard in the fields, and we could not engage in business because we lacked the funds. As a result we all joined the bandits.

Not long ago we came to Guangxi (Kwangsi) to try to make a living. We met others who had come from our hometowns. We pitied each other because of our sad situation, and together we began to imitate outlaws in order to relieve our hungry stomachs. In other words, no one forced us to join the outlaws. We were driven to join them because we were desperate. Given the chance, we would have returned gladly to our normal way of life.

We thought constantly of our families, but we could not return to them. Indeed, we were drifting on a

SOURCE: Patricia Buckley Ebrey, ed., *Chinese Civilization and Society: A Sourcebook* (New York: The Free Press, 1981), pp. 225–26.

hungry, painful sea and knew not when we would reach the other side. We hope Your Excellency will forgive our past sins. We hope you will think of the great benevolence of our imperial house and give us a chance to start a new life. Grass and trees are without feeling, yet they still appreciate the dew and rain that falls upon them to nourish them. Men are conscious beings; therefore how could we forget your great benevolence if you should allow us a new life? We are laying out our situation sincerely to you. We hope you can state clearly your intention. If you are willing to forgive us, please issue a statement of amnesty. If we could again become children of Heaven and return to the kingdom of benevolence and longevity, we will serve you as loyally as your dogs and horses. We will obey all your orders, and we will be willing to serve in your military camp. We have presented our situation to you. Knowing that we have bothered Your Honor with our petty matters, trembling we await our punishment. We sincerely present our case to Your Excellency. . . .

We hate the army runners who recently made heavy demands on us and disturbed our villages. They used the excuse of establishing a local militia to cause trouble for the good and honest people and create opportunities for the wicked ones. The words they used were virtuous-sounding; yet the deeds they actually perpetrated were most wicked. They allied themselves with government officials and formed cliques so that they could oppress our village and make excessive demands whenever they wished. They falsely reported that certain persons were connected with the bandits. This was due to personal grudges against the accused or to the fact that they wanted to obtain rewards. They burned down our houses and took all we had; they robbed us of our property and threatened our lives. Therefore we banded together to insure our own safety. Those who still remain in the village may run away someday while those who have left can hardly come back. Therefore, for each ordinary person who ran away, there was one more bandit, and the numbers of bandits became greater and greater. Since there are so many of us, we could not survive except by pillage, nor could we save our lives if we did not fight against the imperial troops that were sent out to exterminate us. As a consequence, we have offended the court and hurt the merchants.

## Manifesto of the United League
*Sun Yat-sen*

*In the end, no rebel movement brought down the Qing (Ch'ing) Dynasty; it fell of its own corruption and ineptitude in 1911. But all the rebellions had the combined effect of pushing the dynasty to its final collapse.*

*No rebel was more prominent, fought longer, and was more determined than Sun Yat-sen (1865–1925). Born near Macao, Sun was a Western-educated medical doctor and convert to Christianity who spoke fluent English. Having lived and traveled in Europe and the United States, Sun dreamed of establishing a modern republican form of government in China. To this end he devoted his last 35 years and, as a result, is known as the Father of Modern China. This reading from Sun's "Manifesto of the Tong Menghui (T'ung-Meng-Hui)" (United League) was written in 1905 and meant to lay out Sun's goals for a new China.*

CONSIDER: *Sun's vision of a new China; how that vision fit into traditional Chinese culture; ways in which Sun's vision was influenced by Western ideas.*

"National revolution" means that all people in the nation will have the spirit of freedom, equality, and fraternity; that is, they will all bear the responsibility of revolution. . . . Therefore we proclaim to the world in utmost sincerity the outline of the present revolution and the fundamental plan for the future administration of the nation.

1. *Drive out the Tartars:* The Manchus of today were originally the eastern barbarians beyond the Great Wall. They frequently caused border troubles during the Ming dynasty; then when China was in a disturbed state they came inside Shanhaikuan, conquered China, and enslaved our Chinese people. Those who opposed them were killed by the hundreds of thousands, and our Chinese have been a people without a nation for two hundred and sixty years. The extreme cruelties and tyrannies of the Manchu government have now reached their limit. With the righteous army poised against them, we will overthrow that government, and restore our sovereign rights. . . .

2. *Restore China:* China is the China of the Chinese. The government of China should be in the hands of the Chinese. After driving out the Tartars we must restore our national state. . . .

3. *Establish the Republic:* Now our revolution is based on equality, in order to establish a republican government. All our people are equal and all enjoy political rights. The president will be publicly chosen by the people of the country. The parliament will be made up of members publicly chosen by the people of the country. A constitution of the Chinese Republic will be enacted, and every person must abide by it. Whoever

SOURCE: Sun Yat-sen, "Manifesto of the T'ung-Meng-Hui [Tong Menghui]," in Ssu-Yu Teng and John K. Fairbank in *China's Response to the West: A Documentary Survey, 1839–1923* (New York: Atheneum, 1963), pp. 227–29.

dares to make himself a monarch shall be attacked by the whole country.

4. *Equalize land ownership:* The good fortune of civilization is to be shared equally by all the people of the nation. We should improve our social and economic organization, and assess the value of all the land in the country. Its present price shall be received by the owner, but all increases in value resulting from reform and social improvements after the revolution shall belong to the state, to be shared by all the people, in order to create a socialist state, where each family within the empire can be well supported, each person satisfied, and no one fail to secure employment. . . .

The above four points will be carried out in three steps in due order. The first period is government by military law. When the righteous army has arisen, various places will join the cause. . . . Evils like the oppression of the government, the greed and graft of officials, the squeeze of government clerks and runners, the cruelty of tortures and penalties, the tyranny of tax collectors, the humiliation of the queue—shall all be exterminated together with the Manchu rule. Evils in social customs, such as the keeping of slaves, the cruelty of foot-binding, the spread of the poison of opium, the obstructions of geomancy (*feng-shui*), should also all be prohibited. . . .

The second period is that of government by a provisional constitution. When military law is lifted in each xian (*hsien*), the Military Government shall return the right of self-government to the local people. The members of local councils and local officials shall all be elected by the people. All rights and duties of the Military Government toward the people and those of the people toward the government shall be regulated by the provisional constitution, which shall be observed by the Military Government, the local councils, and the people. . . .

The third period will be government under the constitution. Six years after the provisional constitution has been enforced a constitution shall be made. The military and administrative powers of the Military Government shall be annulled; the people shall elect the president, and elect the members of parliament to organize the parliament. The administrative matters of the nation shall proceed according to the provisions of the constitution.

. . . It is hoped that our people will proceed in due order and cultivate their free and equal status; the foundation of the Chinese Republic will be entirely based on this.

## Japan, Reject the Westerners
*Tokugawa Nariaki*

*After over two centuries of self-imposed isolation, Japan suddenly found itself the object of Western curiosity as British,* *Russian, and American ships began to arrive, uninvited and unwanted. The Japanese watched events unfolding in China in the early 19th century with tremendous trepidation. Seeing that resistance to the arrival of foreigners was useless due to their superior military technology, Japan's response to the arrival of American ships and its forced opening was relatively calm. However, as we see from the following selection, not everyone was reconciled to it. Written in 1853, this memorandum was from Tokugawa Nariaki, a high official to the Bakufu (the military government led by a Shogun). He urged an immediate and aggressive response to the foreign ships attempting to land on Japanese soil.*

CONSIDER: *The reason for rejecting Westerners; what this reveals about Japanese culture and attitudes; similarities and differences between Japanese and Chinese responses to Western imperialism.*

It is my belief that the first and most urgent of our tasks is for the Bakufu to make its choice between peace and war, and having determined its policy to pursue it unwaveringly thereafter. When we consider the respective advantages and disadvantages of war and peace, we find that if we put our trust in war the whole country's morale will be increased and even if we sustain an initial defeat we will in the end expel the foreigner; while if we put our trust in peace, even though things may seem tranquil for a time, the morale of the country will be greatly lowered and we will come in the end to complete collapse. This has been amply demonstrated in the history of China. . . . However, I propose to give here in outline the ten reasons why in my view we must never choose the policy of peace.

1. Although our country's territory is not extensive, foreigners both fear and respect us. . . . Despite this, the Americans who arrived recently, though fully aware of the Bakufu's prohibition, entered Uraga displaying a white flag as a symbol of peace and insisted on presenting their written requests. Moreover they entered Edo Bay, fired heavy guns in salute and even went so far as to conduct surveys without permission. They were arrogant and discourteous, their actions an outrage. Indeed, this was the greatest disgrace we have suffered since the dawn of our history. . . .

2. The prohibition of Christianity is the first rule of the Tokugawa house. . . . Yet if the Americans are allowed to come again this religion will inevitably raise its head once more, however strict the prohibition; and this, I fear, is something we could never justify to the spirits of our ancestors. . . .

SOURCE: G. Beasley, trans. and ed., *Select Documents on Japanese Foreign Policy, 1853–1868* (London: Oxford University Press, 1960), pp. 102–7.

3. To exchange our valuable articles like gold, silver, copper, and iron for useless foreign goods like woollens and satin is to incur great loss while acquiring not the smallest benefit. The best course of all would be for the Bakufu to put a stop to the trade with Holland. . . .

4. For some years Russia, England, and others have sought trade with us, but the Bakufu has not permitted it. Should permission be granted to the Americans, on what grounds would it be possible to refuse if Russia and the others [again] request it? . . .

5. It is widely stated that [apart from trade] the foreigners have no other evil designs and that if only the Bakufu will permit trade there will be no further difficulty. However, it is their practice first to seek a foothold by means of trade and then go on to propagate Christianity and make other unreasonable demands. . . .

6. [Some argue that] Japan . . . clinging to ideas of seclusion in isolation . . . is a constant source of danger to us and that our best course would . . . be to communicate with foreign countries and open an extensive trade; yet, to my mind, if the people of Japan stand firmly united, if we complete our military preparations and return to the state of society that existed before the middle ages, then we will even be able to go out against foreign countries and spread abroad our fame and prestige. . . .

9. I hear that all, even though they be commoners, who have witnessed the recent actions of the foreigners, think them abominable; and if the Bakufu does not expel these insolent foreigners root and branch there may be some who will complain in secret, asking to what purpose have been all the preparations of gun-emplacements. It is inevitable that men should think in this way when they have seen how arrogantly the foreigners acted at Uraga. That, I believe, is because even the humblest are conscious of the debt they owe their country, and it is indeed a promising sign. Since even ignorant commoners are talking in this way, I fear that if the Bakufu does not decide to carry out expulsion, if its handling of the matter shows nothing but excess of leniency and appeasement of the foreigners, then the lower orders may fail to understand its ideas and hence opposition might arise from evil men who had lost their respect for Bakufu authority. It might even be that Bakufu control of the great lords would itself be endangered.

## The Japanese Constitution
*Count Ito*

*For over 200 years Japan lived in self-imposed isolation from the rest of the world. From early in the 17th to the middle of the 19th century, only a tiny handful of Japanese scholars knew of the scientific and military progress of the European powers.*

*Eventually Japan would be forced to end its isolation. In the years after Perry's arrival in Japan (1853), the Tokugawa Shogunate collapsed and the Meiji Restoration (1868) began. Japan's leaders abruptly ended the feudal structure of the country, disarmed the samurai, created a modern conscript army, abolished hereditary social classes, introduced universal education, and initiated a modern industrial economic system. This revolution included the substitution of absolute rule with a written Constitution. This exceptional document codified the rights of the Japanese and ended extraterritoriality (the principle whereby foreigners were subject only to the laws of the countries of which they were citizens). The reasoning behind this system (in China as well) was that Europeans and Americans could not understand the local legal system. Constitutional rule in Japan forced foreigners to end extraterritoriality.*

*In this excerpt from a speech made in 1889, Count Ito, one of Japan's new progressive leaders, comments on the importance of the Constitution to a revitalized Japan.*

CONSIDER: *How Ito justifies the changes that Japan made; what Ito hopes the consequences of these changes are or will be; the significance of having a written constitution.*

. . . Now that the Constitution has been promulgated, it will be of interest to discuss it briefly from a historical point of view, with the object of demonstrating that this momentous event is no mere fortuitous occurrence. . . . That great achievement, resulting in the return of power and rule to the proper hands, was due to two causes; namely, loyalty and foreign intercourse. The loyalty found its expression in a strong desire to revert to that system under which power was vested in the Emperor, while foreign intercourse operated through an earnest wish to substitute for the national policy hitherto pursued (that of seclusion) a course aiming at the extension and development of our relations with foreign peoples. . . . As you are no doubt aware, the affairs of the country were, in the simple days of old, administered under the personal direction of the Emperor, by means of the gun and ken systems. As time went on the military classes, however, acquired a hold on the governing power, and eventually the court became a mere ornament; though the people at large, remembering the facts of history, always entertained a hope that sooner or later the Throne should have its own again. . . . This page of our history cannot be sufficiently regretted, but as a matter of fact the failure of the loyalists then operated beneficially by stimulating to greater enthusiasm the minds of later

SOURCE: W. W. McLaren, ed., *Transactions of the Asiatic Society of Japan*, vol. 92:1 (1914), pp. 614–22.

generations. For feudalism long presented to its enemies a firm and impregnable front; but its end was surely though slowly approaching. Towards the close of the Tokugawa regime, the regency found itself face to face with the disagreeable necessity of opening to foreigners the gates which for so long had been closed against them; and of concluding treaties with some of those whom the Japanese people had been accustomed to despise as "barbarians." The unsatisfactory course pursued by the Shōgunate with regard to foreigners speedily evoked disapprobation, and as its policy went from bad to worse, the old loyal sentiment, which had only been slumbering, was at last roused into action, and the Restoration was accomplished. . . . [I]t became evident that further attempts to maintain the seclusion and isolation of the country from the rest of the world would be highly impolitic. Treaties were therefore concluded with our visitors, and intercourse with them was duly initiated. But those who had now been entrusted by the Emperor with the chief share in the conduct of public affairs were not satisfied with the restoration of power to the Throne and the inauguration of treaty relations with foreign powers. They set themselves to the task of introducing Western civilisation into Japan and of eliminating such undesirable features as became apparent by contrast with the conditions of the West. They saw foreign powers actively engaged in the rivalry of cultivating their strength and resources; and they could not help asking themselves how Japan could hope to hold her own in the struggle, or maintain her independence and integrity so that, in common with other countries, she might enjoy the benefits of civilisation and enlightenment. It was plain to them that if the national dignity was to be demonstrated in the face of the world the national resources must be developed and the national power strengthened by some uniform process of government and administration. . . . So much having been accomplished, the next question was, how should these resources be husbanded and encouraged in their development. The answer plainly was, to educate the people with a view to their becoming factors in the progress of the country. . . . If we carefully regard the method in which public education has advanced, from the cultivation of knowledge in connection with political economy, law, and kindred branches, to commerce, trade, and industries, and compare the present state of affairs with that which existed some twenty years ago, we shall not exaggerate if we say that the country has undergone a complete metamorphosis. . . . It is only by the protection of the law that the happiness of the nation can be promoted and the safety of person and property secured, and to attain these ends the people may elect their representatives and empower the latter to deliberate on laws with a view to the promotion of their own happiness and the safeguarding of their rights. This, gentlemen, is enacted by the Constitution, and I think you will agree that it constitutes a concession to the people of a most invaluable right.

## Proclamation of the Young Turks

*For the Islamic Ottoman Empire, the 19th century was part of a long period of decline. One reaction to that decline was an effort to infuse Turkey, the heart of the Empire, with Western-style nationalism, secularism, and political reform. In the 1860s and 1870s a group of modern reformers, called the Young Ottomans, began to press for a constitutional democracy in Turkey. In 1867 they achieved their aim when a constitution was proclaimed. Unfortunately, the new Sultan, Abdul Hamid II, was not in agreement with the reforms and ignored the Constitution while ruling as an absolute monarch.*

*Nationalists began to organize opposition to the sultan. One such group, the Committee of Union and Progress, was established in 1889. These young people, commonly known as the Young Turks, were persecuted, imprisoned, and forced into exile for their attempts to restore the 1867 Constitution.*

*In 1908 there was an extensive army mutiny. The Young Turks took the opportunity to openly demand a restoration of parliamentary rule; the sultan, unable to resist, was forced to submit. After the reinstatement of the Constitution, the Young Turks issued this proclamation outlining their ideas for the "new" Turkey that they envisioned. The state they created was secular, repressive, and oppressive of racial minorities, although it had the trappings of a democracy.*

CONSIDER: *The nature of the Young Turks' political demands; the similarities and differences between this vision of the state and the democratic, liberal state of western Europe; who might agree with this program.*

1. The basis for the Constitution will be respect for the predominance of the national will. One of the consequences of this principle will be to require without delay the responsibility of the minister before the Chamber, and, consequently, to consider the minister as having resigned, when he does not have a majority of the votes of the Chamber.

2. . . . [T]he Senate will be named . . . as follows: one third by the Sultan and two thirds by the nation, and the term of senators will be of limited duration.

3. . . . [A]ll Ottoman subjects having completed their twentieth year, regardless of whether they possess property or fortune, shall have the right to vote. . . .

4. It will be demanded that the right freely to constitute political groups be inserted in a precise fashion in the constitutional charter. . . .

SOURCE: A. Sarrou, "*La Jeune-Turquie et la Révolution,*" ("The Young Turks,") in *Civilization since Waterloo,* Rondo Cameron, ed. (Paris, 1912), pp. 40–42.

7. The Turkish tongue will remain the official state language. . . .

9. Every citizen will enjoy complete liberty and equality, regardless of nationality or religion, and be submitted to the same obligations. All Ottomans, being equal before the law as regards rights and duties relative to the State, are eligible for government posts, according to their individual capacity and their education. Non-Muslims will be equally liable to the military law.

10. The free exercise of the religious privileges which have been accorded to different nationalities will remain intact. . . .

14. Provided that the property rights of landholders are not infringed upon . . . it will be proposed that peasants be permitted to acquire land, and they will be accorded means to borrow money at a moderate rate. . . .

16. Education will be free. . . .

17. All schools will operate under the surveillance of the state. In order to obtain for Ottoman citizens an education of a homogenous and uniform character, the official schools will be open, their instruction will be free, and all nationalities will be admitted. . . .

Secondary and higher education will be given in the public and official schools indicated above. . . . Schools of commerce, agriculture and industry will be opened with the goal of developing the resources of the country. . . .

Steps shall also be taken for the formation of Roads and Canals to increase the facilities of communication and increase the sources of the wealth of the country. Everything that can impede commerce or agriculture shall be abolished.

# VISUAL SOURCES

## Foreigners at Yokohama
### Gountei Sadahide

When the Westerners arrived in Japan in the 19th century, the Japanese embraced them to the point of making a passion of things Western. Artists rushed to depict the newcomers so that Japanese outside of the treaty ports could see what these strange visitors were like.

This triptych print by Gountei Sadahide (1807–73) portrays, from left to right, families from Russia, the Netherlands, and Britain. Artists enjoyed depicting Europeans and Americans with very sharp facial features, especially noses. They often wore baggy clothes in these pictures and were always carrying exotic items such as telescopes and concertinas. In these renderings, note the women's faces, which are less

European than a standard form adopted for Japanese women in the 19th century by painters of the Utagawa school.

CONSIDER: What these pictures reveal about the Japanese vision of Western men, women, and children.

## Rauneah, A Village in the Punjab
### Ghulam 'Ali Khan

Through high culture we have been able to preserve a record of the lives of the elite and life in towns and urban areas. This is as true of India as anywhere else. However, the vast majority of Indians have always lived, and still do live, in villages—and there are fewer depictions of the lives of these people.

This painting of a 19th-century village, probably by Ghulam 'Ali Khan, is part of a collection of over 100 portrayals of village life commissioned by an eccentric Englishman named William Fraser who lived in India from 1799 until his death in 1835. As Fraser made his rounds among his estates in Harayana Province and elsewhere, he developed the habit of being accompanied by experienced Indian painters trained in the Mogul tradition; their purpose was to record the scenes they encountered as accurately as possible. As a result of these efforts, we have an incomparable record of everyday life in 19th-century India. In this example, Rauneah, A

**Illustration 21–1** © The Trustees of The British Museum.

Village in the Punjab, *we see the mixture of English townscapes, probably at Fraser's insistence, and the precision for detail for which miniaturists in the Mogul tradition were known. Notice the peacock on the thatched roof, the array of animals, and the busy life of the village.*

CONSIDER: *The conditions of village life in 19th-century India; the roles of men and women revealed in this painting.*

## The Weakening of China, 1839–1895

Since the second century B.C.E., Chinese imperial rulers strove to maintain strong central rule. Confucian teaching inculcated in the people the belief that a lack of strong central authority and benevolent rule called for the

**Illustration 21–2**    The British Library.

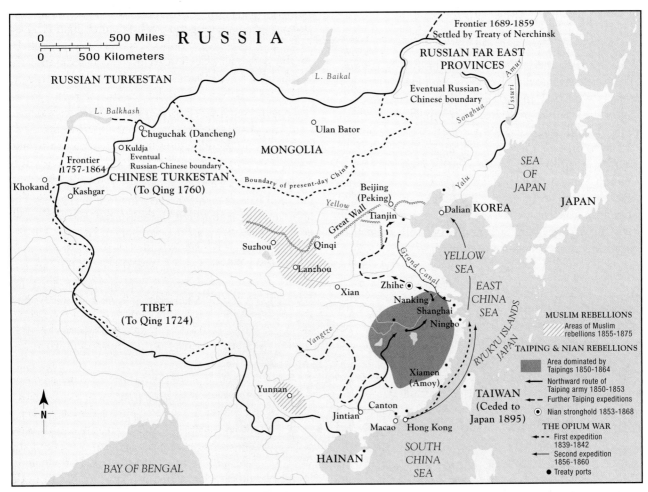

**Map 21–1**

violent overthrow of the dynasty. Indeed, such overthrows occurred over 20 times in Chinese history.

The Qing (Ch'ing) Dynasty had been in power since 1644, but beginning in the late 18th century, the arrival of Europeans led increasingly to a weakening central authority. This weakening was accelerated after 1839 by the developments shown in this map. First, the Qing Emperors were unable to halt Britain's illegal importation of opium into China and suffered humiliation in the two Opium Wars with Great Britain. This weakening, in turn, pressured the government to grant special privileges to Western powers in "treaty ports," all of which led to numerous uprisings around the country. While these internal uprisings were ended by 1873, the cycle toward dissolution had inexorably begun.

CONSIDER: The sorts of forces that can fundamentally undermine a government; the benefits and detriments of trade and cultural contact with outside powers.

## SECONDARY SOURCES

## Being Chinese

*Susan Naquin and Evelyn S. Rawski*

*A strong, centralized rule was not all that held the Chinese together. Several other elements, including Confucianism and the early development of a written script, contributed to a sense of cultural unity and even superiority. In the following selection, Susan Naquin and Evelyn S. Rawski, prominent scholars of China, analyze this sense of unity and focus on what it meant to be Chinese in the 18th century.*

CONSIDER: *What some of the central elements of the Chinese belief system were; how the Chinese linked external forms, such as writing and clothing, with internal values.*

But what was entailed in being Chinese? Some might associate this identity with the written language that had linked the educated elite of this culture for millennia. Even the illiterate peasant had a profound reverence for the written word—written in Chinese characters of course—if not a passing familiarity with it. . . . Despite differences between dialects that were virtually separate languages, being Chinese seemed to involve some commitment to the unified and standardized written character.

The classical formulation for Chineseness identified clothing, diet, and ritual as key components. China's superior textile technology had long since become a hallmark of Chinese culture. The Chinese rejected the dairy products that the nomads ate and took pride in a culinary tradition that considered good eating essential to good health and placed eating at the core of community solidarity. Above all, to be Chinese was to value ritual and to follow tradition, especially in marriage and funerals.

Implicit in the centrality of ritual was a confidence in the linkage between external behavior and internalized values, an assumption by now so ingrained in Chinese culture that performance without belief could be seen to suffice. In a ritual, correct actions were thus more essential than the feelings of the participants. Individuals with widely different educations and background could invest the same ritual with different meanings. Ritual thus subsumed and harmonized differences even as it educated. Community rites cut across class and were not categorized as being associated exclusively either with the elite or with the masses, thus forming the basis for a truly popular (in the sense of pervasive) shared culture. Chinese followed Confucius not only in this faith in ritual but also in the core values expressed in such ceremonies: the asymmetrical and hierarchical relations between ruler and subject, father and child, husband and wife.

Proper behavior expressing orthodox values was associated in Confucian thought with a properly ordered and stable society presided over by a ruler who was in harmony with the cosmos. Harmony, order, and stability were goals not just for the state but for individuals as well. To the Chinese, civilization consisted of imposing order onto chaos, transforming societies in which individuals wore no clothing, "knew their mothers but not their fathers," and made no social distinctions. . . .

By Qing times, filial piety meant a commitment to the patriline, living and dead, so profound that it affected not only behavior but also, as we have seen, many political and social institutions. Family identity was primary and central, and, as we have noted, individualism weak and undeveloped by comparison with the West. . . .

A belief system that de-emphasized personal salvation and stressed the collective patriline, that valued ritual and behavior based on venerable Confucian precepts concerning the sources of order in society and the cosmos, and that encouraged individuals to work hard and improve their lot in life—these are major elements found not just in the eighteenth century but in traditional Chinese society generally.

SOURCE: Susan Naquin and Evelyn S. Rawski, *Chinese Society in the Eighteenth Century* (New Haven: Yale University Press, 1987), pp. 91–93 as excerpted.

## Minorities in the Ottoman Empire
*Bernard Lewis*

*The Ottoman Empire had many different groups of people under its rule. For the most part, it treated them with tolerance. This tolerant attitude allowed these minority peoples to flourish. By the 19th century, however, European ideas of independence, the equality of all citizens of a state, and the preservation of cultural control had been widely disseminated among the Ottoman minorities. These three principles led to conflict within the Ottoman Empire. Noted Arab historian Bernard Lewis discusses these problems in the following excerpt.*

Consider: *The position on "nonbelievers" in traditional Islamic societies; the impact of European ideas on Ottoman society.*

The traditional political and social order which flourished in the Ottoman Empire and, with some modifications, in the realms of the shahs of Iran, had its roots in classical Islamic law and custom, and beyond that in the remoter civilizations of the ancient Middle East. As in other religious cultures, it was based frankly on inequality, since it would be inappropriate and indeed absurd to accord equal treatment to those who accept God's final revelation and those who wilfully reject it. Some modern apologists, in justly praising the religious tolerance of traditional Islamic regimes, have described it as a system of equal rights. It was not, and such equality would indeed have been seen at the time not as a merit but as a dereliction of duty. In refusing equality to the unbeliever, the Islamic state was following the common practice of religions in power. Where it differed from most others was in according to these unbelievers a recognized status in society, defined and maintained by Holy Law, and accepted by the mass of the Muslim populations. This was not equal status, but it did provide a level of toleration which in states guided by other dispensations was not achieved until religion was disestablished or, at the very least, deprived of much of its influence in public affairs. Muslim religious tolerance was of course limited to monotheists who accepted what Islam recognized as earlier revelations. In practice, in the Middle East this meant Christians of various denominations and Jews. In Iran there was also a small surviving community of Zoroastrians. . . .

It was only in modern times, under the impact of European ideas of nationality, that literate city-dwellers began to describe themselves by . . . ethnic terms.

The impact of these European ideas was naturally stronger and more immediate among the Christian peoples of the Ottoman Empire. First, the Greeks and Serbs, later the other Balkan peoples, and eventually the Armenians, encountered and responded to the new and potent ideologies of nationalism. Even the Jews, the smallest, weakest and least disaffected of the non-Muslim minorities, in time developed their own nationalism. In 1843, a rabbi called Yehuda Alkalai wrote a little book in which he advanced the novel idea that the Jews should return to the Holy Land and rebuild it by their own efforts without waiting for divine redemption. Rabbi Alkalai was born and lived in the Ottoman city of Sarajevo.

During the nineteenth century, the Christian minorities in the Ottoman Empire pursued three different and ultimately irreconcilable objectives. The first of these was equal citizenship in the Ottoman state . . .

It was not only new ideas that made the old inequalities unacceptable; it was also a new prosperity. . . . [N]on-Muslim communities on the whole did pretty well. . . . [T]hey were growing more and more prosperous. All this made the social and political inferiority imposed on them by the old order increasingly irksome. . . .

The second objective pursued with increasing energy by more and more of the Ottoman Christians was that of independence, or at least autonomy within a national territory of their own. . . .

The third aim, rarely avowed but nevertheless tenaciously pursued, was the retention of the privileges and autonomies which [they] had had under the old order—the right to the maintenance and enforcement of their own religious laws, to the control of their own educational systems in their own languages, and generally to the maintenance of their own distinctive cultures.

In time, even the Muslim peoples of the Empire—Turks, Arabs and others—lost their previous immunity and succumbed to the infection of European ideas—liberal, patriotic and nationalist.

## Stifling the Voice of Protest in India
*Nemai Sadhan Bose*

*One of the more common justifications for colonialism that the European powers offered was the argument that Europe was bringing "civilization" and "education" to the peoples of the non-European world. Once these non-Europeans achieved a level of sophistication equal to that of the Europeans, so this argument went, they could be treated equally. The reality, however, was that the closer these colonial*

SOURCE: Bernard Lewis, *The Middle East: A Brief History of the Last 2,000 Years* (New York: Scribner's, 1995), pp. 321–27.

SOURCE: Nemai Sadhan Bose, *Racism, Struggle for Equality and Indian Nationalism* (Calcutta: Firma KLM Private Limited, 1981), pp. 130–51.

*citizens emulated their European masters, the more nervous the Europeans became.*

*In India, Britain allowed considerable freedom of the press. As the population became more literate and newspapers became a force to reckon with, Indians began to emulate the British principles of a free press ready to criticize anything and anyone. In particular, the press liked to question British rule in India. At times this criticism bothered the British considerably and, for a brief period in the 19th century, the British colonial administration restricted Indian periodicals. Indian historian Nemai Sadhan Bose tells this story here.*

CONSIDER: *The contradictions of allowing freedom of the press and having to live with, at times, harsh criticisms or offensive materials; why the British wanted to control the Indian press at all.*

The rapid rise of the press was a major factor behind the growth of nationalism in India in the nineteenth century. In 1875, the total number of Indian newspapers was nearly five hundred. These papers and journals carried political discussions and reviewed and analyzed problems and issues from different angles. . . . The link between journalism and nationalism had been so close that Indian journalism may truly be regarded as the "handmaiden" of Indian nationalism.

The vernacular press occupied a distinct position. . . . [That press] had several noticeable features. The foremost of these was a growing consciousness about racial animosity . . . and a concern for the preservation of the rights and honor of the people. The press also expressed a faith in the strength of the combined efforts of the people and underlined the necessity of political organizations. Another feature was that while admitting the blessings of the British rule and pleading loyalty to it, the press also visualized a free India where the people would live with honor and dignity.

The British Indian administration was not happy with the tone and tenor of the vernacular press. Taking cognizance of the impact of the vernacular press on public opinion, an official report for the year 1866–1867 stated, "The Hindu papers fearlessly record their opinions though sometimes crude, regarding public measures. Those opinions are based upon the broad principles of universal equality. And the authorities are often subjects of unceremonious comment, sometimes severe . . . Their opinions are beginning to be felt both at home and abroad, as an index of native public feeling." . . .

There were a number of economic and political issues in the 1870s which agitated the minds of the people and were subjects of criticism in the newspapers, necessitating a fresh review of the question of shackling the press. But by far the most recurring theme was racial discrimination and exposure of instances of crimes committed by the Europeans in India without the least respect for or fear of law.

## Chapter Questions

1. In what ways did Asian civilizations—in particular, their governments—respond to the increasing presence and demands of Westerners? What do these responses reveal about the politics and culture of their civilizations?

2. Using some of the sources in this chapter, how might it be argued that some Asian societies reaped benefits from contacts with the West? How might some of these same sources and others be used to show the opposite—that Asian societies suffered from contacts with the West?

3. How might sources in this chapter and Chapter 15 ("Asia, 1500–1700") be used to show the "rise" of Japan and "decline" of China, India, and the Ottoman Empire during this period? How might this rise and decline be explained?

# Chapter Twenty-Two

# Imperialism and New Global Entanglements, 1880–1914

Between the 15th and the 18th centuries, European nations gained control over most of the Western Hemisphere and established bases and commercial outlets on the west coast of Africa and southern Asia. Then, from the 1760s to the 1870s, there was a relative lull in expansion. Indeed, several imperial powers lost many of their overseas holdings. In the period between 1880 and 1914, however, there was a new burst of imperial expansion, the "new imperialism." The impetus came from Europe, where the powers engaged in a sudden quest for control over new territories in Asia, Africa, and the Pacific. Explorers, missionaries, traders, troops, and government officials quickly followed one another into these lands and established direct and indirect political control. Other lands already partially controlled, such as in India and southeast Asia, were brought under tighter reign. In this process Europe greatly increased its dominance over much of the rest of the world, bringing Western culture and institutions to the non-Western societies whether they wanted them or not. While the impact of the new imperialism varied in different lands, it was intensely felt and inspired resistance that would grow over the course of the 20th century.

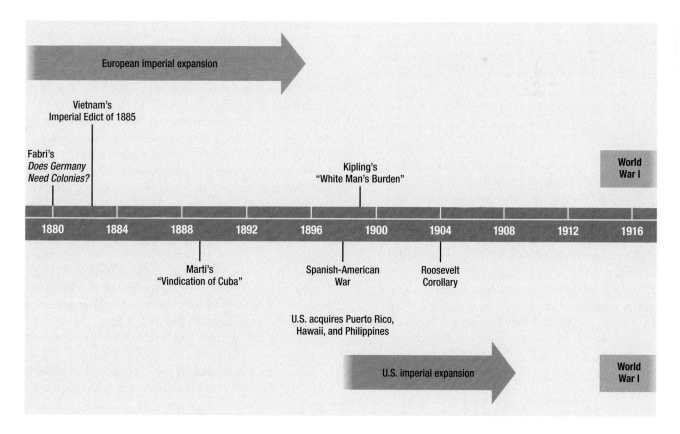

As the United States, long the strongest nation in the Americas, emerged as a dominant economic power in the world, it assumed some of the roles held by European imperial powers. Following the Spanish–American War in 1898, the United States acquired Puerto Rico and the Philippines. It also established a protectorate over Cuba. While opposing European imperialism and expansionism elsewhere in the world, the United States often assumed that it could act as if Latin American countries were only semiautonomous. And as with the European powers, the United States would have to face the consequences of this new imperialism throughout the 20th century.

Certainly imperialism has been a topic of considerable debate among historians, as the questions addressed in this chapter indicate. What were the nationalistic, economic, and political motives for imperialism? What were some of the attitudes toward imperialism, particularly as reflected in materials glorifying it as a Christian and humanitarian movement? How is imperialism understood from a Marxist perspective? In what ways was imperialism opposed as nations struggled for independence from imperial powers?

Here our focus on the competitive struggle between imperial powers leads us toward the outbreak of World War I, which will be examined in Chapter 23. Subsequent chapters will deal with the worldwide impact of imperialism throughout the 20th century.

# PRIMARY SOURCES

## Does Germany Need Colonies?

*Friedrich Fabri*

*Imperialism swept through Europe with extraordinary force in the late 19th century. Probably the most apparent motive for the new imperialism was economic. With each conquest, people expected to develop new commerce and particularly new markets for manufactured goods. But there was another, perhaps even more important motive: nationalism. The step between the increasingly assertive nationalism of the time and the new imperialism was a short one. Both of these views are reflected by Friedrich Fabri in his 1879 pamphlet, "Does Germany Need Colonies?" A former inspector of a German missionary association in South West Africa, Fabri emphasizes Germany's "cultural mission" in becoming an imperial power.*

CONSIDER: *What arguments Fabri mounts to justify Germany's acquisition of colonies; what Fabri means by Germany's "cultural mission" and how that relates to imperialism.*

Should not the German nation, so seaworthy, so industrially and commercially minded, more than other peoples geared to agricultural colonization, and possessing a rich and available supply of labor, all these to a greater extent than other modern culture-peoples, should not this nation successfully hew a new path on the road of imperialism? We are convinced beyond doubt that the colonial question has become a matter of life-or-death for the development of Germany. Colonies will have a salutary effect on our economic situation as well as on our entire national progress.

Here is a solution for many of the problems that face us. In this new Reich of ours there is so much bitterness, so much unfruitful, sour, and poisoned political wrangling, that the opening of a new, promising road of national effort will act as a kind of liberating influence. Our national spirit will be renewed, a gratifying thing, a great asset. A people that has been led to a high level of power can maintain its historical position only as long as it understands and proves itself to be *the bearer of a culture-mission.* At the same time, this is the only way to stability and to the growth of national welfare, the necessary foundation for a lasting expansion of power.

At one time Germany contributed only intellectual and literary activity to the tasks of our century. That era is now over. As a people we have become politically minded and powerful. But if political power becomes the primal goal of a nation, it will lead to harshness, even to barbarism. We must be ready to serve for the ideal, moral, and economic culture-tasks of our time. The French national-economist, Leroy Beaulieu, closed his work on colonization with these words: "That nation is the greatest in the world which colonizes most; if she does not achieve that rank today, she will make it tomorrow."

No one can deny that in this direction England has by far surpassed all other countries. Much has been said,

SOURCE: Louis L. Snyder, *The Imperialism Reader* (New York: D. Van Nostrand, 1962), pp. 18–20 as excerpted.

even in Germany, during the last few decades about the "disintegrating power of England." Indeed, there seems to be something to it when we consider the Palmerston era and Gladstonian politics. It has been customary in our age of military power to evaluate the strength of a state in terms of its combat-ready troops. But anyone who looks at the globe and notes the steadily increasing colonial possessions of Great Britain, how she extracts strength from them, the skill with which she governs them, how the Anglo-Saxon strain occupies a dominant position in the overseas territories, he will begin to see the military argument as the reasoning of a philistine.

The fact is that England tenaciously holds on to its world-wide possessions with scarcely one-fourth the manpower of our continental military state. That is not only a great economic advantage but also a striking proof of the solid power and cultural fiber of England. . . .

It would be wise for us Germans to learn about colonial skills from our Anglo-Saxon cousins and to begin a friendly competition with them. When the German Reich centuries ago stood at the pinnacle of the states of Europe, it was the Number One trade and sea power. If the New Germany wants to protect its newly won position of power for a long time, it must heed its *Kultur-mission* and, above all, delay no longer in the task of renewing the call for colonies.

## The White Man's Burden

*Rudyard Kipling*

*Imperialism was often glorified both by those actively involved in it and by the public at home. Part of this glorification involved perceiving imperialism as a Christian and nationalistic venture. More broadly it involved portraying imperialism as a heroic deed carried out by idealistic leaders of Western civilization in an effort to spread the "benefits" of "true civilization" to "less advanced" peoples of the world. One of the most popular expressions of this is found in the writings of Rudyard Kipling (1865–1936), particularly in his poem "The White Man's Burden," written in 1899 to celebrate the American annexation of the Philippines.*

CONSIDER: *What Kipling means by "the White Man's burden"; how Kipling justifies imperialism; why such a justification might be so appealing.*

Take up the White Man's burden—
    Send forth the best ye breed—
Go, bind your sons to exile

SOURCE: Rudyard Kipling, "The White Man's Burden," *McClure's Magazine,* vol. XII, no. 4 (February 1899), pp. 290–91.

To serve your captives' need;
To wait, in heavy harness,
    On fluttered folk and wild—
Your new-caught sullen peoples,
    Half devil and half child.

Take up the White Man's burden—
    In patience to abide,
To veil the threat of terror
    And check the show of pride;
By open speech and simple,
    An hundred times made plain,
To seek another's profit
    And work another's gain.

Take up the White Man's burden—
    The savage wars of peace—
Fill full the mouth of Famine,
    And bid the sickness cease;
And when your goal is nearest
    (The end for others sought)
Watch sloth and heathen folly
    Bring all your hope to nought.

Take up the White Man's burden—
    No iron rule of kings,
But toil of serf and sweeper—
    The tale of common things.
The ports ye shall not enter,
    The roads ye shall not tread,
Go, make them with your living
    And mark them with your dead.

Take up the White Man's burden,
    And reap his old reward—
The blame of those ye better
    The hate of those ye guard—
The cry of hosts ye humour
    (Ah, slowly!) toward the light:—
"Why brought ye us from bondage,
    Our loved Egyptian night?"

Take up the White Man's burden—
    Ye dare not stoop to less—
Nor call too loud on Freedom
    To cloke your weariness.
By all ye will or whisper,
    By all ye leave or do,
The silent sullen peoples
    Shall weigh your God and you.

Take up the White Man's burden!
    Have done with childish days—
The lightly-proffered laurel,
    The easy ungrudged praise:

Comes now, to search your manhood
   Through all the thankless years,
Cold, edged with dear-bought wisdom,
   The judgment of your peers.

## Nationalism and Colonialism in Vietnam
### Imperial Edict, 1885

*Traditionally in mainland southeast Asia, rivalries between Thailand, Laos, Cambodia, and Vietnam led to shifting patterns of control. The 18th and 19th centuries added the British (in Burma, Malaya, and Singapore) and the French (in Cambodia, Laos, and Vietnam) to the equation. Nationalism was a constant theme throughout the histories of southeast Asia during the 18th and 19th centuries. Yet no nation was more militant in its nationalism than Vietnam. The reasons are easy to discern. Before the French arrived, the Vietnamese had suffered through a thousand years of Chinese colonialism, Mongol invasions, encroachment from Cambodia, and more. Militant nationalism became a central theme of their cultural identity.*

*From the very beginning of their hundred-year colonization of Vietnam, the French had to deal with nationalistic resistance. This reading is from the Loyalty to the King (Can Vuong) Edict promulgated in 1885, which calls on all Vietnamese to resist the French.*

CONSIDER: *Imperial Vietnamese attitudes toward the advancing French colonialists; sources of Vietnamese strength.*

The Emperor proclaims:

From time immemorial there have been only three strategies for opposing the enemy: attack, defense, negotiation. Opportunities for attack were lacking. It was difficult to gather required strength for defense. And in negotiations the enemy demanded everything. In this situation of infinite trouble we have unwillingly been forced to resort to expedients. . . .

Our country recently has faced many critical events. . . . Nevertheless, with every passing day the Western envoys got more and more overbearing. Recently they brought in troops and naval reinforcements, trying to force on Us conditions We could never accept. We received them with normal ceremony, but they refused to accept a single thing. People in the capital became very afraid that trouble was approaching. The high ministers sought ways to retain peace in the country and protect the court. It was decided, rather than bow heads in obedience, sitting around and losing chances, better to ap-

preciate what the enemy was up to and move first. If this did not succeed, then we could still follow the present course to make better plans, acting according to the situation. . . .

Court figures had best follow the righteous path, seeking to live and die for righteousness. . . . Our virtue being insufficient, amidst these events We did not have the strength to hold out and allowed the royal capital to fall, forcing the Empresses to flee for their lives. The fault is Ours entirely, a matter of great shame. But traditional loyalties are strong. Hundreds of mandarins and commanders of all levels, perhaps not having the heart to abandon Me, unite as never before, those with intellect helping to plan, those with strength willing to fight, those with riches contributing for supplies—all of one mind and body in seeking a way out of danger, a solution to all difficulties.

On the other hand, those who fear death more than they love their king, who put concerns of household above concerns of country, mandarins who find excuses to be far away, soldiers who desert, citizens who do not fulfill public duties eagerly for a righteous cause, officers who take the easy way and leave brightness for darkness—all may continue to live in this world, but they will be like animals disguised in clothes and hats. Who can accept such behavior? With rewards generous, punishments will also be severe. The court retains normal usages, so that repentance should not be postponed. All should follow this Edict strictly.

## Letters of a Javanese Princess
### Raden Ajeng Kartini

*By the end of the 19th century, the Dutch had long established colonial rule over an archipelago of thousands of islands (later known as Indonesia) where the South China Sea meets the Indian Ocean. The Dutch reinforced their control in several ways, including rules about the use of the Dutch language.*

*Raden Ajeng Kartini (1879–1904) was a member of the Javanese aristocracy. Her father encouraged her to study Dutch. She became committed to the education of her people and established a school for Javanese girls. In this letter, written in 1901, she describes how the Dutch language was used as a form of colonial domination.*

CONSIDER: *Why, in this colonial situation, language became such a sensitive issue; how the use of language might have fit*

SOURCE: David Marr, *Vietnamese Anticolonialism 1885–1925* (Berkeley: University of California Press, copyright © 1971), The Regents of the University of California.

SOURCE: Raden Ajeng Kartini, *Letters of a Javanese Princess,* tr. by Agnes Louise Symmers (New York: Alfred A. Knopf, 1920), pp. 39–44 as excerpted.

*with other practices that reinforced distinctions between the Dutch and the Javanese.*

I shall relate to you the history of a gifted and educated Javanese. The boy had passed his examinations, and was number one in one of three principal high schools of Java. Both at Semarang, where he went to school, and at Batavia, where he stood his examinations, the doors of the best houses were open to the amiable school-boy, with his agreeable and cultivated manners and great modesty.

Every one spoke Dutch to him, and he could express himself in that language with distinction. Fresh from this environment, he went back to the house of his parents. He thought it would be proper to pay his respects to the authorities of the place and he found himself in the presence of the Resident who had heard of him, and here it was that my friend made a mistake. He dared to address the great man in Dutch.

The following morning notice of an appointment as clerk to a comptroller in the mountains was sent to him. There the young man must remain to think over his "misdeeds" and forget all that he had learned at the schools. After some years a new comptroller or possibly assistant comptroller came; then the measure of his misfortunes was made to overflow. The new chief was a former school-fellow, one who had never shone through his abilities. The young man who had led his classes in everything must now creep upon the ground before the one-time dunce, and speak always high Javanese to him, while he himself was answered in bad Malay. Can you understand the misery of a proud and independent spirit so humbled? And how much strength of character it must have taken to endure that petty and annoying oppression?

But at last he could stand it no longer, he betook himself to Batavia and asked his excellency the Governor General for an audience; it was granted him. The result was that he was sent to Preanger, with a commission to make a study of the rice culture there. He made himself of service through the translation of a pamphlet on the cultivation of water crops from Dutch into Javanese and Sudanese. The government presented him in acknowledgement with several hundred guilders. In the comptroller's school at Batavia, a teacher's place was vacant—a teacher of the Javanese language be it understood—and his friends (among the Javanese) did all in their power to secure this position for him, but without result. It was an absurd idea for a Native to have European pupils who later might become ruling government officials. Perish the thought! I should like to ask who could teach Javanese better than a born Javanese?

The young man went back to his dwelling place; in the meantime another Resident had come, and the tal-ented son of the brown race might at last become an assistant *wedono*.* Not for nothing had he been banished for years to that distant place. He had learned wisdom there; namely, that one cannot serve a European official better than by creeping in the dust before him, and by never speaking a single word of Dutch in his presence. Others have now come into power, and lately when the position of translator of the Javanese language became vacant it was offered to our friend (truly opportunely) now that he does not stand in any one's way! . . .

With heavy hearts, many Europeans here see how the Javanese, whom they regard as their inferiors, are slowly awakening, and at every turn a brown man comes up, who shows that he has just as good brains in his head, and a just as good heart in his body, as the white man. . . .

But we are going forward, and they cannot hold back the current of time. I love the Hollanders very, very much, and I am grateful for everything that we have gained through them. Many of them are among our best friends, but there are also others who dislike us, for no other reason than we are bold enough to emulate them in education and culture.

In many subtle ways they make us feel their dislike. "I am a European, you are a Javanese," they seem to say, or "I am the master, you the governed." Not once, but many times, they speak to us in broken Malay; although they know very well that we understand the Dutch language. It would be a matter of indifference to me in what language they addressed us, if the tone were only polite. . . .

A few days ago we paid a visit to Totokkers (Europeans who are new-comers in Java). Their domestics were old servants of ours, and we knew that they could speak and understand Dutch very well. I told the host this, and what answer did I receive from my gentleman? "No, they must not speak Dutch." "No, why?" I asked. "Because natives ought not to know Dutch." I looked at him in amazement, and a satirical smile quivered at the corners of my mouth. The gentleman grew fiery red, mumbled something into his beard, and discovered something interesting in his boots, at least he devoted all of his attention to them.

## The Roosevelt Corollary: American Imperialism

*Theodore Roosevelt*

*The successful revolutions in Latin America during the early 19th century, combined with the United States' belief in the inevitability of expansion from the Atlantic to the Pacific Oceans, led U.S. President James Monroe to declare in*

---

*Administrative official.

*1823 that European powers should avoid future intrusion into North and South America. This statement, known as the Monroe Doctrine, was little noticed at the time, yet, by the early 1900s, it became a part of a much larger rationale for extending American power throughout Central and South America. The Roosevelt Corollary to the Monroe Doctrine was actually a part of President Theodore Roosevelt's (1901–9) message to Congress in 1904. It stated the new assumptions regarding the conditions under which the United States had the right to intervene in Latin America. This became the rationale for American interventions in Santo Domingo, Haiti, Nicaragua, and Cuba in subsequent years.*

CONSIDER: *How Roosevelt justifies intervention; what Roosevelt meant by the term* civilized; *how Latin Americans might react to such a policy.*

. . . It is not true that the United States feels any land hunger or entertains any projects as regards the other nations of the Western Hemisphere save such as are for their welfare. All that this country desires is to see the neighboring countries stable, orderly, and prosperous. Any country whose people conduct themselves well can count upon our hearty friendship. If a nation shows that it knows how to act with reasonable efficiency and decency in social and political matters, if it keeps order and pays its obligations, it need fear no interference from the United States. Chronic wrongdoing, or an impotence which results in a general loosening of the ties of civilized society, may in America, as elsewhere, ultimately require intervention by some civilized nation, and in the Western Hemisphere the adherence of the United States to the Monroe Doctrine may force the United States, however reluctantly, in flagrant cases of such wrongdoing or impotence, to the exercise of an international police power. . . . It is a mere truism to say that every nation, whether in America or anywhere else, which desires to maintain its freedom, its independence, must ultimately realize that the right of such independence can not be separated from the responsibility of making good use of it.

In asserting the Monroe Doctrine, in taking such steps as we have taken in regard to Cuba, Venezuela, and Panama, and in endeavoring to circumscribe the theater of war in the Far East, and to secure the open door in China, we have acted in our own interest as well as in the interest of humanity at large. There are, however, cases in which, while our own interests are not greatly involved, strong appeal is made to our sympathies. . . . But in extreme cases action may be justifiable and

proper. What form the action shall take must depend upon the circumstances of the case; that is, upon the degree of the atrocity and upon our power to remedy it. The cases in which we could interfere by force of arms as we interfered to put a stop to intolerable conditions in Cuba are necessarily very few.

## A Vindication of Cuba

*Jose Marti*

*Before the Spanish–American War in 1898, Cuba had been engaged in a 10-year struggle of liberation from Spain. Jose Marti (1853–95) was one of the island's most vocal patriots. He was also one of Cuba's great nationalist poets. In this selection, Marti defends his people and rejects the paternalism of U.S. leaders who, under the guise of "aiding" the anti-Spanish forces, actually sought to impose a new form of external rule.*

CONSIDER: *Marti's view of the United States; his view of Cubans and their character; the nature and importance of nationalism for this Latin American poet.*

There are some Cubans who, from honorable motives, from an ardent admiration for progress and liberty, from a prescience of their own powers under better political conditions, from an unhappy ignorance of the history and tendency of annexation, would like to see the island annexed to the United States. But those who have fought in war and learned in exile, who have built, by the work of hands and mind, a virtuous home in the heart of an unfriendly community; who by their successful efforts as scientists and merchants, as railroad builders and engineers, as teachers, artists, lawyers, journalists, orators, and poets, as men of alert intelligence and uncommon activity, are honored wherever their powers have been called into action and the people are just enough to understand them; those who have raised, with their less prepared elements, a town of workingmen where the United States had previously a few huts in a barren cliff; those, more numerous than the others, do not desire the annexation of Cuba to the United States. They do not need it [or] . . . believe that excessive individualism, reverence for wealth, and the protracted exultation of a terrible victory are preparing the United States to be the typical nation of liberty, where no opinion is to be based in greed, and no triumph or acquisition reached against charity and justice. . . .

SOURCE: Theodore Roosevelt, Annual Message, December 6, 1904, *Messages and Papers of the Presidents*, vol. XIV, pp. 6923ff.

SOURCE: Jose Marti, *Our America: Writings on Latin America and the Struggle for Cuban Independence* (New York: Monthly Review Press, 1977), pp. 234–37, as excerpted.

We have suffered impatiently under tyranny; we have fought like men, sometimes like giants, to be freemen; we are passing that period of stormy repose, full of germs of revolt, that naturally follows a period of excessive and unsuccessful action. . . .

But because our government has systematically allowed after the war the triumph of criminals, the occupation of the cities by the scum of the people, the ostentation of ill-gotten riches by the myriad Spanish officeholders and their Cuban accomplices, the conversion of the capital into a gambling den, where the hero and the philosopher walk hungry by the lordly thief of the metropolis; because the healthier farmer, ruined by a war seemingly useless, turns in silence to the plough that he knew well how to exchange for the *machete*; because thousands of exiles, profiting by a period of calm that no human power can quicken until it is naturally exhausted, are practicing in the battle of life in the free countries the art of governing themselves and of building a nation; because our halfbreeds and city-bred young men are generally of delicate physique, of suave courtesy, and ready words, hiding under the glove that polishes the poem the hand that fells the foe—are we to be considered . . . an "effeminate" people? These city-bred young men and poorly built halfbreeds knew in one day how to rise against a cruel government, to pay their passages to the seat of war with the pawning of their watches and trinkets, to work their way in exile while their vessels were being kept from them by the country of the free in the interest of the foes of freedom, to obey as soldiers, sleep in the mud, eat roots, fight ten years without salary, conquer foes with the branch of a tree, die—these men of eighteen, these heirs of wealthy estates, these dusky striplings—a death not to be spoken of without uncovering the head. They died like those other men of ours who, with a stroke of the *machete*, can send a head flying, or by a turn of the hands bring a bull to their feet.

# VISUAL SOURCES

## Imperialism Glorified

### George Harcourt

*This 1900 painting by George Harcourt conveys some of the meaning of imperialism to Europeans. First displayed at the Royal Academy in 1900, it shows British soldiers leaving by train for the Boer War in South Africa. The soldiers are clearly cast in the role of masculine heroes in their own eyes as well as in the eyes of civilians, young and old. This is further evidenced by the couple in the center, representing the epitome of sentimentalized British masculinity and femininity. For many, imperialism enabled Europeans to have a sense of adventure and to prove their superiority to themselves and the rest of the world. Avoided in this picture is the reality of the bloodshed and exploitation to be experienced by these same soldiers and the populations of the colonized lands.*

CONSIDER: *How this painting fits with Kipling's description of "the White Man's burden."*

## The Colonial Battlefield

### Charles Edwin Fripp

*Europeans avidly followed the race for colonies. Newspapers reporting on incidents and conquests in Asia and Africa framed imperial developments as adventures and patriotic causes. Thrilling stories about action overseas sold countless papers and became the subject matter for painters such as Charles Edwin Fripp (1854–1906). In his 1885 canvas (Illustration 22–2), Fripp reveals some of the perceptions of imperialism and the means of conquest. The painting depicts the final moments of the Battle of Isandhlwana on January 22, 1879. The remnants of a 1200-man force of British soldiers stand shoulder to shoulder in a box formation making their last stand before their annihilation by a force of 20,000 Zulus. The steadfast bearing and determined faces of the brave British soldiers indicate that these are masculine heroes, while the Zulus are depicted as ruthless "savages" who brutally kill British soldiers and then gloat over their bodies. The still standing soldiers are portrayed as being at the end of a dramatic "adventure" gone bad, but viewers can see how their tight organization—like the organization of the larger imperial effort—multiplied the power of imperial troops.*

*Viewers of this painting knew that this battle cost the native Zulus dearly, and they assumed that the weapons and quality of men in British uniforms that would follow would lead to victory here as well as in many other such "adventures" over the globe. The painting shows that innovations in weaponry gave the West great clout, enabling so few to hold off so many opponents for so long. Europeans had long possessed more firepower than non-Western peoples. The new breech-loading rifles and machine guns*

SOURCE: Charles Edwin Fripp. *The Battle of Isandhlwana, 22 January 1879.* 1885. National Army Museum, London.

**Illustration 22–1**  Bettmann/Corbis.

multiplied that advantage. Local societies like these Zulus resisted, but with the destructive power of new weapons, European forces numbering in the hundreds could annihilate local forces in the thousands.

CONSIDER: What advantages imperial troops enjoyed in battles; what message to British viewers this painting conveys.

## American Imperialism in Asia: Independence Day 1899

The Spanish–American War of 1898 led to the Spanish defeat and withdrawal from Cuba, Puerto Rico, and the Philippines. It also occasioned an impassioned debate in the United States about whether America should follow in Europe's

**Illustration 22–2**   The National Army Museum, London.

**Illustration 22–3**   General Research Division, The New York Public Library, Astor, Lenox and Tilden Foundations.

footsteps and acquire colonies. The "liberation" of the Philippines led to a 10-year war against Philippine insurgents who fought for independence from both Spain and the United States. American imperialists were interested in the Philippines in large part because it gave them access to trade and investments in other Asian countries, especially the fabled China market that would be able to buy untold quantities of American goods. In this cartoon we see Uncle Sam about to bayonet a Filipino youth who is trying to defend himself with a sword, suggesting the massive difference in power between the U.S. Army and the Philippine insurgents. In back of Uncle Sam, then President McKinley waves the flag, *suggesting the patriotism and jingoism that was seen to be behind American imperialism.*

CONSIDER: *How Americans were able to rationalize their support for colonialism with their long opposition to European imperialism.*

## Imperialism and the Looting of Cultures

In 1897 the British government launched a punitive expedition against the ancient kingdom of Benin in retaliation for the killing of its temporary consul James Philips. Philips had attempted to enter the royal capital, Benin city, unarmed and was killed by Benin forces. The British used the event to launch a war against Benin which resulted in the sacking, burning, and looting of the capital and the conquest of the state. In the picture British officers display part of the hundreds of ivories and bronzes that they had taken from the royal palace. These famous ivories and bronzes later found their way into myriad museums and art dealerships throughout Europe and North America.

CONSIDER: *What the picture suggests about the nature of the "new imperialism"; the debate that such a picture can evoke today about national treasures.*

## Imperialism in Africa

The first of these two maps shows the approximate divisions among indigenous peoples in the centuries prior to European colonization. There were also extremely important cultural and political divisions throughout Africa at this time. The second map shows areas of Africa under European control prior to 1880 and the colonial partition of Africa by European nations by 1914.

Together these maps indicate a number of things about imperialism in Africa. First, the manner and speed with which Africa was divided demonstrate the intense competition involved in this late-19th-century imperial expansion. Second, the European partition of Africa did not take account of the already established social, political, cultural, and ethnic divisions among Africans. From this geopolitical perspective alone, one can imagine some of the disruption to African societies and cultures caused by imperialism. Third, these maps help explain problems experienced by Africans after decolonization occurred. The new African nations were generally formed on the basis of the arbitrary political lines established by European colonizers. Thus, many African countries had to deal with persisting divisions and rivalries among their populations, stemming from the 19th-century partition of Africa.

CONSIDER: *How these maps help explain the effects of imperialism on Africans.*

**Illustration 22–4**   The Pitt Rivers Museum, Oxford, UK.

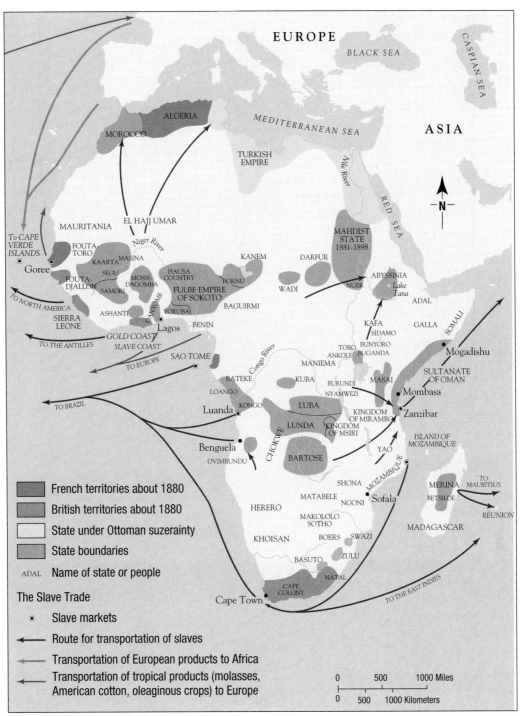

EUROPE

BLACK SEA

CASPIAN SEA

ALGERIA

MOROCCO

MEDITERRANEAN SEA

ASIA

TURKISH EMPIRE

Nile River

RED SEA

N

To CAPE VERDE ISLANDS

MAURITANIA

EL HAJJ UMAR

Niger River

MAHDIST STATE 1881-1898

FOUTA TORO

KAARTA MASINA

KANEM

DARFUR

ABYSSINIA

Goree

SEGU

HAUSA COUNTRY

NUER

Lake Tana

ADAL

FOUTA-DJALLON

MOSSI-DAGOMBA

BORNU

WADI

SAMORI

FULBE EMPIRE OF SOKOTO

KAFA

GALLA

SOMALI

TO NORTH AMERICA

ASHANTI

DAHOMEY

YORUBA

BAGUIRMI

SIDAMO

SIERRA LEONE

BENIN

TORO

BUNYORO

Mogadishu

GOLD COAST

Lagos

ANKOLE

BUGANDA

TO THE ANTILLES

SLAVE COAST

Congo River

MANIEMA

TO EUROPE

SAO TOME

BATEKE

KUBA

MASAI

SULTANATE OF OMAN

LOANGO

BURUNDI

Mombasa

NYAMWEZI

TO BRAZIL

Luanda

KONGO

LUBA

KINGDOM OF MIRAMBO

Zanzibar

CHOKWE

LUNDA

KINGDOM OF MSIRI

ISLAND OF MOZAMBIQUE

Benguela

YAO

OVIMBUNDU

BARTOSE

MOZAMBIQUE

TO MAURITIUS

SHONA

MERINA

MATABELE

Sofala

BETSILOE

HERERO

NGONI

RÉUNION

MAKOLOLO SOTHO

MADAGASCAR

KHOISAN

BOERS

SWAZI

BASUTO

ZULU

NATAL

Cape Town

CAPE COLONY

TO THE EAST INDIES

French territories about 1880

British territories about 1880

State under Ottoman suzerainty

State boundaries

ADAL    Name of state or people

The Slave Trade

▫    Slave markets

←    Route for transportation of slaves

←    Transportation of European products to Africa

←    Transportation of tropical products (molasses, American cotton, oleaginous crops) to Europe

0        500        1000 Miles

0    500    1000 Kilometers

**Map 22–1**

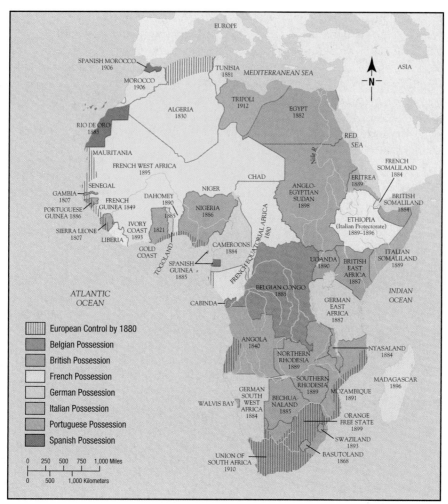

**Map 22–2**

## SECONDARY SOURCES

### The Age of Empire
*Eric J. Hobsbawm*

*Imperialism has been interpreted from a number of perspectives since the early 20th century. The way that scholars view imperialism often reveals much about their own political and ideological views. Some of the earliest interpretations, such as those by J. H. Hobson and V. I. Lenin, were economic. They criticized imperialism as an outgrowth of capitalism—Hobson from the perspective of a liberal socialist, Lenin as a Marxist theorist and political leader. Economic interpretations of imperialism, often in newer versions, remain popu-*

*lar. This is illustrated in the following selection by British historian E. J. Hobsbawm, who has written extensively on 19th-century Western civilization.*

CONSIDER: *Why Hobsbawm considers economic results irrelevant to economic motives for imperialism; why Hobsbawm calls imperialism a natural by-product of the international economy; why political actions are secondary to the economic motives for imperialism.*

A more convincing general motive for colonial expansion was the search for markets. The fact that this was often disappointed is irrelevant. The belief that the 'overproduction' of the Great Depression could be solved by a vast export drive was widespread. Businessmen, always inclined to fill the blank spaces on the map of world trade with vast numbers of potential customers, would naturally look for such unexploited areas: China was one which haunted the imagination of salesmen—what if every one of those 300 millions bought only one box of tin-tacks?—and Africa, the unknown continent, was another. The Chambers of Commerce of British cities in the depressed early 1880s were outraged by the thought that diplomatic negotiations might exclude their traders from access to the Congo basin, which was believed to offer untold sales prospects, all the more so as it was being developed as a paying proposition by that crowned businessman, King Leopold II of the Belgians. . . .

But the crux of the global economic situation was that a number of developed economies simultaneously felt the same need for new markets. If they were sufficiently strong their ideal was 'the open door' on the markets of the underdeveloped world; but if not strong enough, they hoped to carve out for themselves territories which, by virtue of ownership, would give national business a monopoly position or at least a substantial advantage. Partition of the unoccupied parts of the Third World was the logical consequence. In a sense, this was an extension of the protectionism which gained ground almost everywhere after 1879. . . . To this extent the 'new imperialism' was the natural by-product of an international economy based on the rivalry of several competing industrial economies, intensified by the economic pressures of the 1880s. It does not follow that any particular colony was expected to turn into Eldorado by itself, though this is what actually happened in South Africa, which became the world's greatest gold-producer. Colonies might simply provide suitable bases or jumping-off points for regional business penetration. . . .

At this point the economic motive for acquiring some colonial territory becomes difficult to disentangle from the political action required for the purpose, for protectionism of whatever kind is economy operating with the aid of politics. . . .

Once rival powers began to carve up the map of Africa or Oceania, each naturally tried to safeguard against an excessive portion (or a particularly attractive morsel) going to the others. Once the status of a great power thus became associated with raising its flag over some palm-fringed beach (or, more likely, over stretches of dry scrub), the acquisition of colonies itself became a status symbol, irrespective of their value.

## The Scramble for Africa

### M. E. Chamberlain

*The era of European imperialism in Africa (1884–1914) witnessed the military conquest of Africa by different European powers and resulted in the replacement of the various African ruling elites by Europeans. This period has generated significant interest by scholars seeking to explain imperialism*

*by locating it squarely within the realm of European political, economic, and cultural developments. British imperialist expansion has perhaps been subject to more scholarly debates than the actions of any other imperialist power in Africa. In the following selection, Chamberlain, a noted British historian, argues that economic competition was responsible for British actions in west Africa.*

CONSIDER: *The relationship between a restricted group of industrialists and the general public in the democratic politics of Great Britain; the reasons historians would regard the British actions as defensive, not offensive; how unimportant developments in Africa seem to be in this assessment.*

British participation in the Scramble in West Africa was largely defensive, to protect existing interests against new competition. But both the new challenge from the continental powers and the strength of the British response may have had their roots in more general economic factors. Whereas during the greater part of the nineteenth century there had only been one highly industrialised power, Britain, which had supplied a large part of the world with its manufacturing requirements, there were now a number of competing industrial powers. The United States was getting into its stride again after the Civil War. Germany, united in 1871, and helped by the huge indemnity exacted from the defeated French, was industrialising at a rate that left Britain standing still. Even the France of the Third Republic, although slower off the mark than Germany, was modernising quickly. As a natural result of competitive conditions, nations were once again turning to protective tariff policies. Only Britain had committed herself completely to a free trade policy in the middle of the century. For many Britons free trade had indeed become almost a religious doctrine, a necessary precondition of peace, prosperity and international cooperation. In these circumstances Britain could hardly abandon it as an obsolete economic theory, but other nations had no such inhibitions. The United States never really relaxed the high tariffs they had put on during the abnormal circumstances of the Civil War. Germany introduced a protectionist tariff in 1879—partly, it is true, for domestic and revenue reasons. France, which had never been a wholehearted convert to free trade, reverted to traditional protectionist duties in 1882. British traders protested time and time again that their real objection to foreign protectorates was that they meant damage to British trade arising from discriminatory duties.

A shrill note was added to the complaints of the traders, German and French, as well as British, by the

SOURCE: M. E. Chamberlain, *The Scramble for Africa* (New York: Longman, 1974), pp. 60–62.

background fact of the 'Great Depression.' This depression, about which economic historians still argue vigorously, was marked by low prices, low profits, low interest rates, overproduction of certain commodities and, irregularly, high unemployment. It affected most of western Europe. It began with a financial crisis in 1873 and lasted, with varying degrees of intensity, until 1896. Germany and Britain were badly affected in the 1870s. In France the main effect was not felt until the 1880s. In Germany the French indemnity had proved a two-edged weapon. After an initial boom hundreds of companies had gone bankrupt in 1873. By 1879 both British and German economists were seriously alarmed. The depression had already lasted longer than was normal and there seemed no way out of it. Some men in both countries began to think in terms of colonial solutions. A few bold men in Britain began to ask for 'Fair Trade,' a euphemism for the taboo word *protection*. They also began to ask for a parliamentary enquiry. This was eventually set up in 1885 and issued a massive report at the end of 1886. It was one of the most thorough enquiries ever conducted into the state of British industry in the nineteenth century. The Commission called for evidence, not only from government experts but also from chambers of commerce and employers' and working men's associations. The evidence revealed deep and widespread anxieties. There was a great division of opinion as to how the crisis should be met but many spoke of the need for new markets and a few spoke specifically of the existing colonies and of the new possibilities of Africa.

It would be wrong to see a massive or articulate public demand for imperial expansion in the mid-1880s, but the climate of opinion had undoubtedly changed. Britain's industrial position was now challenged and with it the prosperity of all classes of her population, Lancashire cotton workers as much as city businessmen, and this was widely realised. There was a distinct disposition to hang on to everything Britain had and not to shrink from new acquisitions, if this kept them out of the hands of a rival. The government was affected by this as well as the public. There was little logic about Britain's large acquisitions of territory in tropical Africa in the mid-1880s. They were essentially an anxious, even panicky, reaction to new challenges in an already worrying situation.

## The Tools of Empire

*Daniel R. Headrick*

*Recently some historians have focused on exactly how the spread of imperial rule took place during the second half of the 19th century. They argue that the tools of colonial conquest* *constituted an important explanation for that burst of colonial expansion occurring when it did. In the following selection from his influential book,* The Tools of Empire: Technology and European Imperialism in the Nineteenth Century, *Daniel R. Headrick focuses on the ways key inventions and innovations enabled Europeans to conquer new lands with such relative ease.*

CONSIDER: *How, according to Headrick, technology helps explain the events of imperial expansion; whether Headrick's argument undermines an economic or nationalistic interpretation of imperialism or adds to those interpretations.*

Imperialism in the mid-century was predominantly a matter of British tentacles reaching out from India toward Burma, China, Malaya, Afghanistan, Mesopotamia, and the Red Sea. Territorially, at least, a much more impressive demonstration of the new imperialism was the scramble for Africa in the last decades of the century. Historians generally agree that from a profit-making point of view, the scramble was a dubious undertaking. Here also, technology helps explain events.

Inventions are most easily described one by one, each in its own technological and socioeconomic setting. Yet the inner logic of innovations must not blind us to the patterns of chronological coincidence. Though advances occurred in every period, many of the innovations that proved useful to the imperialists of the scramble first had an impact in the two decades from 1860 to 1880. These were the years in which quinine prophylaxis made Africa safer for Europeans; quick-firing breechloaders replaced muzzleloaders among the forces stationed on the imperial frontiers; and the compound engine, the Suez Canal, and the submarine cable made steamships competitive with sailing ships, not only on government-subsidized mail routes, but for ordinary freight on distant seas as well. Europeans who set out to conquer new lands in 1880 had far more power over nature and over the people they encountered than their predecessors twenty years earlier had; they could accomplish their tasks with far greater safety and comfort. . . .

What the breechloader, the machine gun, the steamboat and steamship, and quinine and other innovations did was to lower the cost, in both financial and human terms, of penetrating, conquering, and exploiting new territories. So cost-effective did they make imperialism that not only national governments but lesser groups as well could now play a part in it. The Bombay Presidency opened the Red Sea Route; the Royal Niger Company

SOURCE: Daniel R. Headrick, *The Tools of Empire: Technology and European Imperialism in the Nineteenth Century* (New York: Oxford University Press, 1981), pp. 205–6.

conquered the Caliphate of Sokoto; even individuals like Macgregor Laird, William Mackinnon, Henry Stanley, and Cecil Rhodes could precipitate events and stake out claims to vast territories which later became parts of empires. It is because the flow of new technologies in the nineteenth century made imperialism so cheap that it reached the threshold of acceptance among the peoples and governments of Europe, and led nations to become empires. Is this not as important a factor in the scramble for Africa as the political, diplomatic, and business motives that historians have stressed?

## Imperialism in the Americas

### Manuel Maldonado-Denis

*While U.S. historians generally present U.S. involvement in Latin America as being a product of mistakes or good intentions gone awry, Latin Americans see these political and economic manipulations through a very different lens. Maldonado-Denis, a Puerto Rican historian, uses much starker Marxist concepts of imperialism to explain the subjugation of an island that is ostensibly part of the United States.*

CONSIDER: *How Maldonado-Denis thinks the expansion of the United States should be viewed and understood; how U.S. interests in Puerto Rico should be understood according to Maldonado-Denis; how one might disagree with Maldonado-Denis's interpretation.*

The expansion of the United States must . . . be seen in its proper perspective as a movement destined to gain commercial, industrial, and financial hegemony in the Western Hemisphere, and, as a necessary corollary to that, naval and military bases indispensable to maintaining this hegemony. Nor can this expansionist movement to the south be seen apart from U.S. expansion to the Orient—in search of new markets in the Philippines, Hawaii, China, and other countries for its surplus products. Acquiring influence in all of these geographical areas fell within the great master plan of this empire which, according to its most fervent apologists, sought to extend to "savage and backward" people the immense benefits of its civilization. The rhetoric of the period—stripped of all pretense about the sensibilities and rights of colonized peoples—reveals that . . . North American capitalism had as its motivating force the pressing need to expand its influence beyond its borders or face crises . . . as, for example, the depression of 1893—which shook the system to its roots.

SOURCE: M. Maldonado-Denis, *Puerto Rico: A Socio-Historic Interpretation,* trans., E. Vialo. Translation Copyright © 1972 by Random House, Inc. Reprinted by permission of the publisher.

Imperialism is inherently a global system of domination. Therefore, with successful North American expansion at the end of the nineteenth century there arose a curious mixture of colonialism in the classic sense (Puerto Rico, Hawaii, the Philippines) and what we today know of as neocolonialism (as, for example, in the case of Cuba, and later Santo Domingo, Haiti, etc.). Viewed in perspective, neocolonialism did not first develop in the postwar period; at the time of the War of 1898 it was already germinating in North American foreign policy. The Monroe Doctrine, with its particular corollaries (Olney, T. Roosevelt), and "manifest destiny" are more or less comprehensive examples of the phenomenon referred to. When Olney, because of the dispute between England and Venezuela over British Guiana, issued his famous corollary—"The United States is today practically sovereign in America, and her fiat is the law in those matters in which she intervenes"—he unabashedly admitted that the North American hegemony was already so deeply entrenched that no other power had sufficient strength to oppose its will. . . .

Seen from this point of view, U.S. interest in Puerto Rico can be more clearly understood. First of all, . . . [f]or a system that, as we have seen, needed markets for its surplus products, the smallest of the Antilles could not be unimportant. In the second place, once the United States became a great naval power, it found it necessary to construct coaling stations, provision centers, and so forth, to enable the U.S. Navy to cross the seas with as few stops as possible. In 1891 Blaine wrote to Benjamin Harrison, "I believe that there are only three places of sufficient value to be taken: one is Hawaii and the others are Puerto Rico and Cuba." In addition, Harrison's administration considered acquiring the Dutch West Indies, the Bay of Samaná in Santo Domingo, and the St. Nicholas Mole in Haiti. This preoccupation with the acquisition of strategic areas continued to manifest itself as a major characteristic of U.S. foreign policy with the opening of the Panama Canal some years later. . . .

Therefore, to convert the Caribbean into a "North American Mediterranean" was not something alien to the concerns of the ruling North Americans. Because of her strategic position, Puerto Rico had her importance to the new empire. The same could be said for Cuba, Hawaii, and the Philippines.

## Chapter Questions

1. How might you use the sources in this chapter to explain the rise of the new imperialism in the late 19th century?

2. In what ways was imperialism justified by Westerners? Take care to distinguish between justifications and causes.

3. What do you think were the most important consequences of imperialism during this period, for the imperialized areas of the world as well as for the imperial nations themselves?

4. Compare the new imperialism with the imperial expansion of the 15th and 16th centuries. What were the similarities? What were the differences?

# Chapter Twenty-Three

# War, Revolution, and Authoritarianism in the West, 1914–45

Western historians usually mark the end of the 19th century not at the turn of the century but with the outbreak of World War I in 1914. At first, few expected the war to be so widespread or long-lasting. In the end, the destruction was so unprecedented and the fighting so brutal that one had to question whether Western civilization had progressed at all.

War strains contributed to revolutions occurring during and after the war in a number of areas, most notably in Germany, the Austro-Hungarian Empire, and Russia. The

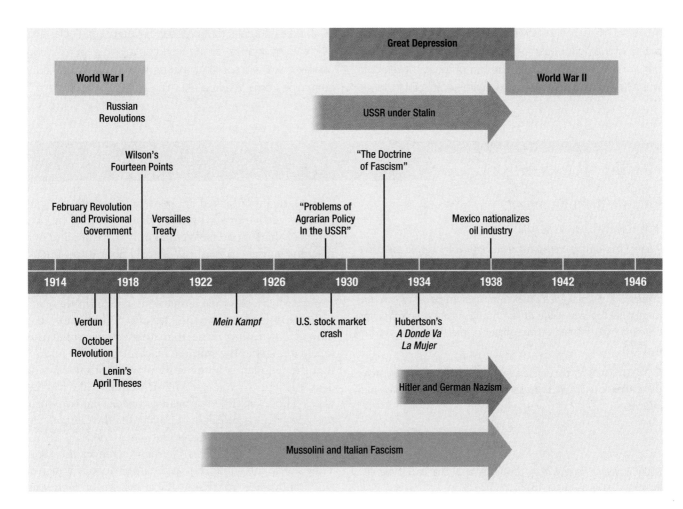

revolutions in Russia were the most important. In March 1917 the tsarist government was swept from power by relatively moderate, liberal groups. In November of that year the new Provisional Government was toppled by the Bolsheviks, who initiated a communist regime that proved surprisingly resilient. Under this government, the Soviet Union was to become a significant force in world politics.

The two decades following World War I were marked by instability and uncertainty. Except in the Soviet Union, where the Bolsheviks had taken power, it appeared that liberal democracy had been established throughout much of the West. But soon a trend toward authoritarianism appeared. The economic problems left from World War I did not disappear, despite a brief period of fragile prosperity in the mid-1920s. In 1929 the stock market crash in New York initiated the Great Depression in the United States, which quickly spread to Europe. Huge numbers of people suffered economically, and governments were pressured to effect radical solutions to the problems. Swept by uncertainty about the present and the future, societies seemed to polarize into opposing classes and around opposing ideologies.

While Communist parties spread throughout the West and were perceived as a great threat, they did not come to power outside of the Soviet Union. Authoritarian movements of the right became the most immediate danger to parliamentary democracies. The first of these movements was Mussolini's fascism, which became dominant in Italy in 1922. By the end of the decade, regimes in eastern and southern Europe were becoming more authoritarian. This trend became stronger during the Depression of the 1930s in both Europe and Latin America. The most extreme of rightist ideologies, Hitler's Nazism, became dominant in Germany in 1933 and spawned a totalitarian form of government there. By the end of that decade, Europe (and soon thereafter most of the West) was embroiled in a new world war even greater than World War I.

The sources in this chapter focus on four topics. The first concerns the two world wars of the period, particularly the causes and consequences of World War I. The second concerns the causes and nature of the revolutions in Russia, which eventually brought the Bolsheviks to power and transformed the country into the Soviet Union. The third involves social and economic problems of the period, including those stemming from World War I and the Great Depression; particular attention is paid to the extent to which changes affected women. The fourth is the rise of authoritarianism and totalitarianism, with emphasis on Fascism in Italy, Nazism in Germany, and Communism under Stalin in the Soviet Union.

As the sources indicate, the period between 1914 and 1945 was traumatic for European nations in particular and of great importance for the world as a whole. In following chapters we will see that this period and developments stemming from it marked a turning point in world history.

# PRIMARY SOURCES

## Reports from the Front:
## The Battle for Verdun, 1916

*The widely anticipated short war typified by heroic offensive thrusts failed to materialize. Instead, it turned into a long, extraordinarily brutal struggle. On the Western front, opposing armies slaughtered each other from their trenches. There are numerous reports of life at the front, such as the following account by a French Army officer of the battle for Verdun in 1916.*

CONSIDER: *Why the defense was at such an advantage; why there was a willingness to sacrifice so much for such small advances.*

---

SOURCE: *Source Records of the Great War,* vol. IV, Charles F. Horne, ed. (New York: National Alumni, 1923), pp. 222–23.

The Germans attacked in massed formation, by big columns of five or six hundred men, preceded by two waves of sharpshooters. We had only our rifles and our machine guns, because the 75's could not get to work.

Fortunately the flank batteries succeeded in catching the Boches on the right. It is absolutely impossible to convey what losses the Germans must suffer in these attacks. Nothing can give the idea of it. Whole ranks are mowed down, and those that follow them suffer the same fate. Under the storm of machine gun, rifle and 75 fire, the German columns were plowed into furrows of death. Imagine if you can what it would be like to rake water. Those gaps filled up again at once. That is enough to show with what disdain of human life the German attacks are planned and carried out.

In these circumstances German advances are sure. They startle the public, but at the front nobody attaches any importance to them. As a matter of fact, our trenches are so near those of the Germans that once the barbed wire is destroyed the distance between them can be covered in a few minutes. Thus, if one is willing to suffer a loss of life corresponding to the number of men necessary to cover the space between the lines, the other trench can always be reached. By sacrificing thousands of men, after a formidable bombardment, an enemy trench can always be taken.

There are slopes on Hill 304 where the level of the ground is raised several meters by mounds of German corpses. Sometimes it happens that the third German wave uses the dead of the second wave as ramparts and shelters. It was behind ramparts of the dead left by the first five attacks, on May 24th, that we saw the Boches take shelter while they organized their next rush.

We make prisoners among these dead during our counterattacks. They are men who have received no hurt, but have been knocked down by the falling of the human wall of their killed and wounded neighbors. They say very little. They are for the most part dazed with fear and alcohol, and it is several days before they recover.

## Dulce et Decorum Est: Disillusionment
*Wilfred Owen*

*The experience of World War I was profoundly disillusioning to those who believed in 19th-century ideals. After World War I, Europe was no longer characterized by the sense of optimism, progress, and glory that had typified Europe for most of the period between the 18th-century and 1914. This is evidenced in war poems that no longer glorified the struggle but instead conveyed a sense of the horror and futility about it. One of the best of these antiwar poets was Wilfred Owen, born in England in 1893 and killed in action in 1918, one week before the armistice. The following poem has the ironic ending, "It is sweet and proper to die for one's country."*

CONSIDER: *The psychological consequences of war for the soldiers; other ways this same disillusionment might be shown in novels, plays, paintings, or even historical analyses of the time.*

DULCE ET DECORUM EST

Bent double, like old beggars under sacks,
Knock-kneed, coughing like hags, we cursed
   through sludge,
Till on the haunting flares we turned our backs

And towards our distant rest began to trudge.
Men marched asleep. Many had lost their boots
But limped on, blood-shod. All went lame; all blind;
Drunk with fatigue; deaf even to the hoots
Of tired, outstripped Five-Nines that dropped behind.

Gas! Gas! Quick, boys!—An Ecstasy of fumbling,
Fitting the clumsy helmets just in time;
But someone still was yelling out and stumbling
And flound'ring like a man in fire or lime . . .
Dim, through the misty panes and thick green light,
As under a green sea, I saw him drowning.
In all my dreams, before my helpless sight,
He plunges at me, guttering, choking, drowning.

If in some smothering dreams you too could pace
Behind the wagon that we flung him in,
And watch the white eyes writhing in his face,
His hanging face, like a devil's sick of sin;
If you could hear, at every jolt, the blood
Come gargling from the froth-corrupted lungs,
Obscene as cancer, bitter as the cud
Of vile, incurable sores on innocent tongues,—
My friend, you would not tell with such high zest
To children ardent for some desperate glory,
The old Lie: Dulce et decorum est
Pro patria mori.

## The Fourteen Points
*Woodrow Wilson*

*Each nation entered World War I for its own mixture of pragmatic and idealistic reasons. In considering their war aims and a possible peace settlement, governments did not anticipate the changes that would occur in this unexpectedly long and costly war. By 1918 various governments had fallen and the United States had entered the conflict. On January 8, 1918, in an address to a joint session of the U.S. Congress, President Woodrow Wilson (1856–1924) presented his Fourteen Points, a delineation of American war aims and proposals for a peace settlement. The Fourteen Points served as a basis for debate at the Paris Peace Conference in 1919 and represented the most idealistic statement of what might be gained in a final peace settlement.*

CONSIDER: *The ideals that hold these points together; the grievances recognized and unrecognized in these points; the assumptions about what measures would preserve peace in the postwar world.*

SOURCE: C. Day Lewis, *Collected Poems of Wilfred Owen.* Reprinted by permission of New Directions and Chatto & Windus, p. 55. Copyright © Chatto & Windus, Ltd., 1946, 1963, and The Owen Estate.

SOURCE: Woodrow Wilson, "Fourteen Points," *Congressional Record,* vol. LVI, part I (1918) (Washington, DC: U.S. Government Printing Office), pp. 680–81.

We entered this war because violations of right had occurred which touched us to the quick and made the life of our own people impossible unless they were corrected and the world secured once for all against their recurrence. What we demand in this war, therefore, is nothing peculiar to ourselves. It is that the world be made fit and safe to live in; and particularly that it be made safe for every peace-loving nation which, like our own, wishes to live its own life, determine its own institutions, be assured of justice and fair dealing by the other peoples of the world as against force and selfish aggression. All the peoples of the world are in effect partners in this interest, and for our own part we see very clearly that unless justice be done to others it will not be done to us. The program of the world's peace, therefore, is our program; and that program, the only possible program, as we see it, is this:

I. Open covenants of peace, openly arrived at, after which there shall be no private international understandings of any kind but diplomacy shall proceed always frankly and in the public view.

II. Absolute freedom of navigation upon the seas, outside territorial waters, alike in peace and in war, except as the seas may be closed in whole or in part by international action. . . .

III. The removal, so far as possible, of all economic barriers and the establishment of an equality of trade conditions among all the nations consenting to the peace and associating themselves for its maintenance.

IV. Adequate guarantees given and taken that national armaments will be reduced to the lowest point consistent with domestic safety.

V. A free, open-minded, and absolutely impartial adjustment of all colonial claims, based upon a strict observance of the principle that in determining all such questions of sovereignty the interests of the populations concerned must have equal weight with the equitable claims of the government whose title is to be determined.

VI. The evacuation of all Russian territory and such a settlement of all questions affecting Russia as will secure the best and freest cooperation of the other nations of the world in obtaining for her an unhampered and unembarrassed opportunity for the independent determination of her own political development and national policy and assure her of a sincere welcome into the society of free nations under institutions of her own choosing; and, more than a welcome, assistance also of every kind that she may need and may herself desire.

VII. Belgium, the whole world will agree, must be evacuated and restored, without any attempt to limit the sovereignty which she enjoys in common with all other free nations. . . .

VIII. All French territory should be freed and the invaded portions restored, and the wrong done to France by Prussia in 1871 in the matter of Alsace-Lorraine, which has unsettled the peace of the world for nearly fifty years, should be righted, in order that peace may once more be made secure in the interest of all.

IX. A readjustment of the frontiers of Italy should be effected along clearly recognizable lines of nationality.

X. The peoples of Austria-Hungary, whose place among the nations we wish to see safeguarded and assured, should be accorded the freest opportunity of autonomous development. . . .

XII. The Turkish portions of the present Ottoman Empire should be assured a secure sovereignty, but the other nationalities which are now under Turkish rule should be assured an undoubted security of life and an absolutely unmolested opportunity of autonomous development. . . .

XIII. An independent Polish state should be erected which should include the territories inhabited by indisputably Polish populations. . . .

XIV. A general association of nations must be formed under specific covenants for the purpose of affording mutual guarantees of political independence and territorial integrity to great and small states alike.

In regard to these essential rectifications of wrong and assertions of right we feel ourselves to be intimate partners of all the governments and peoples associated together against the Imperialists. We cannot be separated in interest or divided in purpose. We stand together until the end.

. . . We have no jealousy of German greatness, and there is nothing in this program that impairs it. We grudge her no achievement or distinction of learning or of pacific enterprise such as have made her record very bright and very enviable. We do not wish to injure her or to block in any way her legitimate influence or power. . . .

Neither do we presume to suggest to her any alteration or modification of her institutions. But it is necessary . . . that we should know whom her spokesmen speak for when they speak to us, whether for the Reich-stag majority or for the military party and the men whose creed is imperial domination.

. . . An evident principle runs through the whole program I have outlined. It is the principle of justice to all peoples and nationalities, and their right to live on equal terms of liberty and safety with one another, whether they be strong or weak. . . . The people of the United States could act upon no other principle; and to the vindication of this principle they are ready to devote their lives, their honor, and everything that they possess. The moral climax of this the culminating and final war for human liberty has come and they are ready to put their own strength, their own highest purpose, their own integrity and devotion to the test.

## April Theses: The Bolshevik Strategy
### V. I. Lenin

*In the spring of 1917 a revolution finally toppled the disintegrating tsarist government in Russia. A relatively moderate, liberal Provisional Government was formed under the leadership of men such as Prince Lvov and Paul Miliukov. While the Provisional Government had to share and even compete for power with the more radical workers' political organizations— the soviets—it initially acted with speed to make important changes. However, faced with a continuing war and deep discontent, the Provisional Government soon came under attack by those such as Vladimir Ilyich Lenin (1870–1924), who called for more radical changes. Lenin, who spent much of his life as a revolutionary—often in exile—had risen to the leadership of the Bolshevik faction of the Russian Marxists. He combined the skills of a superb Marxist theoretician and a revolutionary organizer. In April 1917 the Germans aided his return to Russia in an effort to weaken the new government there. On his arrival, Lenin presented his April Theses, at first criticized by Russian Marxists but eventually accepted by the Bolshevik Central Committee.*

CONSIDER: *Why Lenin rejects support for the Provisional Government; to whom this program might be appealing and why; the ways in which this program is particularly Marxist.*

1. In our attitude towards the war, which under the new government of Lvov and Co. unquestionably remains on Russia's part a predatory imperialist war owing to the capitalist nature of that government, not the slightest concession to a "revolutionary defencism" is permissible. . . .

2. *The specific feature of the present situation in Russia is that the country is* passing from the first stage of the revolution—which, owing to the insufficient class-consciousness and organisation of the proletariat, placed power in the hands of the bourgeoisie—to its *second* stage, which must place power in the hands of the proletariat and the poorest sections of the peasants. . . .

3. No support for the Provisional Government; . . .

5. Not a parliamentary republic—to return to a parliamentary republic from the Soviets of Workers' Deputies would be a retrograde step—but a republic of Soviets of Workers', Agricultural Labourers' and Peasants' Deputies throughout the country, from top to bottom. Abolition of the police, the army and the bureaucracy. The salaries of all officials, all of whom are elective and displaceable at any time, not to exceed the average wage of a competent worker.

6. The weight of emphasis in the agrarian programme to be shifted to the Soviets of Agricultural Labourers' Deputies.
Confiscation of all landed estates.
Nationalisation of *all* lands in the country, the land to be disposed of by the local Soviets of Agricultural Labourers' and Peasants' Deputies. The organisation of separate Soviets of Deputies of Poor Peasants. The setting up of a model farm on each of the large estates ranging in size from 100 to 300 dessiatines, according to local and other conditions, and to the decisions of the local bodies under the control of the Soviets of Agricultural Labourers' Deputies and for the public account.

7. The immediate amalgamation of all banks in the country into a single national bank, and the institution of control over it by the Soviet of Workers' Deputies.

8. It is not our *immediate* task to "introduce" socialism, but only to bring social production and the distribution of products at once under the *control* of the Soviets of Workers' Deputies.

## The Doctrine of Fascism
### Benito Mussolini

*Italy was the first European power to turn to fascism. She was one of the victors in World War I, but the war was costly and Italy did not gain much. After the war the country was*

SOURCE: V. I. Lenin, *Collected Works,* vol. XXIV (Moscow: Progress Publishers, 1964), pp. 21–24. Reprinted by permission of the Copyright Agency of the U.S.S.R.

*marked by instability, weak governments, and an apparent threat from the left. Benito Mussolini (1883–1945), a former leader of the Socialist party and a veteran of the war, organized the Italian Fascist Party in 1919. Strongly nationalistic, the party stood against the Versailles Treaty, left-wing radicalism, and the established government. After leading his Blackshirts in a march on Rome in 1922, Mussolini was invited by King Victor Emmanuel III to form a government. Over the next few years Mussolini effectively eliminated any opposition and installed his fascist state system, which would last some 20 years. The following document contains excerpts from "The Political and Social Doctrine of Fascism," an article signed by Mussolini and written with the philosopher Giovanni Gentile; it originally appeared in the Enciclopedia Italiana in 1932. It describes the ideological foundations of Italian fascism. These excerpts emphasize the rejection of traditional democracy, liberalism, and socialism as well as faith in the authoritarian, fascist state.*

CONSIDER: *The greatest sources of appeal in the doctrine according to Mussolini; the ways in which this doctrine can be considered a rejection of major historical trends developing over the previous century; the government policies that would logically flow from such a doctrine.*

Fascism, the more it considers and observes the future and the development of humanity quite apart from political considerations of the moment, believes neither in the possibility nor the utility of perpetual peace. It thus repudiates the doctrine of Pacifism—born of a renunciation of the struggle and an act of cowardice in the face of sacrifice. War alone brings up to its highest tension all human energy and puts the stamp of nobility upon the peoples who have the courage to meet it. . . .

The Fascist accepts life and loves it, knowing nothing of and depising suicide; he rather conceives of life as duty and struggle and conquest, life which should be high and full, lived for oneself, but above all for others—those who are at hand and those who are far distant, contemporaries, and those who will come after. . . .

Such a conception of life makes Fascism the complete opposite of that doctrine, the base of so-called scientific and Marxian Socialism, the materialist conception of history. . . . Fascism, now and always, believes in holiness and in heroism; that is to say, in actions influenced by no economic motive, direct or indirect. . . .

Fascism repudiates the conception of "economic" happiness, to be realized by Socialism and, as it were, at a given moment in economic evolution to assure to everyone the maximum of well-being. Fascism denies the materialist conception of happiness as a possibility, and abandons it to its inventors, the economists of the first half of the nineteenth century. . . .

After Socialism, Fascism combats the whole complex system of democratic ideology, and repudiates it, whether in its theoretical premises or in its practical application. Fascism denies that the majority, by the simple fact that it is a majority, can direct human society; it denies that numbers alone can govern by means of a periodical consultation, and it affirms the immutable, beneficial, and fruitful inequality of mankind, which can be permanently leveled through the mere operation of a mechanical process such as universal suffrage. . . .

Fascism denies, in democracy, the absurd conventional untruth of political equality dressed out in the garb of collective irresponsibility, and the myth of "happiness" and indefinite progress. But, if democracy may be conceived in diverse forms—that is to say, taking democracy to mean a state of society in which the populace are not reduced to impotence in the State—Fascism may write itself down as "an organized, centralized, and authoritative democracy."

Fascism has taken up an attitude of complete opposition to the doctrines of Liberalism, both in the political field and the field of economics. . . . For if the nineteenth century was a century of individualism (Liberalism always signifying individualism) it may be expected that this will be the century of collectivism, and hence the century of the State. It is a perfectly logical deduction that a new doctrine can utilize all the still vital elements of previous doctrines. . . .

The foundation of Fascism is the conception of the State, its character, its duty, and its aim. Fascism conceives of the State as an absolute, in comparison with which all individuals or groups are relative, only to be conceived of in their relation to the State. The conception of the Liberal State is not that of a directing force, guiding the play and development, both material and spiritual, of a collective body, but merely a force limited to the function of recording results: on the other hand, the Fascist State is itself conscious, and has itself a will and a personality—thus it may be called the "ethic" State. . . .

If every age has its own characteristic doctrine, there are a thousand signs which point to Fascism as the characteristic doctrine of our time. For if a doctrine must be a living thing, this is proved by the fact that Fascism has created a living faith; and that this faith is very powerful in the minds of men, is demonstrated by those who have suffered and died for it.

SOURCE: Benito Mussolini, "The Political and Social Doctrine of Fascism," *International Conciliation,* no. 306 (January 1935), pp. 7–17. Originally published by the Carnegie Endowment for International Peace, as part of the *International Counciliation Series.*

Fascism has henceforth in the world the universality of all those doctrines which, in realizing themselves, have represented a stage in the history of the human spirit.

## The German Woman and National Socialism [Nazism]
*Guida Diehl*

*From the beginning, the Nazi party stood against any expansion of women's political or economic roles. Indeed the Nazi policy was to keep women in their own separate sphere as mothers and wives and remove them from jobs and politics—the man's sphere. Nevertheless, many women supported the Nazi party and joined Nazi women's organizations. The following selection is from a book published in 1933 by Guida Diehl, a leader of pro-Nazi women's organizations.*

CONSIDER: *The ways this might appeal to German women; how this fits with other ideals of Nazism.*

This tumultuous age with all its difficulties and challenges must create a new type of woman capable of partaking in the achievement of the Third Reich and of fulfilling the womanly task that awaits her.

Let us not forget that this new woman holds her honor high above all else. A man's honor rests on fulfilling the tasks of public life entrusted to him. He safeguards his honor by doing his work honorably and with firmness of character and pride. A woman's honor rests on the province specifically entrusted to her, for which she is responsible, the province where new life is to grow: love, marriage, family, motherhood. A woman who does not accept this responsibility, who misuses this province for mere enjoyment, who will not let herself be proudly wooed before she surrenders—which is nature's way—who does not in marriage provide a new generation with the basis of a family—such a woman desecrates her honor. For we live in a time when womanly worth and dignity, womanly honor and pride, are of the utmost importance for the future of the nation, for the next generation. Therefore, the proud safeguarding of her honor must be an essential characteristic of this new type of woman. The German man wants to look up again to the German maid, the German woman. He wants to admire

in her this dignity, this pride, this safeguarding of her honor and her heroic fighting spirit along with her native, cheerful simplicity. He wants to know again that German women and German fidelity go hand in hand, and that it is worthwhile to live and die for such German womanhood.

## The Informed Heart: Nazi Concentration Camps
*Bruno Bettelheim*

*Organized, official racial persecution was a direct consequence of Nazi theories, attitudes, and practices. During the 1920s and early 1930s, however, the extent of the persecution was unanticipated. The most extreme form of this occurred in the late 1930s, with the introduction of forced labor and concentration camps, later to be followed by camps in which a policy of literal extermination was pursued. In the following selection, Bruno Bettelheim, a psychoanalyst in Austria at the time and later a leading psychoanalyst in the United States, describes his experiences in the concentration camps at Dachau and Buchenwald. He focuses on the dehumanizing processes involved and some of the ways prisoners adapted in an effort to survive.*

CONSIDER: *The methods used to gain control over the prisoners; the psychological means developed by Bettelheim and other prisoners to cope with and survive this experience; how the existence, nature, and functioning of these camps reflect the theory and practice of Nazi totalitarianism.*

Usually the standard initiation of prisoners took place during transit from the local prison to the camp. If the distance was short, the transport was often slowed down to allow enough time to break the prisoners. During their initial transport to the camp, prisoners were exposed to nearly constant torture. The nature of the abuse depended on the fantasy of the particular SS man in charge of a group of prisoners. Still, they all had a definite pattern. Physical punishment consisted of whipping, frequent kicking (abdomen or groin), slaps in the face, shooting, or wounding with the bayonet. These alternated with attempts to produce extreme exhaustion. For instance, prisoners were forced to stare for hours into glaring lights, to kneel for hours, and so on.

From time to time a prisoner got killed, but no prisoner was allowed to care for his or another's wounds. The guards also forced prisoners to hit one another and to defile what the SS considered the prisoners' most cherished values. They were forced to curse their God, to accuse themselves and one another of vile actions, and their wives of adultery and prostitution. . . .

The purpose of this massive initial abuse was to traumatize the prisoners and break their resistance; to change at least their behavior if not yet their personalities. This could be seen from the fact that tortures became less and less violent to the degree that prisoners stopped resisting and complied immediately with any SS order, even the most outrageous. . . .

It is hard to say just how much the process of personality change was speeded up by what prisoners experienced during the initiation. Most of them were soon totally exhausted; physically from abuse, loss of blood, thirst, etc.; psychologically from the need to control their anger and desperation before it could lead to a suicidal resistance. . . .

If I should try to sum up in one sentence what my main problem was during the whole time I spent in the camps, it would be: to protect my inner self in such a way that if, by any good fortune, I should regain liberty, I would be approximately the same person I was when deprived of liberty. So it seems that a split was soon forced upon me, the split between the inner self that might be able to retain its integrity, and the rest of the personality that would have to submit and adjust for survival. . . .

I have no doubt that I was able to endure the horrors of the transport and all that followed, because right from the beginning I became convinced that these dreadful and degrading experiences were somehow not happening to "me" as a subject, but only "me" as an object. . . .

All thoughts and feelings I had during the transport were extremely detached. It was as if I watched things happening in which I took part only vaguely. . . .

This was taught me by a German political prisoner, a communist worker who by then had been at Dachau for four years. I arrived there in a sorry condition because of experiences on the transport. I think that this man, by then an "old" prisoner, decided that, given my condition, the chances of my surviving without help were slim. So when he noticed that I could not swallow food because of physical pain and psychological revulsion, he spoke to me out of his rich experience: "Listen you, make up your mind: do you want to live or do you want to die? If you don't care, don't eat the stuff. But if you want to live, there's only one way: make up your mind to eat whenever and whatever you can, never mind how disgusting. Whenever you have a chance, defecate, so you'll be sure your body works. And whenever you have a minute, don't blabber, read by yourself, or flop down and sleep."

## Problems of Agrarian Policy in the U.S.S.R.: Soviet Collectivization

### Joseph Stalin

*Joseph Stalin (1879–1953) rose from his working-class origins to become a leading member of the Bolsheviks before the 1917 revolution, the general secretary of the Russian Communist party in 1922, and the unchallenged dictator of the U.S.S.R. by 1929. In 1927 Stalin and the leadership of the Russian Communist party decided on a policy for the planned industrialization of the U.S.S.R.—the First Five-Year Plan. At the same time they decided on a policy favoring the collectivization of agriculture. By 1929 Stalin made that policy more drastic, using massive coercion against the kulaks (relatively rich independent peasants). Kulaks resisted this enforced collectivization; widespread death and destruction resulted. Nevertheless, by 1932 much of Russian agriculture was collectivized. Here is an excerpt from a 1929 speech delivered by Stalin at the Conference of Marxist Students of the Agrarian Question. In it he explains and justifies the policy of collectivization and the need to eliminate the kulaks as a class.*

CONSIDER: *How this policy toward the kulaks relates to the policy for the planned industrialization of the U.S.S.R.; how Stalin justifies this policy as "socialist" as opposed to "capitalist"; the differences between Stalin's attitudes and ideas toward the kulaks and Hitler's toward the Jews.*

Can we advance our socialized industry at an accelerated rate while having to rely on an agricultural base, such as is provided by small peasant farming, which is incapable of expanded reproduction, and which, in addition, is the predominant force in our national economy? No, we cannot. Can the Soviet government and the work of Socialist construction be, for any length of time, based on two *different* foundations; on the foundation of the most large-scale and concentrated Socialist industry and on the foundation of the most scattered and backward, small-commodity peasant farming? No, they cannot. Sooner or later this would be bound to end in the complete collapse of the whole national economy. What, then, is the solution? The solution lies in enlarging the agricultural units, in making agriculture capable of accumulation, of expanded reproduction, and in thus changing the agricultural base of our national economy. But how are the agricultural units to be enlarged? There are

SOURCE: J. V. Stalin, "Problems of Agrarian Policy in the U.S.S.R.," in *Problems of Leninism*, J. V. Stalin, ed. (Moscow: Foreign Languages, 1940), pp. 303–5, 318–21. Reprinted by permission of the Copyright Agency of the U.S.S.R.

two ways of doing this. There is the *capitalist* way, which is to enlarge the agricultural units by introducing capitalism in agriculture—a way which leads to the impoverishment of the peasantry and to the development of capitalist enterprises in agriculture. We reject this way as incompatible with the Soviet economic system. There is a second way: the *Socialist* way, which is to set up collective farms and state farms, the way which leads to the amalgamation of the small peasant farms into large collective farms, technically and scientifically equipped, and to the squeezing out of the capitalist elements from agriculture. We are in favour of this second way.

And so, the question stands as follows: either one way or the other, either *back*—to capitalism or *forward*—to Socialism. There is no third way, nor can there be. The "equilibrium" theory makes an attempt to indicate a third way. And precisely because it is based on a third (non-existent) way, it is Utopian and anti-Marxian. . . .

Now, as you see, we have the material base which enables us to *substitute* for kulak output the output of the collective farms and state farms. That is why our offensive against the kulaks is now meeting with undeniable success. That is how the offensive against the kulaks must be carried on, if we mean a real offensive and not futile declamations against the kulaks.

That is why we have recently passed from the policy of *restricting* the exploiting proclivities of the kulaks to the policy of *eliminating the kulaks as a class.*

Well, what about the policy of expropriating the kulaks? Can we permit the expropriation of kulaks in the regions of solid collectivization? This question is asked in various quarters. A ridiculous question! We could not permit the expropriation of the kulaks as long as we were pursuing the policy of restricting the exploiting proclivities of the kulaks, as long as we were unable to launch a determined offensive against the kulaks, as long as we were unable to substitute for kulak output the output of the collective farms and state farms. At that time the policy of not permitting the expropriation of the kulaks was necessary and correct. But now? Now the situation is different. Now we are able to carry on a determined offensive against the kulaks, to break their resistance, to eliminate them as a class and substitute for their output the output of the collective farms and state farms. Now, the kulaks are being expropriated by the masses of poor and middle peasants themselves, by the masses who are putting solid collectivization into practice. Now, the expropriation of the kulaks in the regions of solid collectivization is no longer just an administrative measure. Now, the expropriation of the kulaks is an integral part of the formation and development of the collective farms. That is why it is ridiculous and fatuous

to expatiate today on the expropriation of the kulaks. You do not lament the loss of the hair of one who has been beheaded.

There is another question which seems no less ridiculous: whether the kulak should be permitted to join the collective farms. Of course not, for he is a sworn enemy of the collective-farm movement. Clear, one would think.

## Labor and Social Welfare
### Political Constitution of the United States of Mexico

*Article 123 of the Mexican Constitution of 1917 proposed the most advanced social welfare and labor laws in the Western Hemisphere. Twenty years before the United States and other Latin American nations acted, Mexico sought to ensure basic rights for Mexico's laboring classes. Note that although Mexican culture is often seen as embracing machismo, the Constitution called for equal pay for equal work for women.*

CONSIDER: *How these provisions reflect concerns common to industrializing societies of the 19th and 20th centuries; which of these "principles" would have been most difficult to enact into law and why.*

REGARDING LABOR AND SOCIAL WELFARE

Art. 123. Congress, with due regard for the following principles, shall enact laws on labor, which shall govern in the case of skilled and unskilled workmen, employees, domestic help, and artisans, and in general every labor contract:

(I) Eight hours shall be the maximum duration of a day's work. . . .

(IV) Every workman shall enjoy at least one day's rest for every six days' work. . . .

(VI) The minimum wage to be received by a workman shall be that considered sufficient, according to the conditions prevailing in the respective region of the country, to satisfy his normal needs, his education, and his lawful pleasures, considering him as the head of the family. In all agricultural, commercial, manufacturing, or mining enterprises, the workman shall have the right to participate in the profits in the manner set forth in clause IX of this Article.

(VII) The same remuneration shall be paid for the same work, regardless of sex or nationality. . . .

(XI) When, owing to special circumstances, it becomes necessary to increase the working hours, the wage for overtime shall be one hundred per cent more than that fixed for the ordinary shift. In no case shall overtime exceed three hours or continue for more than three consecutive days. No women of whatever age or boys under sixteen may be employed for overtime work. . . .

(XIV) Employers shall be liable for labor accidents and occupational diseases contracted by reason of or in the fulfillment of work; employers, therefore, must pay the proper indemnity, in accordance with the provisions of law, depending on whether death or merely temporary or permanent disability has ensued. This liability of the employer shall not cease if he contracts for the work through an agent.

(XV) Employers shall be bound to observe in the installation of their establishments all the provisions of law governing hygiene and sanitation, and to adopt adequate measures to prevent accidents due to the use of machinery, tools, and working materials, as well as to organize the work in such a manner as to assure the greatest guarantees possible for the health and lives of workmen compatible with the nature of the work, under penalties which the law shall determine.

(XVI) Both workmen and employers shall have the right to unite for the defense of their respective interests, by forming syndicates, unions, professional associations, etc.

(XVII) The law shall recognize the right of workmen and of employers to strike and to lock-out.

(XVIII) Strikes shall be lawful when they aim to bring about the balancing of the various factors of production, harmonizing the rights of labor with those of capital. In the case of public services, the workmen shall be obliged to give notice to the board of conciliation and arbitration ten days in advance of the date set for the stoppage of work. Strikes shall only be considered unlawful when the majority of the workers resort to acts of violence against persons or property, or, in case of war, when the strikers belong to establishments and services dependent on the government. . . .

(XX) Differences or disputes between capital and labor shall be submitted for settlement to a board of conciliation and arbitration composed of an equal number of representatives of the workmen and of the employers and one representative of the government. . . .

(XXIX) The passing of the law of social insurance shall be deemed as public utility. Such law shall provide for life insurance and old age, unemployment, illness and accident insurance, and the like.

## Mexico Nationalizes Its Oil Industry

### Lazlo Cardenas

*During the early 20th century, European and U.S. companies bought up large sections of Latin American countries in search of natural resources such as copper and other heavy metals and, more significantly, oil. In the midst of the worldwide economic depression, and in an environment of growing nationalism, many Latin American countries tried to regain control over companies that controlled valued resources and enormous political power. In this excerpt, Lazlo Cardenas (president of Mexico from 1934 to 1940) announced the reasons for the nationalization of Mexico's oil industry. Until this point, North American and British companies controlled the oil industry of this poverty-stricken nation.*

CONSIDER: *How Cardenas justifies the nationalization; the effects of the foreign companies on Mexico's social, economic, and political life; how this reflects a turning inward typical of many nations during this period.*

For additional justification of the measure herein announced, let us trace briefly the history of the oil companies' growth in Mexico and of the resources with which they have developed their activities.

It has been repeated *ad nauseam* that the oil industry has brought additional capital for the development and progress of the country. This assertion is an exaggeration. For many years, throughout the major period of their existence, the oil companies have enjoyed great privileges for development and expansion, including customs and tax exemptions and innumerable prerogatives; it is these factors of special privilege, together with the prodigious productivity of the oil deposits granted them by the Nation often against public will and law, that represent almost the total amount of this so-called capital.

Potential wealth of the Nation; miserably underpaid native labor; tax exemptions; economic privileges; governmental tolerance—these are the factors of the boom of the Mexican oil industry.

Let us now examine the social contributions of the companies. In how many of the villages bordering on the oil fields is there a hospital, or school or social center, or a sanitary water supply, or an athletic field, or even an electric plant fed by the millions of cubic meters of natural gas allowed to go to waste?

What center of oil production, on the other hand, does not have its company police force for the protection of private, selfish, and often illegal interests? These organizations, whether authorized by the Government or not, are charged with innumerable outrages, abuses, and murders, always on behalf of the companies that employ them.

SOURCE: Benjamin Keane, ed., *Readings in Latin American Civilization, 1942–Present* (Houghton Mifflin, 1967), pp. 362–64. Used by permission.

Who is not aware of the irritating discrimination governing construction of the company camps? Comfort for the foreign personnel; misery, drabness, and insalubrity for the Mexicans. Refrigeration and protection against tropical insects for the former; indifference and neglect, medical service and supplies always grudgingly provided, for the latter; lower wages and harder, more exhausting labor for our people. . . .

Another inevitable consequence of the presence of the oil companies, strongly characterized by their anti-social tendencies, and even more harmful than all those already mentioned, has been their persistent and improper intervention in national affairs.

The oil companies' support to strong rebel factions against the constituted government in the Huasteca region of Veracruz and in the Isthmus of Tehuantepec during the years 1917 to 1920 is no longer a matter for discussion by anyone. Nor is anyone ignorant of the fact that in later periods and even at the present time, the oil companies have almost openly encouraged the ambitions of elements discontented with the country's government, every time their interests were affected either by taxation or by the modification of their privileges or the withdrawal of the customary tolerance. They have had money, arms, and munitions for rebellion, money for the anti-patriotic press which defends them, money with which to enrich their unconditional defenders. But for the progress of the country, for establishing an economic equilibrium with their workers through a just compensation of labor, for maintaining hygenic conditions in the districts where they themselves operate, or for conserving the vast riches of the natural petroleum gases from destruction, they have neither money, nor financial possibilities, nor the desire to subtract the necessary funds from the volume of their profits.

Nor is there money with which to meet a responsibility imposed upon them by judicial verdict, for they rely on their pride and their economic power to shield them from the dignity and sovereignty of a Nation which has generously placed in their hands its vast natural resources and now finds itself unable to obtain the satisfaction of the most elementary obligations by ordinary legal means.

As a logical consequence of this brief analysis, it was therefore necessary to adopt a definite and legal measure to end this permanent state of affairs in which the country sees its industrial progress held back by those who hold in their hands the power to erect obstacles as well as the motive power of all activity and who, instead of using it to high and worthy purposes, abuse their economic strength to the point of jeopardizing the very life of a Nation endeavoring to bring about the elevation of

its people through its own laws, its own resources, and the free management of its own destinies.

## Slaves of the Depression
### Letters from Workers to the U.S. Government

*The Great Depression begin in 1929 and continued until World War II, causing massive unemployment and suffering for those who lacked an income. Yet, the following two letters show that even the employed population suffered enormously during those terrible 12 years. Workers throughout the land were subjected to extremely poor working conditions, speeded up work, and threats of layoffs.*

CONSIDER: *Why the 1930s were a time of enormous growth for the American labor movement—particularly the Congress of Industrial Organizations (CIO), which organized unskilled workers; the sorts of solutions to these problems available to governments.*

Dear Miss Perkins[1]:

Reading about you as I do I have come to the understanding, that you are a fair and impartial observer of labor conditions in the United States. Well, I'll have to get a load off my chest, and tell you of the labor conditions in a place which is laughingly called a factory. We work in a Woolstock Concern. We handle discarded rags. We work, ten hours a day for six days. In the grime and dirt of a nation. We go home tired and sick—dirty—disgusted—with the world in general, work—work all day, low pay—average wage sixteen dollars. Tired in the train going home, sitting at the dinner table, too tired to even wash ourselves, what for—to keep body and souls together not to depend on charity. What of N.R.A.? What of everything? We handle diseased rags all day. Tuberculosis roaming loose, unsanitary conditions—, slaves—slaves of the depression! I'm even tired as I write this letter—a letter of hope. What am I? I am young—I am twenty, a high school education—no recreation—no fun. Pardon ma'am—but I want to live! Do you deny me that right? As an American citizen I ask you, what—what must we do? Please investigate this matter. I sleep now, yes ma'am with a prayer on my lips, hoping against hope, that you will better our conditions. I'll sign my name, but if my boss finds out—well—Give us a new deal, Miss Perkins.

J. G.

Marshalltown, Iowa, February 3, 1937

SOURCE: National Archives, RG100.
[1]U.S. Secretary of Labor.

Dear President:

I am writing you about work and what they pay. My husband work for 1.00 a day and we must pay 8.00 month rent but we are back, have of the time. We don't have anything to eat but my husband go to work any way and I am pretty weak and we have not been in Marshalltown long to get aid but in April we will be I know Mr. Roosevelt you will understand one must have something to eat and sleep and there ist no other work my husband also belong to Co., H he get 1.00 every Monday night. they pay every 3 months I vote for you the 1st time also for the 2nd time. for you are the man for the office. My husband work from 7:30 till 5:30 for only 1.00 day. I will give you this man address he work for C. K. 205 So. 7th Ave Marshalltown. Please help us this town has no union to keep wages up. it should have. There is where us working man is to day. Maybe if you write hime a letter I think that would help a Married Man just can't live on it yes he is making money he run a gramberg [?] truck so please see if you can do something.

Mrs. F. M.

## Canada and the Great Depression

### R. B. Bennett

*The worldwide depression of the 1930s took as heavy a toll on Canadians as on people elsewhere in the Western Hemisphere. In the early 1930s, opposition victories in Canada's provincial elections threatened to tear the country's fragile confederation apart. In January 1935 conservative Prime Minister R. B. Bennett (a multimillionaire) shocked the nation with a radio address condemning the capitalist system, which is excerpted here. In a subsequent address he proposed specific reforms that the parliament quickly passed, including minimum wages, maximum hours, unemployment insurance, housing support, public works, abolition of child labor, and relief from agricultural debts.*

---

SOURCE: R. B. Bennett, *The Prime Minister Speaks to the People* (Ottawa, 1940), in J. M. Bliss, *Canadian History in Documents, 1763–1966.* (Toronto: Ryerson Press, 1966), pp. 280–82.

CONSIDER: *What would lead a conservative politician to support reform legislation that he had opposed a few years earlier.*

. . . We will examine the system without prejudice of any sort. We neither hate nor love it. It is here to do you service. That is its only purpose. *If it has failed, then we must change it. . . .*

You would agree that free competition and the open market place, as they were known in the old days, have lost their place in the system, and that the only substitute for them, in these modern times, is government regulation and control. You would understand that past depressions were caused by maladjustments in the operation of this system, and were corrected only after intense suffering and hardship, that these depressions were so many crises, dangerous and difficult to surmount, but that, in comparison with them, this depression is a catastrophe, and therefore demands the intervention of the Government. . . .

Selfish men, and this country is not without them—men whose mounting bank rolls loom larger than your happiness, corporations without souls and without virtue—these, fearful that this Government might impinge on what they have grown to regard as their immemorial right of exploitation, will whisper against us. They will call us radicals. They will say that this is the first step on the road to socialism. We fear them not. We think that their ready compliance with our programme would serve their interests better than any ill-timed opposition to it. We invite their cooperation. We want the cooperation of all. . . .

*The agencies of production, of manufacture, of distribution, of finance: all the parts of the capitalist system, have only one purpose and that is to work for the welfare of the people.* And when any of those instruments in any way fails, it is the plain duty of a government which represents the people, to remove the cause of failure. This I do not say by way of threat. I have told you that we hope for the unanimous support of all classes, in this great and difficult task of reform, but I think it is only right to add that opposition from any class which imperils the future of this great undertaking we will not tolerate. The lives and the happiness and the welfare of too many people depend upon our success to allow the selfishness of a few individuals to endanger it.

# VISUAL SOURCES

## World War I: The Home Front and Women

*This picture of a British war plant gives an idea of how industrialization and technology have helped turn any extended war into a massive strain. Large factories had to be built or converted to the production of war munitions, here heavy artillery shells. A new labor force had to be trained, often involving a change of values. Here women and older men predominate to make up for the drain on manpower caused* by the armed services. Finally, this picture suggests the enormous logistical organization and government cooperation with capitalist enterprises necessary to keep a modern war effort going.

The need for labor on the home front resulted in large numbers of women entering the labor force or changing jobs. The following two tables indicate the changing employment of women in Great Britain between 1914 and 1918. The first table is for all employment, the second is for industrial employment.

CONSIDER: The ways in which a modern war effort affects a nation's people and economy even though the war is being fought on foreign soil; the potential significance for women of these changes in employment.

**Illustration 23–1**   The Trustees of the Imperial War Museum.

## Nazi Mythology
*Richard Spitz*

This is an example of Nazi propaganda art, with its characteristic blend of realistic style and romantic vision. It shows Nazi soldiers and civilian folk marching in brotherly comradeship toward Valhalla, the final resting place of Aryan heroes. Above them, Nazi flags and wounded soldiers are being lifted together toward the same heavens. Stereotypes, rather than distinct individuals, are shown. The soldiers all look almost the same, and on the right there are representatives of civilian youth, middle-aged and elderly people, farmers, and workers. Those being glorified are all males and almost all soldiers. Viewers of this picture are supposed to feel proud, to feel that sacrifices for the state will be rewarded and that the greatest glory comes from military service. In subject and style, this picture represents a rejection of the major 20th-century artistic trends.

CONSIDER: How this picture fits the image and ideals of Nazism and Fascism.

## Revolutionary Propaganda

This 1922 poster (Illustration 23–3) celebrating the fifth anniversary of the Russian revolution reflects some of the message and appeal of the Communists during the revolution of 1917 and the years that followed. Here Lenin, in a worker's suit, tie, and cap, stands on a globe as if leading a worldwide Communist revolution. He proclaims, "Let the ruling class tremble before the Communist revolution." Behind him the rising sun marks the glorious dawn of the communist era. To his left

**Table 23–1   Women in the Labor Force, Great Britain, 1914–18**

| Number of Women Working | In July 1914 | In July 1918 | In July, 1918, over (+) or under (−) Numbers in July 1914 |
|---|---|---|---|
| On their own account or as employers | 430,000 | 470,000 | +40,000 |
| In industry | 2,178,600 | 2,970,000 | +792,000 |
| In domestic service | 1,658,000 | 1,258,000 | −400,000 |
| In commerce, etc. | 505,500 | 934,500 | +429,000 |
| In national and local government, including education | 262,200 | 460,200 | +198,000 |
| In agriculture | 190,000 | 228,000 | +38,000 |
| In employment of hotels, public houses, theaters, etc. | 181,000 | 220,000 | +39,000 |
| In transport | 18,200 | 117,200 | +99,000 |
| In other, including professional employment and as home workers | 542,500 | 652,500 | +110,000 |
| Altogether in occupations | 5,966,000 | 7,311,000 | +1,345,000 |
| Not in occupations but over 10 | 12,946,000 | 12,496,000 | −450,000 |
| Under 10 | 4,809,000 | 4,731,000 | −78,000 |
| Total females | 23,721,000 | 24,538,000 | +817,000 |

Table 23–2    Women in Industry, Great Britain, 1914–18

| Trades | Estimated Number of Females Employed in July 1914 | Estimated Number of Females Employed in July 1918 | Difference between Numbers of Females Employed in July 1914 and July 1918 | Percentage of Females to Total Number of Workpeople Employed | | Estimated Number of Females Directly Replacing Males in Jan. 1918 |
|---|---|---|---|---|---|---|
| | | | | July 1914 | July 1918 | |
| Metal | 170,000 | 594,000 | +424,000 | 9 | 25 | 195,000 |
| Chemical | 40,000 | 104,000 | +64,000 | 20 | 39 | 35,000 |
| Textile | 863,000 | 827,000 | −36,000 | 58 | 67 | 64,000 |
| Clothing | 612,000 | 568,000 | −44,000 | 68 | 76 | 43,000 |
| Food, drink, and tobacco | 196,000 | 235,000 | +39,000 | 35 | 49 | 60,000 |
| Paper and printing | 147,500 | 141,500 | −6,000 | 36 | 48 | 21,000 |
| Wood | 44,000 | 79,000 | +35,000 | 15 | 32 | 23,000 |
| China and earthenware | 32,000 | | | | | |
| Leather | 23,100 | 197,100 | +93,000 | 4 | 10 | 62,000 |
| Other | 49,000 | | | | | |
| Government establishments | 2,000 | 225,000 | +223,000 | 3 | 47 | 197,000 |
| Total | 2,178,600 | 2,970,600 | +792,000 | 26 | 37 | 704,000 |

SOURCE: *Women in Industry: Report of the War Cabinet Committee on Women in Industry* (London: His Majesty's Stationery Office, 1919).

**Illustration 23–2**    Photograph by Garner. Courtesy of Army Art Collection, U.S. Army Center of Military History.

**Illustration 23–3** © Sovfoto/Eastfoto

and right, together in alliance, are agricultural and industrial workers—the revolutionary mainstays and beneficiaries of the new order—carrying a banner proclaiming, "Proletariat of All Countries, Unite." Below are the tools of their trades and symbols of Russia's Communist revolution—the hammer and sickle.

Consider: *What might be particularly appealing about this poster; what image of the Russian revolution it incorporates.*

## Socialist Realism

### K. I. Finogenov

*This example of socialist realism has great similarities to Nazi art: its realistic style, its romantic vision, its propagandistic purpose. In this case, however, economic themes are emphasized more than military themes. Painted in 1935 by K. I. Finogenov, it shows Communist party and government leaders, led by Stalin, on a modern Soviet farm. On the right, an expert checks the soil. In the background a new tractor is displayed. All figures are relatively well dressed; no one looks like a peasant farmer.*

Consider: *How this picture relates to the role of the government in the Soviet Union and to Stalin's place in it; what insight into the agricultural policy during the 1930s the picture is supposed to convey; how the image presented here fits with Stalin's explanation of collectivization.*

**Illustration 23–4**  Tass/Sovfoto/Eastfoto.

## Authoritarianism and Totalitarianism, 1919–37

*This map shows the spread of authoritarian and totalitarian governments in Europe between 1919 and 1937. Although no firm rules apply here, those countries retaining parliamentary democratic forms of government generally had a longer tradition of democratic institutions, were more satisfied winners in World War I, and were located in more advanced industrialized areas in northwestern Europe.*

CONSIDER: *Taking account of the relevant geography, historical background, and experience of World War I, the commonalities of two or more countries that became dictatorships or changed to right-wing authoritarian regimes.*

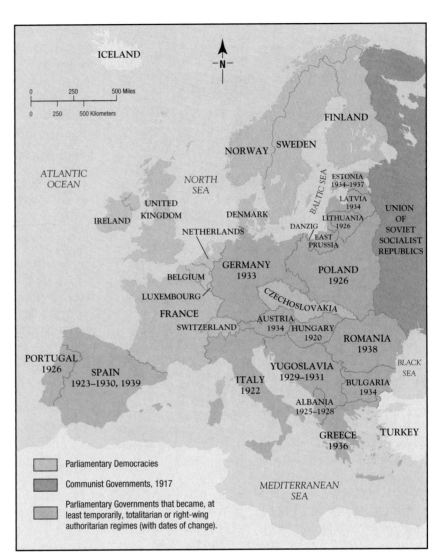

**Map 23–1  The Spread of Authoritarian Governments.**

# SECONDARY SOURCES

## The Origins of World War I: Militant Patriotism

*Roland Stromberg*

Many observers were struck by the almost universal enthusiasm with which people greeted the news that war had been declared in August 1914. This has led some scholars to reevaluate traditional interpretations of the causes for World War I and emphasize the underlying social forces that led people to welcome its outbreak. In the following selection, Roland Stromberg, a historian of modern Europe at the Uni-

versity of Wisconsin, examines various attempts to explain the outbreak of war and suggests that the willingness of European peoples to go to war may have been more important than "the system of sovereign states" or any other cause for World War I.

CONSIDER: *The explanations that Stromberg rejects and why he rejects them; how militant patriotism played a role in the outbreak of the war.*

No wonder the sudden outbreak of a major international war at the beginning of August caught everyone by surprise. The sobering lesson was that war could happen without anybody seeming to want it or to will it. All kinds of myths grew up later, as bewildered people attempted to explain the outbreak of war. As usual,

SOURCE: Roland N. Stromberg, *Europe in the Twentieth Century* (Englewood Cliffs, NJ: Prentice-Hall, Inc., 1980), pp. 43–44, 74.

conspiracy theories flourished. In particular it was alleged that the Germans plotted war; Wilhelm II, the unhappy German monarch, was depicted in the Allied countries as a monster with tentacles reaching out to ensnare small countries. That "Prussian militarism" was the canker in the olive branch became an article of faith in France and England and later, after she had joined the war, in the United States. For their part, the Germans believed that jealous neighbors plotted to encircle and destroy a country whose only crime was her economic success.

Then, too, the theory arose that the capitalistic economic system, far from being a force for peace, had engineered the war because war was profitable or because there was competition for markets and raw materials. Although they may contain germs of truth, all such simple-minded "devil theories" must be dismissed as inadequate to the serious study of events, more interesting as folklore than as history.

Though it is tempting to look for it, no single all-embracing cause can successfully explain the war or any other major historical event. . . .

The states of Europe were like individuals living in a primeval state of nature marked by incessant strife between one and another. They acknowledged no higher authority that might have forced them to keep the peace. What was called "international law" was not in fact binding on them, being backed by no more than a moral or customary sanction. . . .

More and more people had acquired a larger stake in defending the state. This was the natural result of democratization and increase in wealth. However imperfectly or inequitably these had come about, the large majority of citizens had some interest in defending the political community of which they were a part. All over Europe, 1914 was to prove that the masses as well as the classes were militantly patriotic when they thought their country was being attacked. . . .

Virtually no one had expected war; it came with dramatic suddenness. When it did come, . . . a sense of joy rather than of gloom prevailed. Huge cheering crowds surrounded the kaiser, stood outside Buckingham Palace, saluted departing French troops at the railroad stations, made love publicly in St. Petersburg. A Parisian observer on August 2 described a "human torrent, swelling at every corner" screaming, shouting, singing the "Marseillaise." In Berlin, crowds passed through the streets incessantly for two days singing "Deutschland über alles" and "Wacht am Rhein." A mob attacked the German embassy in St. Petersburg. An "indescribable crowd" blocked the streets around government offices in London a few minutes after midnight August 4–5, and continued to fill the streets for days. It was with exultation, not sorrow, that the peoples of Europe greeted the war, a fact that in the last analysis may go farther to explain its coming than all the details of diplomacy. . . .

## Women, Work, and World War I
### Bonnie S. Anderson and Judith P. Zinsser

*As men were drawn into the armed forces during World War I and there were new demands for arms and other goods to support the war effort, the demand for women workers grew. Women entered the workforce in great numbers, often taking jobs previously only offered to men. Historians have pointed to this as a crucial change for women, but recently other historians question how much women, in the long run, benefited from their experiences as workers during World War I. In the following excerpt from* A History of Their Own, *Bonnie S. Anderson and Judith P. Zinsser argue that the changes for women were fewer and less permanent than generally assumed.*

CONSIDER: *Why, according to Anderson and Zinsser, changes for women were more apparent than real, more short-term than long-lasting; how employers, governments, and the mass media undermined changes for women; how this document relates to the visual sources on the home front and women.*

The improved standard of living, smaller family size, maternity benefits, protective legislation, union, and new jobs comprised the most important changes in the lives of urban working-class women between the 1870s and the 1920s. Compared to these changes, the impact of World War I (1914–1918) on these women's lives was relatively minor. While middle- and upper-class women often reported that the war freed them from nineteenth-century attitudes limiting both work and personal life, working-class women's lives changed relatively little. Unlike more privileged women, working-class women were used to earning income outside the home, and their entry into war work was more likely to be exploitative than liberating. Unlike more privileged women, working-class women and girls had rarely been shielded by a "double standard" of sexual behavior for women and men; rather, working-class women made the maintenance of the double standard possible for men of property. For working-class women in the cities, the growth of the new white-collar jobs was the one new trend fostered by the war which was not reversed afterward. Otherwise, World War I brought only a temporary suspension of the normal conditions of work outside the home, and traditional patterns returned in the postwar era.

As soon as the war broke out, European governments moved to suspend protective legislation for women for the duration. Just as nations expected working-class men to serve in the military, so they exhorted working-class women to serve in the factories, taking the places of the men who had joined the armed forces. Drawn by high wages as well as patriotism, women thronged into these new, previously male jobs. . . .

Governments initially insisted that women receive equal pay for doing a job formerly done by a man, but this policy was largely ineffective: factories tended to divide up jobs into smaller operations and pay women at a lesser rate. Women's industrial wages rose during the war, both relative to men's and absolutely, but they still remained measurable as a percentage of male earnings. In Paris, women in metallurgy earned only 45 percent of what men earned before the war; by 1918, the women earned 84 percent of what men earned. In Germany, women's industrial earnings relative to men's rose by about 5 percent. Both women and men seemed to view the changes brought by the war as temporary. After the war, the men would return to their jobs, the women would leave men's work, and all would return to normal. . . .

As soon as the war was over, all belligerent governments acted quickly to remove women from "men's" jobs. In England, these women were made "redundant" and let go; in France, they were offered a bonus payment if they left factory work; and in Germany, the government issued regulations calling for women to be dismissed before men if necessary. These policies were effective: by 1921, fewer French and English women worked in industry than had before the war. Women's earnings decreased to return to lower percentages of men's, and the promise of "equal remuneration for work of equal value" made in the Versailles Treaty of 1919 remained a dead letter. Mass media concentrated on the relatively superficial changes in women's clothing, hair styles, and use of cosmetics and ignored the deeper continuities which structured most women's lives.

## Women in Latin America
### Amanda LaBarca Hubertson

*The struggle for equality between the sexes was fought on many levels throughout the Western Hemisphere. In the United States, women confronted sexism in the political and economic arenas. In Latin America, machismo, the cultural glorification of male domination, was important in holding back the progress of women throughout the 19th and 20th centuries. In this excerpt, from her 1934 book,* A Donde Va

SOURCE: Benjamin Keane, ed., *Readings in Latin American Civilization, 1942–Present* (Houghton Mifflin, 1967). Used by permission.

la Mujer?, *Amanda LaBarca Hubertson, a well-known Chilean educational reformer and feminist, analyzes the progress of Latin American women and the difficulties of overcoming entrenched opposition in the larger culture.*

CONSIDER: *The "gains" and "losses" of women in Latin America; the causes for these gains and losses; how this analysis compares with that of Anderson and Zinsser.*

. . . Has feminism brought gains or losses to the Latin-American middle-class girl of today?

*Gains.* First of all, the consciousness of her own worth in the totality of human progress. Today's girl knows that there are no insurmountable obstacles to the flight of her intelligence; that the question of whether her entire sex is intelligent will not be raised before she is permitted to engage in any intellectual activity; that in the eyes of the majority her womanhood does not mark her with the stigma of irremediable inferiority, and that if she has talent she will be allowed to display it.

The law codes have returned to her, in large part, control over her life and property. She has well-founded hopes of seeing abolished within her lifetime the laws that still relegate her, in certain aspects, to the position of a second-class citizen, and that accord her unequal legal treatment.

She has made progress in economic liberty, basis of all independence, whether it be a question of a simple individual or one of nations. Today she is gaining admission into fields of labor forbidden to her mother. . . .

*She has lost,* in the first place, the respect of the male majority. One might say that formerly consideration for women formed part of good breeding, and it was denied only to one who by her conduct showed that she did not merit it. Today it is the only way around. In general, woman receives no tribute, and she must prove convincingly that she is a distinguished personage before receiving the homage that once was common.

Which has diminished—the respect or the quality of respectability?

It is worth one's while to analyze the point.

Men used to expect of women a stainless virtue, perfect submission—after God, thy husband, orders the epistle of St. Paul—and a life-long devotion to the orbit in which her man revolved. A saint in the vaulted niche of her home, saint to the world, mistress of her four walls, and slave to her man. In exchange for this—respect and devotion. . . .

It is unnecessary to refer again to the upheavals that the invention of machinery brought to the world, the sharp rise in the cost of living, and the pauperization of the household, which from producer was reduced to being a simple consumer. It became impossible for a man of average means to satisfy the needs of all his womenfolk, and women had to enter offices, the professions, and other remunerative employment that had been men's traditional source of income. Woman has gone out into the world, and although this fact in itself is an economic imperative and does not essentially imply the abandonment of any virtue, the ordinary man has denied her his respect. As if it were not much more difficult, and consequently more meritorious, to preserve one's purity, sweetness, and delicacy amid the turmoil of the world than in the secluded garden of the old-time home!

On entering the economic struggle she rubs shoulders with misery. Yesterday she only knew of it by hearsay. Today it bespatters her. The rawness of life surrounds her. Often she must solve the problem of staying in the path of rectitude without the help of, or even defending herself from, the man who is ready to exploit any of her weaknesses. For the ordinary man, woman's freedom is license; her equality, the right to treat her without courtesy.

She has lost in opportunities for marriage, for establishing a household, and for satisfying that yearning for maternity that is her fundamental instinct. The more cultured a woman, the more difficult for her to find a husband, because it is normal for her to seek refuge, understanding, and guidance in a person superior to herself. And the latter do not always prefer cultured women. They imagine that knowledge makes them unfeeling—an absurd notion—that it makes them domineering—which concerns not acquired knowledge but character—or that it makes them insufferably pedantic. I regret to say that here they have a little justice on their side. Knowledge is such a recent attainment of women that the majority make an excessive show of it. We play the role of the *nouveaux-riches* of the world of culture. For their wives men prefer the "old-fashioned" girl.

That is the pathos of the tragedy of middle-class women in the Latin countries. Evolution has taken place in opposition to the fundamental convictions of men, who only tolerate it—in the case of their daughters, for example—because imperious necessity dictates it, and only with profound chagrin. Men—I repeat that I speak of the majority—continue to judge women from the viewpoint of fifty years ago, and if they retain some respect and esteem in their inner beings, they tender it to the woman who remained faithful to the classic type—the woman who has progressed they place very close to those for whom they have no respect.

## The Russian Revolution

*Robert Service*

*Historians often respond to the challenge of explaining the occurrence of a major revolution by constructing a complex set or theory of causes. For Marxist historians, the Russian Revolution was of extraordinary importance. These historians and others point to long-term economic and social factors as crucial in causing this revolution. Many historians, however, argue that the causes were more immediate and less complex. Robert Service, a respected author of several works on Russian history, takes a middle ground, focusing on a few circumstances as the key causes for the revolution. In the following selection, Service analyzes the revolution that toppled the tsar's government in February 1917, as well as the rise to power of Lenin and the Bolsheviks in October 1917.*

CONSIDER: *The problems facing the Russian Empire; how Tsar Nicholas II placed himself in "double jeopardy"; why the Bolsheviks resorted to terror.*

Under the tsars, the Russian Empire faced many problems and approval of the state's demands and purposes was largely absent from society. The technological gap was widening between Russia and the other capitalist powers. Military security posed acute problems; administrative and educational co-ordination remained frail. Political parties had little impact on popular opinion, and the State Duma was to a large extent ignored. Furthermore, the traditional propertied classes made little effort to engender a sense of civic community among the poorer members of society. While most Russians lacked a strong sense of nationhood, several non-Russian nations had a sharp sense of national resentment. The Russian Empire was a restless, unintegrated society.

Nicholas II, the last tsar, had put himself in double jeopardy. He had seriously obstructed and annoyed the emergent elements of a civil society: the political parties, professional associations and trade unions. But he also stopped trying to suppress them entirely. The result was a constant challenge to the tsarist regime. The social and economic transformation before the First World War merely added to the problems. Those groups in society which had undergone impoverishment were understandably hostile to the authorities. Other groups had enjoyed improvement in their material conditions; but several of these, too, posed a danger since they felt frustrated by the nature of the political order. It was in this situation that the Great War broke out and pulled down the remaining stays of the regime. The result was the February Revolution of 1917 in circumstances of economic collapse, administrative dislocation and military defeat. Vent was given to a surge of local efforts at popular self-rule; and workers, peasants and military conscripts across the empire asserted their demands without impediment.

These same circumstances made liberalism, conservatism and fascism impractical for a number of years ahead: some kind of socialist government was by far

SOURCE: Robert Service, *A History of Twentieth-Century Russia* (Cambridge, MA: Harvard University Press, 1998), pp. 545–47.

the likeliest outcome in those years. Yet it was not inevitable that the most extreme variant of socialism—Bolshevism—should take power. What was scarcely avoidable was that once the Bolsheviks made their revolution, they would not be able to survive without making their policies even more violent and regimentative than they already were. Lenin's party had much too little durable support to remain in government without resort to terror. This in turn placed limits on their ability to solve those many problems identified by nearly all the tsarist regime's enemies as needing to be solved. The Bolsheviks aspired to economic competitiveness, political integration, inter-ethnic co-operation, social tranquility, administrative efficiency, cultural dynamism and universal education. But the means they employed inevitably violated their declared ends.

## The Great Depression in Europe

*James Laux*

*Most scholars agree that the Great Depression was very important, but they disagree over its precise significance. For Marxists, it was the greatest in a series of periodic economic crises inevitably flowing from the capitalist system and an indication that this system would soon collapse. For liberal economic historians, it was an indictment of conservative, nationalistic economic policies that would be forced to give way to modern Keynesian policies characterized by greater government activity and planning. For others, it was a crucial cause of the rise of Nazism and World War II itself. In the following selection, James Laux of the University of Cincinnati analyzes the impact of the Great Depression, emphasizing various changes in attitude that stemmed from it.*

CONSIDER: *Whether, as some scholars argue, the Great Depression forced governments to modify laissez-faire just enough to save capitalism as a whole; why economic planning appeared more attractive after the experience of the Depression.*

The Depression, perhaps, had the most serious impact in Europe on people's thinking about economic matters. Looking back on the experience, most Europeans agreed that the orthodoxy of laissez-faire no longer held. They would not again accept the view that a government must interfere as little as possible in the operation of the economic system. Governments must accept wider responsibilities than balancing their own budgets. The value of the currency in terms of gold must give way to economic expansion if the two appear to conflict.

SOURCE: James M. Laux, from "The Great Depression in Europe" (*The Forum Series*) (St. Louis, MO, 1974), pp. 13–14. Reprinted by permission of Forum Press. Copyright © 1974 by Forum Press.

Laissez-faire already was wheezing and laboring in the 1920s; after the decade of the 1930s it was nearly prostrate. As so often happens, a philosophy came along to justify this changed attitude, a new approach to theoretical economics worked out by the Englishman John Maynard Keynes. The most influential economist of the twentieth century, Keynes published his classic work in 1936, *The General Theory of Employment, Interest and Money.* He argued that governments can and should manipulate capitalist economies, by running surpluses or deficits, by investing heavily in public works, by changing the size of the money and credit supply, and by altering rates of interest. In his analysis he emphasized the total economy, the relations among savings, investment, production, and consumption, what is called macroeconomics, rather than an investigation of a single firm or sector. A critic of socialism, Keynes scorned the significance of government ownership of production facilities, but promoted government intervention in an economy to make capitalism work better.

Bolstering this view were the remarkable production achievements of many European industrial states during the two world wars. In these crises national economies expanded military production enormously under government direction. Many asked why such techniques could not be applied in peacetime also, but to make consumer products rather than tools of destruction.

The upshot was that by 1945 if not 1939 most Europeans abandoned the idea that they lived at the mercy of an impersonal economic system whose rules could not be changed and accepted the proposition that the economy could operate the way people wanted it to. From this it was a short step to the concept of planning the future development of the economy—both the whole and particular segments of it. Economic planning became an acceptable posture for capitalist societies and enjoyed a considerable reputation. Some of those who supported it perhaps underestimated the possible merits of free markets as guiding production decisions and did seem to assume that planners somehow possess more wisdom than ordinary human beings.

Economic nationalism was a more immediate result of the Depression—the policy that short-run national economic interests have highest priority and that international economic cooperation and trade must give way before narrowly conceived national interests. Economic nationalism showed its sharpest teeth in those European states where political nationalism reached a peak—Germany, Italy, and the Soviet Union. Its strength declined in western Europe after the Second World War as people saw once again that economic prosperity among one's neighbors could bring great benefits to oneself. In an expanding continental or world economy everyone can get richer. But one wonders if economic nationalism may not revive in western Europe, especially if it seems a popular policy in a crisis.

The Great Depression had important political repercussions too. In Germany, the Depression's tragic gloom made the dynamism of the Nazi movement seem more attractive. It is difficult to imagine the Nazis achieving power without the Depression and its pervasive unemployment in the background. In France, the Depression convinced many that the regime of the Third Republic had lost its élan and relevance to twentieth-century problems, but the lack of a widely popular alternative meant that the Republic could limp along until a disastrous military defeat brought it down. In Britain, the Depression was less serious and no fundamental challenge to the political regime developed. The Conservatives held power for most of the interwar period and their failure to work actively to absorb the large unemployment that continued there until late in the 1930s brought widespread rancor and bitterness against them. Doubts as to the Conservatives' ability to manage a peacetime economy led to the first majority Labour government in the 1945 election. More profoundly, the years of heavy unemployment bred a very strong anticapitalist sentiment in much of British labor, a sentiment that led them after the war to demand moves toward socialism, such as nationalization of major industries.

The Depression helped convince Europeans that their governments must try to manage their economies. Most agreed that full employment and expanding output should be the goals. They did not agree on the means to achieve these ends.

## The Rise of Fascism

*F. L. Carsten*

*Historians have employed a variety of perspectives in an effort to understand the rise of fascism during the two decades following World War I. Focusing on the appeal of fascism, several historians have analyzed what social classes and groups of people supported fascist movements. In the following selection F. L. Carsten argues that while fascism appealed to all social groups, certain groups responded more strongly to it than others.*

CONSIDER: *Why fascism might have been particularly appealing to the lower middle classes; what other groups it appealed to and why.*

SOURCE: F. L. Carsten, *The Rise of Fascism,* pp. 232–34. Copyright 1980. Reprinted by permission of the Regents of the University of California Press and the University of California.

Unlike many middle-class or working-class parties, the Fascists appealed to all social groups, from the top to the bottom of the social scale. Excluded were only those who were their favourite objects of attack: the profiteers, the parasites, the financial gangsters, the ruling cliques, the rapacious capitalists, the reactionary landowners. But even there exceptions were made if it suited the Leader's book. There is no doubt, however, that certain social groups responded much more strongly to the Fascist appeal than others. This is particularly true of those who were uprooted and threatened by social and economic change, whose position in society was being undermined, who had lost their traditional place, and were frightened of the future. These were, above all, the lower middle classes—or rather certain groups within them: the artisans and independent tradesmen, the small farmers, the lower grade government employees and white-collar workers. Perhaps even more important in the early stages were the former officers and non-commissioned officers of the first world war for whom no jobs were waiting, who had got accustomed to the use of violence, and felt themselves deprived of their "legitimate" rewards. In Italy, in Germany, and elsewhere the "front" generation played a leading part in the rise of Fascism. For its members fighting was a way of life which they transferred to the domestic scene. They loved battles for their own sake. It is no accident that the most important Fascist movements had their origin in the year 1919, the year of the Hungarian and Munich Soviet republics, of civil war which aroused fear and hatred in many hearts. Those who had been badly frightened did not easily forget. The occupation of the factories in northern Italy in the following year had the same effect. . . .

Apart from the groups already mentioned, there were the youngsters at school and university who became ardent believers in Fascism at an early stage. They were fed up with the existing society, bored with their daily duties, and strongly attracted by a movement which promised a radical change, which they could invest with a romantic halo. These youths came from middle-class or lower middle-class families. They could not easily find the way into the Communist camp. But they found the weak and changing governments of the post-war period utterly unattractive. In the Weimar Republic, in the post-war Italian kingdom, in the corrupt governments of Rumania, in the powerless governments of Spain, there was nothing to fire the enthusiasm of youth: they were dreary and pedestrian, the offices filled with mediocrities and time-servers. It was this, rather than any economic threat, that led so many idealist students into the Fascist camp. Similarly, many young officers and soldiers of the post-war generation were attracted by visions of national greatness and the promise of a revision of the peace treaties. A perusal of the autobiographical notes compiled by men who joined the National Socialist Party in its early years shows that pride of place belongs to a strong nationalism, the desire to see Germany strong and united again, freed from the 'chains of Versailles', and also from the faction fights and the 'horse-trading' of the political parties. This often went together with hatred of the Communists and Socialists, and with anti-Semitism. Those who joined the Party were usually very young; they loved the frequent fights and battles in which they got involved together with their comrades, as well as the uniforms and the propaganda marches.

## A World at Arms
*Gerhard L. Weinberg*

*The issues involved with appeasement, which have so often been a focus for analysis, lead to the broader questions of why war broke out in 1939 and whether it could have been prevented. To answer these questions, historians often look back to the whole era that began with the outbreak of World War I in 1914. In the following selection, Gerhard Weinberg of the University of Michigan compares the two wars and emphasizes the differences that separate them. He also leaves no doubt whom he holds responsible for World War II.*

CONSIDER: *In what ways the causes and nature of the two wars differed.*

Although this book contains a chapter on the background of World War II, it defines that war as beginning in 1939 in Europe. While some have argued that the war was merely a continuation of World War I after a temporary interruption created by the armistice of 1918, and that the whole period from 1914 to 1945 should be seen as the age of a new European civil war, a Thirty-one Years War if you will, such a perspective ignores not only the very different origins and nature of the prior conflict but obscures instead of illuminating the special character of the second one. If an important by-product of both wars was the weakening of Europe and its hold on the world, the *intentions* of the belligerents were fundamentally different. It is true that these changed somewhat in the course of each of these lengthy struggles, but a basic differentiation remains.

In World War I, the two sides were fighting over their relative roles in the world, roles defined by possible shifts in boundaries, colonial possessions, and military and naval power. It is true that the Austro-Hungarian empire

SOURCE: Gerhard L. Weinberg, *A World at Arms: A Global History of World War II*. Cambridge: Cambridge University Press, 1994, pp. 1–2, 43–44.

anticipated the elimination of Serbia's independent status, and Germany very quickly came to the conclusion that Belgium would never regain its independence, but beyond this expected disappearance of two of the smaller states which had emerged from larger constructions during the nineteenth century, the other powers—and most especially the major ones—were all expected to survive, even if trimmed by the winners. In this sense, the war, however costly and destructive in its *methods*, was still quite traditional in its aims.

It is also true that the fighting itself, with its unprecedented casualties, its incredible costs, the appearance of such new weapons as poison gas, airplanes, tanks, and submarines, as well as vast shifts in world economic patterns, ended up completely transforming the pre-war world and doing so in ways that none of the belligerents had anticipated. The effects on winners and losers alike were colossal, and the pre-war world could not be revived even if some made valiant and sometimes counterproductive efforts to do so. But neither side had either intended or preferred the massive changes which resulted from the ability of the modern state to utilize the social and mechanical technologies developed in the preceding two centuries to draw vast human and material resources out of their respective societies and employ them—and thereby use them up—in the cauldron of battle.

In World War II, all this was very different indeed. The *intent* was different from the start. A total reordering of the globe was at stake from the very beginning, and the leadership on both sides recognized this. The German dictator Adolf Hitler had himself explicitly asserted on May 23, 1939, that the war he intended would be not for the Free City of Danzig but for living space in the East; his Foreign Minister similarly assured Italy's Foreign Minister that it was war, not Danzig, that Germany wanted. When Germany had conquered Poland and offered a temporary peace to Britain and France, those countries responded by making it clear, as British Prime Minister Neville Chamberlain explained, that there could be no agreement with a German government led by Hitler, a man who had regularly broken his promises. If Chamberlain, who has often been derided for allegedly not grasping the true nature of the National Socialist challenge, saw the issues so clearly, the historian decades later ought not to close his or her eyes to the reality of a very different war. This was, in fact, a struggle not only for control of territory and resources but about who would live and control the resources of the globe and which peoples would vanish entirely because they were believed inferior or undesirable by the victors.

It was in this way that the two wars which originated in Europe differed greatly from each other even if separated by only two decades. . . .

No appeals from prospective neutrals could move Hitler. He not only would not put off war for one day, he was in such a hurry that he gave the orders to begin hostilities hours earlier than the German military timetable required. To justify war in the eyes of the German public, he shared in the preparation of demands on Poland that might sound reasonable to his people—and that he ordered withheld until after they were no longer valid. He would not again run the "danger" of having his ostensible demands agreed to, or made the basis for real negotiations, or be met with counter-offers. Now that there was no longer any chance of splitting the Western Powers from Poland, his focus of attention was on the German home front in the coming war, a reflection of his belief that it had been the collapse there which had produced defeat in the preceding great conflict. . . .

On the morning of September 1 the German offensive into Poland began. . . . To the thunderous applause of the representatives of the German people, he announced that Germany was once more at war.

Almost evey nation eventually participated in the new war, some as victims of attack, some as eager attackers themselves, some at the last moment in order to participate in the post-war world organization. A flood of blood and disaster of unprecedented magnitude had been let loose on the world. If the details of military operations and the localities of combat were often vastly different from those of World War I, the fearful anticipation that a new war would be as horrendous or quite likely even worse than the last proved all too accurate. There would be, however, no agitated discussion this time, as there had been after the crisis of 1914, of the question of who was responsible for the outbreak of war. It was all too clear that Germany had taken the initiative and that others had tried, perhaps too much, but certainly very hard, to avert another great conflict. There would be no second "war guilt" debate.

## Hitler's Willing Executioners
### Daniel J. Goldhagen

*One of the most emotionally charged debates has long been over responsibility for the Holocaust, which cost so many lives. The question involves not only who made the key decisions instituting the policy of extermination, but who carried out that policy, who supported it, who knew, and who should have known. One of the most controversial and widely read books addressing these issues is the recently published Hitler's*

SOURCE: Daniel Johah Goldhagen, *Hitler's Willing Executioners: Ordinary Germans and the Holocaust.* New York: Alfred A. Knopf, Inc., 1996, pp. 9–10, 416–17.

*Willing Executioners: Ordinary Germans and the Holocaust, by Harvard scholar Daniel J. Goldhagen. Here he points to the role of antisemitic beliefs held by "ordinary" Germans in ultimately causing the slaughter of the Jews.*

CONSIDER: *How Goldhagen's views differ from other historians; how Goldhagen's argument might be supported or attacked; why these views might be so controversial.*

This revision calls for us to acknowledge what has for so long been generally denied or obscured by academic and non-academic interpreters alike: Germans' antisemitic beliefs about Jews were the central causal agent of the Holocaust. They were the central causal agent not only of Hitler's decision to annihilate European Jewry (which is accepted by many) but also of the perpetrators' willingness to kill and to brutalize Jews. The conclusion of this book is that antisemitism moved many thousands of "ordinary" Germans—and would have moved millions more, had they been appropriately positioned—to slaughter Jews. Not economic hardship, not the coercive means of a totalitarian state, not social psychological pressure, not invariable psychological propensities, but ideas about Jews that were pervasive in Germany, and had been for decades, induced ordinary Germans to kill unarmed, defenseless Jewish men, women, and children by the thousands, systematically and without pity. . . . [T]he perpetrators, "ordinary Germans," were animated by antisemitism, by a particular *type* of antisemitism that led them to conclude that the Jews *ought to die.* The perpetrators' beliefs, their particular brand of antisemitism, though obviously not the sole source, was, I maintain, a most significant and indispensable source of the perpetrators' actions and must be at the center of any explanation of them. Simply put, the perpetrators, having consulted their own convictions and morality and having judged the mass annihilation of Jews to be right, did not *want* to say "no." . . .

This, it must be emphasized, is not a monocausal account of the perpetration of the Holocaust. Many factors were necessary for Hitler and others to have conceived the genocidal program, for them to have risen to the position from which they could implement it, for its undertaking to have become a realistic possibility, and for it then to have been carried out. Most of these elements are well understood. This book has focused on one of a number of the causes of the Holocaust, the least well-understood one, namely the crucial motivational element which moved the German men and women, without whom it would and could not have occurred, to devote their bodies, souls, and ingenuity to the enterprise. With regard to the *motivational* cause of the Holocaust, for the vast majority of perpetrators, a monocausal explanation does suffice.

When focusing on only the motivational cause of the Holocaust, the following can be said. The claim here is that this virulent brand of German racial antisemitism was in *this historical instance* causally sufficient to provide not only the Nazi leadership in its decision making but also the perpetrators with the requisite motivation to participate willingly in the extermination of the Jews.

## Chapter Questions

1. Utilizing the sources, what were some of the social, economic, and political effects of World War I?

2. In light of this chapter's evidence and interpretations of the natures of authoritarianism and totalitarianism, how would you explain their appeal or relative success in the first half of the 20th century? In what ways should Italian fascism, German Nazism, and Russian communism be distinguished here?

3. In what ways do developments between 1914 and 1945 support the argument that Western civilization reached its apogee between 1789 and 1914, and that starting with World War I it was relatively on the decline? What factors might be pointed out to mitigate or counter this interpretation?

# Chapter Twenty-Four

# Asia and Africa between World Wars I and II

In Asia and Africa, the period between World War I and World War II was marked by the struggle with Western colonialism, by rising nationalism, and, particularly in China, by revolutionary turmoil.

The struggle with Western influence and colonial exploitation differed in various areas. In some places, such as India, southeast Asia, and Africa, both accommodation and resistance to Western colonialism were common. In Africa in particular, these were the years that produced the prototype of European colonial rule. As colonial masters, Europeans sought agents among the African elite and the population at large. They also faced continued resistance from Africans in west, central, and east Africa. European officials used African agents to collect taxes and advise the

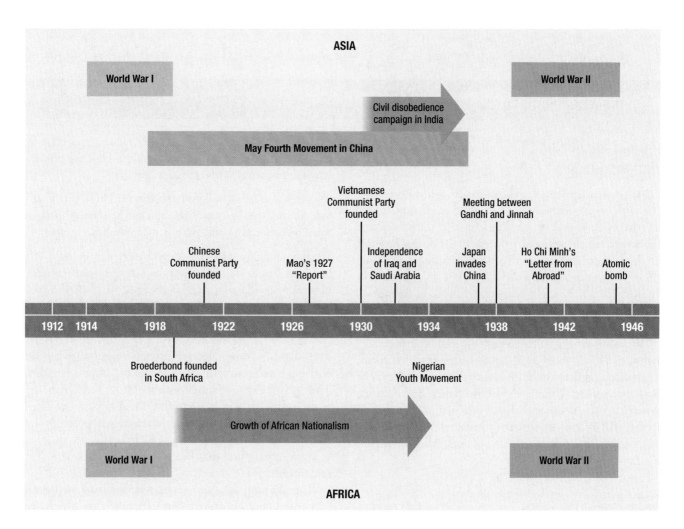

ASIA

World War I

World War II

Civil disobedience campaign in India

May Fourth Movement in China

Vietnamese Communist Party founded

Meeting between Gandhi and Jinnah

Chinese Communist Party founded

Mao's 1927 "Report"

Independence of Iraq and Saudi Arabia

Japan invades China

Ho Chi Minh's "Letter from Abroad"

Atomic bomb

1912 1914 · 1918 · 1922 · 1926 · 1930 · 1934 · 1938 · 1942 · 1946

Broederbond founded in South Africa

Nigerian Youth Movement

Growth of African Nationalism

World War I

World War II

AFRICA

people on what to produce to meet the demands of European industrial centers. In other places, such as parts of the Middle East, the struggle was against Western imperialism. In still other places, such as Iran and Japan, the struggle was with the extent to which Western models and ideas should be copied.

The growth of nationalism was widespread throughout Asia and Africa. West Africa, with its modern elites whose roots went back to the 19th century, led the way in presenting organized challenges to European hegemony. In South Africa, Kenya, and Southern Rhodesia, transplanted European settlers' regimes sought to maintain control of the state, at times by opposing metropolitan plans for the colonies or by seeking metropolitan support for their interests. And throughout Africa, Africans also presented major challenges to the colonial system that had displaced African states of the 19th century. In Asia, like Africa, nationalism was harnessed into the struggle with Western influence. In some places, above all Japan, nationalism was a force for political authoritarianism and foreign expansionism. Paradoxically, it was Japan that fueled nationalism and the struggle against Western colonialism by promising "liberation" while at the same time creating fear of her own empire and military strength.

Revolutionary turmoil was most prominent and of greatest significance in China, Asia's largest and most populated nation. The overthrow of the Qing (Ch'ing) dynasty in 1911 initiated a period of social, political, and military conflict that did not end until the Communists gained control in 1949. For much of that period the internal struggle was between the Kuomintang, headed by General Chiang Kai-shek, and the Chinese Communist Party, under the leadership of Mao Zedong.

The sources in this chapter focus on each of these three developments—the struggle with Western influence, the growth of nationalism, and China's revolutionary turmoil—that affected the peoples of these regions so deeply in the period between World Wars I and II. In the process, the sources will also provide insights into some of this period's social, cultural, and military developments. This sets the stage for the end of colonial rule and the realignments of power that would occur throughout the world in the years following 1945.

# PRIMARY SOURCES

## Japanese Nationalism and Expansionism
### Hashimoto Kingoro

*Japan emerged from its self-imposed exile in the 1850s to being one of the most militarily powerful nations in the world by the 1930s. In the course of this transformation, Japan defeated China and, more importantly, Russia in 1905, and acquired an Asian empire in its quest for equality with the colonial powers of the world. During the 1920s and 1930s, nationalist groups gained influence in Japan and elements of the military became increasingly involved in politics. Overseas, Japan followed a policy of growing adventurism and expansion.*

*Whatever non-Japanese thought of Japan's territorial expansion, the vast majority of Japanese agreed with it. First, there was the attempt to be equal with the major military and economic powers (Britain, the United States, and France); one of the ways to accomplish that goal was to have colonies as they did. Second, there was the feeling that Japanese civilization was superior, and the rest of Asia should appreciate the exporting of it.*

SOURCE: Ryusaku Tsunoda et al., eds., *Sources of Japanese Tradition* (New York and London: Columbia University Press, 1961), pp. 796–98.

*These sentiments are reflected in the following selection by Hashimoto Kingoro, an ultranationalist. Here he justifies Japan's foreign policy of colonial acquisition.*

CONSIDER: *The appeal of this argument; Hashimoto's attitudes toward the West; why, according to Hashimoto, policies based on nationalism and expansion are justified for Japan.*

We have already said that there are only three ways left to Japan to escape from the pressure of surplus population. We are like a great crowd of people packed into a small and narrow room, and there are only three doors through which we might escape, namely emigration, advance into world markets, and expansion of territory. The first door, emigration, has been barred to us by the anti-Japanese immigration policies of other countries. The second door, advance into world markets, is being pushed shut by tariff barriers and the abrogation of commercial treaties. What should Japan do when two of the three doors have been closed against her?

It is quite natural that Japan should rush upon the last remaining door.

It may sound dangerous when we speak of territorial expansion, but the territorial expansion of which we speak does not in any sense of the word involve the occupation of the possessions of other countries, the planting of the Japanese flag thereon, and the declaration of their annexation to Japan. It is just that since the Powers have suppressed the circulation of Japanese materials and merchandise abroad, we are looking for some place overseas where Japanese capital, Japanese skills and Japanese labor can have free play, free from the oppression of the white race.

We would be satisfied with just this much. What moral right do the world powers who have themselves closed to us the two doors of emigration and advance into world markets have to criticize Japan's attempt to rush out of the third and last door?

If they do not approve of this, they should open the doors which they have closed against us and permit the free movement overseas of Japanese emigrants and merchandise. . . .

At the time of the Manchurian incident, the entire world joined in criticism of Japan. They said that Japan was an untrustworthy nation. They said that she had recklessly brought cannon and machine guns into Manchuria, which was the territory of another country, flown airplanes over it, and finally occupied it. But the military action taken by Japan was not in the least a selfish one. Moreover, we do not recall ever having taken so much as an inch of territory belonging to another nation. The result of this incident was the establishment of the splendid new nation of Manchuria. The Powers are still discussing whether or not to recognize this new nation, but regardless of whether or not other nations recognize her, the Manchurian empire has already been established, and now, seven years after its creation, the empire is further consolidating its foundations with the aid of its friend, Japan.

And if it is still protested that our actions in Manchuria were excessively violent, we may wish to ask the white race just which country it was that sent warships and troops to India, South Africa, and Australia and slaughtered innocent natives, bound their hands and feet with iron chains, lashed their backs with iron whips, proclaimed these territories as their own, and still continues to hold them to this very day?

They will invariably reply, these were all lands inhabited by untamed savages. These people did not know how to develop the abundant resources of their land for the benefit of mankind. Therefore it was the wish of God, who created heaven and earth for mankind, for us to develop these undeveloped lands and to promote the happiness of mankind in their stead. God wills it.

This is quite a convenient argument for them. Let us take it at face value. Then there is another question that we must ask them.

Suppose that there is still on this earth land endowed with abundant natural resources that have not been developed at all by the white race. Would it not then be God's will and the will of Providence that Japan go there and develop those resources for the benefit of mankind?

And there still remain many such lands on this earth.

## The Chinese Communist Party Mobilizes the Masses

### Mao Zedong (Mao Tse-tung)

*During the decades between World War I and World War II, China experienced great instability. This environment fostered new political and social movements, one of which was Chinese Communism. The Chinese Communist Party grew after 1927, especially after 1935 under the leadership of Mao Zedong (Mao Tse-tung, 1893–1976). Though its fortunes ebbed and flowed, eventually it would achieve victory. One of the reasons the Chinese Communist Party was able to achieve victory was its recognition, very early in its history, that the Chinese farmer (peasant) would be a major revolutionary force. This was in direct opposition to the orthodox teachings of Karl Marx and Vladimir Lenin, which argued that only an industrial proletariat could be the vanguard of any socialist revolution. The problem in China, however, was that in the 1920s the urban proletariat represented a minute fraction of the workforce where the rural population accounted for over 80 percent of the people. More problematic than the numbers, though, was the Marxist-Leninist view that rural people were not sufficiently politicized or capable of being a revolutionary force.*

*Although not the first to recognize this, Mao Zedong came to appreciate these farmers' potential after visiting his home province of Hunan in 1927. The first selection is from Mao's report of that trip.*

CONSIDER: *The concerns of Chinese peasants; why it might be difficult to see poor farmers as a political force; what kinds of persuasion had to be utilized to get the farmers to see themselves as a revolutionary force.*

During my recent visit to Hunan I made a first-hand investigation of conditions. . . . [T]he present upsurge of the peasant movement is a colossal event. In a very short time, . . . several hundred million peasants will rise like a mighty storm, like a hurricane, a force so swift and violent that no power, however great, will be able to hold it back. They will smash all the trammels that bind them and rush forward along the road to liberation. They will sweep all the imperialists, warlords, corrupt officials, local tyrants and evil gentry into their graves. Every revolutionary party and every revolutionary comrade will be put to the test, to be accepted or rejected as they decide.

SOURCE: Mao Tse-tung, *Selected Works of Mao Tse-tung,* vol. I (Peking: Foreign Languages Press, 1965), pp. 23–28.

There are three alternatives. To march at their head and lead them? To trail behind them, gesticulating and criticizing? Or to stand in their way and oppose them? Every Chinese is free to choose, but events will force you to make the choice quickly. . . .

The main targets of attack by the peasants are the local tyrants, the evil gentry and the lawless landlords, but in passing they also hit out against patriarchal ideas and institutions, against the corrupt officials in the cities and against bad practices and customs in the rural areas. In force and momentum the attack is tempestuous; those who bow before it survive and those who resist perish. . . . With the collapse of the power of the landlords, the peasant associations have now become the sole organs of authority and the popular slogan "All power to the peasant associations" has become a reality. Even trifles such as a quarrel between husband and wife are brought to the peasant association. . . .

. . . [T]he great peasant masses have risen to fulfil their historic mission and that the forces of rural democracy have risen to overthrow the forces of rural feudalism. The patriarchal-feudal class of local tyrants, evil gentry and lawless landlords has formed the basis of autocratic government for thousands of years and is the cornerstone of imperialism, warlordism and corrupt officialdom. To overthrow these feudal forces is the real objective of the national revolution. In a few months the peasants have accomplished what Dr. Sun Yat-sen wanted, but failed, to accomplish in the forty years he devoted to the national revolution. . . .

. . . The peasants are clear-sighted. Who is bad and who is not, who is the worst and who is not quite so vicious, who deserves severe punishment and who deserves to be let off lightly—the peasants keep clear accounts, and very seldom has the punishment exceeded the crime. Secondly, a revolution is not a dinner party, or writing an essay, or painting a picture, or doing embroidery; it cannot be so refined, so leisurely and gentle, so temperate, kind, courteous, restrained and magnanimous. A revolution is an insurrection, an act of violence by which one class overthrows another. A rural revolution is a revolution by which the peasantry overthrows the power of the feudal landlord class. Without using the greatest force, the peasants cannot possibly overthrow the deep-rooted authority of the landlords which has lasted for thousands of years. The rural areas need a mighty revolutionary upsurge, for it alone can rouse the people in their millions to become a powerful force.

## Women and Chinese Communism

*Shan-fei and Agnes Smedley*

*When dynastic rule in China collapsed in 1911, a cultural, social, and political vacuum was created because no new societal forms were available to replace what had just been discredited.*

*One of the newest ideas was the equality of women. No one supported that idea more than the Chinese Communist Party. While it was largely urban women who initially joined this movement, some rural women did as well, but only in cases where male family members were absent or were extraordinarily progressive. Even for the women who joined the Communist Party, total equality was never to be achieved. Nevertheless, the status of these women increased dramatically, if for no other reason than because their original status was so low. Women connected to the party were given positions and responsibilities, and had some power, however limited.*

*This selection was written by American journalist Agnes Smedley, who spent many years in China recording the stories of the people she met. Although somewhat romanticized—because Smedley herself tended to see communist women in a romantic fashion—it nonetheless portrays the changes that some women were able to make in the 1920s and 1930s.*

CONSIDER: *The consequences to a society when one of its major tenets is radically altered.*

This is the story of Shan-fei, daughter of a rich landowner of Hunan, China. Once she went to school and wore silk dresses and had a fountain pen. But then she became a Communist and married a peasant leader. In the years that followed she—but I will begin from the beginning—

Her mother is the beginning. A strange woman. She was old-fashioned, had bound feet, and appeared to bow her head to every wish of her husband who held by all that was old and feudal. Yet she must have been rebellious. She watched her sons grow up, go to school, and return with new ideas. Some of these new ideas were about women—women with natural feet, who studied as men did, who married only when and whom they wished.

When her sons talked the mother would sit listening, her eyes on her little daughter, Shan-fei, . . . we know that at last she died for the freedom of her daughter.

This battle was waged behind the high stone walls that surrounded her home. The enemy was her husband and his brothers. And the mother's weapons were the ancient weapons of subjected women: tears, entreaties, intrigue, cunning. At first she won but one point: her husband consented to Shan-fei's education, provided the teacher was an old-fashioned man who came to the home and taught only the Chinese characters. But Shan-fei's feet must be bound, and she must be betrothed in marriage according to ancient custom. . . .

SOURCE: Agnes Smedley, *Chinese Destinies: Sketches of Present Day China* (New York: The Vanguard Press, 1933), pp. 35–42.

Until Shan-fei was eleven years old, her father ruled as tyrants rule. But then he suddenly died. Yet the funeral was not finished before the bandages were taken off the feet of the little girl, and the earth on the grave was still damp when Shan-fei was put in a school one hundred *li* away. . . .

. . . [T]he news came that Shan-fei had led a students' strike against the corrupt administration of her school. She was nearing sixteen at the time, the proper age for marriage. Yet she was expelled in disgrace from the school, and returned home with her head high and proud. And her mother, instead of subduing her, whispered with her alone, then merely transferred her to a still more modern school in faraway Wuchang on the Yangzi (Yangtze), where rumor further had it that she was becoming notorious as a leader in the students' movement. Moreover, men and women students studied together in Wuchang.

. . . [In] the late summer of 1926, . . . China was swept by winds of revolution. . . . Shan-fei gave up her studies and . . . became a member of the Communist Youth, and in this work she met a peasant leader whom she loved and who was loved by the peasants. She defied the old customs . . . and announced her free marriage to the man she loved. . . .

In those days the Guomindang (Kuomintang) and the Communist Parties still worked together, and, as one of the most active woman revolutionaries, Shan-fei was sent back to her ancestral home as head of the Woman's Department of the Guomindang. There she was made a member of the Revolutionary Tribunal that tried the enemies of the revolution, confiscated the lands of the rich landlords and distributed them among the poor peasants. She helped confiscate all the lands of her own family and of the family of her former fiancé.

When the revolution became a social revolution, the Communists and the Guomindang split, and the dread White Terror began. . . . Shan-fei worked openly as the head of the Woman's Department of the Guomindang; secretly, she carried on propaganda amongst the troops and the workers. Then in this city the chief of the judicial department met her and fell in love with her. He was a rich militarist, but she listened carefully to his lovemaking and did not forget to ask him about the plans to crush the peasants. He told her—and she sent the news to the peasant army beyond. One of the leaders of this army beyond was her husband.

## Letter from Abroad: Revolutionary Nationalism in Vietnam

*Ho Chi Minh*

*With the Japanese, French, and Chinese all busy warring amongst themselves, the Vietnamese nationalists saw an op-*

*portunity to aggressively pursue their struggle for independence. Moreover, the ease with which the Japanese overcame the French forces early in World War II demonstrated the latter's severe vulnerability. Nationalists used this to rally to their cause more people—particularly those who believed that the Vietnamese would never possess the capabilities to overcome French colonial rule.*

*Ho Chi Minh (1892–1969), who founded the Indochinese Communist Party in 1930, understood that now was the time to strike. Consequently, in May 1941, the Viet Nam Doc Lap Dong Minh Hoi (Vietnamese Independence League)—or Viet Minh—was established. On June 6, Ho Chi Minh, then in southern China, issued this "Letter from Abroad" as a clarion call to his countrymen and women to combine nationalism with revolutionary goals as the only means to achieve independence.*

CONSIDER: *The force of Ho's appeal; how this must have sounded to those looking for leadership in the struggle against colonialism.*

Venerable elders!
Patriotic personalities!
Intellectuals, peasants, workers, traders and soldiers!
Dear fellow-countrymen!

Since France was defeated by Germany, its power has completely collapsed. Nevertheless, with regard to our people, the French rulers have become even more ruthless in carrying out their policy of exploitation, repression and massacre. They bleed us white and carry out a barbarous policy of all-out terrorism and massacre. In the foreign field, bowing their heads and bending their knees, they resign themselves to ceding part of our land to Siam and shamelessly surrendering our country to Japan. As a result our people are writhing under a double yoke of oppression. They serve not only as beasts of burden to the French bandits but also as slaves to the Japanese robbers. Alas! What sin have our people committed to be doomed to such a wretched fate? Plunging into such tragic suffering, are we to await death with folded arms?

No! Certainly not! The twenty-odd million descendants of the Lac and the Hong are resolved not to let themselves be kept in servitude. For nearly eighty years under the French pirates' iron heels we have unceasingly and selflessly struggled for national independence and freedom. . . . The recent uprisings in the South and at Do Luong and Bac Son testify to the determination of our compatriots to follow the glorious example of their ancestors and to annihilate the enemy. If we were not successful, it was not because the French bandits were

SOURCE: Ho Chi Minh, *Ho Chi Minh: Selected Writings, 1920–1969,* "Letter from Abroad," June 6, 1941 (Hanoi: Foreign Languages Publishing House, 1977), pp. 44–46.

strong, but only because the situation was not yet ripe and our people throughout the country were not yet of one mind.

Now, the opportunity has come for our liberation. France itself is unable to help the French colonialists rule over our country. As for the Japanese, on the one hand, bogged down in China, on the other, hampered by the British and American forces, they certainly cannot use all their strength against us. If our entire people are solidly united we can certainly get the better of the best-trained armies of the French and the Japanese. . . .

Dear fellow-countrymen! A few hundred years ago, in the reign of the Tran, when our country faced the great danger of invasion by Yuan armies the elders ardently called on their sons and daughters throughout the country to stand up as one man to kill the enemy. Finally they saved their people and their glorious memory will live forever. Let our elders and patriotic personalities follow the illustrious example set by our forefathers. . . .

The hour has struck! Raise aloft the banner of insurrection and lead the people throughout the country to overthrow the Japanese and the French! The sacred call of the Fatherland is resounding in our ears; the ardent blood of our heroic predecessors is seething in our hearts! The fighting spirit of the people is mounting before our eyes! Let us unite and unify our action to overthrow the Japanese and the French.

The Vietnamese revolution will certainly triumph!
The world revolution will certainly triumph!

## Hindus, Muslims, and Nationalism in India
*Mohandas K. Gandhi*

*While the European colonial nations were recovering from the First World War and, shortly thereafter, trying to avoid a second world war, Indian nationalists were trying to develop their movement for independence. During these two decades, the nationalist movement was shaken by a split in the ranks between Hindus and Muslims. Muslims felt that they would be a minority in an Indian state that encompassed all of British India. To protect their rights, they wanted a separate Muslim state, Pakistan.*

*Hindus objected, fearing that two countries would be weaker than a single, large nation. Additionally, the split caused growing concern about the possibility of communal violence. Perhaps no one was more concerned about the possibilities of violence than Mohandas K. Gandhi (1869–1948), the most important Indian leader of the period. The following is a statement made by Gandhi in 1938 just prior to a meet-*

SOURCE: M. K. Gandhi, *Communal Unity* (Ahmedabad: Navajivan Publishing House, 1949), pp. 217–18.

*ing with Mohammed Ali Jinnah, leader of India's Muslim League.*

CONSIDER: *Why Gandhi's views might be appealing; how Gandhi tries to gain credibility for his views; the problems this statement reflects.*

My Hinduism is not sectarian. It includes all that I know to be best in Islam, Christianity, Buddhism, and Zoroastrianism. I approach politics as everything else in a religious spirit. Truth is my religion and *ahimsa* is the only way of its realization. I have rejected once and for all the doctrine of the sword. The secret stabbings of innocent persons, and the speeches I read in the papers are hardly the thing leading to peace or an honourable settlement.

Again I am not approaching the forthcoming interview in any representative capacity. I have purposely divested myself of any such. If there are to be any formal negotiations, they will be between the president of the Congress and the president of the Muslim League. I go as a lifelong worker in the cause of Hindu–Muslim unity. It has been my passion from early youth. I count some of the noblest of Muslims as my friends. I have a devout daughter of Islam as more than a daughter to me. She lives for that unity and would cheerfully die for it. I had the son of the late Muazzin of the Juma Masjid of Bombay as a staunch inmate of the Ashram. I have not met a nobler man. His morning *Azan* in the Ashram rings in my ears as I write these lines during midnight. It is for such reasons that I wait on Shree Jinnah.

I may not leave a single stone unturned to achieve Hindu–Muslim unity. God fulfils Himself in strange ways. He may, in a manner least known to us, both fulfil Himself through the interview and open a way to an honourable understanding between the two communities. It is in that hope that I am looking forward to the forthcoming talk. We are friends, not strangers. It does not matter to me that we see things from different angles of vision. I ask the public not to attach any exaggerated importance to the interview. But I ask all lovers of communal peace to pray that the God of truth and love may give us both the right spirit and the right word and use us for the good of the dumb millions of India.

## Britain and the Origins of the Modern Middle East
*The Balfour Declaration and The Churchill White Paper of 1922*

*The modern Zionist movement could be said to have been launched with the First Zionist Congress in 1897. The chief proponent of Zionism at the time, Theodor Herzl, knew international recognition was essential for success, as the projected Jewish homeland was then controlled by the Ottoman Empire. In World War I the Ottomans allied with Germany against Britain and its allies. Zionist leaders looked to Britain for support for their idea of a Jewish homeland.*

*In the midst of the war, the British Cabinet decided to have Foreign Secretary Arthur James Balfour write to Lord Rothschild, a British Zionist leader, declaring British support for the establishment of a "national home for the Jewish people" in what was then Palestine. "The Balfour Declaration represented the convinced policy of all parties in our country and also in America," recalled Prime Minister Lloyd George in his memoirs, "but the launching of it in 1917 was due . . . to propagandist reasons."*

*But Britain was not only making promises to the Jews. In 1915 Sir Henry McMahon, the British High Commissioner in Egypt, had exchanged letters with Hussein ibn Ali, Sheriff of Mecca, in which he promised Arab control of the Arab lands, exclusive of the Mediterranean coast. In later years the British government, with all new members, tried to backtrack from these various promises, particularly since it had been given control of the region as a "mandate" by the League of Nations after the end of World War I. The official expressions of this change of heart came with a series of "White Papers," beginning with the Churchill "White Paper of 1922" which tried to satisfy the Jews and the Arabs while maintaining British rule.*

CONSIDER: *How people's fates in the Middle East were determined by international politics and the interests of the British state without any consultation with the inhabitants of these lands.*

## The Balfour Declaration

Foreign Office
November 2nd, 1917

Dear Lord Rothschild,
I have much pleasure in conveying to you, on behalf of His Majesty's Government, the following declaration of sympathy with Jewish Zionist aspirations which has been submitted to, and approved by, the Cabinet.

"His Majesty's Government view with favour the establishment in Palestine of a national home for the Jewish people, and will use their best endeavours to facilitate the achievement of this object, it being clearly understood that nothing shall be done which may prejudice the civil and religious rights of existing non-Jewish communities in Palestine, or the rights and political status enjoyed by Jews in any other country."

I should be grateful if you would bring this declaration to the knowledge of the Zionist Federation.

Yours sincerely,
Arthur James Balfour

## The White Paper of 1922
(the "Churchill White Paper")

The Secretary of State for the Colonies has given renewed consideration to the existing political situation in Palestine, with a very earnest desire to arrive at a settlement of the outstanding questions which have given rise to uncertainty and unrest among certain sections of the population. . . . The tension which has prevailed from time to time in Palestine is mainly due to apprehensions, which are entertained both by sections of the Arab and by sections of the Jewish population. These apprehensions, so far as the Arabs are concerned, are partly based upon exaggerated interpretations of the meaning of the Balfour Declaration favouring the establishment of a Jewish National Home in Palestine, made on behalf of His Majesty's Government on 2nd November, 1917. . . . Nor have they at any time contemplated, as appears to be feared by the Arab delegation, the disappearance or the subordination of the Arabic population, language, or culture in Palestine. They would draw attention to the fact that the terms of the Declaration referred to do not contemplate that Palestine as a whole should be converted into a Jewish National Home, but that such a Home should be founded in, Palestine, . . . Further, it is contemplated that the status of all citizens of Palestine in the eyes of the law shall be Palestinian, and it has never been intended that they, or any section of them, should possess any other juridical status. So far as the Jewish population of Palestine are concerned it appears that some among them are apprehensive that His Majesty's Government may depart from the policy embodied in the Declaration of 1917. It is necessary, therefore, once more to affirm that these fears are unfounded, and that that Declaration . . . is not susceptible of change. . . . When it is asked what is meant by the development of the Jewish National Home in Palestine, it may be answered that it is not the imposition of a Jewish nationality upon the inhabitants of Palestine as a whole, but the further development of the existing Jewish community, with the assistance of Jews in other parts of the world, in order that it may become a centre in which the Jewish people as a whole may take, on grounds of religion and race, an interest and a pride. . . . This, then, is the interpretation which His Majesty's Government place upon the Declaration of 1917, and, so understood, the Secretary of State is of opinion that it does not contain or imply anything which need cause either alarm to the Arab population of Palestine or disappointment to the Jews. . . . The Secretary of State believes that a policy upon these lines, coupled with the maintenance of the fullest religious liberty in Palestine and with scrupulous regard for the rights of each community with reference to its Holy Places, cannot but commend itself to the various sections of the population, and that upon this basis may be built up that a spirit of cooperation upon which the future progress and prosperity of the Holy Land must largely depend.

## Africans and the Colonial State

### Jesse Chilula Chipenda

*The following is an excerpt from the autobiography of Jesse Chilula Chipenda. Chipenda wrote his autobiography in 1938 in fulfillment of the requirement that the Protestant Church of central Angola imposed on all candidates for ordination. The excerpt was originally written in Umbundu, the language of the Ovimbundu of central Angola.*

CONSIDER: *What Chipenda's experience tells us about the status of educated Christian converts during the colonial period; the continuation of certain forms of un-free labor in colonial Africa even as Europeans were arguing that the colonial states they imposed brought an end to African forms of slavery; what Chipenda's experience reveals about the relationship between Africans and the colonial state.*

I am Jesse Chilula Chipenda, child of Chipenda and Carvoli. . . . My father, Chipenda, was a trader who had 18 wives. He begat 51 children. When trading was no longer profitable, he became chief of Lomanda. . . .

While working on this program Father sent word to me saying: "We must go to the Administration because the Portuguese official has called all the chiefs and village headmen. We must go to Bailundo." When we entered the administration office the Administrator said that there was a problem about the payment of taxes. I explained the matter of the taxes to the Administrator to his satisfaction, because I was with my father at Lomanda when he was receiving the tax money.

The Administrator asked: "O Chief, whose son is this?" My father said: "He is my son." Then the Administrator said: "All your children should study like this son of yours."

When we arrived at the encampment, Father told the village elders who were gathered what the Administrator had said about all the young people studying. Then Father added that even the slaves and nieces and nephews could study. . . .

When we left the Bailundo Administration, the Administrator came to our village to write up taxes. He asked me if I would help him, and I agreed. When we finished in our village, he asked me to go to the other

villages. So we went to five other villages doing the same work. When we got to King Bunju's village I said that I would not continue. I asked to return to my village. The Administrator urged me to continue working with him, but I would not agree because of three things that bothered me.

1. He would not let me walk from village to village, but insisted that I be carried in a hammock. I am a common youth and shouldn't be carried by elders.

2. This would mean abandoning my teaching.

3. I would have to go wherever the administrator went and reside at the administration.

## Resentment in Colonial Nigeria

### Obafemi Awolowo

*The interwar period was a time when Africans in all the colonial regions were facing the realities of European colonial occupation. For the majority of Africans, colonialism meant forced cultivation of agricultural products and migrant labor in mines and plantations owned and operated by Europeans. There were restrictions in all areas of occupational specialization. Moreover, legal codes enforced residential segregation and second-class citizenship for the few Africans who survived the array of examinations required from early childhood onward. As a result of their frustration with the colonial system, Africans began to organize to challenge colonialism. The following selection from Chief Awolowo's autobiography reveals some of the contending aspects of African resentment in colonial Nigeria during the 1930s.*

CONSIDER: *What Awolowo's recollections suggest about the strategies Africans adopted; what this illustrates about African perceptions of colonial rule; the role of the educated elite in the emergence of anticolonial sentiments.*

The Nigerian Youth Movement was the first nationalist organisation ever to make real efforts to bring within its fold all the nationalists and politically conscious elements in Nigeria. . . .

In 1934, the Nigerian Government inaugurated the Yaba Higher College. This institution, which was not affiliated to any British university, was to award its own Nigerian diplomas in a number of faculties, including medicine, arts, agriculture, economics and engineering. This institution was assailed by Nigerian nationalists. In the first place, it was inferior in status to a British university; and under no circumstance would an institution of higher learning which bore the stamp of inferiority be

SOURCE: Lawrence Henderson, *Development and the Church in Angola: Jesse Chipenda the Trailblazer* (Nairobi: Action Publishers, 2000), pp. 1–8, as excerpted.

SOURCE: Obafemi Awolowo, AWO, *The Autobiography of Chief Obafemi Awolowo* (Cambridge, England: Cambridge University Press, 1960), pp. 113, 115–16.

tolerated by Nigerians. In the second place, the diplomas to be awarded by the institution were also inferior, since the holders of these diplomas were only expected, in various government departments and institutions, to occupy posts which were permanently subordinate to those filled by the holders of British university degrees (mostly expatriates) in the same faculties and professions. Africanisation of the civil service had been in the air for some time, and it was believed that the Yaba Higher College was an infernal device by British imperialism to foil this legitimate aspiration. This view was further strengthened by the fact that, only five years previously, the Nigerian government had planned to introduce a Nigerian School Certificate in place and to the exclusion of the then Cambridge and Oxford School Certificates. The plan was dropped as a result of the undivided opposition to it by all the political leaders in Lagos, irrespective of their party leanings, . . . In the third place, the diplomas to be awarded by the college would only enjoy an inferior recognition in Nigeria and would not command any respect, much less recognition, outside the country. In the fourth place, though the diplomas were in all respects to be inferior to university degrees, the time required to do a course was longer than was the case for a university degree in the same subject. There

was, therefore, widespread resentment in political circles in Lagos, and in some circles in Southern Nigeria. It was in order to canalise this resentment, and to present a united front to the Nigerian government in representing the feelings of the people, that the Lagos Youth Movement was founded by Dr. J. C. Vaughan, Mr. Ernest Ikoli, Oba Samuel Akisanya, and others. I remember the memorandum submitted by the Lagos Youth Movement, the Movement's rejoinder to the government's reply, and Oba Samuel Akisanya's open letter to Duse Mohamed Ali Effendi, who in his paper *Comet* had criticised the leaders of the Movement and had described them as "half-baked critics." All these remonstrances were analytical, constructive, scathing and crushing. In them, the Movement elaborated its reasons for opposing the establishment of the college as it was then constituted, and made suggestions for its improvement. The Nigerian government, however, persisted in going on with its scheme as originally conceived. The Lagos Youth Movement, on the other hand, continued in existence to initiate and conduct agitations against other unjust manifestations of British rule in Nigeria. In 1936, as a result of clamour from different parts of the country, the name "Lagos Youth Movement" was changed to "Nigerian Youth Movement."

## VISUAL SOURCES

### The Foolish Old Man Removes the Mountain
*Xu Beihong (Hsü Pei-hung)*

*The cultural vacuum created in China after the 1911 revolution extended to art. For the first time, Chinese artists began to seriously study European art—some went to study in Europe. Soon schools were established in China—the most famous being the Tian Han (T'ien Han) Academie du*

*Midi in Nanjing (Nanking)—that ridged the two traditions.*

*In 1927 this school invited artist Xu Beihong (Hsü Pei-hung) to establish a fine arts department. Xu had studied in Paris and Berlin and soon after his return had begun painting Chinese historical subjects in oils in the European tradition. His paintings reflected the dilemma of modernization for modern Chinese artists. Before too long he returned to some of the traditional Chinese methods and eventually developed*

**Illustration 24–1** Xu Beihong Museum, Beijing, China.

*a style that combined European realism with Chinese brushwork.*

*Illustration 24–1 below is a good example of this syncretic method. Painted in the late 1930s, this scroll depicts the old Daoist (Taoist) tale whose moral is that everything is possible. The story was also a favorite of Mao Zedong (Mao Tsetung), who liked to tell it when he was trying to empower the peasantry of China.*

CONSIDER: *Why Mao may have found these paintings appealing; the difficulties of finding new cultural patterns when the traditional ones have been discarded.*

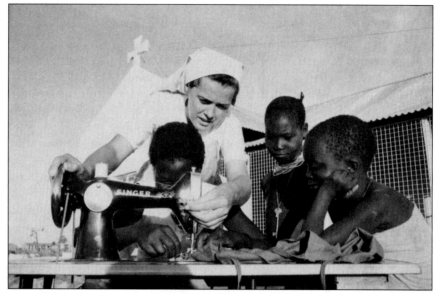

**Illustration 24–2**   Marc & Evelyne Bernheim/Woodfin Camp & Associates.

## Western Technology and Christianity in Colonial Africa

*During the period of conquest and early colonial years, western nations brought not only their troops and administrators but also their technology, religion, and attitudes to Africa. Europeans usually assumed that their own institutions were superior to African institutions. These European institutions were often spread by apparently well-meaning individuals who believed they were improving the lot of the colonized Africans. This is reflected in this photograph of a Christian missionary showing young Africans how to use a sewing machine.*

CONSIDER: *The effects of this introduction of Christianity and technology on African society; the importance of the connection between Christianity, technology, and the role this missionary is playing.*

## The Expansion of Japan

*Ever since Japan emerged from its self-imposed isolation in the middle of the 19th century, one of its major goals was to achieve equality with the major powers in the world. Given*

**Map 24–1**

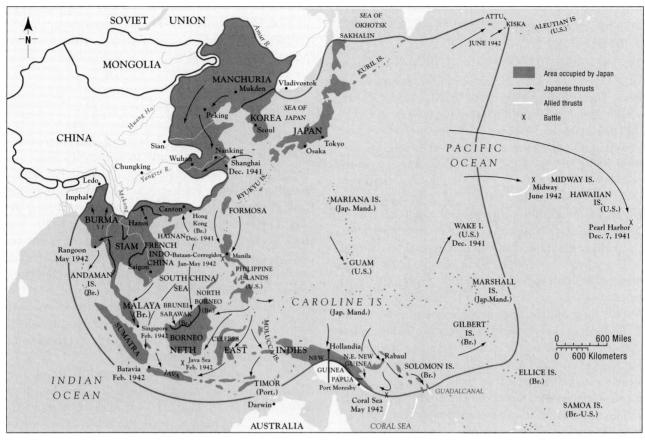

**Map 24–2**

that period in history, one key way to achieve that was to acquire a colonial empire. As Map 24–1 shows, Japan initiated its expansion in the last quarter of the 19th century, continued during the first decade of the 20th century after its successes in the Sino–Japanese War of 1894–95 and the Russo–Japanese War of 1904–5, and pushed on during the early 1930s with acquisitions in Manchuria and northern China. As Map 24–2 indicates, by 1942 Japan was in control of a vast empire and was involved in World War II. Japan's defeat in that war would spell the end of its empire and reduce Japan almost to its mid-19th-century boundaries.

CONSIDER: *The possible justifications the Japanese might have used for the expansion shown by these maps; ways this expansion may have made Japan increasingly vulnerable.*

# SECONDARY SOURCES

## Asia in World War I

### *L. M. Panikkar*

Although the war of 1914–18, otherwise known as World War I, did not take place in Asia, Asia was not unaffected. The colonized nations of Asia were forced to join their colonial masters in the war, while China and Siam allied themselves with what they believed would be the winning side. Japan had treaty obligations. The Asian war effort consisted of dispatching soldiers from the colonized nations or labor brigades from nations such as China. Japan sent neither, but helped protect British interests in Asia, took over German interests, and economically replaced European businesses unable to continue in east Asia.

The war had considerable consequences for Asia. In this selection, L. M. Panikkar, the well-known Indian scholar and diplomat, describes them.

SOURCE: L. M. Panikkar, *Asia and Western Dominance* (London: G. Allen & Unwin, 1959 [Taylor & Francis]).

CONSIDER: *The Asian perception of this war according to Panikkar; the effects on Asians of the ending of the myth of European supremacy.*

The Great War of 1914–18 was from the Asian point of view a civil war within the European community of nations. The direct participation of Asian countries, during some stages of this conflict, was at the invitation and by the encouragement of one of the parties, the *entente* Powers, and was greatly resented by the Germans. . . . [A]t the beginning of the twentieth century . . . European nations . . . remained unshakably convinced that they had inherited the earth, . . . It was the age of Kipling and the white man's burden, and it seemed the manifest destiny of the white race to hold the East in fee.

In 1914, when the German invaders had reached the Marne, divisions of the Indian Army under British officers had been rushed to France. . . . Later, they were extensively used in the defence of the Suez Canal and the Middle East and in campaigns elsewhere in Africa. In 1917, Siam declared war on Germany. An Indo-Chinese labour force had been recruited and was working in France. On August 14, 1917, China also joined the Allies. . . . However, opinion in India, China and even in Japan was at the time more pro-German than pro-Ally. In India, . . . public opinion rejoiced at every report of German victory and felt depressed when the Allies were winning. . . . [P]ublic opinion in the East looked upon the conflict as a civil war in which neither party had a claim to the friendship of the peoples of Asia, and if any party could appeal to the sympathy of Asians it was the Germanic alliance which had no tradition of Asian conquest and was allied with the chief Muslim power, Turkey.

But the participation of Asian people in the war had far-reaching consequences. The Indian soldier who fought on the Marne came back to India with other ideas of the *Sahib* than those he was taught to believe by decades of official propaganda. Indo-Chinese Labour Corps in the South of France returned to Annam with notions of democracy and republicanism which they had not entertained before. Among the Chinese who went to France at the time was a young man named Chou Enlai [Zhou Enlai], who stayed on to become a Communist and had to be expelled for activities among the members of the Chinese Labour Corps. . . .

Politically, a further weakening of the colonial and imperialist position came about as a result of President Wilson's declaration of fourteen points. In 1917, the doctrine of the "self-determination of peoples" had the ring of a new revelation. . . . [I]n Asia it was acclaimed as a doctrine of liberation. . . .

Apart from these political considerations economic forces generated by the war were also helping to undermine the supremacy of the West. Japan utilized the four years of war for a planned expansion of her trade in the East. India gained her first major start on the industrial road and, with the strain on British economy, Indian national capital was placed in a position of some advantage. . . .

[T]he growth of a powerful left-wing movement in the countries of Western Europe had a direct effect on shaping events in the Eastern Empire. The Labour Party in England during the days of its growth had been closely associated with the nationalist movement in India. . . . Annamite nationalism had worked hand in hand with left-wing parties in France. . . . [T]he influence of the Russian Revolution. Imperialism meant something totally different after Lenin's definition of it as the last phase of capitalism and his insistence that the liberation of subject peoples from colonial domination was a part of the struggle against capitalism. Also, Russia's call for and practice of racial equality, abolition of the special privileges that Tsarist Russia had acquired in Persia and China, . . . made it difficult for Western nations which had so long claimed to stand for liberty and progress to deny the claims of Eastern nations. . . .

One fact which stands out clear and illustrates this chasm in thought is the lack of faith in imperialist ideals in the period that followed the war. With the solitary exception of Churchill, there was not one major figure in any of the British parties who confessed to a faith in the white man's mission to rule. Successive Viceroys of India, Liberal, Conservative and non-party, professed publicly their adherence to the cause of Indian freedom. . . . There was no conviction left of the European's superiority or sense of vision.

## Chinese Intellectuals as Agents of Enlightenment

*Vera Schwarcz*

*When the Qing (Ch'ing) Dynasty collapsed in 1911, it left an enormous vacuum in the political, educational, social, and literary life of China. Before that time all aspects of Chinese society were tied to Confucianism. The collapse of the dynastic cycle in the face of Western imperialism made this a bankrupt philosophy.*

*This vacuum was filled by a variety of philosophies so China enjoyed a range of debate and literary renaissance that it had rarely seen before. This movement, which began late in the 1910s and lasted until the Japanese invasion in 1937, is called the May Fourth Movement. The name comes from an*

SOURCE: Vera Schwarcz, *The Chinese Enlightenment: Intellectuals and the Legacy of the May Fourth Movement of 1919* (Berkeley: University of California Press, 1986), pp. 3–10.

incident on May 4, 1919, when the Chinese learned that German concessions in China were being given to the Japanese rather than being restored to China even though China had been on the winning side during World War I. That day produced strikes and demonstrations in Beijing (Peking) and sparked a nationwide anti-Japanese movement.

For the intellectuals who sparked this movement, the gap between their theoretical concepts and the realities of the communities they lived in was far larger than they ever imagined. Here Vera Schwarcz (an intellectual historian of China) discusses the dilemma these young intellectuals faced.

CONSIDER: The ways in which this was an important intellectual movement; the social and economic changes stemming from this movement; what happens to a society that loses trust in its institutions.

Modern China's answer to Kant's question "What is Enlightenment?" reflects the exigencies of its own history. This is a history marked by the rise of modern nationalism, by the unfolding of a rural-based revolution, and by the quest for emancipation from a feudal worldview. . . . One dimension of that tension, most apparent in the lives and work of critical intellectuals, is the conflict between nationalism and cultural critique—or, in Chinese terms, between the external imperatives of jiuguo (national salvation) and the internal prerequisites of qimeng (enlightenment). The Chinese intellectuals who wrestled with this disparity most consciously were themselves beneficiaries of modern education at home and abroad. They shared their compatriots' commitment to a strong and independent China and proved that commitment by active participation in the twentieth-century Chinese revolution. . . .

During the decades that followed the May Fourth movement of 1919, Chinese advocates of enlightenment were forced to reconsider and to refashion, at times even to abandon, their vision of intellectual emancipation. The twin phenomena of political violence and anti-imperialist mobilization created a climate of urgency that challenged the intellectuals' commitment to a slow-paced revolution of ideas. It also called into question their image of themselves as forerunners of cultural awakening. Having set out to reform the mental habits of their countrymen, May Fourth intellectuals ended up changing their own outlook on the relationship between already-enlightened thinkers and the still-to-be-awakened populace. [T]hey had to revise their image of themselves as leaders of new culture, ahead of and above the common people (pingmin), and learn to accept a more circumscribed role as fellow travelers among the ranks of the revolutionary masses.

At the beginning of the May Fourth movement, self-styled "new youths" still saw themselves in terms of a tra-

ditional model, that of . . . those first to know and first to become enlightened. Although they rebelled against much of the Confucian content of this model, modern intellectuals retained the conviction that they had a unique cultural mission. . . . In the wake of the social revolution of the 1920s, however, they discovered that both their knowledge and their courage were more limited than what they had imagined at the height of May Fourth. . . .

As mere fragments of a politicized society, May Fourth veterans still retained their distinctive cultural mission: the mission of enlightenment. During the dispirited 1930s, when the domestic White Terror inaugurated by the Guomindang became aggravated by Japanese aggression in North China, they managed to bring about a revival of May Fourth concerns. They pressed on with the call for emancipation from feudal values even when such values were attacked as inimical to the goal of mobilization against foreign enemies. The more strident the voice of cultural conservatives in this period, the more cogent the argument of those who believed that there could be no national salvation, without enlightment.

In fact, . . . the New Enlightenment movement of 1937–39 was able to combine in a novel way the political imperatives of resistance to Japan with an anti-feudal culture movement. This effort, however, was short-lived. As so often before, critically minded intellectuals were accused of eroding national self-confidence, or more simply, of not being Chinese enough. They and their enlightenment movement became subject to "sinification"—a code word for enforced abandonment of cosmopolitan commitments and of dispassionate criticism of national shortcomings. Once enlightenment and enlighteners became "sinified," they became less effective in reminding China of its incomplete emancipation from feudal culture.

## The Creation of Iraq
### Amal Vinogradov

After World War I the Allies created an entity called Iraq out of the territory of the three former Ottoman administrative districts of Mosul, Baghdad, and Al Basrah and entrusted it to British Mandate. The League of Nations had taken official control over territories ruled by the losing powers (Germany, Austro-Hungary, Ottoman Empire) and transferred control (mandate) to the winning nations with an understanding that

Amal Vinogradov, "The 1920 Revolt in Iraq Reconsidered," *International Journal of Middle East Studies,* Vol. 3, no. 2 (Apr., 1972), pp. 136–9 as excerpted.

*the new rulers would create independent states after several years. The British Mandate in Iraq was confirmed in April 1920 at a conference in San Remo, Italy.*

*When news reached Iraq in July, the people began an armed uprising that the British had considerable troubling quelling. After much expense, the British decided to terminate their mandate in Mesopotamia. The chief British official in the region drew up a plan for a provisional government of the new state of Iraq. It was to be a kingdom, with a government directed by a council of Arab ministers under the supervision of a British high commissioner.*

*Faisal (1885–1933) was born in Mecca to a Saudi royal family and had been King of Syria until ousted by the French. He went to live in exile in Britain, from where he was invited to become the ruler of the new state. In an August 1921 plebiscite Faisal was elected king of the newly created nation of Iraq with 96 percent of the votes cast in the election. Historian Amal Vinogradov discusses the response of the people of Iraq to the establishment of their state by outside powers.*

CONSIDER: *How the people of the region might have felt when they heard that they were being constituted into a new state.*

The first shot signalling the revolt was fired on 30 June 1920 at Rumaytha in the Diwaniya Province. A *sheikh* of the Zawalim tribe, well known for his nationalist activities, was arrested by the Political Officer and thrown into jail, on the accusation that he had not paid his taxes to the British. On the same day, an armed band of his men stormed the mud prison and set him free; they then declared rebellion and began to destroy the railroad tracks and nearby bridges. Soon, the fighting spread to Samawa where the British garrison, taken by surprise, surrendered after having suffered several casualties. . . .

. . . On 11 July 1920, several of the leading *shuyukh* met and drafted a petition which they presented to the British Political Officer in the district. Their petition asked for complete independence for Iraq, and when Major Norbury dismissed their demand, they declared their rebellion and laid siege to Qasba bu Sukhair, the local military post. In Najaf, the British governor withdrew, and the town proceeded to set up a Provisional Revolutionary Government with four departments, Administrative, Municipal, Executive and Educational. . . .

By now, the revolt had spread and the rebels were engaging the British on several fronts simultaneously, at Kûfa, Rustamiya, and Hindiya. . . . Worried about the safety of Baghdad, British Commander Lieutenant-General Aylmer Haldane decided that only a swift and massive display of coordinated force would prevent a large snowball effect from overtaking the whole country. The urgency of the crisis was impressed on the British War Minister, Winston S. Churchill, who authorized immediate reinforcements from Iran. . . . Bombs were dropped on the city mosque that was serving as a refuge for tribesmen who had escaped their burned villages. The use of aircraft unequivocally shifted the balance of force between the two protagonists and signalled the beginning of the end of the revolt. Under air cover, Haldane proceeded to withdraw his forces and regroup them in Fallûja in anticipation of a possible attack on Baghdad. As the British detachments retreated, they were harassed by rebel attacks on their supply lines and transport accommodations. In retaliation, the British set fire to whole villages and settlements that lay along the demolished railway. The Army then gathered at Hilla and prepared for the massive offensive. . . .

Well supplied with men and ammunition and under the protection of the R.A.F., Haldane launched his counter offensive. Five months had passed since the first outbreak; the rebel's supplies were depleted, their ammunition was running low and funds were very scarce. In Baghdad, Sir Percy Cox had replaced the rigid Arnold Wilson, and a more accommodating line was proclaimed. The British Army had surrounded Karbala and cut off its water supply, forcing its surrender. Najaf, full of refugees from the rural areas surrounding it, was given an ultimatum to surrender or be bombarded. Fearful of famine and possible plague, the leaders met and decided to give up. A heavy indemnity was placed on the city: 3,000 guns or 81,000 gold pounds. With the fall of Najaf, the backbone of the rebellion was broken and rebelling centers soon surrendered one by one.

The British had decided by now on a political solution for Iraq and they deputized Sir Percy Cox and his assistant Gertrude Bell to put it into effect. . . .

It was not until the end of November that the revolt was fully brought to an end. Sir Percy Cox and Gertrude Bell, aided by a large number of Political Officers, proceeded to paint a native façade over the British apparatus in Baghdad, and a provisional government was established. The Iraqi Revolt had cost the exchequer 40,000,000 pounds, twice the annual budget allotted for Iraq. . . .

The British proceeded to prepare the ground for installing Faisal as king. . . . The machinery started preparing the ground for his acceptance in Iraq while he was being officially confirmed at the Cairo Conference over which Winston Churchill presided. On 13 June 1921, on the first anniversary of the Revolt, Faisal left Mecca for his new throne in Iraq. . . .

The British military presence was made less visible as the ground troops were pulled out and replaced by the R.A.F., stationed to the west of Baghdad at Habaniyya. A constitution was drafted, governmental departments were set up and staffed, and the country was divided into fourteen provinces (*liwa*), each with a governor. The Euphrates region was neglected by the government and left to the mercy of absentee landlords. History books, newly printed, did not teach about the 1920 Revolt, and there was no official celebration of its anniversary. Thus, modern Iraq began in 1921.

## Propaganda and Racism in the Pacific War

*John W. Dower*

*In time of war, or in preparation for war, all countries use propaganda as a means to instill in their people a willingness to fight and die for their country. One of the many ways to accomplish this goal is to depict the enemy as vicious, cruel, and savage.*

*Leading up to and immediately after Pearl Harbor, the U.S. government was engaged in just such efforts, depicting Japanese as subhuman lemmings with a cultlike dedication to the Emperor. One of the most influential ways in which this was done was through a series of films entitled* Know Your Enemy—Japan *by famed movie director Frank Capra. The Japanese in turn invoked images of Americans as inhuman and barbaric. In this excerpt from a prize-winning book* War without Mercy: Race and Power in the Pacific War, *American Japanologist John Dower examines Japanese propaganda to that end and comments on the use of racial stereotypes by both sides.*

CONSIDER: *The arguments used by the Japanese against their Anglo-American opponents; why such propaganda might have been effective.*

. . . [I]n August 1941, the [Japanese] Ministry of Education issued a major ideological manifesto entitled *The Way of the Subject* . . . [which] told the Japanese who they were—or should aspire to be—as a people, nation, and race. At the same time, it offered a critical analysis of modern Western history and culture. In Japanese eyes, it was the non-Axis West that aimed at world domination and had been engaged in that quest, with conspicuous success, for centuries, and it was the value system of the modern West, rooted in acquisitiveness and self-gratification, that explained a large part of its bloody history of war and repression, culminating in the current world crisis. The Japanese thus read Western history in much the same way that Westerners were reading the history of Japan: as a chronicle of destructive values, exploitative practices, and brutal wars. The picture of the Anglo-American enemy presented here and in the Army pamphlet persisted through the war. . . . The early

SOURCE: John Dower, *War without Mercy* (New York, 1986). Copyright © 1986 by John W. Dower. Reprinted by permission of Pantheon Books, a division of Random House, Inc.

Western defeats and quick surrenders revealed the flabbiness of Western society, Japanese at home were told. Later, the American bombing of Japanese cities was offered as proof beyond any conceivable question of the bestial nature of the enemy.

The southern region, embarking troops were informed in *Read This and the War Is Won*, was the treasure house of the Far East and a land of everlasting summer. It was also a place where a half million British ruled 350 million Indians, and another few score thousands of Englishmen ruled 6 million Malayans; where two hundred thousand Dutchmen governed a native population of 60 million in the East Indies; where twenty thousand Frenchmen controlled 23 million Indochinese, and a few tens of thousands of Americans ruled over 13 million Filipinos. Eight hundred thousand whites, the tally went, controlled 450 million Asians; if India was excluded, the count was 100 million oppressed by three hundred thousand. "Money squeezed from the blood of Asians maintains these small white minorities in their luxurious mode of life—or disappears to the respective home-countries," the Japanese soldiers were told. The white men were described as arrogant colonials who dwelled in splendid houses on mountainsides and hilltops, from which they looked down on the tiny thatched huts of the natives. They took it as their birthright to be allotted a score or so natives as personal slaves. Ties of blood and color linked the Japanese to these oppressed peoples of Asia. And because the latter had been all but emasculated by generations of colonial subjugation, it was left to Japan "to make men of them again" and lead them along the path of liberation—in short, to "liberate East Asia from white invasion and oppression." In the final analysis, this was "a struggle between races."

. . . The Japanese were informed that Western expansion was inspired partly by love of adventure, but more by desire for local resources as well as markets. And they were reminded that the heavy hand of the Occidental expansionists did not fall on Asians alone. Here the Ministry of Education posed two rhetorical questions that would remain effective propaganda to the end of the war: "How were American Indians treated? What about African Negroes?" . . .

Each of these exercises in ideology and propaganda can be seen as a tapestry of truths, half-truths, and empty spaces. When the American and Japanese examples are set side by side, the points each neglected to cover become clearer; and it becomes plain that both sides reveal more about themselves than about the enemy they are portraying. . . . Whether as film, radio broadcast, or written text, such discourse was ideological and overt, calculated and carefully edited, explicitly designed for public consumption. More refined than visceral expressions of race hate, it was also less frank and densely detailed than the calculations of power and interest made in secret at high levels. Yet it was not simply a tissue of lies or purely cynical manipulation of emotional rhetoric. Speakers, viewers, listeners alike (so long as they were all on the same side) generally took these statements seriously, and there is much to be learned here in retrospect about language, stereotyping, and the making of modern myths. Because World War Two is the context, the consequences of such seemingly abstract concerns emerge with special harshness. To people at war, after all, the major purpose in knowing one's enemies is to be better able to control or kill them.

## The Politics of Race, Class, and Nationalism in Twentieth-Century South Africa

### Shula Marks and Stanley Trapido

*Between World Wars I and II, Afrikaners (Boers—white settlers, primarily of Dutch rather than English origin) became increasingly assertive in south Africa. Not only did they struggle to maintain a separation of white and nonwhite peoples there, they attempted to wrestle power from the British who were still in control. One part of these efforts was the further development of Afrikaner nationalism in south Africa. It was an avowedly racist philosophy, drawing on a Christian heritage and racial ideologies emanating from Europe at the time. Its focus was to institutionalize apartheid (racial segregation) by exploiting British democratic institutions. In the following excerpt, Shula Marks and Stanley Trapido trace the roots of Afrikaner nationalism, particularly the role played by the Afrikaner intelligentsia of the period.*

CONSIDER: *Why Afrikaners felt the need to formulate their own ideology; how the elements of Afrikaner nationalism served Afrikaner needs; connections made between ethnicity, religion, economics, and the state.*

To meet the challenge of cheaply purveyed British culture, daily life had to be redefined and an alien world transformed into one in which Afrikaner sensibilities ruled. . . . [N]o artefact was too substantial or too small not to have its Afrikaans version, no occupation too eminent or too humble, not to have its Afrikaans mutation. This coincided with the creation and re-creation of Afrikaner history, fiction, the language and cultural institutions, as well as with the increasingly successful economic movement in the Cape, based on the first Afrikaner insurance company, SANLAM. The activities of both cultural and economic nationalists were further developed through the Christian National ideology adopted by the Broederbond, a secret society founded in 1919 and devoted to mobilising Afrikaners for the nationalist programme. . . .

Much of what they wrote was confused and contradictory, but the general directions were clear. Nations and cultures were divine creations, each was sovereign and had its own calling and destiny. Service to the nation was service to God. Not only was the Almighty best served by worshipping Him in the language He had created; without maintaining this language, the culture and nation He had created would not survive. Language, culture and nation were endangered by an alien capitalism and an equally alien communism. . . .

It was not capitalism *per se* which was the enemy of the Afrikaner people, according to the leading Bond member, L. J. du Plessis, but the control of the capitalist system by non-Afrikaners. Afrikaners had to take control of what was their rightful share, through *Volkskapitalisme,* the mobilisation of ethnic resources to foster Afrikaner accumulation. To do this, the northern Broederbond, with its weak financial resources, turned to the Cape-based SANLAM in the calling of the 1939 Ekonomiese Volkskongres (People's Economic Congress). . . .

At the Volkskongres, SANLAM launched the first Afrikaner-owned financial house, the Federale Volksbelegging, which by 1981 had become the second-largest single conglomerate in South Africa. The embryonic entrepreneurs of the north were largely excluded from this, and could only look forward to the small business of the one-man firm also advocated by the Kongress. For the Afrikaner poor, the "solution" offered was employment in the Afrikaner enterprises they were exhorted to patronise. There was a symbiotic relationship between Afrikaner capital and the growing Afrikaner petty bourgeoisie, but it was not a relationship without tension and conflict.

## African Women and the Law

### Martin Chanock

*The period between the wars also witnessed the creation of social systems in the African colonies that had tremendous impact on the lives of ordinary men and women. Besides having to deal with taxation, forced labor, and the like, Africans were also subject to an array of new legal codes as well as*

SOURCE: Shula Marks and Stanley Trapido, *The Politics of Race, Class, and Nationalism in Twentieth Century South Africa* (Essex, United Kingdom: Longman Group Publishers, 1987).

SOURCE: Martin Chanock, *Law, Custom and Social Order: The Colonial Experience in Malawi and Zambia* (Cambridge, England: Cambridge University Press, 1985), pp. 186–87.

*changing customs relating to division of labor, marriage, divorce, inheritance, and every aspect of household management. Most of the new statutes were a combination of "traditional" legal norms interpreted according to European legal codes. For African women especially, the institutionalization of "customary laws" deprived them of much of their former independence and imposed a system of patriarchy that had no precedent in African society. Moreover, these laws were being imposed on African women at a time when European women had openly challenged the Victorian underpinning of male dominance. In the following excerpt, Martin Chanock describes some of the contradictions inherent in any such social engineering.*

CONSIDER: *The argument that these policies lessened the status of women; the likelihood that such social engineering could be successful; the arguments that women might have made against the new laws.*

The Marriage and Divorce Ordinances of 1902 and 1905 in Malawi made female consent (which could be given by the father, who would not normally have been the guardian) necessary for a valid marriage and lack of consent grounds for annulment. These gave legal backing to the early ambition to establish the free status of women. In the mind of early administrators the status of a 'free woman' was something to be defended against the institutions of African marriage, with its apparent ignoring of female consent, and with the 'inheriting' of widows by the husband's heirs. There are however relatively few cases reported in which women specifically complained about the kind of restraints which the administration would interpret as absence of consent. As women, usually through their matrikin, appeared to have brought all other kinds of matrimonial cases to the courts, the few consent cases that did come to court must have been those which involved the special perception of status of the newly converted Christian women who were complainants or reflected the spread of bridewealth marriage. The mission churches, and the early administrators, did put an emphasis on the autonomy of female consent to marriage and regarded many of the rights and duties existing in all forms of African marriage as conflicting with this. Emily Maliwa has written that the deepest conflict between Malawian and British ideas about law was over marriage and she emphasises a total conflict between the missions' idea of marriage and the "traditional" one. Women, she writes, looked to the missionaries as protectors and to the missions as a ladder to great equality of status. Chiefs and male adults generally much resented, she says, the erosion of their authority inherent in the way the missions treated women. But Christian marriage and mission influence affected only a small minority, as Maliwa herself notes. While the Churches may have im-

proved the marital position of a small number of women, this was not the main thrust of "western" influence.

In February 1931, as a consequence of the interest being taken in Britain and at the League of Nations in the position of women in tropical Africa, district officers were circulated with a questionnaire on the rights of women. It seemed clear to them that women were free. In the eyes of the chief secretary it was precisely the establishment of the jural status of women at the Boma which had given them this freedom. "One of the strongest arguments in support of the claim that native women have much independence," he wrote, "is the way in which they bring cases, and often win them, before administrative officers or in the Courts." There was general satisfaction that there were no forced marriages or inheritance of widows; that women could own property; and that "where complaint is made of slavery it is usually the insult that is objected to and not the fact of slavery." Some of the answers commented on the advantages women enjoyed in predominantly "matrilineal" areas. The Blantyre district officer reported that the lot of Yao women, who lived with their *nkhoswe* in their own villages, was far happier than that of Ngoni women, and others emphasised that Ngoni women, unlike others in the protectorate, could not hold property independently, could not inherit, and were normally inherited. In "matrilineal" areas, the Mlanje report said, the mother took the children after divorce even where she had been "entirely to blame . . . exceptions to this are very rare: and almost always due to European influence." This gives the essential clue to British attitudes. While they saw themselves as having established the free status of women, they were not at all enamoured by what they appeared to do with it. From Cholo the district officer wrote:

In my opinion Native women in Nyasaland have much, in fact too much, independence. Husbands find it increasingly difficult to maintain order and good behaviour in their households. Women often attend beer drinks, dances, and similar functions against their husbands' wishes and neglect their wifely duties. At the slightest remonstrance or correction they are apt to fly into a rage, become abusive, cause a breach of the peace, and then fly to the Headman or the Boma and complain of cruelty.

In the face of such an attitude jural status was not going to be particularly useful.

## Chapter Questions

1. How did nationalism play a role in Asian and African political developments during the decades spanned by World Wars I and II?

2. In what ways did Japan constitute a force against imperialism, and in what ways was Japan a force propagating imperialism?

3. In what ways did Western ideas have an impact on Chinese developments in particular and Asian and African developments in general during this period?

4. Drawing on materials from this and the previous chapter, compare developments in the Western and the non-Western worlds. What sorts of forces in the non-Western world are being created or unleashed by developments in the Western world? What might be the long-term significance of these developments?

## Chapter Twenty-Five

# Global Transformations and the Struggles of Superpowers: The Post–World War II Era, 1945–89

The year 1945 marked the end of World War II and the decades of turmoil that had begun with the outbreak of World War I in 1914. It also marked the beginning of an age of rapidly growing global interdependence brought on by expanding communications, economic dependence, international organizations, systems of alliances, ideological competition, and cultural exchanges. In this chapter we will examine the three decades following World War II by focusing on five developments.

First, almost immediately following the war, the United States and the Soviet Union became engaged in a bitter ideological and political battle of global proportions—the "Cold

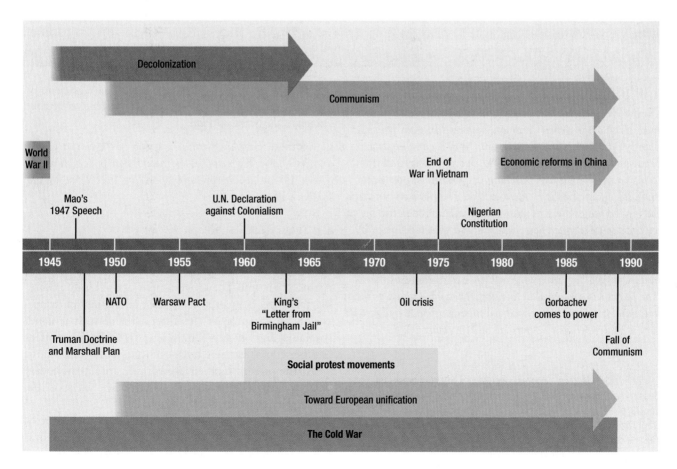

World War II

Decolonization

Communism

End of War in Vietnam

Economic reforms in China

Mao's 1947 Speech

U.N. Declaration against Colonialism

Nigerian Constitution

| 1945 | 1950 | 1955 | 1960 | 1965 | 1970 | 1975 | 1980 | 1985 | 1990 |

NATO

Warsaw Pact

King's "Letter from Birmingham Jail"

Oil crisis

Gorbachev comes to power

Truman Doctrine and Marshall Plan

Fall of Communism

Social protest movements

Toward European unification

The Cold War

War." It seemed as if no political development, whether occurring in Europe, Latin America, Asia, Africa, or elsewhere, was free of Cold War connotations.

In the Americas, the United States was now the world's leading military and economic power and Latin America had been spared most of the losses from World War II that others suffered. Yet these decades witnessed some important political and social instability. In Latin America, the struggle was usually between the elites, supported by authoritarian governments, and the rural and urban poor, supported by revolutionary movements. In the United States, the Civil Rights Movement, the Womens Liberation Movement, and the war in Vietnam spawned major social and political conflicts.

In Asia and Africa, the devastation of two world wars and the rising movements for independence were too much for Western imperial powers to handle. Sometimes gracefully and sometimes only after protracted violence, Europe and the United States relinquished almost all their colonies during these decades.

However, the successful struggles for independence throughout Asia and Africa more often than not carried in their wakes ethnic, political, religious, communal, and economic woes. In some cases, such as Japan, South Korea, Hong Kong, Taiwan, Singapore, Israel, and oil-rich areas of the Middle East, nations would come to enjoy relative prosperity. In other cases, such as Vietnam, Cambodia, Laos, India, Bangladesh, and Afghanistan, peace and prosperity would remain elusive. In China, the communists were victorious and set about creating a "new China" not only economically, socially, and politically, but also philosophically. Along the way their policies also produced innumerable deaths and chaos during the Great Leap Forward (1959–62) and the Great Proletarian Cultural Revolution (1966–76). In Africa, the nationalistic struggles for independence were often more protracted. As African nations achieved independence, the overriding concern became how to devise state systems that would bring not only stability but economic prosperity as well.

The sources in this chapter deal with each of these developments, which were of such global importance, as well as some of the connections between these developments. In Chapter 26 the story of some of these developments will be carried forward in an attempt to analyze the present from a historical perspective.

# PRIMARY SOURCES

## The Truman Doctrine *and* The Marshall Plan

*During World War II the Soviet Union and the United States were allied against their common enemies, the Axis powers. Shortly after the end of the war, animosity began to reappear between the former allies. By 1947 that animosity had risen to the point where it was formalized in government programs and international policies; the Cold War had broken out. In the United States this was most clearly announced in two policy decisions excerpted here. The first is a speech delivered by President Truman on March 12, 1947, to Congress, concerning proposed aid to Greece and Turkey, which appeared in danger of falling under the influence of the Soviet Union. The principles contained in this speech became known as the Truman Doctrine. The second is a statement made by Secretary of State George C. Marshall on November 10, 1947, to Senate and House Committees on Foreign Relations. Proposing massive aid to Europe, his statement became known as the Marshall Plan.*

CONSIDER: *The American perception of the Soviet Union and its allies; the purposes of this foreign policy; how the Soviet Union would probably perceive and react to this foreign policy.*

### THE TRUMAN DOCTRINE

The peoples of a number of countries of the world have recently had totalitarian regimes forced upon them against their will. The Government of the United States has made frequent protests against coercion and intimidation, in violation of the Yalta agreement, in Poland, Rumania, and Bulgaria. I must also state that in a number of other countries there have been similar developments.

At the present moment in world history nearly every nation must choose between alternative ways of life. The choice is too often not a free one.

One way of life is based upon the will of the majority, and is distinguished by free institutions, representative government, free elections, guaranties of individual

SOURCE: U.S. Congress, *Congressional Record*, 80th Congress, 1st Session (Washington, DC: U.S. Government Printing Office, 1947), vol. 93, p. 1981.
SOURCE: U.S. Congress, Senate Committee on Foreign Relations, *A Decade of American Foreign Policy: Basic Documents, 1941–1949* (Washington, DC: U.S. Government Printing Office, 1950), pp. 1270–71.

liberty, freedom of speech and religion, and freedom from political oppression.

The second way of life is based upon the will of a minority forcibly imposed upon the majority. It relies upon terror and oppression, a controlled press and radio, fixed elections, and the suppression of personal freedoms.

I believe that it must be the policy of the United States to support free peoples who are resisting attempted subjugation by armed minorities or by outside pressures.

I believe that we must assist free peoples to work out their own destinies in their own way.

I believe that our help should be primarily through economic and financial aid, which is essential to economic stability and orderly political processes.

THE MARSHALL PLAN

As a result of the war, the European community which for centuries had been one of the most productive and indeed creative portions of the inhabited world was left prostrate. This area, despite its diversity of national cultures and its series of internecine conflicts and wars, nonetheless enjoys a common heritage and a common civilization.

The war ended with the armies of the major Allies meeting in the heart of this community. The policies of three of them have been directed to the restoration of that European community. It is now clear that only one power, the Soviet Union, does not for its own reasons share this aim.

We have become involved in two wars which have had their origins in the European continent. The free peoples of Europe have fought two wars to prevent the forcible domination of their community by a single great power. Such domination would have inevitably menaced the stability and security of the world. To deny today our interest in their ability to defend their own heritage would be to disclaim the efforts and sacrifices of two generations of Americans. We wish to see this community restored as one of the pillars of world security; in a position to renew its contribution to the advancement of mankind and to the development of a world order based on law and respect for the individual.

The record of the endeavors of the United States Government to bring about a restoration of the whole of that European community is clear for all who wish to see. We must face the fact, however, that despite our efforts, not all of the European nations have been left free to take their place in the community of which they form a natural part.

Thus the geographic scope of our recovery program is limited to those nations which are free to act in accordance with their national traditions and their own estimates of their national interests. If there is any doubt as to this situation, a glance at the present map of the European continent will provide the answer.

The present line of division in Europe is roughly the line upon which the Anglo-American armies coming from the west met those of the Soviet Union coming from the east. To the west of that line the nations of the continental European community have been grappling with the vast and difficult problem resulting from the war in conformity with their own national traditions without pressure or menace from the United States or Great Britain. Developments in the European countries to the east of that line bear the unmistakable imprint of an alien hand.

## The Cold War: A Soviet Perspective

### B. N. Ponomaryov

*The Cold War and indeed modern history were seen differently in the Soviet Union than in the West. The following excerpt is from* History of the Communist Party of the Soviet Union (1960), *an official publication of the Soviet government. Here the focus is on the end of World War II and the early Cold War period.*

CONSIDER: *The elements of this interpretation most likely to be accepted by Western non-Marxist historians; how this interpretation differs from Truman's and Marshall's perceptions; how these differences help explain the existence of the Cold War.*

As a result of the war the capitalist system sustained enormous losses and became weaker. *The second stage of the general crisis of capitalism set in,* manifesting itself chiefly in a new wave of revolutions. Albania, Bulgaria, Eastern Germany, Hungary, Czechoslovakia. Poland, Rumania and Yugoslavia broke away from the system of capitalism. . . .

In their relations with the People's Democracies the Communist Party and the Soviet Government strictly adhered to the principle of non-interference in their internal affairs. The U.S.S.R. recognised the people's governments in these States and supported them politically. True to its internationalist duty, the U.S.S.R. came to the aid of the People's Democracies with grain, seed and raw materials, although its own stocks had been badly depleted during the war. This helped to provide the population with foodstuffs and also to speed up the recommissioning of many industrial enterprises. The presence of the Soviet armed forces in the People's Democracies prevented domestic counter-revolution from unleashing

SOURCE: B. N. Ponomaryov et al., *History of the Communist Party of the Soviet Union,* Andrew Rothstein, trans. (Moscow: Foreign Languages Publishing House, 1960), pp. 599, 606–12.

a civil war and averted intervention. The Soviet Union paralysed the attempts of the foreign imperialists to interfere in the internal affairs of the democratic States. . . .

The U.S.A. decided to take advantage of the economic and political difficulties in the other leading capitalist countries and bring them under its sway. Under the pretext of economic aid the U.S.A. began to infiltrate into their economy and interfere in their internal affairs. Such big capitalist countries as Japan, West Germany, Italy, France and Britain all became dependent on the U.S.A. to a greater or lesser degree. The people of Western Europe were confronted with the task of defending their national sovereignty against the encroachments of American imperialism. . . .

The radical changes that took place after the second world war substantially altered the political map of the world. There emerged *two* main *world* social and political camps: the *Socialist* and democratic camp, and the *imperialist* and anti-democratic camp. . . .

The ruling circles of the U.S.A., striving for world supremacy, openly declared that they could achieve their aims only from "positions of strength." The American imperialists unleashed the so-called cold war, and sought to kindle the flames of a third world War. In 1949, the U.S.A. set up an aggressive military bloc known as the North Atlantic Treaty Organisation (NATO). As early as 1946, the Western States began to pursue a policy of splitting Germany, which was essentially completed in 1949 with the creation of a West German State. Subsequently they set out to militarise West Germany. This further deepened the division of Germany and made her reunification exceptionally difficult. A dangerous hotbed of war began to form in Europe. In the Far East the United States strove to create a hotbed of war in Japan, stationing its armed forces and building military bases on her territory.

In 1950, the United States resorted to open aggression in the Far East. It occupied the Chinese island of Taiwan, provoked an armed clash between the Korean People's Democratic Republic and South Korea and began an aggressive war against the Korean people. The war in Korea was a threat to the People's Republic of China, and Chinese people's volunteers came to the assistance of the Korean people.

The military adventure of the U.S.A. in Korea sharply aggravated international tension. The U.S.A. started a frantic arms drive and stepped up the production of atomic, thermonuclear, bacteriological and other types of weapons of mass annihilation. American military bases, spearheaded primarily against the U.S.S.R., China and the other Socialist countries, were hastily built at various points of the capitalist world. Military blocs were rapidly knocked together. The threat of a third world war with the use of mass destruction weapons increased considerably.

## Communism in China
### *Mao Zedong (Mao Tse-tung)*

*When the Chinese Communist Party achieved victory in the civil war in 1949, it set about immediately to create a new and completely different China. The tasks were enormous, especially since many of the attitudes that the communists wanted to change (the role of women, for example) had been ingrained in Chinese culture for almost 4,000 years. Undaunted, the communists launched a series of mass political and social campaigns from 1949 to the present.*

*The following reading is from a speech on China's future given in 1947 by Mao Zedong (Mao Tse-tung) to the party's leadership. Here the emphasis is on land reform and rewarding the rural population whose sacrifices and aid made victory possible for the communists.*

CONSIDER: *How Mao proposes to reward his supporters; whom he identifies as his enemies and why; the policies he recommends and the changes that would flow from such policies.*

The Chinese people's revolutionary war has now reached a turning point. That is, the Chinese People's Liberation Army has beaten back the offensive of several million reactionary troops of Chiang Kai-shek, the running dog of the United States of America, and gone over to the offensive. . . .

After the Japanese surrender, the peasants urgently demanded land, and we made a timely decision to change our land policy from reducing rent and interest to confiscating the land of the landlord class for distribution among the peasants. The directive issued by the Central Committee of our party on May 4, 1946, marked this change. In September 1947 our party called the National Land Conference and drew up the Outline Land Law of China, which was promptly carried out in all areas. . . . The Outline Land Law provides for equal distribution of land per head, based on the principle of abolishing the land system of feudal and semifeudal exploitation and putting into effect the system of land to the tillers. This is a method which most thoroughly abolishes the feudal system and fully meets the demands of the broad masses of China's peasants. To carry out the land reform resolutely and thoroughly, it is necessary to organize in the villages, as lawful bodies for carrying out the reform, not only peasant associations on the broadest mass basis, including farm laborers, poor peasants, and middle peasants and their elected committees, but first of all poor peasant leagues composed of poor peasants and farm laborers and their elected committees; and these poor peasants' leagues should be the backbone of leadership in all rural struggles. Our policy is to rely on the poor peasants and unite solidly with the middle peasants to abolish the feu-

SOURCE: Mao Tse-tung, *Selected Works of Mao Tse-tung*, vol. 4 (Peking: Foreign Languages Press, 1961), pp. 170–74.

dal and semifeudal system of exploitation by the landlord class and by the old-type rich peasants. Landlords or rich peasants must not be allotted more land and property than the peasant masses. . . . Although the proportion of landlords and rich peasants in the rural population varies from place to place, it is generally only about 8 percent (in terms of households), while their holdings usually amount to 70 to 80 percent of all the land. . . .

Confiscate the land of the feudal class and turn it over to the peasants. Confiscate monopoly capital, . . . and turn it over to the new democratic state. Protect the industry and commerce of the national bourgeoisie. These are the three major economic policies of the new democratic revolution. . . . The new democratic revolution aims at wiping out only feudalism and monopoly capitalism, only the landlord class and the bureaucrat-capitalist class (the big bourgeoisie), and not at wiping out capitalism in general, the upper petty bourgeoisie or the middle bourgeoisie. In view of China's economic backwardness, even after the country-wide victory of the revolution, it will still be necessary to permit the existence for a long time of a capitalist sector of the economy represented by the extensive petty bourgeoisie and middle bourgeoisie. In accordance with the division of labor in the national economy, a certain development of all parts of this capitalist sector which are beneficial to the national economy will still be needed.

## China's Marriage Law: New Rules for the Women of China

*From its earliest days in 1921, the Chinese Communist Party supported the notion that women were equal to men. This concept was particularly revolutionary in a society that bound women's feet, thereby restricting their mobility; that practiced the sale of young girls into marriage, concubinage, or prostitution; that sanctioned female infanticide; and that generally considered women as almost subhuman.*

*In putting its theories into practice, the Communist Party did offer women a higher status than they had previously. Some women achieved positions of responsibility, some women fought alongside men, and the worst abuses against women, such as child betrothal and foot binding, were indeed eliminated in areas controlled by the communists.*

*However, women never achieved equality. Even within the ranks of party officials, the men could not bring themselves to share power completely. Nevertheless, the communists were committed to an ideal and when they came to power in 1949, one of their first acts was to pass the following "Marriage Law," which, in legal terms at least, afforded Chinese women the equality they sought.*

SOURCE: *The Marriage Law of the People's Republic of China* (Peking: Foreign Languages Press, 1959).

CONSIDER: *The significance of these changes for Chinese raised according to the old traditions; how these principles, rights, and duties reflect an effort to enact communism in China.*

### CHAPTER I. GENERAL PRINCIPLES

*Article 1.* The arbitrary and compulsory feudal marriage system, which is based on the superiority of man over woman and which ignores the children's interests, shall be abolished.

The new democratic marriage system, which is based on free choice of partners, on monogamy, on equal rights for both sexes, and on protection of the lawful interests of women and children, shall be put into effect.

*Article 2.* Bigamy, concubinage, child betrothal, interference with the remarriage of widows, and the exaction of money or gifts in connection with marriage shall be prohibited. . . .

### CHAPTER III. RIGHTS AND DUTIES OF HUSBAND AND WIFE

*Article 7.* Husband and wife are companions living together and shall enjoy equal status in the home.

*Article 8.* Husband and wife are in duty bound to love, respect, assist, and look after each other, to live in harmony, to engage in production, to care for the children, and to strive jointly for the welfare of the family and for the building up of a new society.

*Article 9.* Both husband and wife shall have the right to free choice of occupation and free participation in work or in social activities.

*Article 10.* Both husband and wife shall have equal right in the possession and management of family property.

*Article 11.* Both husband and wife shall have the right to use his or her own family name.

*Article 12.* Both husband and wife shall have the right to inherit each other's property.

## U.N. Resolution 242 and A Palestinian Memoir: Israel, Palestine, and the Middle East

*Since World War II, the Middle East has been a center of violent conflict as well as a source of great concern for the world. One of the main sources of conflict has been the struggle over the creation of Israel and the Palestinian problem that resulted. The roots of this Israeli–Palestinian struggle stretch back at least as far as the late 19th century, when the Zionist movement—a movement to make Palestine the national home of the Jews—began. The struggle over the creation of Israel came to a head in 1948 when the British, who controlled Palestine, left it in the hands of the United Nations. A United Nations resolution and the first Arab–Israeli war resulted in the creation of Israel, a massive number of Palestinian refugees, and decades of conflict between Arabs and Israelis.*

*The first of the following two documents on this topic is Resolution 242 (passed by the United Nations in 1967), which recognized Israel's existence and its need for security but at the same time called on Israel to withdraw from the territories captured in the 1967 Arab–Israeli War. The second document contains excerpts from a memoir of a Palestinian exile, Fawaz Turki. He describes the flight from Palestine in 1948, the years of exile that followed, and his continuing sense of Palestinian consciousness.*

CONSIDER: *Why Israel has been reluctant to accept U.N. Resolution 242; the source and importance of Turki's sense of Palestinian consciousness.*

U.N. RESOLUTION 242

*The Security Council, . . .*

1. *Affirms* that the fulfilment of Charter principles requires the establishment of a just and lasting peace in the Middle East which should include the application of both the following principles:
   (i)  Withdrawal of Israel armed forces from territories occupied in the recent conflict;
   (ii) Termination of all claims or states of belligerency and respect for and acknowledgement of the sovereignty, territorial integrity and political independence of every State in the area and their right to live in peace within secure and recognized boundaries free from threats or acts of force;
2. *Affirms further* the necessity
   (*a*) For guaranteeing freedom of navigation through international waterways in the area;
   (*b*) For achieving a just settlement of the refugee problem;
   (*c*) For guaranteeing the territorial inviolability and political independence of every State in the area, through measures including the establishment of demilitarized zones.

A PALESTINIAN MEMOIR

A breeze began to blow as we moved slowly along the coast road, heading to the Lebanese border—my mother and father, my two sisters, my brother and I. Behind us lay the city of Haifa, long the scene of bombing, sniper fire, ambushes, raids, and bitter fighting between Palestinians and Zionists. Before us lay the city of Sidon and indefinite exile. Around us the waters of the Mediter-

SOURCE: *International Documents on Palestine, 1968,* Zuhair Diab, ed. (New York, 1971). Fawaz Turki, *The Disinherited: Journal of a Palestinian Exile* (New York: Monthly Review Press, 1972), pp. 43–45, 54, as excerpted.

ranean sparkled in the sun. Above us eternity moved on unconcerned, as if God in his heavens watched the agonies of men, as they walked on crutches, and smiled. And our world had burst, like a bubble, a bubble that had engulfed us within its warmth. From then on I would know only crazy sorrow and watch the glazed eyes of my fellow Palestinians burdened by loss and devastated by pain.

April 1948. And so it was the cruelest month of the year, but there were crueler months, then years. . . .

After a few months in Sidon, we moved again, a Palestinian family of six heading to a refugee camp in Beirut, impotent with hunger, frustration, and incomprehension. But there we encountered other families equally helpless, equally baffled, who like us never had enough to eat, never enough to offer books and education to their children, never enough to face an imminent winter. In later years, when we left the camp and found better housing and a better life outside and grew up into our early teens, we would complain about not having this or that and would be told by our mothers: "You are well off, boy! Think of those still living there in the camps. Just think of them and stop making demands." We would look out the window and see the rain falling and hear the thunder. And we would remember. We would understand. We would relent as we thought "of those still living there."

Man adapts. We adapted, the first few months, to life in a refugee camp. In the adaptation we were also reduced as men, as women, as children, as human beings. At times we dreamed. Reduced dreams. Distorted ambitions. One day, we hoped, our parents would succeed in buying two beds for me and my sister to save us the agonies of asthma, intensified from sleeping on blankets on the cold floor. One day, we hoped, there would be enough to buy a few pounds of pears or apples as we had done on those special occasions when we fought and sulked and complained because one of us was given a smaller piece of fruit than the others. One day soon, we hoped, it would be the end of the month when the UNRWA rations arrived and there was enough to eat for a week. One day soon, we argued, we would be back in our homeland.

The days stretched into months and those into a year and yet another. Kids would play in the mud of the winters and the dust of the summers, while "our problem" was debated at the UN and moths died around the kerosene lamps. . . .

Our Palestinian consciousness, instead of dissipating, was enhanced and acquired a subtle nuance and a new dimension. It was buoyed by two concepts: the preservation of our memory of Palestine and our acquisition of education. We persisted in refusing the houses and monetary compensation offered by the UN to settle us in our host countries. We wanted nothing short of returning to our homeland. And from Syria, Lebanon, and Jordan, we would see, a few miles, a few yards, across the border, a land where we had been born, where we had lived, and where we felt the earth. "This is my land," we would shout, or cry, or sing, or plead, or reason. And to that land a people had come, a foreign community of colonizers, aided by a Western world in a hurry to rid itself of guilt and shame, demanding independence from history, from heaven, and from us.

## Declaration against Colonialism
### *The General Assembly of the United Nations*

*Most colonized peoples gained their independence from Western powers during the 20 years that followed World War II. This reflected both the weakness of Europe after the war and the strength of anti-imperialist sentiments around the world. Yet the process of decolonization was difficult in itself and was complicated by the ideological differences that divided nations. In 1960, after a bitter debate, the United Nations adopted the following "Declaration against Colonialism." Although no nation voted against the resolution, Australia, Belgium, the Dominican Republic, France, Great Britain, Portugal, South Africa, Spain, and the United States abstained.*

CONSIDER: *Possible reasons why these nations abstained; justifications used by nations for not giving up their colonial possessions; what this declaration reveals about the strengths and weaknesses of the United Nations.*

THE GENERAL ASSEMBLY

*Mindful* of the determination proclaimed by the peoples of the world in the Charter of the United Nations to reaffirm faith in fundamental human rights, in the dignity and worth of the human person, in the equal rights of men and women and of nations large and small and to promote social progress and better standards of life in larger freedom,

*Conscious* of the need for the creation of conditions of stability and well-being and peaceful and friendly relations based on respect for the principles of equal rights and self-determination of all peoples, and of universal respect for, and observance of, human rights and fundamental freedoms for all without distinction as to race, sex, language or religion,

SOURCE: General Assembly of the United Nations, "Declaration against Colonialism," *Official Records of the General Assembly,* Fifteenth Session, Resolution 1514, December 14, 1960.

*Recognizing* the passionate yearning for freedom in all dependent peoples and the decisive role of such peoples in the attainment of their independence,

*Aware* of the increasing conflicts resulting from the denial of or impediments in the way of the freedom of such peoples, which constitute a serious threat to world peace,

*Considering* the important role of the United Nations in assisting the movement for independence in Trust and Non-Self-Governing Territories,

*Recognizing* that the people of the world ardently desire the end of colonialism in all its manifestations,

*Convinced* that the continued existence of colonialism prevents the development of international economic co-operation, impedes the social, cultural, and economic development of dependent peoples and militates against the United Nations ideal of universal peace,

*Affirming* that peoples may, for their own ends, freely dispose of their natural wealth and resources without prejudice to any obligations arising out of international economic co-operation, based upon the principle of mutual benefit, and the international law,

*Believing* that the process of liberation is irresistible and irreversible and that, in order to avoid serious crises, an end must be put to colonialism and all practices of segregation and discrimination associated therewith,

*Welcoming* the emergence in recent years of a large number of dependent territories into freedom and independence, and recognizing the increasingly powerful trends toward freedom in such territories which have not yet attained independence,

*Convinced* that all peoples have an inalienable right to complete freedom, the exercise of their sovereignty and the integrity of their national territory,

*Solemnly proclaims* the necessity of bringing to a speedy and unconditional end colonialism in all its forms and manifestations;

And to this end

*Declares* that:

1. The subjection of peoples to alien subjugation, domination and exploitation constitutes a denial of fundamental human rights, is contrary to the Charter of the United Nations and is an impediment to the promotion of world peace and co-operation.

2. All peoples have the right to self-determination; by virtue of that right they freely determine their political status and freely pursue their economic, social and cultural development.

3. Inadequacy of political, economic, social or educational preparedness should never serve as a pretext for delaying independence.

4. All armed action or repressive measures of all kinds directed against dependent peoples shall cease in order to enable them to exercise peacefully and freely their right to complete independence, and the integrity of their national territory shall be respected.

5. Immediate steps shall be taken, in Trust and Non-Self-Governing Territories or all other territories which have not yet attained independence, to transfer all powers to the peoples of those territories, without any conditions or reservations, in accordance with their freely expressed will and desire, without any distinction as to race, creed or color, in order to enable them to enjoy complete independence and freedom.

6. Any attempt aimed at the partial or total disruption of the national unity and the territorial integrity of a country is incompatible with the purposes and principles of the Charter of the United Nations.

7. All States shall observe faithfully and strictly the provisions of the Charter of the United Nations, the Universal Declaration of Human Rights and the present Declaration on the basis of equality, noninterference in the internal affairs of all States, and respect for the sovereign rights of all peoples and their territorial integrity.

## From Independence to Statehood: Ethnic Conflict in Nigeria

*The years between 1957 and the 1980s witnessed the end of European colonial rule in Africa. In some regions, the new leaders hoped to maintain colonial boundaries while changing the system of rewards to benefit Africans, while in other regions, the nationalist leaders wished to depart radically from the former colonial economic and political systems. In the three decades since independence, however, African countries have been ravaged by numerous civil wars, ethnic conflicts, economic collapse and military dictatorships that have contributed to weak postcolonial states. Despite these problems, some African leaders have continued to take the steps to bring about national cohesion. Nigeria, one of the earliest independent countries to overcome a civil war, has been in the forefront of these attempts. The following selection concerning Nigeria's 1979 Constitution details some of the problems in nation building.*

CONSIDER: *The role the state seeks to play in controlling regionalism and ethnicity; how these principles compare with the rise of democracy in other areas of the world.*

SOURCE: Robert B. Goldmann and A. J. Wilson, eds., *From Independence to Statehood: Managing Ethnic Conflict in Five African and Asian States* (New York: St. Martin's Press, 1984), p. 6.

In inaugurating the drafting committee on 18 October 1975, the Military Head of State suggested these basic approaches to the problems of national cohesion:

The major political parties of the past emerged with regional and ethnic support.

The main political parties of the past were in fact little more than (regional or ethnic) armies organised for fighting elections in the regions for the regional and federal legislatures.

So vile was the abuse of the electoral process in the past that this has raised the question as to whether we need continue to accept simple majorities as a basis for political selection especially at the centre.

Given our commitment to a Federal System of Government; to a free democratic and lawful system which guarantees fundamental human rights; and to the emergence of a stable system through constitutional law, the creation of viable political consensus and orderly succession to political power. We should:

seek to eliminate cut-throat competition in the political process; discourage institutionalised opposition to the government in power, and instead develop consensus politics and government based on a community of all interests rather than interests of sections of the country;

eliminate over-centralisation of power and as a matter of principle decentralise power wherever possible as a means of diffusing tensions;

evolve an electoral system which is free and fair and ensures adequate representation of our peoples;

evolve a system from which will emerge genuine and truly national political parties;

recommend the establishment of an executive presidential system of government in which the president and vice-president are assigned clearly defined powers and made accountable directly to the people, and in which the making of the president, the vice-president and the members of the executive council deliberately reflect the federal character of the country.

Finally, the Head of the Military Government advised the CDC[1] and the country:

Past events have shown that we cannot build a future for this country on a rigid political ideology. Such an approach would be unrealistic. The

---

[1]The Constitution Drafting Committee.

evolution of a doctrinal concept is usually predicated upon the general acceptance by the people of a national political philosophy . . . consequently, until all of our people, or a large majority of them, have acknowledged a common ideological motivation, it would be fruitless to proclaim any particular philosophy or ideology in our Constitution.

These fundamental elements of Nigeria's origins, growth and development provide the framework for analysing how this vast, complex system has survived and intends to continue its cohesion in the future.

Chapter II of the Constitution re-states the country's commitment to the principles of federalism, republicanism, democracy and social justice; the fostering of "national integration" together with the directive that the Nigerian State should "promote or encourage the formation of associations that cut across ethnic, linguistic, religious or other sectional barriers . . . foster a feeling of belonging and of involvement among the various peoples of the Federation, to the end that loyalty to the (Nigerian) nation shall override sectional loyalties." Having acknowledged the cultural pluralism of Nigeria, Section 20 of the Constitution directs that "The State shall protect and enhance Nigerian culture."

Section 14 (3) and (4) is even more compelling:

The composition of the Government of the Federation or any of its agencies and the conduct of its affairs shall be carried out in such a manner as to reflect the federal character of Nigeria and the need to promote national unity, and also to command national loyalty, thereby ensuring that there shall be no predominance of persons from a few states or from a few ethnic or other sectional groups in that government or in any of its agencies.

The composition of the Government of a State, a local government council, or any of the agencies of such government or council, and the conduct of the affairs of the government or council shall be carried out in such manner as to recognise the diversity of the peoples within its area of authority and the need to promote a sense of belonging and loyalty among all the peoples of the Federation.

The preceding citations from the provisions of the 1979 Constitution illustrate the many objectives and intentions in the Constitution designed to relate constitutional structures to the problems of national cohesion.

## Growing Up in Algeria

*Assia Djebar*

*Numerous people in lands colonized by Western powers grew up in an environment of two cultures and two languages.*

*Problems stemming from this environment would persist for years after independence was gained in the post–World War II era. In the following selection from her autobiographical novel, the Algerian author Assia Djebar describes the divisions that remain within her and that she lives with: between the Arabic and French languages as well as the Arabic Muslim and French cultures. Here she is reflecting back on her childhood in Algeria during the late 1940s and early 1950s before the revolution for independence from France. In those years, she attended both a Koranic religious school and a French school.*

CONSIDER: *Why language makes such a difference for her; the problems facing someone brought up in this colonial culture that is in the process of changing.*

[W]hen I sit curled up like this to study my native language it is as though my body reproduces the architecture of my native city: the *medinas* with their tortuous alleyways closed off to the outside world, living their secret life. When I write and read the foreign language, my body travels far in subversive space, in spite of the neighbours and suspicious matrons; it would not need much for it to take wing and fly away!

As I approach a marriageable age, these two different apprenticeships, undertaken simultaneously, land me in a dichotomy of location. My father's preference will decide for me: light rather than darkness. I do not realize that an irrevocable choice is being made: the outdoors and the risk, instead of the prison of my peers. This stroke of luck brings me to the verge of breakdown.

I write and speak French outside: The words I use convey no flesh-and-blood reality. I learn the names of birds I've never seen, trees I shall take ten years or more to identify, lists of flowers and plants that I shall never smell until I travel north of the Mediterranean. In this respect, all vocabulary expresses what is missing in my life, exoticism without mystery, causing a kind of visual humiliation that it is not seemly to admit to. . . . Settings and episodes in children's books are nothing but theoretical concepts; in the French family the mother comes to fetch her daughter or son from school; in the French street, the parents walk quite naturally side by side. . . . So, the world of the school is expunged from the daily life of my native city, as it is from the life of my family. The latter is refused any referential rôle.

My conscious mind is here, huddled against my mother's knees, in the darkest corners of the flat which she never leaves. The ambit of the school is elsewhere: My search, my eyes are fixed on other regions. I do not

SOURCE: Assia Djebar, "Growing Up in Algeria," in *Fantasia: An Algerian Cavalcade*, tr. Dorothy S. Blair (Portsmouth, NH: Heinemann, 1993), pp. 184–85.

realize, no-one around me realizes, that, in the conflict between these two worlds, lies an incipient vertigo.

## Christianity, Communism, and Revolution in Latin America

### Camilo Torres

*Camilo Torres was a Colombian priest who became a leading revolutionary in the mid-1960s following the Cuban Revolution. In this excerpt he explains to the Colombian people why he refused to join the Catholic hierarchy in opposing the goals of communist insurgents. Although he refused to join the Communist Party, Torres believed that attacks on communists only served to keep the poor and dispossessed from gaining their own political freedom. He felt so strongly that the reigning oligarchies should be overthrown that he joined with the revolutionaries as a guerilla fighter in 1965.*

CONSIDER: *What Torres saw as the "common objectives" that could unite Catholic and revolutionary; what arguments Torres used in rejecting anticommunism.*

Because of the traditional relations between Christians and Marxists, and between the Church and the Communist Party, it is quite likely that erroneous suspicions and suppositions will arise regarding the relations of Christians and Marxists within the United Front, and of a priest and the Communist Party.

This is why I want to clarify to the Colombian people my relations with the Communist Party and its position within the United Front.

I have said that I am a revolutionary as a Colombian, as a sociologist, as a Christian, and as a priest. I believe that there are elements within the Communist Party which are genuinely revolutionary. Consequently, I cannot be anti-Communist either as a Colombian, as a sociologist, as a Christian, or as a priest.

I am not anti-Communist as a Colombian because anti-Communism in my country is bent on persecuting the dissatisfied, whether they be Communists or not, who in the main are poor people.

I am not anti-Communist as a sociologist because the Communist proposals to combat poverty, hunger, illiteracy, and lack of housing and public services are effective and scientific.

I am not anti-Communist as a Christian, because I believe that anti-Communism condemns the whole of Communism, without acknowledging that there is some justice in its cause, as well as injustice. By condemning

the whole we condemn the just and the unjust, and this is anti-Christian.

I am not anti-Communist as a priest because, whether the Communists realize it or not, there are within their ranks some authentic Christians. If they are working in good faith, they might well be the recipients of sanctifying grace. Should this be true, and should they love their neighbor, they would be saved. My role as a priest, even though I am not exercising its prerogatives externally, is to lead all men to God. The most effective way to do this is to get men to serve the people in keeping with their conscience.

I do not intend to proselytize among the Communists and to try to get them to accept the dogma and teachings of the Catholic Church. I do want all men to act in accordance with their conscience, to look in earnest for the truth, and to love their neighbor effectively.

The Communists must be fully aware of the fact that I will not join their ranks, that I am not nor will I ever be a Communist, either as a Colombian, as a sociologist, as a Christian, or as a priest.

Yet I am disposed to fight with them for common objectives: against the oligarchy and the domination of the United States, and for the takeover of power by the popular class.

I do not want public opinion to identify me with the Communists. This is why in all my public appearances I have wanted to be surrounded not only by the Communists but by all revolutionaries, be they independent or followers of other movements. . . .

Once the popular class assumes power, with the help of all revolutionaries, then our people will be ready to discuss the religious orientation they should give their lives.

Poland is an example of how socialism can be established without destroying what is essential in Christianity. As a Polish priest once said: "As Christians we have the obligation of contributing to the construction of a socialist state so long as we are allowed to adore God as we wish."

## Letter from Birmingham Jail: The Civil Rights Movement in the United States

### Martin Luther King, Jr.

*The late 1950s and early 1960s witnessed one of the greatest social movements in American history. African Americans*

SOURCE: John Alvarez Garcia and Christian Restrepo Calle, eds., *Camilo Torres: His Life and His Message* (Springfield, IL: Templegate, 1968), pp. 74–78.

SOURCE: Martin Luther King, Jr., "Letter from Birmingham Jail," in *Why We Can't Wait.* Copyright © 1963, 1964 by Martin Luther King, Jr. Reprinted by permission of HarperCollins Publishers.

*and whites joined in an effort to overcome the lasting legacy of slavery and racial oppression, organizing the Civil Rights Movement. Using legal challenges, civil disobedience, passive resistance and mass demonstrations, they toppled legal segregation. Martin Luther King, Jr. (1929–68), was unquestionably the moral leader of the civil rights movement. Like Gandhi, he went to jail dozens of times to bear personal witness against the segregation system that he considered immoral and unconstitutional. In this excerpt, written by King while in jail in Birmingham, Alabama, he explains to his fellow clergymen why he was willing, and they should be willing, to break immoral laws and go to jail.*

CONSIDER: *King's distinction between a just and an unjust law.*

You express a great deal of anxiety over our willingness to break laws. This is certainly a legitimate concern. Since we so diligently urge people to obey the Supreme Court's decision of 1954 outlawing segregation in the public schools, at first glance it may seem rather paradoxical for us consciously to break laws. One may well ask: "How can you advocate breaking some laws and obeying others?" The answer lies in the fact that there are two types of laws: just and unjust. I would be the first to advocate obeying just laws. One has not only a legal but a moral responsibility to obey just laws. Conversely, one has a moral responsibility to disobey unjust laws. I would agree with St. Augustine that "an unjust law is no law at all."

Now, what is the difference between the two? How does one determine whether a law is just or unjust? A just law is a man-made code that squares with the moral law or the law of God. An unjust law is a code that is out of harmony with the moral law. . . . All segregation statutes are unjust because segregation distorts the soul and damages the personality. It gives the segregator a false sense of superiority and the segregated a false sense of inferiority. . . . Hence segregation is not only politically, economically and sociologically unsound, it is morally wrong and sinful. . . . Thus it is that I can urge men to obey the 1954 decision of the Supreme Court, for it is morally right; and I can urge them to disobey segregation ordinances, for they are morally wrong. . . .

Let me give another explanation. A law is unjust if it is inflicted on a minority that, as a result of being denied the right to vote, had no part in enacting or devising the law. Who can say that the legislature of Alabama which set up that state's segregation laws, was democratically elected? Throughout Alabama all sorts of devious methods are used to prevent Negroes from becoming registered voters, and there are some counties in which, even though Negroes constitute a majority of the population, not a single Negro is registered. Can any law enacted under such circumstances be considered democratically structured?

Sometimes a law is just on its face and unjust in its application. For instance, I have been arrested on a charge of parading without a permit. Now, there is nothing wrong in having an ordinance which requires a permit for a parade. But such an ordinance becomes unjust when it is used to maintain segregation and to deny citizens the First-Amendment privilege of peaceful assembly and protest.

I hope you are able to see the distinction I am trying to point out. In no sense do I advocate evading or defying the law, as would the rabid segregationist. That would lead to anarchy. One who breaks an unjust law must do so openly, lovingly, and with a willingness to accept the penalty. I submit that an individual who breaks a law that conscience tells him is unjust, and who willingly accepts the penalty of imprisonment in order to arouse the conscience of the community over its injustice, is in reality expressing the highest respect for law. . . .

I must make two honest confessions to you, my Christian and Jewish brothers. First, I must confess that over the past few years I have been gravely disappointed with the white moderate. I have almost reached the regrettable conclusion that the Negro's great stumbling block in his stride toward freedom is not the White Citizen's Counciler or the Ku Klux Klanner, but the white moderate, who is more devoted to "order" than to justice; who prefers a negative peace which is the absence of tension to a positive peace which is the presence of justice; who constantly says: "I agree with you in the goal you seek, but I cannot agree with your methods of direct action"; who paternalistically believes he can set the timetable for another man's freedom; who lives by a mythical concept of time and who constantly advises the Negro to wait for a "more convenient season." Shallow understanding from people of good will is more frustrating than absolute misunderstanding from people of ill will. Lukewarm acceptance is much more bewildering than outright rejection.

## A Feminist Manifesto
### Redstockings

*It is increasingly recognized that women, both individually and in organizations, have been struggling for changes for a long time. The effort to gain consciousness and understanding of what it means to be a woman—politically, socially, economically, and sexually—became central to women's*

SOURCE: Redstockings, July 7, 1969, mimeograph.

*struggles for change in the mid-20th century. During the 1960s and 1970s women's struggle for change spread and took on a new militancy. Throughout the West, women were arguing for change in what came to be known, especially in the United States, as the women's liberation movement. Numerous women's organizations formed, and many issued publications stating their views.*

*The following selection is an example of one of the more radical statements of feminism. It was issued in July 1969 by Redstockings, an organization of New York feminists.*

CONSIDER: *The primary demands of the Redstockings; how this group justifies its demands; how men might react to this selection.*

I. After centuries of individual and preliminary political struggle, women are uniting to achieve their final liberation from male supremacy. Redstockings is dedicated to building their unity and winning our freedom.

II. Women are an oppressed class. Our oppression is total, affecting every facet of our lives. We are exploited as sex objects, breeders, domestic servants, and cheap labor. We are considered inferior beings, whose only purpose is to enhance men's lives. Our humanity is denied. Our prescribed behavior is enforced by the threat of physical violence.

Because we have lived so intimately with our oppressors, in isolation from each other, we have been kept from seeing our personal suffering as a political condition. This creates the illusion that a woman's relationship with her man is a matter of interplay between two unique personalities, and can be worked out individually. In reality, every such relationship is a class relationship, and the conflicts between individual men and women are political conflicts that can only be solved collectively.

III. We identify the agents of our oppression as men. Male supremacy is the oldest, most basic form of domination. All other forms of exploitation and oppression (racism, capitalism, imperialism, and the like) are extensions of male supremacy: men dominate women, a few men dominate the rest. All power structures throughout history have been male-dominated and male-oriented. Men have controlled all political, economic, and cultural institutions and backed up this control with physical force. They have used their power to keep women in an inferior position. *All men* receive economic, sexual, and psychological benefits from male supremacy. *All men* have oppressed women.

IV. Attempts have been made to shift the burden of responsibility from men to institutions or to women themselves. We condemn these arguments as evasions. Institutions alone do not oppress; they are merely tools of the oppressor. To blame institutions implies that men and women are equally victimized, obscures the fact that men benefit from the subordination of women, and gives men the excuse that they are forced to be oppressors. On the contrary, any man is free to renounce his superior position provided that he is willing to be treated like a woman by other men.

We also reject the idea that women consent to or are to blame for their own oppression. Women's submission is not the result of brainwashing, stupidity, or mental illness but of continual, daily pressure from men. We do not need to change ourselves, but to change men.

The most slanderous evasion of all is that women can oppress men. The basis for this illusion is the isolation of individual relationships from their political context and the tendency of men to see any legitimate challenge to their privileges as persecution.

V. We regard our personal experience, and our feelings about that experience, as the basis for an analysis of our common situation. We cannot rely on existing ideologies as they are all products of male supremacist culture. We question every generalization and accept none that are not confirmed by our experience.

Our chief task at present is to develop female class consciousness through sharing experience and publicly exposing the sexist foundation of all our institutions. Consciousness-raising is not "therapy," which implies the existence of individual solutions and falsely assumes that the male–female relationship is purely personal, but the only method by which we can ensure that our program for liberation is based on the concrete realities of our lives.

The first requirement for raising class consciousness is honesty, in private and in public, with ourselves and other women.

VI. We identify with all women. We define our best interest as that of the poorest, most brutally exploited woman.

We repudiate all economic, racial, educational, or status privileges that divide us from other women. We are determined to recognize and eliminate any prejudices we may hold against other women.

We are committed to achieving internal democracy. We will do whatever is necessary to ensure that every woman in our movement has an equal chance to participate, assume responsibility, and develop her political potential.

VII. We call on all our sisters to unite with us in struggle.

We call on all men to give up their male privileges and support women's liberation in the interests of our humanity and their own.

In fighting for our liberation we will always take the side of women against their oppressors. We will not ask what is "revolutionary" or "reformist," only what is good for women.

The time for individual skirmishes has passed. This time we are going all the way.

# The Vietnam War: A Reporter with the Vietcong

## James Cameron

*The years after World War II in southern Asia were marked by struggles to end colonial rule and achieve independence. In northern Vietnam, the French withdrew in 1954 after years of fighting, leaving the forces of Ho Chi Minh victorious. But in southern Vietnam, Americans, concerned with containing communism, increasingly took the place of the French. By 1965 war, characterized by continuing bombing raids by Americans and guerilla war tactics by the Vietcong, raged in Vietnam. In the following selection, James Cameron describes a 1965 visit to a village in North Vietnam that was in the path of many bombing raids.*

CONSIDER: *What this reveals about how struggles such as these were conducted; the methods used by the Vietcong to withstand American military power; how the people in North Vietnam perceived these bombings.*

Through the daylight hours nothing moves on the roads of North Vietnam, not a car nor a truck. It must look from the air as though the country had no wheeled transport at all. That, of course, is the idea, it is the roads and bridges that are being bombed; it is no longer safe after sunrise to be anywhere near either.

In the paddies the farmers are reaping their third harvest of the year, which has been particularly abundant. They move among the rice with their sickles, bowed under a shawl of foliage, the camouflage that gives everyone a faintly carnival air, like so many Jacks-in-the-Green.

At the corners of the paddies stand what look like sheaves of corn and are stacks of rifles. The roads stretch long and empty, leading from nowhere to nowhere.

Then the sun goes down and everything starts to move.

At dusk the roads become alive. The engines are started and the convoys grind away through the darkness

behind the pinpoints of masked headlamps. There are miles of them, heavy Russian-built trucks, anti-aircraft batteries, all deeply buried under piles of branches and leaves; processions of huge green haystacks. North Vietnam by day is abandoned; by night it thuds and grinds with movement. It is a fatiguing routine: working by day and moving by night.

In this fashion I drove down to what is called the 'fighting areas' in the central province of Thanh Hoa. . . .

The great showplace of Thanh Hoa is the famous Ham Rong bridge. It has been attacked more than 100 times, by at least 1000 aircraft; it is scarred and pitted and twisted and the area around is a terrible mess, but the bridge still carries the road and the railroad. It lies between two very steep hills, and must be extremely difficult to hit; it would need a very steep and oblique bombing run. . . .

At the village of Nanh Ngang, hard by the bridge, I was presented to Miss Nguyen Thi Hang, who is a Labour Hero and a People's Hero, and is clearly adjusted to a measure of local celebrity as the nation's Resistance pin-up. She once led a delegation to Moscow. . . .

Miss Hang commands the women's corps of the Nanh Ngang militia, and she put them through their paces for me—a mock alert, a covey of most nubile little girls popping into foxholes and pointing their rifles at the sky, with Miss Hang gesturing upwards, exactly as in her pictures.

It all seemed so palpably make-believe—this vital bridge defended by a chorus of sweet little girls; I felt awkward and rueful.

And then, in the middle of the performance, as I walked back from the river to the village—the alarm went in all truth, and the war game was real after all, in the sighing howl of jets overhead, the thud of ack-ack, and for all I know, for I could not be sure, a tiny volley from Miss Hang's young ladies in the foxholes.

The aeroplanes were not after us this time, but streaking homeward south. The village took cover philosophically, but by the time the children were herded into the earth dugouts, the flight was, doubtless, miles away.

There were several such raids while I moved about the country, and it is fair to try to analyse one's reaction. It is not easy. What supervened, I think, was not the emotion of fear (for I was in no particular danger) nor high-minded horror—there was somehow a sense of outrage against civility: what an *impertinence*, one felt, what arrogance, what an offence against manners. These people in North Vietnam are agreeable, shy people, and very poor. Will this sort of thing blow Communism out of their heads?

SOURCE: James Cameron, "The Vietnam War: A Reporter with the Vietcong, Near Hanoi, 10 December 1965," in *Eyewitness to History*, John Carey, ed. (Cambridge, MA: Harvard University Press, 1987), pp. 670–71.

# VISUAL SOURCES

## The Cold War and European Integration

*This map gives some idea of the movements toward the Cold War and toward European integration in the two decades following World War II. Militarily, west and east divided into NATO, led by the United States, and the Warsaw Pact Organization, led by the USSR. Economically, western European nations became increasingly tied together through organizations such as the Benelux Customs Union, the European Coal and Steel Community, the European Economic Community (Common Market), and the European Free Trade Association; the East joined in the Council for Mutual Economic Assistance (Comecon). Although military cooperation and economic cooperation were not always linked together, such linkage often did take place.*

CONSIDER: *The geographic logic, if any, of the political and economic decisions that were made by the various countries; how maps of the world indicating regional economic cooperation, military alliances, political upheavals, and international "hotspots" might show the extent and intensity of the Cold War and regional cooperation even more fully than this map of Europe.*

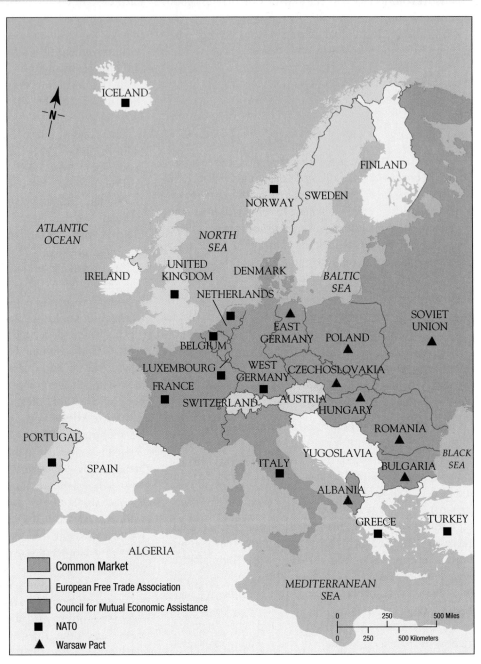

**Map 25–1  The Economic and Military Division of Postwar Europe.**

## Decolonization in Asia and Africa

*Weakened by World War II and faced with growing movements for national liberation, Western imperial powers were forced to start giving up their colonial holdings in the late 1940s. As indicated by this map, the process of decolonization was in some ways rapid—witness the large areas that gained independence in the few years around 1960—and in some ways delayed—it took some three decades for the process to be almost complete with some areas (e.g., Namibia, Hong Kong) still under external control into the 1990s.*

CONSIDER: *Possible explanations for some areas gaining independence sooner, others later; possible problems new countries faced following independence.*

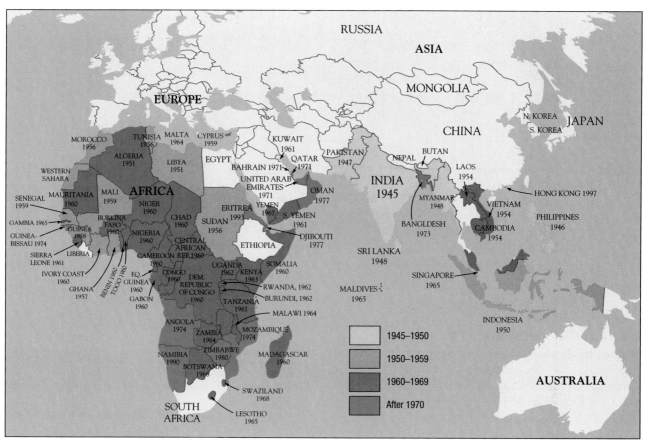

**Map 25–2    Decolonization in Asia and Africa.**

## Rent Collection Courtyard: Art and Politics in China

One of the most important aspects of Chinese Communist belief was that art should serve politics. Art should, Mao Zedong (Mao Tse-tung) argued, show people how to act; who their enemies were; who their friends were; and how they should view their own society. Art for art's sake was considered bourgeois and against the interests of the majority of China's population. These notions were taken to an extreme during the period known as the Cultural Revolution (1966–76) when art was confined to a handful of acceptable works. Moreover, it was deemed appropriate for the subjects of the art to participate in its creation.

Although "Rent Collection Courtyard" was originally done in 1965, just prior to the Cultural Revolution, it was to serve as a model for that period. The original work consisted of 114 life-sized figures created by sculptors at the Sichuan (Szechwan) Institute of Fine Arts. They were aided by provincial Communist Party officials and by local peasants who followed the creations closely, describing their experiences and guiding the sculptors artistically as well as politically. For example, it was the peasants who suggested the use of glass eyes for more realism.

These stark, gripping, and very obvious figures were meant to portray the bitterness of the past, which people were then to compare to the much better present realities. The message is very clear. Photographs and copies were later distributed widely throughout the country.

CONSIDER: What the viewer was to understand about pre-Communist China in looking at this scene; how art is used for political purposes.

**Illustration 25–1**   Sichuan Institute of Fine Arts, China.

# SECONDARY SOURCES

## Origins of the Cold War

*James L. Gormly*

*The period between the end of World War II and the late 1980s was marked by the Cold War between the two superpowers emerging from World War II: the United States and the USSR. Initially American historians analyzed the Cold War with assumptions not too different from policymakers': The United States was only responding defensively to an aggressive Soviet Union intent on spreading its control and Communist ideology over the world. But by the 1960s other interpretations were being offered, most notably a revisionist position holding the Cold War to be at least in part a result of an aggressive, provocative American foreign policy. In the following selection James Gormly describes the competing interpretations and suggests how the controversy might be analyzed.*

CONSIDER: *Whether the Cold War was inevitable or could have been avoided; how the speeches by Truman and Marshall or the views of Ponomaryov support one side or the other; which view makes the most sense to you.*

Those who place the major responsibility for the Cold War on the Soviet Union argue that Stalin, as dictator and leader of a totalitarian system, easily could have moderated the nation's interests to meet U.S. objections and ensure peace. According to this view, if the generalissimo was not an expansionist wanting to overrun central and Western Europe, he should have articulated the defensive and limited nature of his goals to the Truman administration and the American public. Instead, the Russians would not accept the U.S. vision for a stable and prosperous world or trust that Washington accepted the legitimacy of the Soviet Union and recognized its need for some degree of influence over regions along its borders. Moscow needed "a hostile international environment" to maintain control and the integrity of the Soviet state. Thus, Stalin was either an expansionist or unwilling to communicate his aims, and the United States, supported by Britain, had no other option than to react aggressively. . . .

Other analysts place a large amount of the blame on the United States and its unwillingness to accept expressed Soviet needs and to articulate to the Russians and Stalin that Washington trusted them and recognized the legitimacy of their system and state. Some explain U.S. behavior as an outgrowth of the American Open Door ideology, which sought to ensure for the nation's businesses access to world markets. Still others credit U.S. actions to a general arrogance of power that translated the country's tremendous economic and military strength and accomplishments into a moral, ideological superiority. According to this theory, many Soviets feared that the West still hoped to destroy their state. To convince them that America intended to be a friend and thereby avoid the Cold War, the United States should have shelved its presumptuousness and global goals and demonstrated an affirmation of the Soviet Union's right to rule and enjoy the fruits of its victory. To ease fears and mistrust, Washington needed to recognize Russia's new borders, its diplomatic equality, and its spheres of influence in Eastern Europe. Instead, the U.S. government continued to follow the path suggested by Ambassador Harriman, who stated that the administration should supply assistance to the Soviets only if they "played the international game with us in accordance with our standards." . . .

Given the situation, the belief that U.S. actions divided the world into two camps and necessitated a rapid Sovietization of Eastern Europe seems as logical as the view that Russian expansionism forced the United States to institute its containment policy. To evaluate and assess either theory fully and to determine if the Cold War international system could have been avoided requires an examination of Soviet records, but, even without such information, and using existing American and British documents, one can conclude that U.S. policymakers made few efforts after the Potsdam Conference to reassure Moscow that mutual cooperation was possible and that Washington had no intention of seeking the destruction of the Soviet state.

## The Last Japan

*Hasegawa Nyozekan*

*Perhaps no country has gone through so many cataclysmic changes in such a short span of years as Japan. In 100 years (1850s–1950s), Japan went from a feudal, preindustrial, hermit nation to a major industrial and military power, to a conqueror and colonial master, to ignominious defeat, and finally to a democratic economic power with a pacifist foreign policy.*

*Hasegawa Nyozekan was a leading radical journalist, novelist, and critic who, having been born in 1875, lived through many of those events. This selection is from* The Last Japan, *written in 1952 when he was 77 years old. He reflects on the changes in Japan over his lifetime and wonders if traditional Japanese culture is conducive to democratic in-*

SOURCE: Ryusaku Tsunoda et al., eds., *Sources of Japanese Tradition* (New York and London: Columbia University Press, 1961), pp. 891–900.

*stitutions. Hasegawa also raises the issue of Japan's historical tendency to adopt cultural values from other peoples and wonders if the time has not come to work harder on developing indigenous forms of science and culture.*

CONSIDER: *What modernization in the post–World War II decades meant for Japan; the problems facing Japan in trying to modernize and democratize; the possible effects of modernization on Japanese culture and character.*

The American decrees issued with respect to freedom and democratization in the internal administration of Japan resulted in five major changes: the enfranchisement of Japanese women (through granting of the vote); the encouragement given to the formation of labor unions; the liberalization of school instruction; the abolition of institutions which tended to cause the people to live in fear; and the democratization of the economic structure.

These five great changes in the government of the nation followed a course which the history of the modernization of Japan and of the Japanese themselves would have taken anyway if left to its natural tendency; they were, in fact, the direction towards which Japanese history was pointed. The history of Japan since the early '30s was distorted by the mistaken designs of the men in power, but the process of modernization itself was uncompromisingly carried out. We must, therefore, examine whether or not the culture of the Japanese people today is of a nature capable of turning Japan into a truly and completely modern nation. We must also make ourselves aware of those elements in both our strong points and our shortcomings which must be changed.

During the Meiji Era the nation and people advanced boldly in the historical process of modernization which permitted Japan to break out of her isolation and stand among the nations of the world. When we reached the '30s, however, Japan was carried away by the tide of an age of world reaction, and there ensued a revival of feudalistic Japanese institutions. That our nation should have been plunged into destruction by the coercive force of a union of the military and civil proves that there had been no break in the "feudalistic" nature of the forms of our characteristic racial, political and social activities. This factor lent a special quality to our national culture, a quality destined to determine Japanese national and racial characteristics and to lead Japan to its tragic fate. Thus, as a basic condition for the reconstruction of Japan as a free and democratic nation, a change in our cultural nature itself must be planned and executed. . . .

. . . [T]he discovery of a new means of freeing ourselves from an attitude of subordination and of developing cultural characteristics of independence which can be shared by the entire people is a prerequisite to the reconstruction of the nation.

The first essential to achieve is an educational and cultural program which will permit the free development of the feelings and intellect of the Japanese. We must restore the cultural attitude held by the Japan of ancient times with respect to all aspects of life: that is, to maintain a receptivity which is free, unbiased, and diverse.

Second, there must be a switch from imitativeness to creativity. Japanese culture, now as in former days, has been said to be imitative in character. This is because Japan during the period from the earliest days to the Middle Ages was always in the position of being obliged to take in the cultural nourishment of China. In modern times she has been in the same position with respect to the West. However, the Japanese have invariably digested and absorbed these cultural influences once they had passed the stage of imitation, and thereby succeeded in creating a new and purely Japanese culture. . . .

. . . The real reason why Japanese politics, philosophy, literature, and art from the Meiji Period to the present have always been engaged in such a frantic pursuit of Western trends is that we have not been able to display sufficient creativity in the development of our own cultural nature.

This failing was not in the least compensated for by the pretended "discovery" or "creation" of "truly Japanese" things, stemming from the cultural commands of the military clique during the war. Such activities were no more than a kind of "cultural self-consolation." . . . The "truly Japanese" things are not things which can be "discovered" or "created" in this manner; they must be a natural product obtained from a nationwide ability and means to create. Education and research must be for the sake of fostering such an ability throughout the country and for the promotion of a structure, organization, form, and content which would permit such a process to take place throughout the country. . . .

We must change the world of the daily life of the Japanese into an environment for living in which we, who up to now have led most unscientific lives, will be given a scientific purpose and form. We will thus be enabled to breathe in a scientific atmosphere, just as a newborn babe drinks its mother's milk. . . .

It is impossible to deny that most of the better educated classes of Japanese society were unhappy over the blind acts of the military clique and sought to prevent them. That their strength was inadequate to the task was due not so much to a deficiency of intellect as to a weakness of the will.

This will power can be strengthened by cultural education or by means quite outside the realm of culture. . . .

Viewed in this light, the difficult conditions under which the Japanese have lived since the defeat may be said to contain hope if we think of them as the environment for strengthening our will power and for molding us.

## Economic Decolonization and Arrested Development in Africa

### D. K. Fieldhouse

*The political instability that independent Africa experienced was evident not only in the political sphere, but in the economy as well. Many supporters of African independence became disillusioned with the steady economic decline that formerly rich colonial regions experienced and sought to identify the causes. Although some scholars and loan agencies have linked the economic disasters to the unstable political climate, more recent analyses have sought the causes in the economic policies of the colonial period. According to this view, African independent leaders inherited from the Europeans an economy with an intrusive state system that they have been unable to alter. According to critics of colonialism, the structure inherited from the period of colonialism has limited the economic choices of Africans and is responsible for Africa's relative economic backwardness. In the following discussion, D. K. Fieldhouse, a noted British historian of imperialism, adds another dimension to the debate.*

CONSIDER: *Where the author lays the blame for the "arrested development" of African states; African nationalists' possible reaction to the deterioration of the economy; why this question of the economy is so important.*

[W]hile the seeds of Africa's dependence on foreign concessionary loans and grants were sown in the late-colonial period, the most important single consequence of decolonization was its grotesque flowering into unmanageable overspending and indebtedness. Colonialism, for most of its course, had kept colonial public expenditure, investment and borrowing in line with a colony's capacity to pay; and this capacity was closely related to the health of the international economy, since this determined a colony's balance of payments position and the size of government revenues. After independence these constraints were gradually thrown off: need and ambition rather than ability to meet the costs became the criteria of policy-making. During the first decade and a half after 1960 international conditions generally concealed the dangers. Commodity prices remained generally good, interest rates and repayment terms on foreign borrowing low, the flow of foreign equity capital high. By the later 1970s most of this had changed. Black Africa found itself

SOURCE: D. K. Fieldhouse, *Black Africa 1945–1980: Economic Decolonization and Arrested Development* (London: Allen & Unwin, 1986), pp. 244–45.

in a position no colonial government would ever have permitted, heavily indebted, deeply committed to continuing large expenditure, but facing greatly increased interest charges, lower commodity prices and a virtual stoppage of fresh equity capital as a consequence of the compulsory indigenization of foreign private capital.

It is at this point that the economic consequences of decolonization became for the first time really obvious. Colonial economic policy had been cautious to the point of inertia; but caution had at least provided insurance against disaster. Most new African states preferred to gamble. The superficially impressive achievements of the first two decades after independence, which had made colonialism appear to have achieved so little, were built on sand. Growth resulted from booming exports, unexploited domestic tax potential and huge injections of foreign capital; it did not reflect structural development in Black Africa. When it was no longer possible to extract so large a surplus from the peasants and foreign borrowing became prohibitively expensive at a time when the commodity markets were depressed, most African states found themselves virtually bankrupt.

This, then, is the main link between decolonization and economic failure in Black Africa. Colonial rulers, afraid of the political and social consequences of economic recession, were probably too reluctant to innovate at the cost of indebtedness. Their successors, impelled rather by the political need to demonstrate progress, to reward supporters and to employ growing urban populations, went to the other extreme. Because the development they planned was, in many cases, ill-conceived and based on wildly over-optimistic assessments of what was possible, it was bound sooner or later to slow up or be checked. But that is not to say that it was "arrested" and therefore could not be resumed: merely that development in Black Africa was at all times bound to be slow and that it could only be sustained when governments tackled the underlying weaknesses which neither colonial nor postcolonial regimes had been able to remove by the mid-1980s.

## Inequality, Repression, and Rebellion in Latin America

### Hernando de Soto

*Maldistribution of land and wealth has been a major problem in Latin America in the post–World War II decades. Some historians argue that many Latin American countries' political and legal systems, far from helping to alleviate this in-*equality, *merely reinforce it or make it worse. De Soto, an economist, examines the origins of social injustice and economic failure in his native Peru and elsewhere.*

CONSIDER: *The sources of economic and social divisions in Latin America; why the call for land reform has had such power throughout Latin American history; connections between repression and rebellion in Latin America.*

It is essential . . . that political and social scientists investigate whether the lack of opportunity and the absence of legal facilities and protection for the majority of Peruvians is contributing importantly to the violence in the country. . . .

The poorest and most discontented members of the population are not prepared to accept a society in which opportunities, property, and power are distributed arbitrarily. People realize that the country's legal institutions do not allow them to fulfill rational expectations or afford them minimum facilities and protection. The frustration engendered can easily result in violence, either in complicity or relative indifference to it. After all, if the main reason for the existence of legal institutions is to protect individual rights and property from third parties, permit orderly access to productive activity, and facilitate harmonious interaction with other individuals, it is understandable that, when people are discriminated against, many will rebel.

It is obvious to even the most formal and peaceful of citizens that the existing legal system—the red tape, the widespread mistreatment on waiting lines, the bribes, the rudeness—are a Kafkaesque trap which prevent their and the country's resources from being used efficiently. This is unacceptable to the poorest, because the most discriminatory laws and institutions are those governing economic activities—the main channel for upward mobility. The resulting frustration, at best, gives rise to informal activity; at worst, to criminality and subversion. Aggression is a human response to frustration which, in turn, is caused less by suffering and poverty than by the difference between what people have and what they think they are entitled to. . . .

If opportunities for mass migration, such as those available in Mexico, do not exist and the necessary institutional reforms do not occur, the most likely outcome of a failed mercantilist system will be violence in one or another of its manifestations: revolution or repression. After all, we know that it is mainly young people from rural areas who are drawn to the cities, because they do not have to take a family with them. Since those who migrate are the most enterprising, they may also prove to be the most aggressive and belligerent. Both their age and the difficulty of establishing personal relationships and a home far from their place of origin make them the easiest prey to the rhetoric of violence. Casual employment with

SOURCE: Hernando de Soto, *The Other Path: The Invisible Revolution in the Third World* (New York: Harper & Row, 1989).

no future gradually wears down their tolerance and buries their hopes.

## The War in Vietnam

*The United States became involved in the wars of Indochina in 1947 in support of the French efforts to regain colonial rule. American officials wanted a strong France in Europe and believed that continued colonial possessions would add to that strength. By 1954 the United States was paying for over 80 percent of the French war effort and was unhappy about France's decision to end its involvement after the defeat at Dien Bien Phu.*

*The United States saw Vietnam as a potential battleground in the Cold War and viewed it as a surrogate of the Chinese, if not the Russians. So Washington subverted the planned elections in 1956 and created a new government in the south of Vietnam, importing a leader handpicked by U.S. officials in Washington. Those decisions led only to disaster and the defeat of the Americans in 1973. A civil war between the two governments of Vietnam finally ended in 1975 after the southern forces were defeated.*

*After the enormous amount of human life expended to fight this Indochinese war, most Americans (unlike the Vietnamese, who knew they were fighting for an end to foreign involvement in their country) still didn't understand what the war was about. This confusion is evident in this excerpt from an editorial in* The New Yorker *on May 5, 1975.*

CONSIDER: *How Americans could fight for so long and know so little about the Vietnamese people and culture, which were considered their "enemy."*

Last week, the war in Vietnam seemed to be moving toward its end, but something stranger than the victory of one side over the other was going on. Not only was the side supported by the United States collapsing; the world view that had given the war its importance in the eyes of American officialdom was collapsing, too. The system of friendships and enmities that had provided the policy with what Secretary of State Henry Kissinger calls its "coherence" was in disarray. The confusion was visible in microcosm in the positions taken on the issue of the Americans who remained in Saigon. The threats to these Americans came from some unexpected quarters. The principal threat, it seemed, came not from the North Vietnamese but from the South Vietnamese, America's ally. Drew Middleton, the military-affairs analyst for the *Times*, wrote of the mood of the South Vietnamese soldiers who had retreated from Danang to Saigon, "Ironically, these forces, who fought better than

any other Government troops in the five-week campaign, are now regarded as the most serious danger to Americans in Saigon, as well as to politicians seeking an accommodation with the Communists infiltrating into the city." There was even fear that the South Vietnamese might hold the Americans hostage. Stranger still were reports that Mr. Graham Martin, the American Ambassador to South Vietnam, was slowing the evacuation—that he was holding the Americans hostage, in the hope of getting more aid for the South from Congress. Meanwhile, the "enemy"—the North Vietnamese—were promising a safe withdrawal for the Americans. The North Vietnamese, of course, have been trying to get Westerners out of Vietnam for some thirty years now.

The enmity of the South Vietnamese against the Americans was fast becoming the predominant emotion in Saigon. President Thieu, in his speech of resignation, put the blame for his government's plight not on the North Vietnamese but on the United States. The North Vietnamese may have had a supporting role, he seemed to be suggesting, but it was the United States that had "led the South Vietnamese people to death." He sounded as though the United States had been at war with South Vietnam, not North Vietnam, these last fifteen years. Thieu's opinion was apparently shared by the Ford Administration. In Washington, not long before, Mr. Kissinger—whom Thieu bitterly attacked in his resignation speech—had said that the United States must give Thieu more aid if it did not want to "destroy an ally." But while Thieu was blaming Kissinger for the collapse of the Saigon regime, Kissinger was blaming Congress. He contended that it was Congress that had not lived up to the American "commitment" to South Vietnam. (Congress, meanwhile, was learning of the "commitment" for the first time, and was surprised at being accused of not having upheld a promise it did not know that the United States had made.) Moreover, as Kissinger was blaming Congress for its failures in the past, another member of the Administration, Vice-President Rockefeller, was looking to the future failures of Congress. Speculating that some thousands of Americans might be killed or captured in Saigon, he said that such an eventuality would make a campaign issue in the Presidential race of 1976; he also said that if Congress did not vote funds "and the Communists take over and there are a million people liquidated, we know where the responsibility will lie." Then, shortly afterward, President Ford said that Vietnam should not be a campaign issue in 1976.

Oddly, amid all this recrimination and talk of prospective massacres and campaign issues, there was very little mention of Russia, China, and North Viet-

---

SOURCE: "Notes and Comment" from the May 5, 1975, issue of *The New Yorker.*

nam—the nations whose influence the United States had supposedly been opposing in South Vietnam. Indeed, President Ford, in his recent State of the World address, said that America's wounds were "self-inflicted." The foe had apparently been read out of the picture. We had been battling ourselves, it seemed, and had lost. What mention there was of the Communist powers tended to be cordial and understanding. Secretary of Defense James Schlesinger set the tone when he said, a few weeks back, during a discussion of the American presence in Asia, that the Chinese and the Russians sometimes found their Asian allies prone to "exuberance" and welcomed having the United States step in as a restraining influence. President Ford struck the same note in some remarks not long afterward. Speaking of the collapse of the Saigon forces in the northern part of South Vietnam, he said, "I don't think we can blame the Soviet Union and the People's Republic of China in this case. If we had done with our allies what we promised, I think this whole tragedy could have been eliminated." Instead, we could blame the members of our own Congress, who had voted down the extra military aid.

The remarks of the President and the Secretary of Defense seemed to evoke nothing less than a vision of a new world order. At one time, the government had told the public that the United States was fighting against Moscow and Peking in Vietnam, but now it seemed to be saying that these countries were our partners in the war. In the new world order, the great powers had apparently agreed that each would support its own allies in whatever wars were going on. Thus, a balance had been struck in which the Americans and the Russians and the Chinese were to live in peace while the Vietnamese would go on killing each other forever. The name of this order was "détente." But if the United States was in Asia to protect Chinese and Russian interests, as Mr. Schlesinger had said, Mr. Kissinger had not been told, for the day after the President had said we could not blame

Russia and China for what was happening in Vietnam, Kissinger did blame them. "We shall not forget who supplied the arms which North Vietnam used to make a mockery of its signature on the Paris accords," he said.

The regime in Saigon was falling, but official Washington seemed at a loss to explain why. Some people were pointing the finger of blame at Russia and China, but others were saying that those countries were innocent. Some were saying that the fault was President Thieu's (while he was saying that the fault was ours). Some were saying that Congress was to blame, but then they were saying that there was enough blame for all Americans to share. The longest war in our history was at last coming to an end, and we did not know who the enemy had been.

## Chapter Questions

1. What argument could be made for the assertion that the fundamental historical shift in the past 200 years did not come with World War I, as some historians argue, but with World War II, as indicated by the consequences of that war and the developments of the postwar period?

2. What were some alternatives available to societies trying to deal with modernization during this period? What role might the Cold War have played in choosing among these alternatives? What role might the experience of colonization and decolonization have played in this choice?

3. Drawing from the sources in this chapter, in what ways was the period one of struggle between the elites in power and those below them demanding recognition? What are some of the similarities and differences in these struggles in various parts of the world?

# Chapter Twenty-Six

# The Present in Perspective and the Beginnings of the 21st Century

The most recent years in world history are particularly difficult to evaluate. They are so much a part of the present that it is almost impossible to gain a historical perspective on them.

While many of the basic trends of the postwar era examined in the previous two chapters have continued, some important changes have become apparent—particularly in the past two decades. The Cold War between the United States and the Soviet Union waned during the late 1980s, and revolutionary changes took place in what was the Soviet Union and in eastern Europe. At least for the West, these changes are so far-reaching as to constitute a historical watershed—a marking of the end of the 20th century and the beginning of the 21st century. The rest of Europe, and indeed much of the world, has pursued an increasingly independent course from the two superpowers. The strife-ridden, oil-rich Middle East has become an area of great concern and importance to the world community. Certain areas in Asia (such as Japan, South Korea, Taiwan, and Singapore) have developed strong economies, helping to shift the economic balance of power in the world. In South Africa, black democratic rule has opened a new era. New technological accomplishments, ranging from space exploration to the production of computers, affect our civilizations in many ways. Numerous other recent trends and events—particularly the rise of international terrorism—could be added to this necessarily brief list.

This chapter is not organized in the usual way, for the sources are so much a part of the present that the usual distinctions between primary and secondary sources are no longer useful. The selections deal with four kinds of developments. The first concerns changes in the communist world, particularly the former Soviet Union and China. The second has to do with social, cultural, and ecological trends that have been of particular significance and still affect us today. The third focuses on the rise of international terrorism and developments in the Middle East. The fourth involves interpreting the present era as a whole and predicting the future.

**Illustration 26–1**   Bruno Barbey/Magnum Photos.

There is much ambivalence about recent developments. Our own involvement makes evaluation of the present particularly difficult. At best, the selections in this chapter can help put elements of the present into perspective.

## Modernization: The Western and Non-Western Worlds

*Although almost all areas of the world that were once colonies of the Western powers gained independence during the quarter century following World War II, the penetration of the rest of the world by Western ideas, values, institutions, and products has been extremely widespread. This is illustrated in this photograph showing a citizen of Kuwait, an oil-rich sheikdom of the Persian Gulf, carrying a Western television set across a road. He is wearing Western-style tennis shoes that were probably manufactured in the Far East. In the background are a bilingual store sign and Western automobiles. Reflected in the glass of the television set is a modern building probably designed by a Western architect and built under the direction of an international construction firm using both foreign and domestic labor and materials. This photograph suggests that some of the formerly colonized areas are taking economic, political, and social steps in the same direction as Western industrialized states.*

CONSIDER: *The effects of westernization on non-Western culture as illustrated by this photo.*

## Communist China: The Four Modernizations

*Communique of the Central Committee, December 1978*

*Over the past three decades, there have been some striking changes within the communist world. One of the most important was initiated in China in 1978. Since the 1950s, under the leadership of Mao Zedong (Mao Tse-tung), China had pursued a policy of economic development similar to the Soviet Union's Five-Year Plans emphasizing centralized planning, heavy industry, and agricultural collectivization. After a power struggle following Mao's death in 1976, more moderate officials, led by Deng Xiaoping (Teng Hsiao-p'ing), came to power. In 1978 they initiated the policy of the "Four Modernizations." As indicated in the following official statement of this policy, China would be abandoning many elements of its old program of economic development in favor of more pragmatic methods.*

CONSIDER: *By implication, what sorts of economic problems China was having; ways in which the old policy of centralized planning is being attacked; the significance of changes in agricultural policy.*

[N]ow is an appropriate time . . . to shift the emphasis of our Party's work and the attention of the people of the whole country to socialist modernization. This is of major significance for fulfilment of the three-year and eight-year programmes for the development of the national economy and the outline for 23 years, for the modernization of agriculture, industry, national defence and science and technology and for the consolidation of the dictatorship of the proletariat in our country. The general task put forward by our Party for the new period reflects the demands of history and the people's aspirations and represents their fundamental interests. Whether or not we can carry this general task to completion, speed socialist modernization and on the basis of a rapid growth in production improve the people's living standards significantly and strengthen national defence—this is a major issue which is of paramount concern to all our people and of great significance to the cause of world peace and progress. Carrying out the four modernizations requires great growth in the productive forces, which in turn requires diverse changes in those aspects of the relations of production and the superstructure not in harmony with the growth of the productive forces, and requires changes in all methods of management, actions and thinking which stand in the way of such growth. Socialist modernization is therefore a profound and extensive revolution. . . .

. . . [W]e are now, in the light of the new historical conditions and practical experience, adopting a number of major new economic measures, conscientiously transforming the system and methods of economic management, actively expanding economic co-operation on terms of equality and mutual benefit with other countries on the basis of self-reliance, striving to adopt the world's advanced technologies and equipment and greatly strengthening scientific and educational work to meet the needs of modernization. . . .

The session points out that one of the serious shortcomings in the structure of economic management in our country is the overconcentration of authority, and it is necessary boldly to shift it under guidance from the leadership to lower levels so that the local authorities and industrial and agricultural enterprises will have greater power of decision in management under the guidance of unified state planning; big efforts should be made to simplify bodies at various levels charged with economic administration and transfer most of their functions to such enterprises as specialized companies or complexes; it is necessary to act firmly in line with economic law, attach importance to the role of the law of value, consciously combine ideological and political

SOURCE: *The Peking Review,* July 28, 1978.

work with economic methods and give full play to the enthusiasm of cadres and workers for production; it is necessary, under the centralized leadership of the Party, to tackle conscientiously the failure to make a distinction between the Party, the government and the enterprise and to put a stop to the substitution of Party for government and the substitution of government for enterprise administration, to institute a division of responsibilities among different levels, types of work and individuals, increase the authority and responsibility of administrative bodies and managerial personnel, reduce the number of meetings and amount of paper work to raise work efficiency, and conscientiously adopt the practices of examination, reward and punishment, promotion and demotion. . . .

The plenary session holds that the whole Party should concentrate its main energy and efforts on advancing agriculture as fast as possible because agriculture, the foundation of the national economy, has been seriously damaged in recent years and remains very weak on the whole. . . . This requires first of all releasing the socialist enthusiasm of our country's several hundred million peasants, paying full attention to their material well-being economically and giving effective protection to their democratic rights politically. Taking this as the guideline, the plenary session set forth a series of policies and economic measures aimed at raising present agricultural production. The most important are as follows: The right of ownership by the people's communes, production brigades and production teams and their power of decision must be protected effectively by the laws of the state; it is not permitted to commandeer the manpower, funds, products and material of any production team; the economic organizations at various levels of the people's commune must conscientiously implement the socialist principle of "to each according to his work," work out payment in accordance with the amount and quality of work done, and overcome equalitarianism; small plots of land for private use by commune members, their domestic side-occupations, and village fairs are necessary adjuncts of the socialist economy, and must not be interfered with; the people's communes must resolutely implement the system of three levels of ownership with the production team as the basic accounting unit, and this should remain unchanged.

## The End of the Cold War
*Raymond L. Garthoff*

*For over four decades after World War II international affairs were dominated by the Cold War between the United States and the Soviet Union. While there were times—particularly in the 1970s—when tensions between these two*

*superpowers seemed to ease, conflicts persisted until the mid-1980s. In 1985 Mikhail Gorbachev rose to power in the Soviet Union and initiated major reform policies: glasnost (political and cultural openness) and perestroika (economic restructuring). Major changes within the Soviet Union, in other eastern European countries, and in international affairs streamed from these reform policies. By 1991 the Soviet Union had lost control over the states of Eastern Europe and was itself disintegrating—the Cold War was over. In the following selection, Raymond L. Garthoff analyzes the roles played by Gorbachev and American diplomacy in ending the Cold War.*

CONSIDER: *Why, according to Garthoff, Gorbachev set out deliberately to end the Cold War; what sorts of perceptions influenced American foreign policy during the Cold War according to Garthoff; what other factors might help to explain why the Cold War ended.*

In the final analysis, only a Soviet leader could have ended the Cold War, and Gorbachev set out deliberately to do so. Although earlier Soviet leaders had understood the impermissibility of war in the nuclear age, Gorbachev was the first to recognize that reciprocal political accommodation, rather than military power for deterrence or "counterdeterrence," was the defining core of the Soviet Union's relationship with the rest of the world. The conclusions that Gorbachev drew from this recognition, and the subsequent Soviet actions, finally permitted the Iron Curtain to be dismantled and ended the global confrontation of the Cold War.

Gorbachev, to be sure, seriously underestimated the task of changing the Soviet Union, and this led to policy errors that contributed to the failure of his program for the transformation of Soviet society and polity. His vision of a resurrected socialism built on the foundation of successful *perestroika* and *demokratizatsiya* was never a realistic possibility. A revitalized Soviet political union was beyond realization as well. Whether Gorbachev would have modified his goals or changed his means had he foreseen this disjunction is not clear, probably even to him. In the external political arena, however, Gorbachev both understood and successfully charted the course that led to the end of the Cold War, even though in this area, too, he almost certainly exaggerated the capacity for reform on the part of the Communist governments in Eastern Europe.

As the preceding discussion suggests, the Western and above all the American role in ending the Cold War was

SOURCE: Raymond L. Garthoff, "Why Did the Cold War Arise, and Why Did It End?" in *The End of the Cold War: Its Meaning and Implications*, Michael J. Hogan, ed. (Cambridge, England: Cambridge University Press, 1992), pp. 131–32.

necessary but not primary. There are a number of reasons for this conclusion, but the basic one is that the American worldview was derivative of the Communist worldview. Containment was hollow without an expansionist power to contain. In this sense, it was the Soviet threat, real or imagined, that generated the American dedication to waging the Cold War. . . .

American policymakers were guilty of accepting far too much of the Communist worldview in constructing an anti-Communist antipode, and of being too ready to fight fire with fire. Indeed, once the Cold War became the dominant factor in global politics (and above all in American and Soviet perceptions), each side viewed every development around the world in terms of its relationship to that great struggle, and each was inclined to act according to a self-fulfilling prophecy. The Americans, for example, often viewed local and regional conflicts of indigenous origins as Cold War battles. Like the Soviets, they distrusted the neutral and nonaligned nations and were always more comfortable when countries around the world were either their allies or the satellites and surrogates of the other side. Thus, many traditional diplomatic relationships not essentially attendant on the superpower rivalry were swept into the vortex of the Cold War, at least in the eyes of the protagonists and partly by their actions.

## After Communism: Causes for the Collapse
*Robert Heilbroner*

*The rapid collapse of communism in the Soviet Union and eastern Europe has stunned most observers. Only in retrospect have reasons for this collapse been presented with any conviction. Scholars are now struggling to interpret what has happened. One of these, Robert Heilbroner, has written extensively on economics, economic history, and current affairs. In the following selection, he focuses on the Soviet economic system, particularly the Soviet central planning system as the key to the collapse.*

CONSIDER: *Why the Soviet central planning system might have worked well enough in the early stages of industrialization or for specific projects, but not well enough for a mature industrialized economy; why the collapse of communism in the Soviet Union has such widespread significance.*

Socialism has been a great tragedy this century, its calamitous finale the collapse of Communism in the Soviet Union and Eastern Europe. I doubt very much whether socialism has now disappeared from history, but

SOURCE: Robert Heilbroner, "After Communism," *The New Yorker,* September 10, 1990.

there is no doubt that the collapse marks its end as a model of economic clarity. Moreover, I suspect that its economic failure may haunt socialism longer than the pathologies of Communism. Early on, one could see that the Soviets were headed toward political disaster, but much of that disaster seemed attributable to the hopeless political heritage of Russian history, not to socialism per se. It was the economic side of the Russian collapse that came as a shock. The prodigies of Russian prewar industrialization appeared to be an incontrovertible argument for the capacity of a planned economic system to achieve growth, and the argument appeared to be confirmed by the spectacular performance of the Soviets during the years of reconstruction immediately following the Second World War. Thus, there may have been discomfiture but there was not much surprise when the Soviet economy during the nineteen-fifties grew twice as fast as the American economy. Surprise did not appear until the nineteen-seventies, when the Soviet growth rate slipped to only half of ours, and consternation was not evident until the middle to late nineteen-eighties, when C.I.A. and academic specialists alike began to report something very close to zero growth. But collapse! No one expected collapse.

There is still no definitive account as to exactly why the Soviet economic system collapsed—one can never find the nail for whose want the shoe was lost. There were undoubtedly elements of this economic disaster with their roots in history: the bureaucrat is well known to Russian literature. Perhaps the final blow was delivered by *glasnost*, which released long-pent-up anger against economic conditions; or perhaps by the Soviet attempt to meet the Star Wars initiative—one hears many such guesses. All we know for certain is that the system deteriorated to a point far beyond the worst economic crisis ever experienced by capitalism, and that the villain in this deterioration was the central planning system itself. The conclusion one inevitably comes to is that to whatever extent socialism depends on such a system it will not work. . . .

The great problem of central planning lies buried in the procedures by which the economy is given its marching orders. As in a military campaign, which central planning resembles in many ways, production is brought about by a series of commands from the top, not by the independent decisions of regimental commanders, company captains, and platoon sergeants. This means that the economy "works" because—and only to the extent that—the quantity, quality, size, weight, and selling price of every nut, bolt, hinge, beam, tractor, and hydroelectric turbine have been previously determined. At the supreme headquarters, the numbers for gross national product are announced. In considerably lower and dingier offices, the numbers for nuts, bolts, and turbines are calculated, but it is apparent that if the plans for the latter are off, the plans for the former may be impossible to attain.

Planning thus requires that the immense map of desired national output be carved up into millions of individual pieces, like a jigsaw puzzle—the pieces produced by hundreds of thousands of enterprises, and the whole thing finally reassembled in such a way as to fit. That would be an extraordinarily difficult task even if the map of desired output were unchanged from year to year, but, of course, it is not: the chief planners change their objectives, and new technologies or labor shortages or bad weather or simply mistakes get in the way. In 1986, before *perestroika* was officially formulated, Gosplan, the highest planning commission in the Soviet Union, issued two thousand sets of instructions for major "product groups," such as construction materials, metals, and automotive vehicles. Gossnab, the State Material and Technical Supply Commission, then divided these product groups into fifteen thousand categories—lumber, copper, and trucks, for instance—and the various ministries in charge of the categories in turn subdivided them into fifty thousand more finely detailed products (shingles, beams, laths, boards) and then into specific products in each category (large, medium, and small shingles). These plans then percolated down through the hierarchy of production, receiving emendations or protests as they reached the level of plant managers and engineers, and thereafter travelled back up to the ministerial level. In this Byzantine process, perhaps the most difficult single step was to establish "success indicators"—desired performance targets—for enterprises. For many years, targets were given in physical terms—so many yards of cloth or tons of nails—but that led to obvious difficulties. If cloth was rewarded by the yard, it was woven loosely to make the yarn yield more yards. If the output of nails was determined by their number, factories produced huge numbers of pinlike nails; if by weight, smaller numbers of very heavy nails. The satiric magazine *Krokodil* once ran a cartoon of a factory manager proudly displaying his record output, a single gigantic nail suspended from a crane.

The difficulty, of course, was that the inevitable mismatches and mistakes could not be set to rights by the decisions of platoon sergeants or regimental commanders who were able to see that the campaign was not going as expected.

\*

I am not very sanguine about the prospect that socialism will continue as an important form of economic organization now that Communism is finished. This statement will come as a wry commentary to those who remember that Marx defined socialism as the stage that precedes Communism. But the collapse of the planned economies has forced us to rethink the meaning of socialism. As a semireligious vision of a transformed humanity, it has been dealt devastating blows in the twentieth century. As a blueprint for a rationally planned society, it is in tatters.

## War in Bosnia and Ethnic Cleansing
### Robert J. Donia

*Some of the great difficulties facing Eastern European nations are illustrated by the civil wars that broke out in 1991 in former Yugoslavia. The most brutal conflict took place in Bosnia-Herzegovina, where Serbs, in a war for a "Greater Serbia," fought Bosnians (mostly Muslims). There the Serbs followed policies of "ethnic cleansing," driving Muslim Bosnians from their homes, placing them in concentration camps, and subjecting them to mass rape, starvation, and murder: Bosnian Muslims, supported by aid from the Islamic world, fought back against long odds in battles that raged for more than four years. In the following selection, Robert J. Donia examines this conflict and the practice of ethnic cleansing.*

CONSIDER: *How Donia analyzes the causes of this conflict; the nature of ethnic cleansing and who bears responsibility for practicing it.*

The war in Bosnia occurred against a backdrop of three important external developments that altered the prospects and alternatives of Bosnia's political leaders. First, the Yugoslav People's Army (YPA) dramatically changed its mission in the latter half of 1991 from defending Yugoslav ideals to becoming an agent of Greater Serbian nationalism. Secondly, the 1991 war in Croatia strengthened national extremists among the Bosnian Serbs and weakened those who hoped to preserve a multiethnic Bosnian state. Finally, although diplomatic representatives of the international community cited lofty principles and voiced high ideals, their actions drove the major participants in Bosnia to press separatist claims and abandon efforts for a negotiated solution.

Some observers have portrayed the Bosnian conflict as a renewal of age-old mutual hatreds that inexorably resurfaced after the collapse of Tito's Communist regime. In contrast, we assert that the current Bosnian crisis is, in the context of Bosnia's history, an *historical aberration*, albeit with a single important historical precedent: the interethnic slaughter of the World War II era. Armed

SOURCE: Robert J. Donia. *Bosnia and Herzegovina: A Tradition Betrayed.* New York: Columbia University Press, 1994, pp. 220–21, 245–47.

conflict, ethnic cleansing, the bombardment of cities, and atrocities against civilians in Bosnia were not preordained consequences of ethnonational divisions in Bosnian society; they developed as a result of the transformation of the YPA into an instrument of Serbian nationalists, the annexationist ambitions of the Croatian and Serbian governments, and the eagerness of national extremists to conduct unsavory ethnic cleansing campaigns with the endorsement and assistance of organized armies in the region. . . .

The practice of ethnic cleansing, it should be noted, has been employed by all three sides in the conflict in Bosnia; however, the Serbian forces and the rump Yugoslav regime bear responsibility for recruiting, training, enfranchising, and paying the worst perpetrators of this violence, the irregular forces of Arkan and Vojislav Šešelj. Many groups and observers, including Helsinki Watch, Amnesty International, the US State Department, and the International Court of Justice, share the belief that Serbia has been the initiator and principal perpetrator of ethnic cleansing. At the same time, Croatian armed forces and irregulars have engaged in widespread operations of ethnic cleansing. Muslims have also conducted ethnic cleansing operations and committed atrocities, although the Bosnian government, despite the immense stress under which it operated beginning in the spring of 1992, acted on numerous occasions to curb such activities.

The methodology of ethnic cleansing is terror practiced openly and ostentatiously, calculated to drive from their homes those longtime inhabitants belonging to the "wrong" ethnic group. Ethnic cleansing thus differs from the systematic, quiet extermination procedures used by the Germans against Jews, Gypsies, and others during World War II. The Germans set out to kill people without creating public furor; the ethnic cleansers of Bosnia use killings and other atrocities to sow fear and panic and to induce flight.

## Economic Revitalization of East Asia

*Thomas B. Gold*

*More than any other part of the world, east Asia came out of the second world war in a state of extreme disruption and devastation. Japanese leaders had brought their people to the verge of starvation even before the massive American firebombing of Tokyo and the dropping of two atomic bombs. China had been at war with Japan since 1931 only to see the end of that war*

SOURCE: Thomas B. Gold, "Economic Revitalization of East Asia," in *Asia in the Core Curriculum: Case Studies in the Social Sciences*, Myron L. Cohen, ed., pp. 464–69.

*in 1945 followed by five years of brutal civil war. Taiwan, which had been bombed prior to 1945, had its resources stretched even more with the arrival of 2 to 3 million Chinese from the mainland as the Nationalists (Guomindang/GMD) were losing the war against the communists. Korea went through its own devastating war in 1950–53.*

*Economic recovery seemed very distant indeed, given this desolation, the region's lack of raw materials and sufficient foodstuffs, and the traditional Confucian (in China, Korea, Japan, and Vietnam) view of the merchant (who was at the bottom rung of the social ladder) being immoral because of the pursuit of profits. But Confucianism also placed very high value on education, particularly rote memory. It also taught loyalty to, and dependence on, a collective entity: family, enterprise, and the state.*

*In recent years Japan, Korea (at least South Korea), Hong Kong, Taiwan, and Singapore—all Confucian states—have become enormously successful economically. There are many complicated reasons for this, but one certainly is the shared characteristic of a strong, centrally run state. In this excerpt Thomas B. Gold (professor of sociology at the University of California, Berkeley) examines how this attribute is linked to economic development.*

CONSIDER: *The relationship between economic growth and political democratization; the limitations of terms such as* socialist *and* capitalist *in describing economic systems.*

China, Japan, Taiwan, and South Korea **all share an economic model with a central role for the state.** This is multi-faceted. The strong state role in socialist China is well-known, but many are unaware of the major place of the state in the market-economies of Japan, Taiwan, and South Korea. In each of these countries, the state periodically produces plans for economic development; government agencies collect data on the local and international economies and make predictions as to their evolution. They target certain domestic sectors for special incentives (tax breaks and rebates, low-interest loans, access to foreign exchange, reduced import tariffs, etc.) in order to motivate local businesses to invest in those target industries. The states have considerable control over the banking system (through ownership of major shares in a number of banks and administration of the postal savings systems), which facilitates implementation of fiscal policies. The states also own many enterprises in key sectors, often as monopolies, enabling them to direct certain materials to targeted companies. These are **indicative plans,** not the command-type plans of a Soviet-style economy as in pre-reform PRC. What is more, they are **market-conforming,** that is, they try to anticipate market developments and assist private businesses to take optimal advantage of future trends. In addition to these positive tactics, the states can use various sanctions to elicit the desired response. By withholding incentives and licenses, imposing punitive taxes, auditing books, and exercising various forms of political coercion, the states can motivate recalcitrant businesses to conform. These are economies attuned to the market and they have large, vibrant private sectors, but they are not strictly free enterprise economies as is often argued, because the state, directly and indirectly, is a major actor. Its role has shrunk since the 1950s, but it nonetheless continues to be a determinant.

An additional important role of the state that has had positive economic consequences has been its **massive investment in education in order to develop human capital.** The literacy rate in Japan, Taiwan, and South Korea exceeds 90 percent. There is severe competition for advanced education, but the governments have also invested in vocational training in order to provide a highly qualified cadre of technicians and workers.

There are a number of reasons for the dominance of the state in East Asian economies. **In East Asian tradition, people expect the state to play a dominant role in their lives, helping to create prosperity and ensuring social harmony; failure to do so is considered grounds for rebellion.** There is the historical legacy of the Confucian bureaucracy placing constraints on the activities of merchants, although one of the revolutionary aspects of contemporary East Asia is the high social prestige given to private businessmen. Bureaucrats still enjoy high status and a certain degree of insulation from politics, enabling them to work according to objective criteria.

As part of the 1868 Meiji Reform in Japan, the central leadership took a forceful approach to developing the country's economy in order to make it wealthy and strong and thereby able to fend off Western imperialists. Japan took Taiwan, Korea, and Manchuria as colonies and implemented similar statist policies for their economies, introducing a structure which subsequent postcolonial governments adopted and continued. As in many underdeveloped economies, only the state had the necessary capital to establish key enterprises and build the infrastructure required for industrialization. This legacy of state-owned enterprises in crucial sectors has continued to the present.

Also, the governments of Taiwan and South Korea see themselves as under continued threat from their Communist enemies. This garrison mentality stimulates their efforts for economic development and legitimizes policies which interfere in private business decisions and activities in the name of national security. These governments are highly militarized and have created vast internal security networks, which frequently serve, through intimidation, to ensure compliance with state policies. It has also resulted in severe labor repression

and the maintenance of labor peace, at least as long as incomes keep ahead of inflation. In China, the Communist party controls labor unions tightly. Defining itself as the party of the proletariat, it legitimizes labor repression by claiming that strikes work against the workers' own interests. . . .

Japan, Taiwan, South Korea, and, now to a greater degree than ever, China have mixed planned and market economies, and a powerful state sector alongside a vibrant private sector. **The old dichotomies of capitalism and socialism are breaking down.** Other developing economies of various political stripes are increasingly attempting to adopt aspects of the East Asian systems. . . .

Perhaps the major shortcoming of the East Asian development experience has been the strict and often brutal political authoritarianism that has accompanied rapid economic growth. It has been suggested that this authoritarianism facilitated, indeed, is indispensable to growth, and is a small price to pay for the tremendous economic reward it has brought. In order for the state to play a strong role in guiding the economy and channelling resources efficiently, the argument goes, it needs to have unquestioned authority and force. This reasoning runs counter to the assumption, popular in the 1950s, that economic development would be accompanied by political "modernization," meaning the introduction of Western-style democratic institutions and practices. Although postwar Japan has instituted a democratic electoral system, in the 1930s its industrialization was led by a militarized fascistic state.

The KMT [GMD] brought to Taiwan a militarized state with a far-flung internal security network. Comprised of a small cohort of mainland émigrés, it monopolized political power over 85 percent of the population who, while also Chinese, had lived on the island prior to its retrocession in 1945 from Japanese to Chinese control. Similar in structure to a Leninist communist party, it penetrated Taiwan's society to stifle dissent and mobilize the people. It did not permit other parties and maintained its rule by martial law, dealing ruthlessly with its enemies.

The year 1987 proved to be a watershed for both Taiwan and South Korea. On Taiwan, the KMT abolished martial law and tacitly recognized the legitimacy of the opposition party, which until then had been illegal. It also began to step up exchanges with the Communist mainland, a sign of renewed confidence in itself and in its people. In January of 1988, President and KMT Chairman Chiang Ching-kuo died and was succeeded by Lee Teng-hui, a Taiwanese technocrat without military experience. The succession was peaceful, and the process of democratization and opening to the mainland continued and even accelerated. In South Korea, President

Chun Doo-hwan bowed to public pressure to permit a constitutional change allowing the direct election of his successor. After a campaign in which two leading opposition figures opposed each other as well as Chun's hand-picked candidate, Roh Tae-woo, it was Roh who emerged victorious. He proceeded to speed up political liberalization and in 1988 did not prevent the public censure of his predecessor. In both Taiwan and South Korea, street demonstrations have increased, and there is a very visible radical component among Korean students. But in both societies, the process of political democratization has definitely begun; political modernization is catching up with economic and social development.

## The Short Century—It's Over

### John Lukacs

*Historians have traditionally been interested in dividing their study and analysis of civilizations into eras or periods that make some sense—ideally that begin and end with some watershed developments and have some unifying characteristics. This is particularly difficult to do for our own time, for we lack some historical perspective. In the following selection, John Lukacs argues that in 1989 watershed events occurred in the West, bringing the 20th century to an end and initiating the 21st century.*

CONSIDER: *How Lukacs supports his argument; whether his argument works as well for the non-Western world; what this might mean for the future.*

The 20th century is now over, and there are two extraordinary matters about this.

First, this was a short century. It lasted 75 years, from 1914 to 1989. Its two principal events were the two world wars. They were the two enormous mountain ranges that dominated its landscape. The Russian Revolution, the atom bomb, the end of the colonial empires, the establishment of the Communist states, the emergence of the two superpowers, the division of Europe and of Germany—all of these were the consequences of the two world wars, in the shadow of which we were living, until now.

The 19th century lasted exactly 99 years, from 1815 to 1914, from the end of Napoleon's wars to the start of the—so-called—First World War. The 18th century lasted 126 years, from 1689 to 1815, from the beginning of the world wars between England and France (of which the American War of Independence was but part) until their end at Waterloo.

Second, we know that the 20th century is over. In 1815, no one knew that this was the end of the Atlantic world wars and the beginning of the Hundred Years' Peace. At that time, everyone, friends as well as enemies of the French Revolution, were concerned with the prospect of great revolutions surfacing again. There were revolutions after 1815, but the entire history of the 19th century was marked by the absence of world wars during 99 years. Its exceptional prosperity and progress were due to that.

In 1689, the very word *century* was hardly known. The *Oxford English Dictionary* notes its first present usage, in English, in 1626. Before that the word meant a Roman military unit of 100 men; then it began to have another meaning, that of 100 years. It marked the beginning of our modern historical consciousness.

We know that the 20th century is over—not merely because of our historical consciousness (which is something different from a widespread knowledge of history) but mainly because the confrontation of the two superpowers, the outcome of the Second World War, has died down. The Russians have retreated from Eastern Europe and Germany has been reunited. Outside Europe, even the Korean and the Vietnam wars, the missile crisis in Cuba and other political crises such as Nicaragua were, directly or indirectly, involved with that confrontation.

In 1991, we live in a very different world, in which, both the U.S. and the Soviet Union face grave problems with peoples and dictators in the so-called third world. Keep in mind that the ugly events in Lithuania are no exception to this: They involve the political structure of the Soviet Union itself. Even its name, the Union of Soviet Socialist Republics, is becoming an anachronism, as once happened with the Holy Roman Empire.

Keep in mind, too, that no matter when and how the Gulf war ends, the so-called Middle East will remain a serious problem both for the U.S. and the Soviet Union. Even in the case of a smashing American political or military victory, its beneficial results will be ephemeral. To think—let alone speak—of a Pax Americana in the Middle East is puerile nonsense.

Not only the configuration of great powers and their alliances but the very structure of political history has changed. Both superpowers have plenty of domestic problems. In the Soviet Union, this has now become frighteningly actual; in the U.S., the internal problems are different but not superficial. The very sovereignty and cohesion of states, the authority and efficacy of the governments are not what they were.

Are we going to see ever larger and larger political units? "Europe" will, at best, become a free-trade economic zone, but a Union of Europe is a mirage. Or are we more likely going to see the break-up of several states into small national ones? Are we going to see a large-scale migration of millions of peoples, something that has not happened since the last centuries of the Roman Empire? This is at least possible. The very texture of history is changing before our very eyes.

Are we on the threshold of a new Dark Ages? We must hope not. The main task before us is the rethinking of the word *progress*. Like that of *century*, the meaning of that word, too, is more recent than we have been accustomed to think. Before the 16th century, that is, before the opening of the so-called modern age (another misnomer, suggesting that this age would last forever) *progress* simply meant an advance in distance, not in time, without the sense of evolutionary improvement.

Thereafter, the word *progress* began to carry the unquestionable optimistic meaning of endless material and scientific promise, until, during the 20th century, it began to lose some of its shine, because of the increasingly questionable benefits of technology. At the beginning of the 20th century, technology and barbarism seemed to be antitheses. They no longer are. But technology and its threat to the natural environment are only part of the larger problem of progress, a word and an ideal whose more proper and true application is the task of the 21st century that has already begun.

## Revolution and the Intellectual in Latin America

*Alan Riding*

*The political boundaries of Latin American nations have produced national identities and rivalries. But over the course of the past century, a broader Latin American nationalism has survived and even flourished. Common language, interlocked histories, and cultures have led Latin Americans—especially intellectuals—to articulate a common identity. This excerpt by Alan Riding looks at the importance of this special identity for Latin American intellectuals, who are central political as well as literary figures.*

CONSIDER: *Why intellectuals in Latin America are so concerned with political issues; why there is not a greater distinction between art and politics in Latin American culture.*

[I]ntellectuals exercise enormous political influence in Latin America. It is they who provide respectability to governments in power and legitimacy to revolts and revolutionary movements, they who articulate the ideas and contribute the images through which Latin Americans

SOURCE: Alan Riding, "Revolution and the Intellectual in Latin America," *The New York Times,* March 13, 1963. Copyright © 1963 by The New York Times Company. Reprinted by permission.

relate to power, they who satisfy the decidedly Latin need for a romantic and idealistic raison d'être. . . .

"Why is it like this?" Mario Vargas Llosa, the Peruvian novelist, asked in a recent essay. "Why is it that instead of being basically creators and artists, writers in Peru and other Latin American countries must above all be politicians, agitators, reformers, social publicists and moralists?"

The question may be even more puzzling to people in the United States, where the political influence of writers and other intellectuals is exercised far more subtly and indirectly, and politics mainly has to do with specific issues rather than ideologies. . . .

Intellectuals may not be the principal actors in the Latin drama, but they define the issues. Before causes win out, it is their ideas that triumph. Nothing less than the continent's long-range political evolution may be at stake.

The Latin intellectual's position grows out of the society in which he lives. In a region characterized by weak social institutions, inadequate public education and little democratic tradition, intellectuals automatically belong to a prestigious elite. And because Latin American politics invariably revolves around personalities, men of talent are looked to for wisdom and leadership.

Taken together, the intellectuals of Latin America form a kind of unofficial parliament in which the major political events of the day are discussed, integrated into the regional agenda, or allowed to fade from the public consciousness. . . .

This kind of political eminence rarely brings wealth—few Latin writers can survive on their royalties and only García Márquez, whose books have been translated into many languages, can be called rich. But it does make writers into powerful political symbols, particularly if they have been recognized abroad, and few of today's top Latin American authors show many qualms about making full use of this power. . . .

While they come from different countries, the writers' audience is continental, not only because they project a strong sense of a common Latin American identity but because the issues they raise are familiar throughout the region. Almost without exception, they write widely syndicated columns and give frequent interviews—more often about politics than about literature—that are read across Latin America. They frequently gather at conferences that issue sweeping declarations on world issues. And while their political opinions may be challenged, their moral authority is rarely questioned. . . .

Thus, the Latin American intellectual owes his role not only to the fact that so relatively few others in his society are well educated: He is also heir to a general European tradition. What distinguishes him even from the

European intellectual, however, is the special tradition of dogma that he inherited from Catholic Spain and that still weighs down political thought in the hemisphere.

For three centuries after the Spanish Conquest, most Latin intellectuals came from the ranks of the clergy and observed the limitations on free thought dictated by the Spanish Inquisition. Such minimal dissent as existed could only come from within the church. Priests, for example, were the first to protest the enslavement of the Indians in colonial Mexico. Yet whatever the intellectual debate at the time, it revolved around the prevailing Catholic dogma. Priests organized Mexico's independence movement against Spain, but their troops followed the standard of the Virgin of Guadalupe. Even the Liberal Reforms that swept across Latin America in the 19th century became almost dogmatic in their anticlericalism.

This doctrinaire past facilitated the transition to Marxism following the 1917 Bolshevik revolution in Moscow. In Latin America, Marxism became the new creed and intellectuals its new priests, while the state was assigned the church's old role of organizing society. "We are the sons of rigid ecclesiastic societies," says the Mexican novelist Carlos Fuentes. "This is the burden of Latin America—to go from one church to another, from Catholicism to Marxism, with all its dogma and ritual. This way we feel protected."

## Reviving African Culture

### Ali A. Mazrui and Michael Tidy

*Modern African nationalists have expressed concern over continuing "cultural imperialism" whereby colonial regimes had set a cultural agenda for Africa that was rooted not in African but in Western experience. Many intellectuals and scholars have called for cultural emancipation or liberation, a return to traditional values, a greater use of African languages, and a development of new philosophies and ideologies based in the African experience. Others, however, seek a more balanced development of existing cultural forms, including continued use of European languages for international communication, higher education, and national unity. Ali Mazrui, one of the authors of this excerpt, is a well-known proponent of the rediscovery and fuller use of the African traditional background. He lays out some of his thoughts in the following selection.*

CONSIDER: *To what extent the ideology of national culture is a practical idea; how Africans might work within a cultural*

*policy that stressed both Western and African elements; Ali's concern for the integrity of national cultures.*

The cultural tyranny of a Eurocentric world culture that was imposed on Africa during the colonial period has largely withstood the fairly tame assaults launched against it by independent African governments and African writers. In the fields of language policy, education and even literature only limited efforts have been made so far toward cultural liberation.

One of the obstacles to cultural liberation has been an excessive emphasis on the part of writers and scholars on political and economic liberation as processes in themselves, divorced from the struggle for cultural independence. Much of the earlier literature on modernization in Africa concentrated on political development, and too readily assumed that the road to political development lay through Westernization. Political development was envisaged in terms of building institutions comparable to those of Western systems. More recently there has grown up a new rival literature based on the concept of dependency, in which the whole concept of development has been either rejected or drastically redefined. Where it has been redefined, development is now conceived in terms of a progressive reduction in economic dependence. . . . Although some writers have emphasized economic decolonization, cultural decolonization is more fundamental than many have assumed. Mental and intellectual dependency, a lack of readiness to break loose from the metropolitan power, and a compulsive urge to imitate and emulate the West are factors that have on the whole had grave economic and political consequences for societies which are still unwilling to take drastic decisions for their own transformation; they are also phenomena with deep cultural causes. . . .

Another obstacle to cultural liberation has been the confusion of the concept of modernization with Westernization. In fact, retraditionalization of African culture can take modernizing forms, especially if it becomes an aspect of decolonization. Retraditionalization does not mean returning Africa to what it was before the Europeans came. In hard assessment, it would be suicidal for Africa to attempt such a backward leap. But a move towards renewed respect for indigenous ways and the conquest of cultural self-contempt may be the minimal conditions for cultural decolonization.

Amílcar Cabral, the Guinea-Bissau freedom fighter, pointed out that the African Westernized élite led the struggle for political independence because, having experienced Western education, it was the sector which most rapidly became aware of the need to win freedom from foreign domination. But this élite was culturally alienated and therefore fell victim to a neo-colonialist mentality and it therefore needed to be "reborn." Cabral's solution to the problem of the rebirth of the

SOURCE: Ali A. Mazrui and Michael Tidy, *Nationalism and New States in Africa* (Portsmouth, NH: Heinemann Educational Books, 1984). Reprinted with permission.

élite was to return "to the source," to the culture of the mass of the people. Colonialism was short-lived, lasting only about 70 years in most of Africa, and the colonial social structure and European culture affected the rural masses very little. "Repressed, persecuted, humiliated, betrayed by certain social groups who have compromised with the foreign power, culture took refuge in the villages, in the forests, and in the spirits of the victims of domination." The culturally alienated élite must repossess much of the culture of the villages in order to achieve identification with the masses, understand their needs and problems and mobilize them for social and economic development.

Almost every African state has a long way to go on the road to cultural emancipation, to adopt a language policy of relevance to African culture, to transform its educational system, to develop literature and arts of relevant kinds, as well as to pursue an ideology which puts a premium on autonomy and to build a political system which gives weight to the culturally more authentic peasants.

## Democracy in South Africa

### Nelson Mandela

*Nelson Mandela, who became the first president of a democratic South Africa in 1994 at the age of 78, had spent his entire adult life fighting for a democratic and multiracial South Africa. As a member of the African National Congress (ANC), a multiethnic organization founded in 1912, Mandela became one of the most influential leaders of the organization. He spearheaded most of the nonviolent campaigns the organization undertook in its attempts to bring an end to the apartheid system that Boers had instituted after 1948. Mandela was responsible for the development of the military wing of the ANC, and he, along with many members of the ANC leadership, spent a total of 28 years in the infamous Robben Island prison as political prisoners. Imprisonment did not stop Mandela and his fellow inmates, for they continued the fight. In 1990 Mandela and other political prisoners gained their freedom, and the ANC, along with other anti-apartheid organizations, was legalized. In the following excerpt Mandela describes his emotions on the day he was inaugurated as the first president of a democratic South Africa.*

CONSIDER: *The lack of bitterness in Mandela's speech; Mandela's reflection on the meaning of struggle; Mandela's notion of courage.*

MAY 10 DAWNED bright and clear. For the past few days, I had been pleasantly besieged by arriving dignitaries and world leaders who were coming to pay their respects before the inauguration. The inauguration would be the largest gathering ever of international leaders on South African soil. . . .

I said:

Today, all of us do, by our presence here . . . confer glory and hope to newborn liberty. Out of the experience of an extraordinary human disaster that lasted too long, must be born a society of which all humanity will be proud.

. . . We, who were outlaws not so long ago, have today been given the rare privilege to be host to the nations of the world on our own soil. We thank all of our distinguished international guests for having come to take possession with the people of our country of what is, after all, a common victory for justice, for peace, for human dignity.

We have, at last, achieved our political emancipation. We pledge ourselves to liberate all our people from the continuing bondage of poverty, deprivation, suffering, gender, and other discrimination.

Never, never, and never again shall it be that this beautiful land will again experience the oppression of one by another. . . . The sun shall never set on so glorious a human achievement.

Let freedom reign. God bless Africa!

A few moments later we all lifted our eyes in awe as a spectacular array of South African jets, helicopters, and troop carriers roared in perfect formation over the Union Buildings. It was not only a display of pinpoint precision and military force, but a demonstration of the military's loyalty to democracy, to a new government that had been freely and fairly elected. Only moments before, the highest generals of the South African Defense Force and police, their chests bedecked with ribbons and medals from days gone by, saluted me and pledged their loyalty. I was not unmindful of the fact that not so many years before they would not have saluted but arrested me. Finally a chevron of Impala jets left a smoke trail of the black, red, green, blue, white, and gold of the new South African flag.

The day was symbolized for me by the playing of our two national anthems, and the vision of whites singing "Nkosi Sikelel' iAfrika" and blacks singing "Die Stem," the old anthem of the republic. Although that day, neither group knew the lyrics of the anthem they once despised, they would soon know the words by heart.

On the day of the inauguration, I was overwhelmed with a sense of history. In the first decade of the twentieth century, a few years after the bitter Anglo-Boer War and before my own birth, the white-skinned peoples of South Africa patched up their differences and erected a system of racial domination against the dark-skinned peoples of their own land. The structure they created

SOURCE: Nelson Mandela, *Long Walk to Freedom* (Little, Brown and Co., 1995), pp. 620–22.

formed the basis of one of the harshest, most inhumane societies the world has ever known. Now, in the last decade of the twentieth century, and my own eighth decade as a man, that system had been overturned forever and replaced by one that recognized the rights and freedoms of all peoples regardless of the color of their skin.

That day had come about through the unimaginable sacrifices of thousands of my people, people whose suffering and courage can never be counted or repaid. I felt that day, as I have on so many other days, that I was simply the sum of all those African patriots who had gone before me. That long and noble line ended and now began again with me. I was pained that I was not able to thank them and that they were not able to see what their sacrifices had wrought.

The policy of apartheid created a deep and lasting wound in my country and my people. All of us will spend many years, if not generations, recovering from that profound hurt. But the decades of oppression and brutality had another, unintended effect, and that was that it produced the Oliver Tambos, the Walter Sisulus, the Chief Luthulis, the Yusuf Dadoos, the Bram Fischers, the Robert Sobukwes of our time—men of such extraordinary courage, wisdom, and generosity that their like may never be known again. Perhaps it requires such depth of oppression to create such heights of character. My country is rich in the minerals and gems that lie beneath its soil, but I have always known that its greatest wealth is its people, finer and truer than the purest diamonds.

死ね——っ
チビ野郎!!

**Illustration 26–2** "Die Punk!" from comic book *Football Taka* (Football Hawk) by Noboru Kawasaki.

## Football Hawk: The Japanese Comic Book
*Noboru Kawasaki*

*In contemporary Japan one of the most important forms of popular culture is comic books—manga. Japanese comic books are not like American ones; they are designed largely for adults of all social strata and convey a wide array of stories from pornography to sports. They were so popular that in 1984 one billion were published—27 for every household in Japan.*

*Their popularity has much to do with the nature of Japanese society. There is little physical space, inhabitable land is at a premium, and houses are very small. In addition, school and after-school tutoring leave children little time for play. For adults, the rules of society are extremely rigid. Comic books are thus easy forms of escape for everyone.*

*Comic books are also avenues of transmitting traditional Japanese values, even if they are wrapped in a new format. For example, values of bushido, the martial spirit of the samurai, are conveyed in fantasies concerning team sports. American football—Amefukami—is especially popular. Engaging in combat, men dressed in uniforms learn about team spirit, strategy, and tactics.*

This drawing is from a comic book called Football Taka (Football Hawk) by Noboru Kawasaki. It portrays a Japanese hero named Taka who is smaller than his American opponent but fearless nevertheless. He is shouting "die punk" as he charges. Taka represents the spirit of the kamikaze pilots who used their tiny planes against the behemoth American battleships.

CONSIDER: The use of modern images and metaphors to transmit traditional values and how this perpetuates a culture.

## The Growth of Cities

World population in 1999 passed 6 billion—more than double that at the end of World War II. The poorer southern half of the globe carried the heaviest burden of population growth. The distinction between Europe and the rest of the world in population trends is also reflected in the process of urbanization. This map shows those areas with the largest urban populations and the growth of population in the world's largest cities.

CONSIDER: Where the greatest growth of large cities has been and is expected to occur; what problems this growth of urban population poses for the West and the world.

## Global Environmental Problems

Economic growth, population increases, and urbanization created alarming environmental problems in the late 20th century. The earth's air, water, and seas became more and more polluted, while acid raid, caused by smoke and fumes, damaged forests. Asia has been particularly hard hit; 13 of the 15 cities with the worst air pollution in the world were in Asia, while the majority of the estimated 2.7 million people worldwide who died each year from illnesses caused by air pollution were Asians. This map reveals the spread of these environmental problems.

CONSIDER: Which areas of the world are affected more than others by environmental problems; how some of these problems might be interconnected; what other environmental problems are not adequately revealed by this map.

## Ecological Threats

*Edward O. Wilson*

In recent decades, many people and organizations have turned their attention to ecological problems facing the world. Population growth and the depletion of the earth's living

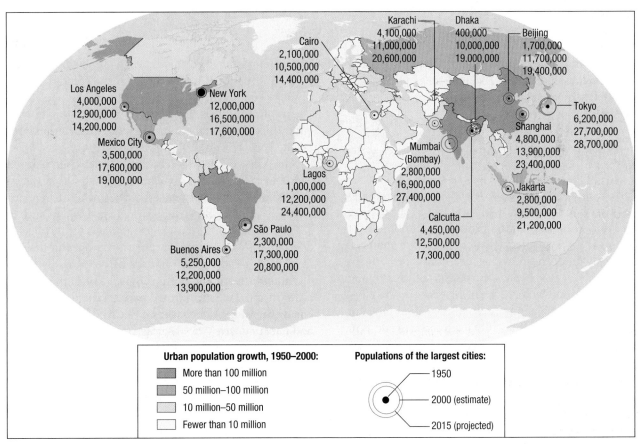

Map 26–1

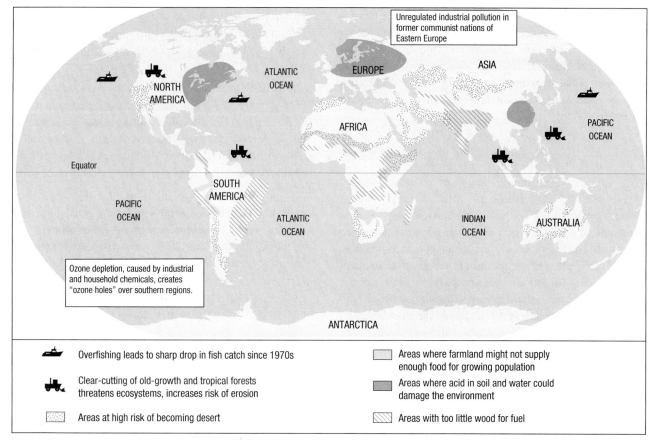

Unregulated industrial pollution in former communist nations of Eastern Europe

Ozone depletion, caused by industrial and household chemicals, creates "ozone holes" over southern regions.

Overfishing leads to sharp drop in fish catch since 1970s

Clear-cutting of old-growth and tropical forests threatens ecosystems, increases risk of erosion

Areas at high risk of becoming desert

Areas where farmland might not supply enough food for growing population

Areas where acid in soil and water could damage the environment

Areas with too little wood for fuel

Map 26–2

*resources are two of the most important problems. In the following selection, Edward O. Wilson, a well-known biologist, addresses these and suggests some steps that need to be taken.*

CONSIDER: *Why population growth in some parts of the world poses particularly great difficulties; why deforestation is so important; Wilson's solutions and whether you agree they will work.*

The pace of population growth and environmental destruction has continued with no visible pause, having become a case study in the principle of unintended results wherein mass effects float up from vast numbers of seemingly innocent individual decisions. . . .

. . . [E]very country has three forms of wealth: material, cultural, and biological. The first two are the basis of almost all our economic and political life. The third, composed of the fauna and flora and the uses put to natural diversity, is far more potent for long-term human welfare than generally appreciated, and it is declining irreversibly through the accelerating extinction of species

and genetic strains. Furthermore, the problem is distinctively international in scope. By far the greatest variety of life occurs in the developing countries, especially in the tropics, and it is there also that population growth, environmental degradation, and species extinction have reached crisis levels.

The scope of the problem can be briefly summarized as follows: The rate of population growth has begun to slow on every continent except Africa, where it remains as rapid as ever. But even with a modest amount of global amelioration, most demographers still project a doubling of the standing population, from the present five billion to at least ten billion, before it finally levels off around the middle of the 2100s. Most of the growth is destined to be concentrated in just a few regions, principally the Indian subcontinent, the Middle East, Africa, and Latin America. So disproportionate is this distribution that the projected growth for North America, all of Europe, and the Soviet Union is less than the additions expected in either Bangladesh or Nigeria. . . .

Well over two billion people have already been added in the developing countries since 1932, more than the entire world population of that time. This spurt of growth is entirely unprecedented in the history of the

SOURCE: Edward O. Wilson, "Conservation: The Next Hundred Years," in *Conservation for the Twenty-First Century*, ed. David Western and Mary Pearl (Oxford: Oxford University Press, 1989), pp. 3–7 as excerpted.

world, and it has already led to a great deal of poverty and failed hopes. According to The World Bank, of the 2.5 billion people now living in the tropics, one billion live in a condition of absolute poverty. This means that the family head is unable to count on being able to provide food, shelter, and clothing for himself and his family from one day to the next. . . .

. . . The rate of tropical forest destruction is now reasonably well known, thanks to improvements in satellite scanning and increasingly accurate ground surveys. By the late 1970s, according to estimates from the Food and Agricultural Organization and United Nations Environmental Programme, 76,000 square kilometers, or nearly 1 percent of the total cover per annum, were being permanently cleared or converted into the shifting-cultivation cycle. The absolute amount is greater than the area of West Virginia or the entire country of Costa Rica. In effect, most of this land is being permanently cleared, that is, reduced to a state in which natural reforestation will be very difficult if not impossible to achieve. . . .

The current reduction of diversity thus seems destined to approach that of the great natural catastrophes at the end of the Paleozoic and Mesozoic eras—in other words, the most extreme for 65 million years. . . .

*What Is to Be Done?*

1. A complete biotic survey. I am convinced that the needs of humanity in the context of the biodiversity crisis demand nothing less than a complete catalog of life on the earth. . . .

2. . . . The biotic survey should be accompanied by a more nearly comprehensive effort to build larger seed banks than now exist, as well as to expand populations of some of the most threatened species of plants and animals in zoos and botanical gardens. . . .

3. Combining conservation and economic development. Conservation is inseparably linked to the future of economic development by a form of mutualistic symbiosis. Biodiversity will be impoverished without the shaping of land use in a form that preserves it, and economic development will be hindered and eventually reversed if it omits the kind of environmental policy that reserves and uses biodiversity. . . .

4. Pressures from assistance and lending agencies. It is in the interest of each country in turn to use its natural resources so as to get a sustained yield rather than a short-term yield, even when the latter may be very high. The question for the pure utilitarian is whether to take a tidy one-time profit or a vastly larger profit over generations of time. There is only one moral choice. To cut down a virgin rain forest may produce a few million dollars during a ten-year period, but then it is gone forever, the age-old patrimony of the country having been diminished by the loss of many of its native species, the soil having been impoverished, and the hydrological cycle and water tables soon to be altered unfavorably. . . .

5. Restoration ecology. . . . National parks and biosphere reserves can be expanded. Natural ecosystems can be reconstituted in forms that both restore the original biodiversity and add to productivity in agriculture and forestry. . . .

6. Engagement by the social sciences. One of the many weaknesses of the social sciences is their failure to make realistic assessments of the environment, including biodiversity. They have virtually nothing to say about how behavior and economic health are related to the living world in which the human mind evolved over millions of years. In this respect neoclassical economics is bankrupt. . . .

7. Aesthetic and moral reasoning. Environmental ethics, still a small and neglected branch of intellectual activity, deserves to become a major branch of the humanities during the next hundred years. In the end, when all the accounting is done, conservation will boil down to a decision of ethics based on empirical knowledge: How we value the natural world in which we evolved and now, increasingly, how we regard our status as individuals.

## The AIDS Epidemic

*This map shows the number of adult people living with HIV/AIDS in various parts of the world at the end of 1999. The accompanying chart details some of the damage this epidemic has caused and what looms in the future.*

CONSIDER: *What areas of the world have been hardest hit by AIDS; what social problems might stem from this epidemic.*

## Globalization

*Thomas L. Friedman*

*Scholars looking at Western history since the fall of Communism have tried to come up with terms that best characterize the period. Several scholars have focused on "globalization" as the outstanding quality of this period. While some historians also use the term in descriptions of the post-1945 world and even the world during the decades just before World War I, globalization now refers to something different in quantity*

SOURCE: Thomas L. Friedman, *The Lexus and the Olive Tree* (New York: Farrar, Straus, Giroux, 1999), pp. 7–12.

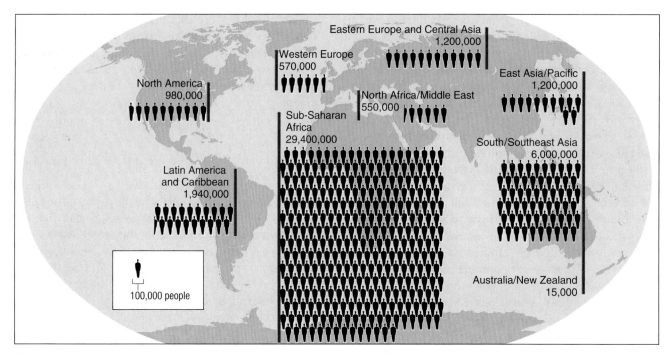

**Map 26–3**

and quality. In the following selection from his well-received book, The Lexus and the Olive Tree, Thomas L. Friedman analyzes the meaning of the globalization system by comparing it with its predecessor, the Cold War system.

CONSIDER: What Friedman means by the "globalization system"; how it differs from the "Cold War system"; the three "balances" that structure the globalization system.

Today's era of globalization, which replaced the Cold War, is a similar international system, with its own unique attributes.

To begin with, the globalization system, unlike the Cold War system, is not static, but a dynamic ongoing process: globalization involves the inexorable integration of markets, nation-states and technologies to a degree never witnessed before—in a way that is enabling individuals, corporations and nation-states to reach around the world farther, faster, deeper and cheaper than ever before, and in a way that is also producing a powerful backlash from those brutalized or left behind by this new system.

The driving idea behind globalization is free-market capitalism—the more you let market forces rule and the more you open your economy to free trade and competition, the more efficient and flourishing your economy will be. Globalization means the spread of free-market capitalism to virtually every country in the world. Globalization also has its own set of economic rules—rules that revolve around opening, deregulating and privatizing your economy.

**Chart 26–1 Global Summary of the HIV/AIDS Epidemic, 1999**

| People newly infected with HIV in 1999 | Total | 5.4 million |
| | Adults | 4.7 million |
| | *Women* | *2.3 million* |
| | Children < 15 years | 620,000 |
| Number of people living with HIV/AIDS | Total | 34.3 million |
| | Adults | 33.0 million |
| | *Women* | *15.7 million* |
| | Children < 15 years | 1.3 million |
| AIDS deaths in 1999 | Total | 2.8 million |
| | Adults | 2.3 million |
| | *Women* | *1.2 million* |
| | Children < 15 years | 500,000 |
| Total number of AIDS deaths since the beginning of the epidemic | Total | 18.8 million |
| | Adults | 15.0 million |
| | *Women* | *7.7 million* |
| | Children < 15 years | 3.8 million |
| Total number of AIDS orphans[1] since the beginning of the epidemic | | 13.2 million[1] |

[1]Children who lost their mother or both parents to AIDS when they were under the age of 15.

Unlike the Cold War system, globalization has its own dominant culture, which is why it tends to be homogenizing. In previous eras this sort of cultural homogenization happened on a regional scale—the Hellenization of the Near East and the Mediterranean world under the Greeks, the Turkification of Central

Asia, North Africa, Europe and the Middle East by the Ortomans, or the Russification of Eastern and Central Europe and parts of Eurasia under the Soviets. Culturally speaking, globalization is largely, though not entirely, the spread of Americanization—from Big Macs to iMacs to Mickey Mouse—on a global scale.

Globalization has its own defining technologies: computerization, miniaturization, digitization, satellite communications, fiber optics and the Internet. And those technologies helped to create the defining perspective of globalization. If the defining perspective of the Cold War world was "division," the defining perspective of globalization is "integration." The symbol of the Cold War system was a wall, which divided everyone. The symbol of the globalization system is a World Wide Web, which unites everyone. The defining document of the Cold War system was "The Treaty." The defining document of the globalization system is "The Deal." . . .

Last, and most important, globalization has its own defining structure of power, which is much more complex than the Cold War structure. The Cold War system was built exclusively around nation-states, and it was balanced at the center by two superpowers: the United States and the Soviet Union.

The globalization system, by contrast, is built around three balances, which overlap and affect one another. The first is the traditional balance between nation-states. In the globalization system, the United States is now the sole and dominant superpower and all other nations are subordinate to it to one degree or another. The balance of power between the United States and the other states still matters for the stability of this system. . . .

The second balance in the globalization system is between nation-states and global markets. These global markets are made up of millions of investors moving money around the world with the click of a mouse. I call them "the Electronic Herd," and this herd gathers in key global financial centers, such as Wall Street, Hong Kong, London and Frankfurt, which I call "the Supermarkets." The attitudes and actions of the Electronic Herd and the Supermarkets can have a huge impact on nation-states today, even to the point of triggering the downfall of governments. . . .

The United States can destroy you by dropping bombs and the Supermarkets can destroy you by downgrading your bonds. The United States is the dominant player in maintaining the globalization gameboard, but it is not alone in influencing the moves on that gameboard. This globalization gameboard today is a lot like a Ouija board—sometimes pieces are moved around by the obvious hand of the superpower, and sometimes they are moved around by hidden hands of the Supermarkets.

The third balance that you have to pay attention to in the globalization system—the one that is really the newest of all—is the balance between individuals and nation-states. Because globalization has brought down many of the walls that limited the movement and reach of people, and because it has simultaneously wired the world into networks, it gives more power to individuals to influence both markets and nation-states than at any time in history. So you have today not only a superpower, not only Supermarkets, but, as I will also demonstrate later in the book, you have Super-empowered individuals. Some of these Super-empowered individuals are quite angry, some of them quite wonderful—but all of then are now able to act directly on the world stage without the traditional mediation of governments, corporations or any other public or private institutions.

## The Future after 9-11-01
### Niall Ferguson

*During the period after the September 11, 2001, terrorist attack on the United States, it seemed to many people that the country and large parts of the world were entering a new era with all sorts of changes radiating out from that attack. In the following selection, Oxford scholar Niall Ferguson argues that the importance of this event must be placed in the context of preexisting historical trends. He goes on to analyze what trends are likely to prove most important ten years after 9-11-01.*

CONSIDER: *Whether you agree with the key trends that Ferguson identifies; what you think was the significance of 9-11-01; the risks of historical prediction.*

In its immediate aftermath, the destruction of the World Trade Center looked like one of those events—the assassination at Sarajevo, the bombing of Pearl Harbor—that set history on a new course. Some excitable commentators began talking about "World War III" almost the same day the twin towers fell. . . . Tragic and spectacular though it was, that event was far less of a turning point than is generally believed.

We should be wary, in fact, of ever attaching too much importance to any single event. . . . The attacks on New York and Washington, however shocking, did not alter the direction of several underlying historical trends. In many respects the world will not be so very different in 2011 from the world as it would have evolved under the influence of those trends, even had the attacks not happened.

SOURCE: Niall Ferguson, "2011," *The New York Times Magazine*, December 2, 2001, pp. 76–79.

The first deep trend is obvious enough: the spread of terrorism—that is to say the use of violence by nonstate organizations in the pursuit of extreme political goals— to the United States. This kind of terrorism has been around for quite a while. Hijacking planes is certainly not new: since the late 1960's, when the tactic first began to be used systematically by the Palestine Liberation Organization and its sympathizers, there have been some 500 hijackings. As for the tactic of flying planes directly at populous targets, what else were the 3,913 Japanese pilots doing who killed themselves and many more American servicemen flying kamikaze missions in 1944 and 1945?

All that was really new on Sept. 11 was that these tried-and-tested tactics were applied in combination and in the United States. Between 1995 and 2000, according to State Department figures, there were more than 2,100 international terrorist attacks. But just 15 of them occurred in North America, causing just seven casualties. It was the successful extension of international terrorism to the United States that was the novelty. . . .

The bad news is that no amount of warfare against the states that harbor terrorists will rule out further attacks. The Western European experience of combating leftist and nationalist terrorism shows that the real war against terrorism has to be fought on the home front by domestic intelligence agencies, police forces and humdrum security guards around all potential targets. . . .

The second trend that Sept. 11 did nothing to change is the economic downturn. The asset bubble of the late 1990's peaked a year and a half before the terrorists struck. And despite their proximity to Wall Street the real crashes of Sept. 11 did not cause a metaphorical crash on the stock market—just its temporary closure. . . .

Nevertheless, the world economy has two serious economic weaknesses—also predating Sept. 11—that cannot be ignored.

The first is the nonglobal nature of globalization. Far from being perfectly integrated, the world's markets for goods, capital and labor appear to have become remarkably segmented. Thus, the overwhelming bulk of American, Canadian and Mexican trade now takes place within the North American Free Trade Area, just as most European trade takes place within Europe. Back in 1913, international capital was truly international: about 63 percent of foreign direct investment in 1913 went to developing countries. But in 1996, the proportion was just 28 percent. Labor mobility is also distorted, with the United States able to cherry-pick the best-qualified and most-talented workers from European and Asian economies under its various visa programs while letting in many more unskilled (and untaxed) Latino workers through the Mexican back door.

This is one key reason that the process we call globalization has tended to result in widening inequality between nations. In the 1960's, the richest fifth of the world's population had a total income 30 times as great as the poorest fifth's; in 1998, the ratio was 74:1. In 1965, real gross domestic product per capita in Chad was one-fifteenth of the U.S.'s; in 1990, *one-fiftieth*. If there was a substantial measure of convergence of incomes during the first age of globalization, in this age there is a pronounced divergence. And such inequality seems likely to increase the resentment felt in poorer countries toward the super-rich United States. . . .

Even more worrying is the medium-term outlook for global energy supplies. The rise of the S.U.V. as a status symbol shows how complacent Americans are about their supply of oil and petroleum. . . .

The realities are stark. The Middle East accounts for 31 percent of world oil production but just 6 percent of consumption. North America accounts for about 18 percent of world oil production but consumes 30 percent. Even more sobering, however, are the figures for world oil reserves: North America has just 6 percent of them; the Middle East 65 percent. . . . Kenneth S. Deffeyes of Princeton University predicts that global oil production will start to decline from 2004. At a conference at the Royal United Services Institute in London in October, experts warned that from 2008 supplies of non-OPEC oil will fall steeply—reaching close to zero in 2040—and that, barring some major technological breakthroughs, there will be an effective world shortage from 2010. . . .

There is a third trend that has been at work for more than a decade: the transition of American global power from informal to formal imperialism.

Since 1945, the United States has largely been content to exercise influence around the world indirectly: exercising economic leverage through multinational corporations and international agencies like the International Monetary Fund and political power through "friendly" indigenous regimes.

As Britain discovered in the 19th century, however, there are limits to what can be achieved by informal imperialism. Revolutions can overthrow the puppet rulers New regimes can default on their debts, disrupt trade, go to war with their neighbors—even sponsor terrorism.

Slowly and rather unreflectively, the United States has been responding to crises of this sort by intervening directly in the internal affairs of faraway countries. True, it has tended to do so behind a veil of multilateralism, acting in the name of the United Nations or NATO. But the precedents set in Bosnia and Kosovo are crucial. What happened in the 1990's was that those territories became a new kind of colony: international protectorates underwritten by U.S. military and monetary might. . . .

I have not yet raised one trend, much commented on—the supposedly inescapable "clash" between a democratic West and an intolerant Islam. From this viewpoint, Sept. 11 was a moment of *revelation* rather than redirection, as America belatedly woke up to a struggle the Muslim world has been fighting for years. I don't buy this.

Primarily that's because the most striking features of modern Islam are its amazing heterogeneity and geographical dispersion. Violence between ethnic or religious groups is not dividing the world into great blocs. As we have already seen in the Balkans (where we were inclined to side with the Muslims, don't forget), the tendency is for existing political units to fragment. So any clash of civilizations will occur not on conventional battlefields but in the streets of multicultural states like Bosnia—or even cities like Bradford in England, where gangs of Muslim youths rioted last summer. . . .

In this context, the main significance of movements like Islamic fundamentalism may lie in their centrifugal as opposed to centripetal effects. Rather than at anticipating a clash between monolithic civilizations, we should expect a continued process of political disintegration as religious and ethnic conflicts challenge the integrity of existing multicultural nation-states. Civil war has, after all, been the most frequent kind of war since 1945: something like two-thirds of all postwar conflicts have been *within* rather than between states. From Yugoslavia to Iraq to Afghanistan, what the United States keeps having to confront is not a united Islam but a succession of fractured polities, racked by internecine war. (The same could be said about Somalia, Sierra Leone and Rwanda.)

## Islam and Democracy

*Bahgat Korany*

*The West has long sought, rhetorically at least, to spread democracy and pluralism throughout the world. This effort has been intensified since the collapse of communism and the rise of globalism. But there is a huge gap between rhetoric and reality. Moreover, what works in Europe or the United States does not necessarily fit with other cultures, traditions, religions, and societies. Since Western colonialism and imperialism are also associated with democracy, its introduction is bound to be influenced by Muslim hostility to anything having to do with the West.*

*While there are some vivid examples of democracy in Islamic states (Turkey, Malaysia, and Indonesia, for example), the question of whether Islam and democracy are*

SOURCE: Bahgat Korany, "Arab Democratization," *Political Science and Politics*, Vol 27, No. 3 (September 1994), pp. 511–13 as excerpted.

*compatible is the subject of considerable debate both outside and inside the Muslim world, where reformers have been calling in recent years for a "liberal Islam." Any attempt to introduce liberal democracy into most of the Islamic world will be challenged by both religious authorities and the traditional power-holders. Moreover, traditional authoritarian rule possesses a measure of social legitimacy in these societies. In the end modernization and all its attributes will only succeed in some form of compromise with the theological forces and the traditional elites who will battle furiously to prevent any diminution in their power, even if it is for the betterment of their people. In the following excerpt, Bahgat Korany, professor of political science and the director of the Inter-University Consortium of Arab Studies at the Université de Montréal, argues that the introduction of democracy will be long and costly and, in the end, may not succeed.*

CONSIDER: *How the introduction of radically new ideas into a traditional society can upset the delicate balance of the society.*

The view adopted in this short paper assumes that the democratization process in the Arab countries will be both long and costly. The contagion effect might transform governments' piecemeal concessions into substantive democracy, but this is less probable than a situation of democratic breakdowns and incumbent governments presenting formal pluralism and controlled multipartism as the real thing. . . .

Democratization goes beyond a type of pluralist political system to denote a type of society based on respect of basic civil rights and an institutionalized political culture accepting and negotiating differences. The process in the Arab world presents on the whole altogether different characteristics.

1. The present process is not yet political democracy, nor even polyarchy, but at best a limited and shy process of organizational political pluralism (ta'addudiyya).

2. This ta'addudiyya is a regime response to crises— political and economic.

3. As a result, the whole democratization process is defensive, truncated, and tactical.

4. It can easily break down, i.e., it is neither linear nor irreversible. . . .

By using a shorthand like "the Arabs," or "Arab democratization," we tend to overhomogenize regimes. But a common characteristic—admittedly with varying degrees—is their extraversion or dependency. They are directly or indirectly rentier states. . . . Thus, the oil-based rentier state is not dependent on its citizens for financial resources. Quite the opposite. . . . If public finance is the basis of governability and political power, civil society is inescapably weak in the face of the rentier state's hegemony. . . .

In both primary and secondary rentier states, the road to democracy is full of stumbling blocks. For if democracy—rather than pluralism—begins from the bottom up, with the creation of a civil society consisting of a complex web of interrelationships and mutual responsibilities formed by the free choices of individuals and by the natural relationship among them, political participation at the top level of government is not enough. Democracy must grow from the grass roots of society upward through the creation and mediation of structures of community life. . . .

By all conventional indicators of modernization, from communication to education, Arab society has been going through a social revolution. Yet at the apex of the political pyramid, there is almost stagnation. . . .

In the face of this gap between social transformation and political stagnation, democratization is not only of academic interest; on the contrary, it is a political necessity to manage the transition. . . . For one of the dangers inherent in transition without the presence of strong opposition forces and viable political alternatives is the possibility of anarchy. . . .

In facing up to this ordeal of transformation and the engineering of peaceful transition, the taking into consideration of Islam and Islamic groups is unavoidable. . . . This brings us to the controversial relationship between Islam and democracy. . . .

The opposition between Islam and Western democracy is not a creation of the imagination or image-forgery. Between a sacred faith and a political doctrine, there are bound to be differences. But at the level of general norms, Islamic and Western democratic values tend to overlap, e.g., Islam's basic concepts of equality, justice. . . . Hassan El-Banna, the Egyptian founder of the Moslem Brotherhood in the late 1920s, affirmed in writing that parliamentary democracy and the holding of elections are not incompatible with Islam. . . .

Historically the practice of Western or political democracy in the Arab world cannot be separated from this region's encounter with a renascent colonial West, of advancing Christianity and defensives weakened Dar El-Islam (world of Islam). . . . Western democratization is inevitably associated in some sectors of the public psyche with outside intervention and coercion.

If anything, the colonial domination of the successor states—the empire's ex-Arab provinces—reinforced negative perceptions of Western democracy. Democratic form was artificially transplanted and was usually manipulated to serve the objectives of political control.

At the time of independence, indigenous elites inherited this paraphernalia of democracy without adding to its content. . . . The new state authorities continued pre-colonial and colonial practices of containing and controlling civil society, if not suppressing it. . . .

As a result, the historical legacy entails ambiguity toward the West and its mode of export. At one level the West is a model of power, progress, and civil liberties. At another level it is a symbol of past humiliation, repeated double standards, and empty political slogans. . . .

## The Middle East and Iraq, 2003

*Map 25–4 shows the Middle East, estimated oil reserves in several nations, and ethno-religious groups in Iraq. The oil reserves suggest one reason why the Middle East might be of such strategic importance to many areas in the world that depend on foreign sources for their energy needs. The war in Iraq, Iraq's internal divisions, the conflicts between Palestinians and Israelis, and the growth of international terrorism stemming from this region also reflect the instability and complexity of the Middle East.*

CONSIDER: *The ways war in Iraq might change this region; the problems facing those in Iraq who are trying to establish a stable, unified nation.*

## Religious Terrorism
### Mark Juergensmeyer

*Terrorism is not new. However, terrorist organizations grew alarmingly in the 1980s and 1990s and adopted bolder tactics aimed at both military and civilian targets. Events during the first years of the 21st century, such as the attacks on the United States on September 11, 2001, and those on Spain on March 11, 2004, suggest how deadly terrorism can become. In the following selection from* Terror in the Mind of God: The Global Rise of Religious Violence, *Mark Juergensmeyer focuses on religious terrorism.*

CONSIDER: *The meaning of religious terrorism according the Juergensmeyer; the possible causes for terrorism; what enables people to carry out acts of terrorism.*

Terrorism is meant to terrify. The word comes from the Latin *terrere*, "to cause to tremble," and came into common usage in the political sense, as an assault on civil order, during the Reign of Terror in the French Revolution at the close of the eighteenth century. Hence the public response to the violence—the trembling that terrorism effects—is part of the meaning of the term. It is appropriate, then, that the definition of a terrorist act is provided by us, the witnesses—the ones terrified—and not by the party committing the act. It is we—or more often our

SOURCE: Mark Juergensmeyer, *Terror in the Mind of God: The Global Rise of Violence* (Berkeley: The University of California Press, 2001), pp. 5–6, 11.

public agents, the news media—who affix the label on acts of violence that makes them terrorism. (These are public acts of destruction, committed without a clear military objective, that arouse a widespread sense of fear.)

This fear often turns to anger when we discover the other characteristic that frequently attends these acts of public violence: their justification by religion. Most people feel that religion should provide tranquility and peace, not terror. Yet in many of these cases religion has supplied not only the ideology but also the motivation and the organizational structure for the perpetrators. It is true that some terrorist acts are committed by public officials invoking a sort of "state terrorism" in order to subjugate the populace. The pogroms of Stalin, the government-supported death squads in El Salvador, the genocidal killings of the Khmer Rouge in Cambodia, ethnic cleansing in Bosnia and Kosovo, and government-spurred violence of the Hutus and Tutsis in Central Africa all come to mind. The United States has rightfully been accused of terrorism in the atrocities committed during the Vietnam War, and there is some basis for considering the nuclear bombings of Hiroshima and Nagasaki as terrorist acts.

But the term "terrorism" has more frequently been associated with violence committed by disenfranchised groups desperately attempting to gain a shred of power or influence. Although these groups cannot kill on the scale that governments with all their military power can, their sheer numbers, their intense dedication, and their dangerous unpredictability have given them influence vastly out of proportion with their meager military resources. Sonic of these groups have been inspired by purely secular causes. They have been motivated by leftist ideologies, as in the cases of the Shining Path and the Tupac Amaru in Peru, and the Red Army in Japan; and they have been propelled by a desire for ethnic or regional separatism, as in the cases of Basque militants in Spain and the Kurdish nationalists in the Middle East.

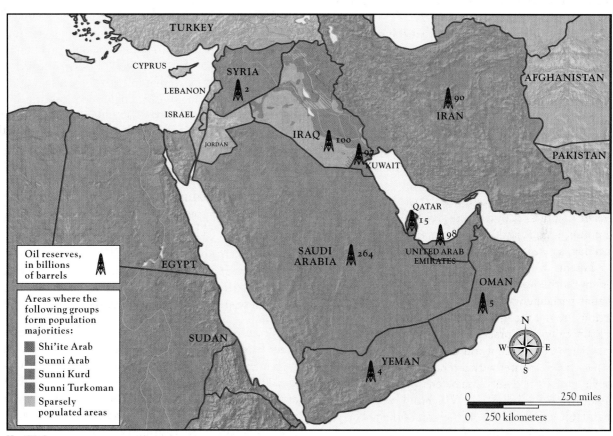

**Map 25–4**

But more often it has been religion—sometimes in combination with these other factors, sometimes as the primary motivation—that has incited terrorist acts. . . .

As these instances show, it takes a community of support and, in many cases, a large organizational network for an act of terrorism to succeed. It also requires an enormous amount of moral presumption for the perpetrators of these acts to justify the destruction of property on a massive scale or to condone a brutal attack on another life, especially the life of someone one scarcely knows and against whom one bears no personal enmity. And it requires a great deal of internal conviction, social acknowledgment, and the stamp of approval from a legitimizing ideology or authority one respects. Because of the moral, ideological, and organizational support necessary for such acts, most of them come as collective decisions—such as the conspiracy that led to the release of nerve gas in the Tokyo subways and the Hamas organization's carefully devised bombings.

## The War in Iraq

*Michael Ignatieff*

*In March 2003, the United States took a major step in the name of its "war on terrorism." The U.S. military, backed by British forces and the token support of other nations, attacked Iraq. Within weeks, U.S. and British air and ground forces overwhelmed Iraqi defenders and toppled Saddam Hussein and the Baathist Party, which had ruled Iraq with an iron fist for more than 20 years. From the beginning, many debated the reasons and wisdom of the attack on Iraq. In the following selection, Michael Ignatieff analyzes the reasons for the war. Ignatieff is director of the Carr Center at the Kennedy School of Government at Harvard University. He describes himself as a liberal and a reluctant, yet convinced supporter of the war in Iraq.*

SOURCE: Michael Ignatieff, "Why Are We in Iraq?" *The New York Times Magazine,* September 7, 2003, p. 7.

CONSIDER: *What, according to Ignatieff, is the most important reason the Bush administration invaded Iraq; what role September 11 played in the invasion of Iraq.*

Human rights could well be improved in Iraq as a result of the intervention. But the Bush administration did not invade Iraq just to establish human rights. Nor, ultimately, was this intervention about establishing a democracy or saving lives as such. And here we come to the heart of the matter—to where the Bush administration's interventions fit into America's long history of intervention. All such interventions have occurred because a president has believed going in that it would increase both his and his country's power and influence. To use Joseph S. Nye Jr.'s definition, "power is the ability to obtain the outcomes one wants." Presidents intervene because successful interventions enhance America's ability to obtain the outcomes it wants.

The Iraq intervention was the work of conservative radicals, who believed that the status quo in the Middle East was untenable—for strategic reasons, security reasons and economic reasons. They wanted intervention to bring about a revolution in American power in the entire region. What made a president take the gamble was Sept. 11 and the realization, with 15 of the hijackers originating in Saudi Arabia, that American interests based since 1945 on a presumed Saudi pillar were actually built on sand. The new pillar was to be a democratic Iraq, at peace with Israel, Turkey and Iran, harboring no terrorists, pumping oil for the world economy at the right price and abjuring any nasty designs on its neighbors.

As Paul Wolfowitz has all but admitted, the "bureaucratic" reason for war—weapons of mass destruction—was not the main one. The real reason was to rebuild the pillars of American influence in the Middle East. Americans may have figured this out for themselves, but it was certainly not what they were told. Nor were they told that building this new pillar might take years and years. What they were told—misleadingly and simplistically—was that force was justified to fight "terrorism" and to destroy arsenals of mass destruction targeted at America and at Israel.

## Chapter Questions

1. The closeness of the past 15 years makes it difficult to know what trends and developments will be the most significant historically. Those selected for this chapter are just a few of the possibilities. What others might have been selected? What evidence would demonstrate their importance?

2. It is possible to argue that most of what is claimed to be new about the past 15 years is not really so new, that it is just our impression that it is new because we have been living through it. How might this argument be supported? How might it be refuted?

3. Using sources in this and the previous chapter, evaluate the significance of recent events in the communist and formerly communist states of the world.

4. What might be the connections between globalism, international terrorism, and developments in the Middle East?